A Constructional Approach To Resultatives

STANFORD MONOGRAPHS IN LINGUISTICS

The aim of this series is to make exploratory work
that employs new linguistic data, extending the scope or domain
of current theoretical proposals, available to a wide audience.
These monographs will provide an insightful generalization of the
problem and data in question which will be of
interest to people working in a variety of frameworks.

STANFORD MONOGRAPHS IN LINGUISTICS

A CONSTRUCTIONAL APPROACH TO RESULTATIVES

Hans C. Boas

CSLI PUBLICATIONS
Center for the Study of
Language and Information
Stanford, California

Center for the Study of Language and Information
Leland Stanford Junior University
Printed in the United States
07 06 05 04 03   5 4 3 2 1

Library of Congress Cataloging-in-Publication Data

Boas, Hans Christian, 1971–
A constructional approach to resultatives / by Hans C. Boas.
p. cm. – (Stanford monographs in linguistics)

ISBN 1-57586-408-8 (pbk. : alk. paper)
ISBN 1-57586-407-X (hbk. : alk. paper)

1. Grammar, Comparative and general–Resultative constructions.
I. Title. II. Series.
P293.4.B6 2003
425–dc21 2003010621

∞ The acid-free paper used in this book meets the minimum requirements of the American National Standard for Information Sciences—Permanence of Paper for Printed Library Materials, ANSI Z39.48-1984.

CSLI was founded in 1983 by researchers from Stanford University, SRI International, and Xerox PARC to further the research and development of integrated theories of language, information, and computation. CSLI headquarters and CSLI Publications are located on the campus of Stanford University.

CSLI Publications reports new developments in the study of language, information, and computation. In addition to lecture notes, our publications include monographs, working papers, revised dissertations, and conference proceedings. Our aim is to make new results, ideas, and approaches available as quickly as possible. Please visit our web site at
http://cslipublications.stanford.edu/
for comments on this and other titles, as well as for changes and corrections by the author and publisher.

To my parents, Ursula Boas and Hans Ulrich Boas,
for all of their love and support.

There is something fascinating about science. One gets such wholesale returns of conjecture out of such a trifling investment of fact.

(Mark Twain)

Contents

Acknowledgments

This book grew out of my Ph.D. thesis (Boas, 2000b), which was completed at the University of North Carolina at Chapel Hill. I am deeply indebted to my advisor, Gert Webelhuth, for his invaluable advice, enthusiasm, and encouragement. The many hours that he spent discussing my work helped me to come a step closer to a solution without being driven insane. Randy Hendrick has given me many thoughtful comments and suggestions, especially during the early phase of my dissertation while I was still in Chapel Hill. As an exchange student in the fall of 1993 I took a morphology class with Randy, which opened up a new world to me. Without his excellent teaching and ability to get students excited about every aspect of linguistics, I would never have considered pursuing a graduate career in linguistics. During my time in Berkeley, Andreas Kathol has given me many invaluable comments on various drafts of my dissertation. The long discussions with him have helped me to rethink several aspects of my analysis and have been a great source of inspiration.

Other members of the UNC faculty contributed in countless ways to my education. I am grateful to Maria Tsiapera for teaching me about the history and philosophy of linguistics and for giving me her experienced advice on every aspect of academic life. I'd like to thank Craig Melchert for instilling in me a deep respect for the complexities of historical data. Megan Crowhurst's enthusiasm for phonology sparked my interest in this field and got me more involved with phonological issues than I could ever have imagined. I am extremely grateful to Walt Wolfram for letting me work with him and his associates on the Lumbee English fieldwork site in Robeson County, North Carolina. His love and enthusiasm for studying dialects has not only been a great inspiration to me, but also always reminds me of the difficulties formal linguistics is faced with when it comes to analyzing 'language.' Finally, I would like to thank Laura Janda for teaching me about Cognitive Linguistics. Without her enthusiastic teaching, my education in linguistics would be lacking an important and meaningful part. I am fortunate to have enjoyed the friendship and support of my colleagues Kristin Reichardt, Pat Murphy, Julie St. John, Donna Salisbury, Melissa Lucas, Soo-Jung Kim, Kirk Hazen, Clare Dannenberg, Natalie Schilling-Estes, Tenney Deane, Eric Bloemeke, Della Chambless, Jenny Palmer, Rod Edwards, and Kirk Baker.

This book would have never reached its present format had I not gone to Berkeley for my research. I am deeply indebted to Chuck Fillmore who made my stay at the FrameNet project at the International Computer Science Institute (ICSI) at Berkeley possible. His love for doing linguistics, his thoughtful comments and his advice have greatly influenced my thinking about linguistics. Seeing linguistic theory being applied in practice at FrameNet to produce valuable resources for linguists and non-linguists alike has kept me going all these years. It has been a pleasure to work with Chuck and other members of the FrameNet project in the very energetic, open-minded, friendly, supportive, and productive atmosphere at ICSI. I am grateful for having had the opportunity to work with Josef Ruppenhofer, Collin Baker, Margaret Urban, Tess Wood, Jane Edwards, Christopher Johnson, Susanne Gahl, Sue Atkins, Uli Heid, J.B. Lowe, Sato Hiroaki, Jerome Feldman, Ben Bergen, Nancy Chang, Srini Narayanan, and Lila Finhill at ICSI. Without the support of the National Science Foundation, the FrameNet project would not have been realized (NSF IRI #9618838, NSF ITR/HCI #0086132). The right to use the British National Corpus on the part of FrameNet researchers was arranged through Oxford University Press. I am thankful for access to this invaluable resource.

The Berkeley linguistics community has been a great source of inspiration for my work. In particular, I am grateful to Paul Kay, George Lakoff, Eve Sweetser, Dan Slobin, Len Talmy, Seizi Iwata, and Michael Ellsworth for intense and stimulating discussions about linguistics in general and resultative constructions in particular.

At the beginning of my university education I had my first contact and subsequent interest in linguistics at the Georg-August-Universität Göttingen in Germany. Many thanks to Thomas Gardner, Theo Janßen, Wolfgang Schmid, and Bernhard Shaw for teaching me the basics of linguistics. Thanks to my father, Hans Ulrich Boas, for many interesting and inspiring discussions about linguistics.

It is with great pleasure that I thank the members of my home base, the Department of Germanic Studies at the University of Texas at Austin, for their support and collegiality. In particular, Katherine Ahrens and Janet

Swaffar have been a constant source of advice and support ever since I got to Austin.

I feel extremely lucky to publish this book with CSLI Publications. An anonymous reviewer provided invaluable feedback on a previous draft of this book. Dikran Karagueuzian, Tony Gee, Christine Sosa, and Lauri Kanerva have been the greatest pleasure to work with. I would like to thank them for their advice and their patience throughout the whole process. For help preparing the final manuscript I would like to thank Claire Colton and Doug Simms for proof reading. For the most careful formatting job I could have imagined, I thank Jana Thompson.

I gratefully acknowledge the support of the 'Deutsche Akademische Auslandsdienst' (DAAD) (German Academic Exchange Service) which awarded me a postdoctoral fellowship that enabled me to conduct post-dissertation research with FrameNet at the International Computer Science Institute (ICSI) in Berkeley. During my time at ICSI, I began with the substantial revisions of my dissertation which lead to the publication of several papers on resultatives (see Boas (2001, 2002a, 2002b, 2002c, 2002d)), as well as the book itself.

This book would have never been completed without the love and support of my family and friends. First and foremost I feel blessed with such wonderful parents who have always been there for me to support me with everything I ever needed. I thank one of my best friends, Christian Ohlendorf, for his support and for reminding me that there are other things in life besides academics. He generously loaned me one of his computers so I could write my dissertation which formed the basis for this book. Other friends that have been a source of constant support over all these years include Bernd von Garmissen, Stefan Brunner, Anabel and Jürgen Aliaga-Buchenau, Chris Prang, and Samer Ali.

Finally, I am immensely grateful to Claire Colton, for always being there for me and for being so understanding and supportive! Thank you, Claire!!!

Austin, May 2003
H.C.B.

1

Introduction

> The analysis of resultatives is only beginning to receive wide attention. The debates are bound to change, perhaps drastically, over the next few years, as additional languages are examined.
>
> (Napoli 1999: 329)

1.1 Aim and Scope

The main goal of this monograph is to arrive at an analysis capable of capturing the syntactic and semantic distribution of resultative constructions in English. Based on an in-depth investigation of the distribution of more than 6000 resultative constructions in the 100 Mio. word British National Corpus (BNC), I develop a constructional analysis which regards the multiple conventionalized senses associated with verbs as central to accounting for the full range of English resultatives.[1] The following sentences are examples of resultative constructions which describe the state of an argument resulting from the action denoted by the verb.

(1.1)
a. I dyed my grey school skirt *dark red.* (BNC)
b. Calm down or you'll drive me *insane*. (BNC)
c. Guatemala mob stones tourist, driver *to death.* (SF Examiner, 2.5.2000)
d. Tom had swept the room *clean*, ... (BNC)
e. Then a big storm likely blew the cracks *shut* and trapped the whales for about 60 days. (National Geographic, January 2000, p. 18)
f. He had run himself *out of breath* ... (BNC)

[1] Throughout this monograph, I will use the terms *resultative construction* and *resultative* interchangeably.

g. Sculpting winds have salted the snow *gray* with swirling ash and rippled it like the sea. (National Geographic, May 2000, p. 111)

The italicized phrases in (1.1) are resultative phrases that describe the resultant state (change of state) of the postverbal N(oun) P(hrase), i.e., the argument of the verb, that is caused by the action denoted by the verb. Thus, (1.1a) means *I dyed my grey school skirt and as a result of my dying the skirt it became dark red.* Resultative constructions belong to the class of secondary predication constructions in which a phrase (XP) following the postverbal NP is in a subject-predicate relation with this NP.

(1.2) [NP V NP XP]
where X = A, N, or P

Constructions exhibiting structures as in (1.2) are called secondary predication constructions because there are two basic dependency relations between the postverbal NP and the two constituents surrounding it.[2] The first dependency relation is a primary predication which holds between the verb and the postverbal NP. Thus, in a sentence like *She dyed her skirt*, it is *her skirt* which is the object of the verb *dye*. The second dependency relation is a secondary predication which holds between the postverbal NP and the XP following it. Thus, in a sentence like *She dyed her skirt red*, the word *red* is analyzed as a secondary predicate because it predicates a property of a constituent of the primary predication. Diagram (1.3) illustrates the primary and secondary predication relations that hold between the verb, the postverbal NP, and the resultative phrase.

(1.3) Primary and secondary predication relations

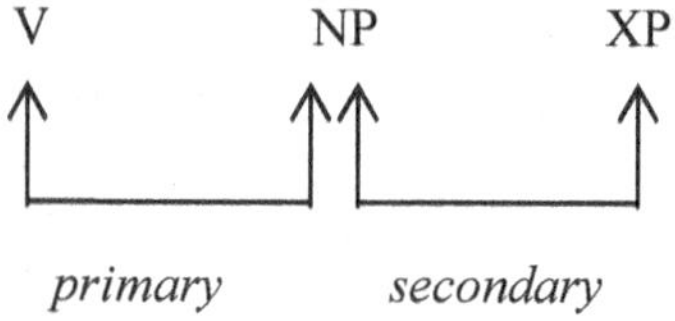

Resultative constructions of the type in (1.1) exhibit the same observable syntactic structure as other types of secondary predication constructions,

[2]The structure in (1.2) only covers transitive resultative constructions. In this monograph we will also be concerned with the licensing of intransitive resultative constructions of the form [NP V XP].

most notably depictive secondary predication constructions as in the following examples.

(1.4) a. Jack considers Flora *intelligent.*
b. Tom ate the steak *raw.*
c. Dave finds warm beer *unbearable.*

Depictive secondary predication constructions differ from resultative constructions in that the italicized phrases in (1.4) do not denote the resultant state of the postverbal NP. Instead, depictive secondary predicates 'modify an entity at the time of the (initiation of the) action denoted by the verb.' (Rapoport 1999: 654). Thus, (1.4b) means *Tom ate the steak, and at the time that he ate it, it was raw.*[3] The observation that in sentences such as (1.4a)-(1.4c) the postverbal NP and the depictive predicate are in a predication relationship has led Jespersen (1961) to the proposal that the two constituents form a syntactic constituent. He points out that

> ... if we ask in each case [of the examples with a verb followed by a noun phrase and a so-called complement] what is the object of the verb, many grammars say that (...) it is the word placed immediately after the verb, and the rest is called 'a complement' of the object, or an 'adjective or noun used predicatively of the object.' (...) The correct analysis is that all these are analogous and contain not two objects (as in 'I gave (made) her a ring'), but only one, which is a nexus containing the same two parts as a nexus that forms a complete sentence or clause (...).
>
> (Jespersen 1961: 7-8)

Jespersen's proposal that the two postverbal constituents form a clause functioning as the object of the preceding verb has given rise to a series of different analyses of resultative constructions as we will see throughout this monograph.[4] However, before turning our attention to the details of the different accounts postulated for resultatives, we first take a more detailed look at the syntactic and semantic distribution of English resultative constructions.

---

[3]For a more detailed discussion about the differences between resultative and depictive predication, see Halliday (1967: 63) and Rothstein (1983: 17, 83).

[4]For proposals that categorize the two postverbal constituents in terms of separate constituents on traditional, theory-independent grounds, see Onions (1904), Sonnenschein (1916), Curme (1931), Hornby (1954), Close (1975), and Quirk et al. (1972, 1985). See Jackendoff (1977) for an early analysis of secondary predication constructions in terms of separate constituents.

1.2 Three Classes of Resultative Constructions

The main question addressed by most accounts of English resultatives is concerned with the factors that license the two postverbal constituents, namely the postverbal NP and the resultative phrase. In this section we thus turn to the different types of syntactic and semantic relationships that hold between the matrix verb and its postverbal constituents. We will see that the distribution of postverbal NPs and resultative phrases is often difficult to predict on the basis of a verb's membership in a verb class.[5] To begin with, consider the distribution of resultative phrases that may occur in post-object position of transitive verbs.

(1.5)
a. She turned the spray and stained the white front of his shirt *blood red.* (BNC)
b. Tearing some cotton wool off a roll, Polly carefully wiped the area *dry*. (BNC)
c. An earthquake destroys buildings by shaking them *to pieces*. (BNC)
d. The next morning Benjamin shook me *awake*. (BNC)
e. Break the chocolate *into pieces* and place in a basin over hot water. (BNC)
f. The distraught family of a young woman prison officer who shot herself *dead* last week have demanded to know why she was given a gun. (BNC)
g. What sort of a person would stab a child *to death*? (BNC)

In contrast to the examples in (1.5a) – (1.5g), other transitive verbs do not allow any phrases in postverbal position that yield a resultative interpretation. Compare, e.g., the following sentences.

(1.6)
a. *Claire touched the vase to madness.
b. *Dawn played her video game broken.
c. *Christian saw Frank nice.
d. *Stefan devoured his grits to pieces.

As we will see throughout this monograph, a great deal of attention has been paid to the question of how resultative phrases are licensed with transi-

---

[5]With respect to the idiosyncratic distribution of resultatives, Levin (1993: 101) points out: 'A wide range of verbs is found in the resultative construction, so no specific classes of verbs are identified here.'

tive verbs. The problem is related to the question of how verbs that are typically transitive and only subcategorize for an object NP may occur with an additional nonsubcategorized phrase. Whereas adherents of the Small Clause Theory (Chomsky 1986, Hoekstra 1988, Aarts 1992, Bowers 1997, and Staudinger 1997, among others) suggest that the licensing of the postverbal constituents is due to the fact that they are part of a clausal constituent which is subcategorized for by the verb, proponents of Predication Theory postulate that the postverbal constituents are licensed in terms of syntactic coindexing between the postverbal NP and the resultative phrase (Williams 1983, Rothstein 1985, Napoli 1988, 1989, 1992, and Carrier and Randall 1992, among others). Another line of syntacticocentric analyses accounts for resultatives in terms of complex predicates (Chomsky 1955, Neeleman and Van de Koot 2001, and Müller 2002).

In contrast to these syntactic analyses, other accounts seek to explain the licensing of resultatives with lexical, semantic, and aspectual conditions (Dowty 1979, Bresnan and Zaenen 1990, Pustejovsky 1995, Jackendoff 1997, Rapp 1997, Wechsler 1997, Winkler 1997, Verspoor 1997, Rappaport Hovav and Levin 1998, 1999, 2001, and Wechsler and Noh 2001). Yet another line of research claims the resultative phrase is licensed by a meaningful construction capable of providing a verb with additional argument roles (Goldberg 1995). Although these accounts vary with respect to the mechanisms that are needed to license the occurrence of the resultative phrase, they are also all concerned with the question of how resultatives are licensed with intransitive verbs such as the following.

(1.7)
a. Sadly, wayward genius Georgie Best (...) slickly eluded our lensman and left after about ten minutes to dance *his studded boots off* at some West End nightclub. (BNC)
b. Well, I laughed *myself silly*. (BNC)
c. But most of the dogs were unhappy and would bark *themselves hoarse*. (BNC)
d. But then there was the question of replacing Susy, without James running *himself ragged*. (BNC)
e. In the small hours of the next morning, when they were back at La Gracieuse, after dancing *her feet raw* with Sam, ... (BNC)
f. Dobson and his mob just laughed *you off the street* tonight and we can't afford that. (BNC)

g. Frank sneezed the napkin *off the table*.
(Goldberg 1995: 152)[6]

The examples in (1.7a) – (1.7g) differ from the sentences in (1.6) in that they are based on intransitive verbs that do not subcategorize for objects. Following observations by Simpson (1983), who labels the nonsubcategorized postverbal NPs 'fake objects,' Levin and Rappaport Hovav (1995) posit the Direct Object Restriction (DOR) which requires that resultative phrases always be predicated of objects.[7] This restriction serves to rule out sentences containing intransitive verbs in which the resultative phrase is supposed to predicate over the verb's subject.

(1.8) a. *... without James running ragged.
b. *... after dancing raw with Sam.
c. *... and his mob laughed off the street tonight.

Note that in cases in which the resultative occurs with fake objects, the resultative phrase is obligatory.

(1.9) a. *He danced his studded boots.
b. *I laughed myself.
c. *The dogs barked themselves.

Another interesting point concerning the distribution of the reflexive and the nonreflexive fake objects in (1.7a) - (1.7g) is the fact that they may typically not be substituted for each other. In other words, when an intransitive verb occurs with a resultative phrase to denote a specific semantic concept, no substitutions are allowed. Compare the following sentences.

(1.10) a. *The mob laughed itself off the street tonight.
b. *James ran her ragged.

---

[6]Sentences such as (1.7f) and (1.7g) are typically classified as caused-motion constructions (see Goldberg 1995) because the postverbal NP ends up in a different location as a result of the activity denoted by the main verb. However, since both resultative constructions and caused-motion constructions denote a change in the status of the postverbal NP, we will discuss them both under the term of resultative constructions (because states can be construed as locations (cf. Lakoff and Johnson's (1999) States are Locations metaphor)). See Chapter 4 for details.

[7]Direct Object Restriction (DOR): 'The basic insight that emerges from work on the resultative construction is that a resultative phrase may be predicated of the immediately postverbal NP, but may not be predicated of a subject or of an oblique complement.' (Levin and Rappaport Hovav (1995: 34)). For another implementation of the DOR, see Bresnan and Zaenen (1990). For a critical discussion of the DOR, see Wechsler (1997/2001), Verspoor (1997), Boas (1998), Rappaport Hovav and Levin (2001), and Wechsler and Noh (2001).

c. *The dog barked the postman hoarse.
d. *Well, I laughed her silly.

Whereas the Direct Object Restriction serves to rule out the unacceptable sentences in (1.10), there are some intransitive verbs (often associated with unaccusativity) which do not adhere to the predictions of the Direct Object Restriction.[8] The following examples show that verbs such as *break*, *freeze*, *melt*, and *burn* may occur with a resultative phrase that predicates over the subject of the main verb.[9]

(1.11) a. The lake froze (rock solid).
b. The vase broke (to pieces).
c. The butter melted (to liquid).
d. The branding iron burned (into the calf's skin).
(Croft 1991: 161)

Finally, we turn to a third class of resultative constructions that seems to differ from the two types discussed so far. Based on the observation that the postverbal NPs in sentences such as (1.12a) – (1.12e) do not bear a semantic relation to the transitive main verb, some authors (e.g., Hoekstra 1988a, 1992, Bowers 1997, and Staudinger 1997) propose that there is a class of resultatives based on transitive verbs with nonsubcategorized postverbal NPs.

(1.12) a. She drank him under the table.
b. He rubbed the sleep out of his eyes.
c. They drank the pub dry.
d. They wrung a confession out of him.
e. Sue swept the broom to pieces.

---

[8]The fact that these verbs may occur without a resultative phrase and still be interpreted resultatively leads Rappaport Hovav and Levin (1998/2001) to classify these verbs as result verbs. These verbs differ from so-called manner verbs in that they lexically specify for a result state. See Chapter 3 for details.

[9]In order to explain this violation of the Direct Object Restriction, Rappaport Hovav and Levin (1995) follow ideas put forward by Simpson (1983), Bresnan and Zaenen (1990), and Hoekstra (1988) which give accounts in terms of syntactic classifications of the respective verbs. This proposal builds on the assumption that unaccusative verbs have underlying objects which are realized as syntactic subjects (cf. the Unaccusative Hypothesis as put forward by Perlmutter (1978), Burzio (1986), and Rappaport Hovav and Levin (1995), among others) which means that resultative phrases are predicated of an object at some level of representation. On this view, verbs which require a fake object (cf. (1.7a)-(1.7g)) are unergative verbs whereas those which do not require a fake object (cf. (1.11a)-(1.11d)) are unaccusative verbs.

The fact that these transitive verbs typically do not occur with the same types of postverbal NPs outside of resultative constructions leads Hoekstra and others to conclude that such resultatives form a separate class. Thus, in combination with these specific types of NPs, the resultative phrase is obligatory as the following examples illustrate.

(1.13) a. *She drank him.
b. *He rubbed the sleep.
c. *They drank the pub.
d. *They wrung a confession.
e. ?Sue swept the broom.

The data surveyed so far show that transitive resultative constructions belong in principle to three different classes. The *first* class consists of resultatives which are based on transitive verbs occurring with an additional phrase supplying the resultative interpretation. The *second* class contains intransitive verbs occurring with both a nonsubcategorized object and a resultative phrase to yield the resultative interpretation. The *third* class consists of transitive verbs occurring with both a nonsubcategorized object as well as a resultative phrase. The analysis I will be developing in the remainder of this monograph will be primarily concerned with the question of how postverbal NPs and resultative phrases are licensed in the three different types of resultative constructions.

1.3 Syntactic, Semantic, and Pragmatic Restrictions on Resultatives

We now turn to the syntactic and semantic selection restrictions that hold for the constituents of each of the three main classes of resultative construction. We turn first to the syntactic status of the resultative phrase which, in principle, can either be an AP (cf. (14a, b)), an NP (cf. (14c, d)), or a PP (cf. (14e, f)).

(1.14) a. For Italian Vogue he dyed the skin of Linda Evangelista *nearly black*. (BNC)
b. Perhaps he could drive Gina *insane* with a little more work. (BNC)
c. I asked Quasimodo recently how he accomplished this, and he replied that he had painted his model *a beautiful shade of red*. (BNC)

d. Her hair was dyed *an incredible brutal red.* (BNC)
e. A pregnant mum who threatened to starve herself and her unborn child *to death* in an immigration row is toasting victory this weekend. (BNC)
f. When the whole side has been removed, pull off the backbone and cut the remaining salmon *into pieces.* (BNC)

Note, however, that not every category of resultative phrase may occur with a given verb. Whereas some verbs such as *dye* or *paint* allow both APs and NPs as their resultative phrases, other verbs are more selective. The following sentences illustrate that some verbs show a strong preference for APs whereas other verbs show a strong preference for PPs as their resultative predicates.

(1.15) a. He used to drive his cousins *crazy/*to craziness* with its mythology. (BNC)
b. And I recall a certain ship, in a certain time, that we were supposed to go down with, as the strings played "Autumn" and we danced ourselves *to dust/*dusty.* (Message-ID: 19980918191301.PAA27679 @ladder01.news.aol.com)
c. Denny Butler nearly crushed you *flat/*to flatness.* (BNC)
d. You've screamed yourself *hoarse/*to hoarseness.* (BNC)
e. Supermodels can make you *sick/*to sickness.* (BNC)
f. Congratulations to your golf score, but we don't have to run ourselves *into extinction/*extinct.* (Message-ID: 85i2m4rj1@nnrp1.deja.com)
g. I never knew she was going to fall through the bloody ceiling and get knocked *soft/*to softness.* (BNC)
h. For the past five years Volkov has been drinking himself *to death/*dead.* (BNC)

Note, moreover, that there are more general semantic and pragmatic constraints at work which determine the range of acceptable resultative phrases in (1.16a)-(1.16i) and postverbal NPs in (1.17a) – (1.17h).

(1.16) a. Pat broke the vase {to pieces /*yellow/*peaceful/ *wooden /*out of the house /*over the lamp}.
b. Julie swept the floor {clean/?red/*old/*wooden}.
c. Donna ran her Nikes {threadbare/?smelly/*green/*clean}.

d. Melissa sneezed the napkin {off the table/*into the ground/*to liquid/*blue}.
e. Kristin ran her feet {sore/*to pieces/*shredded/*off the street}.
f. Eric drank himself {silly/under the table/*dark/*broken /*out of bed}.
g. Della danced herself {tired/?sober/??old/*smart}.
h. Jenny cried herself {to sleep/*awake/*hungry/*around the corner}.
i. The dog barked itself {hoarse/?tired/*young/ *unconscious/*under the table}.

(1.17) a. Ed drove {Jonathan/*his car} crazy.
b. Rachel sneezed {the napkin/?the book/*the plates}off the table.
c. They laughed {him/?the camel/*the beer keg /*themselves} off the stage.
d. Jim ran {his feet/?his hair/*Rich}sore.
e. Dave frowned away {the compliment/?the insult/??the news}.
f. Chelsea broke {the eggs/*the vase/*the branch} into the bowl.
g. Louis hammered {the metal/*a hole} flat.
h. Montgomery hammered {a hole/the metal} through the wall.

The above sentences illustrate that speakers often have strong intuitions about what types of resultative phrases and NPs may occur in combination with a verb in order to form an acceptable and interpretable resultative construction. The same can be observed for the influence of contextual background information with respect to yielding an acceptable interpretation of a resultative as the following examples from Aarts (1992) illustrate.

(1.18) A I was surprised to see Clara clean the kitchen table this morning.
B Yes, I asked her to tidy up, but she didn't do a very good job. At one point she was wiping the tables, but rather than wiping them clean she was wiping them dirty by using that filthy rag which is normally used for the loo!

(1.19) A I hear that loony shepherd was shooting at people again the other day.

B Yes, that's right, but this time things got out of hand: he shot Tom in the arm and Jeff is now lame.
A He shot Jeff lame? That man should be put behind bars!
(Aarts 1992: 63)

In the above examples, lack of contextual background information makes the resultatives sound odd. However, once they are contextualized, the sentences are fairly straightforward. In Chapter 7, we will discuss the role of contextual background information for the licensing of resultative constructions in more detail. In particular, we will address the mechanisms responsible for supplying pragmatic information capable of 'fixing' sentences that would otherwise be unacceptable. With the overview of the types of data to be analyzed in this monograph in mind, we now turn to the methodology that will be used to arrive at an account capable of adequately capturing the syntactic and semantic distribution of English resultative constructions.

1.4 Methodology

An analysis of the phenomenon under investigation necessitates a brief discussion of data collection. After I finished reviewing the data presented by previous approaches to resultatives, I noticed that most accounts were based on a somewhat small set of typically thirty or less constructed example sentences containing the same verbs. Even notable exceptions such as Goldberg (1995) and Rappaport Hovav and Levin (2001) who used corpus examples to support their analyses used limited sets of (corpus) data that did not always take into consideration the full range of argument patterns found with particular verbs. Thus, when I found counterexamples to predictions made by previous accounts, I was often reminded of an observation made by Van Valin and LaPolla about the types of data necessary to conduct a thorough linguistic analysis. The two authors point out that '[d]eveloping serious explanatory theories of language is impossible in the absence of descriptions of the object of explanation.' (Van Valin and LaPolla 1997: 3) In other words, in order to construct an adequate theory of resultative constructions, we should not restrict ourselves to a limited set of data, but should instead aim at collecting large amounts of empirical data in order to cover the subject of study in its entirety. To this end, a theory of resultative constructions should comply with the following criterion identified by Lees (1957) for scientific theories.

> Maximal coverage is desirable because it is the very purpose of scientific theories to explain by means of generalizations our understanding of particular events and our intuitive perception of their interrelations.
>
> (Lees 1957: 376)

Syntacticians have traditionally relied on native speaker elicitations in combination with constructed sentences confirmed by their own linguistic intuitions about acceptability in order to collect relevant data. During the initial period of data collection I found this method not only very time consuming but also very problematic from an empirical point of view.[10] One of the main problems while collecting data on resultatives has been the varying acceptability judgments by native speakers. Whereas some speakers seemed to intuitively accept a wide range of resultatives, other speakers were much more conservative and judged a large number of resultative constructions to be unacceptable. This led to frustrating periods of data collection during which I found that of 20 native speakers asked within one hour about the acceptability of a few resultative constructions, I would get varying answers with respect to the acceptability of the same constructions. Answers ranged from 'acceptable' to 'unacceptable,' and included 'well, maybe,' 'but only if,' 'I've never heard that before,' 'wrong,' and 'I just wouldn't say it like that.' At the beginning, it seemed as if the initial phase of this work – the data collection – was irreversibly caught in what Martinet (1953) described as one of the fundamental problems linguists are faced with when describing language, namely language variation.

> There was a time when the progress of research required that each community should be considered linguistically self-contained and homogeneous (...) Linguists will always have to revert at times to this pragmatic assumption. But we shall now have to stress the fact that a linguistic community is never homogenous and hardly ever self-contained (...) It is not enough to point out that each individual is a battleground for conflicting types and habits (...) What we heedlessly and somewhat rashly call 'a language' is the aggregate of millions of such microcosms many of which

[10] An additional problem with native speaker intuitions is the fact that any given native speaker typically comes to different judgments about the acceptability of the same piece of data on different occasions. For example, Boberg (2002: 12) in his analysis of reliability of native speakers' intuitions points out that 'while it may sometimes be necessary or even desirable to turn to native speakers' intuitions as evidence in linguistics, such evidence should always be interpreted with caution and even skepticism, and should be checked against empirical data whenever possible.'

> evince such aberrant linguistic comportment that the question arises whether they should not be grouped together as 'languages'.
>
> (Martinet 1953: vii)[11]

In order to systematically 'filter out' dialectal differences, native speaker elicitations, and their respective acceptability, judgments were grouped according to dialectal areas. However, even within somewhat clearer defined dialectal areas such as 'White Appalachian English of North Carolina' or 'Lumbee English of Robeson County, North Carolina' there was still widespread disagreement among speakers about the acceptability of certain resultative constructions.[12] Therefore, I realized it would be necessary to acquire a large and quantifiable range of data on resultative constructions.

This realization has led to my adaptation of a usage-based approach to linguistic analysis as proposed by Leisi (1954), Firth (1957), Langacker (1988, 2000), Fillmore (1989), Hunston and Francis (2000), and Stubbs (2001), among others. The following quote from Leisi (1954), pointing out the necessity of developing a framework capable of explaining how words are used in daily discourse, nicely summarizes the goals of a usage-based approach.

> Und doch bedürfen wir dringend einer Lehre vom richtigen Gebrauch der Wörter. Wir möchten Auskunft haben etwa über die folgenden brennenden Fragen: Warum müssen wir eines Tages entdecken, daß wir trotz Lexikon ein gegebenes Wort jahrelang falsch verwendet haben? Warum gebraucht ein Engländer die deutschen Wörter *Stuhl, Tisch, Philosoph* ohne weiteres richtig, scheut sich aber etwas vor *Zipfel, Brocken, stellen*? Wenn also manche Wörter leicht, andere schwer oder gar nicht übersetzbar sind: lassen sich Gesetze aufstellen, sind solche Wörter in Gruppen zu vereinigen und auf eine generelle Formel zu bringen? Weiter: warum gibt dieses Wort an dieser Stelle einen besonderen dichterischen, ironischen oder sonst auffallenden Effekt? Eine Wortlehre sollte dann also Antwort auf solche Fragen geben, und zwar sollte sie nicht nur Einzelfälle behandeln, sondern einen systematischen Rahmen von Wortgesetzen

---

[11]Cited by Le Page (1997: 18) as Martinet's preface to Weinreich's (1953) thesis *Languages in Contact.*

[12]The elicitations of resultative constructions were set up by using comic strips showing scenes in which objects or people underwent a change of state or location. These comic strips contained no text. Speakers were then asked to naturally produce a text that fits the respective scenes under consideration. For a discussion regarding linguistic data collection, see, e.g., L. Milroy (1987).

> geben, die sich auf alle später auftauchenden Fälle erklärend anwenden lassen. (Leisi 1954: 8)[13]

For the purpose of systematically gathering large amounts of usage-based data for this monograph, I chose to adopt a corpus-based approach to resultative constructions. By using large electronic corpora I was not limited to studying what is theoretically possible in a language or to rely on intuitions or anecdotal evidence alone. Instead, I could focus on how actual language is used by a broad variety of speakers in naturally occurring texts and discourse. As Leech (1992) points out, corpus linguistics refers 'not to a domain of study, but rather to a methodological basis for pursuing linguistic research.' (Leech 1992: 105) More specifically, this means that corpus linguistics focuses on:

> 1) linguistic performance, rather than competence;
> 2) linguistic description, rather than universals;
> 3) quantitative, as well as qualitative models of language, and
> 4) a more empiricist, rather than a rationalist view of scientific inquiry. (Ooi 1998: 35)

Another advantage of the corpus linguistic approach lies in the fact that it not only allows assessing the extent to which a pattern is found, but it also makes it possible to analyze the contextual factors that influence variability (see Biber, Conrad, and Reppen 1998: 3). The latter point will be shown to be extremely important for explaining the distribution of resultative constructions in a variety of different contexts. Besides analyzing different structural patterns of resultatives, the alternative approach proposed in this monograph is also concerned with quantifying the occurrence of certain

---

[13] (Rough) translation: We are in dire need of a theory about the proper use of words. We would like to have information about the following important questions: How come we have to discover one day that we have used a given word incorrectly although we had a dictionary? How come an Englishman uses the German words *Stuhl* (chair), *Tisch* (table), and *Philosoph* (philosopher) correctly but has problems with *Zipfel* (tip), *Brocken* (piece), *stellen* (put)? If some words are easily translatable, but other words are hard if not impossible to translate: Is there any way of arriving at laws, is it possible to group these words into larger groups, and to arrive at a general formula for them? And: How come this word has in this position a specific poetic, ironic, or otherwise unusual effect? A theory of words should then give answers to these questions. It should not only be concerned with individual cases, but it should give a systematic framework for laws concerning words that can be systematically applied to all other cases that will occur in the future.

resultative phrases with different types of verbs.[14] In order to find such patterns, I have turned to a number of electronic corpora, dictionaries, and sources on the Internet.[15]

The largest amount of data used in this work stems from the British National Corpus (BNC), an electronic corpus containing ca. 100 million words of contemporary spoken (10%) and written (90%) English.[16] The BNC was chosen because it is currently one of the largest commercially available electronic corpora of English which is both balanced and representative.[17] In order to arrive at a somewhat quantifiable basis for our analysis of resultative constructions in this monograph, the BNC is taken as the basis for determining what types of resultative phrases occur with a given verb and in what quantities certain collocational patterns appear.[18] Following Sinclair (1991: 170), a collocation is understood to be the 'occurrence of two or more words within a short space of each other in a text.' A more detailed discussion of different collocational patterns found with verbs and their resultative phrases will be given in Chapter 5.

The method of data extraction to determine the distribution of resultative phrases with their respective verbs is as follows. Based on examples cited in the literature (ranging from Simpson (1983) to Rappaport Hovav and Levin (1998/2001)) I compiled a list of fifty-one APs and PPs that can function as resultative phrases. In creating that list, I searched for the most

---

[14]See Cowart (1997) for an illustration of how statistical grammaticality judgments can be drawn from data containing dialectal variation.

[15]In reality, the corpus-based approach has a number of limitations which is why it should not be regarded as a substitute for traditional discovery procedures that rely on elicitation or intuition. One problem of the corpus-based approach has to do with the size of the corpus and how well the corpus is balanced. That is, just because a given structure under investigation does not occur in a corpus does not automatically mean that it is not attested or acceptable. To this end, I have combined results from my corpus-based investigations with intuitions and anecdotal evidence whenever necessary.

[16]For more information on the BNC, see Kennedy (1998: 50-53) and http://www.hcu.ox.ac.uk/BNC. The use of the BNC has been made possible by the FrameNet project (P.I. Charles Fillmore, sponsored by the National Science Foundation under Grant IRI #9618838 and ITR/HCI #0086132) at the International Computer Science Institute, Berkeley, California. The right to use the BNC on the part of FrameNet researchers was arranged through Oxford University Press. I am grateful for access to this invaluable resource.

[17]Other large electronic corpora that are balanced and commercially available include the COBUILD Bank of English (ca. 200 Mio. Words). For detailed discussions of corpus size and representativeness of a corpus, see Heid and McNaught (1991: 59), Atkins et al. (1992: 6), Biber (1993: 243, 256), Ooi (1998: 55-56), and Stubbs (2001: 223-224), among others.

[18]See Renouf and Sinclair (1991: 128-143), Kennedy (1998: 108-121), and Stubbs (2001: 29-30, 117-120) for detailed discussions about the relevance of corpus-based studies of collocations for a general theory of language.

frequently occurring resultative phrases such as *dead*, *flat*, *hoarse*, *into pieces*, *mad*, *tired*, etc. as well as other less frequently occurring APs and PPs such as *sleepy*, *empty*, and *to suicide*. Whenever appropriate, I included a given resultative phrase's counterpart belonging to a different syntactic category in order to determine whether verbs would prefer one syntactic type over the other.

For each of the fifty-one APs and PPs, I conducted an exhaustive corpus search in the BNC by using the Corpus Query Processor (CQP) developed at the Institute for Natural Language Processing at the University of Stuttgart, Germany (see Christ (1994) and Christ and Schulze (1995)). The goal of this search was to determine the types of verbs occurring with a given resultative phrase. Using CQP, I first created a subcorpus for each phrase ranging from 35 examples (*to suicide*) to up to almost 70,000 examples (*off*) depending on how often the phrase occurred in the BNC. For each subcorpus, I then specified a verbal parameter for CQP that searched for verbs within five words to the left of the phrase under investigation. The final list returned by CQP thus consisted of sentences that included the target AP or PP and verbs within five words to the left of the target phrase. Since CQP and other electronic query systems do not allow specifications that filter out resultative usages of APs and PPs in combination with a given verb, I then had to extract the resultative constructions manually from the final list. In other words, all sentences in which the target phrase was used resultatively were extracted by hand in order to count the types and numbers of verbs occurring with the target phrase (e.g., *into pieces*). Each manual counting was repeated twice in order to avoid errors in determining the types and numbers of resultative phrases occurring with a given verb. The procedure described here resulted for each resultatives phrase in a table listing the verbs in order of frequency that occur with the resultative phrase as well as the extracted corpus sentences exemplifying the occurrence of verb and resultative phrase (see Appendix A). Because the procedure to determine the distribution of resultative phrases with different verbs could not be fully automated and was therefore time-consuming, I decided to limit this part of my investigation to fifty-one resultative phrases as they occur with different verbs in the British National Corpus.

A similar procedure was followed for a few target verbs that occur repeatedly in the literature on resultatives in order to find out with which resultative phrases they occur in the BNC. Using CQP, I created subcorpora for the semantically related verbs *sweep* and *wipe*, as well as for *drive*.[19] I

[19] For *drive*, I searched the subcorpus for the so-called 'drive-mental-state' of *drive* as in *This topic is driving me nuts* in order to determine which types of resultative phrases are used to express a mental state with this specific sense of the verb.

then searched in each subcorpus for APs and PPs occurring within five words to the right of the target verb. The resulting lists were searched manually for resultative uses of APs and PPs occurring within five words to the right of the target verb. This search allowed me to create tables for each verb detailing the frequency with which it occurred in specific types of resultative phrases (see Appendix B). Each manual counting was repeated twice in order to avoid errors. Again, as this procedure could not be fully automated, I chose to analyze only a few selected verbs that frequently occur with resultative phrases.

In addition to arriving at a statistical distribution of resultative constructions, the present study also contains resultative constructions from sources besides the BNC, such as the COBUILD Bank of English (http://titania.cobuild.collins.co.uk/) and a number of dictionaries. Throughout this monograph each example taken from a corpus or a dictionary is marked with the appropriate citation. Finally, Usenet group archives and websites on the Internet were a very helpful resource for data collection. These archives contain text from e-mails and web pages written by people who are relatively free and creative in their use of language.[20] In cases in which data collected from electronic corpora seemed 'suspicious,' I checked with ten native speakers to see whether they would agree on the acceptability of questionable sentences. Besides these methods of data collection, intuitive and casual elicitation of native speakers in order to trigger innovations of resultative constructions played a role in order to supplement the largely corpus-based approach proposed in this monograph. Thus, the methodology followed in this work can be characterized as what Leech (1991: 74) calls 'a question of corpus *plus* intuition, rather than of corpus *or* intuition.'

Judgments made about the acceptability of resultative constructions in this work reflect the method of data collection. In cases in which the large majority of speakers found a sentence to be unacceptable, a sentence is marked by an asterisk ('*'). The use of the asterisk does not necessarily indicate that the resultative construction is ungrammatical (see Chomsky's (1965: 10-21) discussion of grammaticalness vs. acceptability), but that it sounds unacceptable to the majority of the speech community's members under regular contextual background conditions such as conventionalized knowledge about the usage patterns of the respective verb. The use of question marks ('?') indicates that speakers differ with respect to their acceptability judgments of the respective resultative constructions. Before end-

[20]The messages of different Usenet groups can now be accessed at Google-groups at http://www.google.com. Internet citations are followed by the web-page address or the Message-ID number.

ing this section, a few words of caution are in order with respect to the conclusions drawn from the data collected for our analysis of English resultative constructions. The analysis proposed in this monograph relies mainly on about 6000 corpus-based example sentences and several hundred sentences taken from the literature, dictionaries, the Internet, and native speaker elicitations. In this respect, it is – to my knowledge – the largest data pool of English resultatives collected for the purpose of a comprehensive investigation of this phenomenon to date. This means that the analysis presented in the remaining chapters accounts primarily for the types of resultative constructions exemplified by our data. However, as our discussion of nonconventionalized resultatives in Chapter 7 will show, this does not automatically mean that the analysis proposed in the remaining chapters is in principle capable of predicting the distribution of *every* possible resultative construction. Nevertheless, the current approach provides us with an account that is capable of successfully capturing the syntactic and semantic distribution of more than 6000 English resultative constructions while avoiding a number of problems faced by existing accounts. To this end, the corpus-based analysis presented in this monograph is based on the two principles of empirical observational study identified by Stubbs (2001) as follows:

> (1) The observer must not influence what is observed. Data and analysis must be independent. What is selected for observation admittedly depends on such factors as convenience, personal interests and prior hypotheses. Nevertheless, corpus data were part of natural language use and not produced for purposes of linguistic analysis.
>
> (2) Repeated events are significant. The first task of corpus linguistics is to describe what is usual and typical. Unique events certainly occur, but can be described only against the background of what is normal and expected. The frequent occurrence of lexical or grammatical patterns is good evidence of what is typical and routine in language use. (Stubbs 2001: 21)

The mechanisms proposed for accounting for nonconventionalized resultatives in Chapter 7 are capable of providing us with a comprehensive set of conditions that need to be satisfied in order for nonconventionalized resultatives to be licensed.

1.5 Overview of the Book

The goal of this book is to determine the licensing factors underlying the distribution of English resultative constructions. In the chapters that follow, I first examine the syntactic and semantic distribution of English resultatives, and then develop a lexical-constructional account that distinguishes between conventionalized and nonconventionalized resultative constructions. The former are conventionalized mini-constructions contained in what has traditionally been called 'the lexicon.' The latter are formed by analogy based on existing conventionalized mini-constructions in combination with contextual background information. In particular, I will emphasize the influence of a speaker's lexical knowledge on licensing resultatives and will argue with Bergenholtz and Kaufmann (1996) and Inchaurralde (1997, 2000) that the line between lexical knowledge and world knowledge is fuzzier than previously assumed. This in turn explains why the acceptability of resultatives varies so greatly between speakers. The book is structured as follows.

Chapter 2 surveys various syntactic analyses of resultatives and their theoretical devices. It begins with a discussion of several approaches which take the notion of Small Clauses as central to the analysis of secondary predication structures (Chomsky 1986, Hoekstra 1988, Aarts 1992, Staudinger 1997, Bowers, 1997, among others). I then discuss models that employ Predication Theory as their guiding principle in order to capture the distribution of resultative constructions (Williams 1983, Rothstein 1985, Napoli 1988, 1989, 1992, and Carrier and Randall 1992, among others). Small Clause Theory and Predication Theory both attempt to account for the distribution of resultative constructions primarily in terms of syntactic mechanisms.

In Chapter 3 I take a look at a number of proposals which take event structure to be crucial for the licensing of resultative constructions. In particular, I discuss how Tenny (1994), Pustejovsky (1991, 1995), Winkler (1997), and Rappaport Hovav and Levin (1998, 2001) apply aspectual notions to explain the licensing of resultatives. Based on a detailed discussion of the lexical semantics associated with a broad number of verbs, I argue that an approach to resultatives based solely on aspectual notions such as event structure is problematic on several points, most notably with respect to the licensing of postverbal elements.

Chapter 4 discusses Goldberg's (1995) approach to English resultatives, one of the most prominent analyses of the phenomenon to date. Working within Construction Grammar (Fillmore and Kay 1993, Fillmore, Kay and O'Connor 1988, and Lakoff 1987), Goldberg takes the notion of independently existing meaningful constructions as central to the licensing of a verb's arguments. On this view, resultative constructions are capable of supplying a verb's semantics with additional arguments such as resultative phrases and postverbal NPs.

While this approach arrives at a much more detailed analysis of resultative constructions than previous accounts, I show that it is problematic in terms of the range of application of constructions. More specifically, Goldberg's constraints on the fusion of constructional and verbal semantics are imprecise when it comes to capturing the full semantic and syntactic range of resultative phrases. These observations lead me to argue that the problems are partly due to the fact that lexical entries of the verbs postulated by Goldberg often do not distinguish between individual conventionalized senses. In order to account for the distribution of resultative constructions that may occur with a given verb I suggest shifting the explanatory burden from the level of abstract constructional semantics to the level of concrete verbal semantics. This discussion prepares the ground for the model of resultatives that I develop in the remainder of the book.

In Chapter 5 I propose a usage-based lexical-constructional approach to resultatives. First, I present the main ideas of usage-based approaches to the study of language as advocated by Leisi (1954), Firth (1957), Langacker (1987, 2000), Fillmore (1989), Hunston and Francis (2000), and Stubbs (2001), among others. I then show that a usage-based approach has a number of conceptual as well as empirical advantages over previous accounts of resultatives. Finally, I argue that the multiple conventionalized senses associated with verbs are central to a framework that aims to capture the full range of resultative constructions, thereby laying the groundwork for the lexical-constructional approach developed throughout the rest of the book. Based on corpus data which show that particular senses of verbs subcategorize for distinct semantic and/or syntactic classes of resultative phrases and distinct semantic classes of postverbal NPs, I propose that resultative constructions should be grouped into two main classes, namely conventionalized resultative constructions and nonconventionalized resultative constructions. For the class of conventionalized resultatives I argue for three distinct subclasses based on their communicative function while nonconventionalized resultatives form their own class.

Chapter 6 is devoted to the question of what types of lexical-semantic information are needed to account for the distribution of conventionalized and nonconventionalized resultatives. I discuss in detail the content and structure of lexical-semantic information and its relationship to more general world knowledge (see Langacker 1987, Deane 1992, Pustejovsky 1995, Inchaurralde 1997, 2000). Adopting the main ideas of Frame Semantics (Fillmore 1982, 1985, Fillmore and Atkins 1992), I first introduce the concept of event-frames which contain two types of interrelated information.

The first type of information, which I call *on-stage information*, is linguistically immediately relevant information that needs to be overtly realized because it is conceptually the most salient type of information. The second type of information, *off-stage information*, may only be realized linguistically given the proper contextual conditions because it is conceptually less salient. Then, I propose a splitting approach towards the description of verbal semantics. On this view, each sense of a verb is represented by its own rich idiosyncratic 'packet of semantic information' (an event-frame). It includes information about event participants, force-dynamic relations (Talmy 2000) between event participants, temporal information, world knowledge, and specifications with respect to the types of resultative phrases occurring with a given sense of a verb. Lastly, I take up the question of differences between senses that are associated with the same verb as well as questions of possible generalizations across different verb classes.

Chapter 7 spells out the details of the lexical-constructional approach to resultative constructions. The first part of the chapter concerns the licensing of conventionalized resultatives. The members of the three subclasses outlined in Chapter 5 are accounted for in terms of event-frames which represent the conventionalized semantic/pragmatic as well as syntactic information about a particular sense of a verb. For each of the three subclasses of conventionalized resultatives, I show how different types of licensing mechanisms are responsible for realizing on-stage and off-stage information associated with a number of mini-constructions representing individual senses of a given verb. The second part of the chapter is devoted to the licensing mechanisms underlying nonconventionalized resultative constructions. Based on the distribution of postverbal arguments with a number of air-emission verbs, I argue that nonconventionalized resultatives are formed by analogy on the basis of existing prototypical resultatives that are conventionalized. In these cases, a target event-frame is associated with a new syntactic frame that is capable of overtly realizing a nonprototypical event participant as well as its result state.

In Chapter 8 I examine the distribution of German resultative constructions in order to compare and contrast them with their English counterparts. I argue that the contrasting resultative formations in German and English can be partially accounted for by more general differences between the two languages and are thus not properties particular to resultatives. In particular, I propose that the distinct lexical polysemy networks (cf. Iwata 1998, 2002, Fillmore and Atkins 2000, Boas 2001) of historically related English and German verbs are responsible for differences in the licensing of resultatives. This observation leads me to suggest that general rules and principles used for deriving resultative constructions across languages are problematic.

Finally, Chapter 9 contains a summary and some proposals for future research. The conclusion emerging from this work is that an analysis of resultative constructions does not necessitate generative syntactic rules, event structure augmentation mechanisms, or meaningful constructions adding further roles to a verb's argument structure in order to account for the licensing of resultative phrases and nonsubcategorized NPs. Instead, the relevant information that is contributed to a verb's lexical entry by some mechanism in other frameworks is already contained in one of the various conventionalized event-frames associated with a verb. This information needs only to be highlighted by different sets of perspectivizing mechanisms that are capable of realizing different types of on-stage and off-stage information already contained in a mini-construction associated with a given verb. Although the analysis of resultative constructions that I propose here is developed within the framework of Construction Grammar, it should transfer fairly straightforwardly to other mono-stratal theories of grammar that include a stronger orientation towards more detailed lexical-semantic information such as Head-Driven Phrase Structure Grammar or Lexical Functional Grammar.

2

Syntactic Approaches to Resultatives

> Syntactic investigation of a given language has as its goal the construction of a grammar that can be viewed as a device of some sort for producing the sentences of the language under analysis. (Chomsky 1957: 11)

2.1 Introduction

In this chapter I survey a number of syntactic approaches to resultative constructions and show how they account for the distribution of postverbal arguments in terms of different licensing mechanisms. Section 2.2 begins with a discussion of the Small Clause (SC) Theory as originally developed by Chomsky (1981) and Stowell (1981/1983). This theory proposes that resultative constructions are a subtype of secondary predication constructions that should be analyzed as sentential constituents at the syntactic level which is smaller than a clause. I show that there are a number of empirical as well as theory-internal problems with these accounts, leading me to argue that a SC analysis of resultatives is untenable.

In Section 2.3 I turn to an alternative analysis of resultative constructions in terms of Predication Theory as presented in Williams (1983). On this view, resultative constructions should not be analyzed in terms of a sentential constituent, but rather as 'flat' structures in which the predication relationship between the individual constituents is represented in terms of coindexation. I argue that although the different Predication Theory analyses acknowledge a difference between depictive and resultative secondary predication constructions, they also exhibit a number of problems when it comes to capturing the full distribution of resultative constructions. This shortcoming is caused by largely ignoring lexical semantic information associated with the individual constituents of the resultative construction.[1]

2.2 Small Clause Analyses of Resultative Constructions

Small Clause (SC) Theory proposes that secondary predication constructions should be analyzed as sentential constituents on the syntactic level that are smaller than clauses. Although Williams (1975) originally coined the term SC to describe a small set of constructions containing gerunds and participle constructions, the term's usage was soon expanded to describe a much wider range of sentences including various secondary predication structures.[2] In the following sections, I do not intend to discuss all aspects of SC Theory or its implications for an overall adequate theory of secondary predication in either the Principles and Parameters framework, or syntax in general.[3] Instead, I will focus only on its relevant points in order to illustrate how they relate to the analysis of resultative constructions. The goal of this section is to show that the application of SC Theory to resultatives is problematic for a number of theoretical as well as empirical reasons and should therefore be abandoned.[4]

2.2.1 Small Clause Theory

SC Theory is set in the framework of Government and Binding (GB) (Chomsky 1981), an early version of the Principles and Parameters approach to syntactic theory. In this framework, semantic predication relations

---

[1] Parts of this chapter have been published as Boas (2000a).

[2] Williams later recanted an analysis of secondary predication constructions in terms of Small Clauses (see Williams 1983) and offered an analysis of secondary predication constructions in terms of Predication Theory.

[3] The term 'Principles and Parameters' refers to different versions of the Chomskyan approach to syntactic theory. For a comprehensive overview, see Haegeman (1991), Webelhuth (1995), and Radford (1997). This comprehensive term covers one of Chomsky's earlier versions, namely 'Government and Binding Theory' (GB) (Chomsky 1981), as well as Chomsky's most recent version, namely the 'Minimalist Program' (MP) (Chomsky 1992, 1995).

[4] This is not an entirely new view. Although there have been various convincing counterproposals to a SC analysis of resultatives (e.g., Carrier and Randall (1992), Winkler (1997), Lüdeling (1997), and Kim and Maling (1997), among others), adherents of the SC Theory seem to provide new data and theoretical assumptions that lead them to repeatedly analyze resultatives in terms of SCs. The most recent accounts include Staudinger's (1997) hybrid analysis of resultatives in German, Bowers' (1997) Binary Branching Analysis for English resultatives, and Neeleman and van de Koort's (2001) analysis.

between a predicate and its arguments are interpreted at some level, typically Logical Form.[5] Proponents of this framework suggest that there exists a semantic predication relation between a secondary predicate and a postverbal NP which parallels that of a subject and a predicate in full clauses. Compare the following sentences which include complement SCs (cf. (2.1)), adjunct SCs (cf. (2.2) and (2.3)), and resultative SCs (cf. (2.4)).[6]

(2.1) Mary considers [$_{SC}$ Kim smart].
(2.2) Pat$_i$ ate the steak [$_{SC}$ PRO$_i$ naked].
(2.3) Bart drank his soda$_i$ [$_{SC}$ PRO$_i$ warm].
(2.4) Lisa painted her door$_i$ [$_{SC}$ PRO$_i$ pink].

According to Chomsky's (1986) analysis, the two postverbal elements in (2.1)-(2.4) are categorized as SCs. In SC terminology, *Kim* in (2.1) is the SC subject and *smart* is the SC predicate. On this view, the semantic predication relation between the two postverbal elements is encoded syntactically in terms of a pair of sister constituents which together form a sentential constituent, namely a Small Clause (cf. Stowell 1983). In other words, SCs are similar to full clauses in that they contain a subject and a predicate. They differ, however, in that SCs are morphologically less complex than full clauses as they do not show any tense marking.[7] SC Theory assumes that all of the sentences in (2.1) – (2.4) exhibit the same structure, i.e., they contain SCs consisting of a subject and a predicate:

(2.5) Syntactic Structure of a Small Clause

V [$_{SC}$ NP XP], where X $\in$ {A, N, P, V}

---

[5]GB assumes different levels of syntactic representation (D-structure, S-structure, and Logical Form) that are derived from each other. For a more detailed description, see Webelhuth (1995: 28-51).

[6]For detailed discussions about the structural differences between the three types of SCs, see Hayashi (1991), Kikuchi and Takahashi (1991), Aarts (1992), and Staudinger (1997).

[7]For a discussion of SCs in other languages, in particular with respect to agreement for gender, number, and case within SC structures, see Stowell (1995) and Suzuki (1991) for French, Endo (1991) for Old English, Moro (1988) for Italian, Moro (1995) for Italian and Russian, Staudinger (1997) for German, Hornstein and Lightfoot (1987) for English, Starke (1995) for Slovak, Chung and McKloskey (1987) for Irish, Ramchand (1997) for Scotts Gaelic, Kikuchi and Takahashi (1991) for Korean, Japanese, and Chinese, Schein (1995) for Russian, Levin and Simpson (1981) for Icelandic, Kim and Maling (1997) for Korean, Finnish, and Tamil, Jespersen (1924) for Norwegian and German, and Contreras (1987) for Spanish.

Although the syntactic structure of the SCs in (2.1)-(2.4) appears to be identical, there are two main differences between them. The first is that adjunct SCs as in (2.2) and (2.4) can be omitted whereas complement SCs as in (2.1) cannot. This has to do with the fact that the matrix verb in (2.1) selects for the entire complement SC and theta-marks it as a proposition.[8] Although the matrix verb case-marks the SC subject with accusative case in (2.1) – (2.4), SC Theory claims that the SC subject does not receive a theta-role from the matrix verb. Within the complement SC in (2.1), the SC predicate theta-marks the overt SC. The fact that the SC subject and the SC predicate show agreement has been taken as evidence that the two elements are dominated by some node which indicates that they form a syntactic constituent. It is generally believed that SCs are similar to 'full' clauses in that they exhibit a predication relationship between a predicate and its structural subject. They are different in that SCs, as opposed to 'full' clauses, do not exhibit any overt tense morphology or complementizers.[9]

The second difference between the complement SC in (2.1) and the adjunct SCs in (2.2)-(2.4) is that the latter include a phonetically empty subject PRO (see Hornstein and Lightfoot 1987), which is controlled by either the matrix subject *Pat* in (2.2) or the matrix object *soda* in (2.3). The occurrence of the phonetically empty subject PRO is motivated by theory-internal principles such as the Theta Criterion (Chomsky 1986, Abraham 1995, Eisenberg 1989, Nakajima 1990, and Aarts 1995). Having summarized the main differences between complement and adjunct SCs, we now turn our attention to a number of different approaches arguing for an analysis of resultatives in terms of either complement or adjunct SCs.

---

[8]In the Principles and Parameters framework, semantic predication relations are expressed in terms of theta-marking. It is assumed that verbs lexically require a certain number of arguments to which they assign theta-roles at some level of representation. Chomsky's (1981: 36) original version of the Theta Criterion (Each argument bears assigned one and only one theta-role, and each theta-role is assigned to one and only one argument.) was aimed at insuring that each of a verb's arguments received a theta-role. For an overview, see Schlesinger (1995: 56). For a critical review, see Culicover and Wilkins (1986: 147ff) and Rauh (1988).

[9]There exists some disagreement on the differences between complement SCs and adjunct SCs depending on the language under analysis. See, e.g., Contreras (1987) for SCs in Spanish, Chung and McCloskey (1987) for SCs in Irish, and Staudinger (1997) for SCs in German. For different proposals on the internal structure of SCs, see Stowell (1983), Kitagawa (1985), Chomsky (1986), Hornstein and Lightfoot (1987), Hoekstra (1992a), Bowers (1993), Rapoport (1995), Pesetzky (1995), and Williams (1995a), among many others.

2.2.2 Resultatives as Complement SCs

Hoekstra (1988, 1992b) discusses three different kinds of verb classes that occur in resultative constructions: the first class consists of verbs that are usually intransitive but may combine with a postverbal NP and a predicate to form a resultative construction (cf. (2.6)). The second class includes verbs that are typically transitive but, if combined with a NP alone, do not form a coherent semantic unit (cf. (2.7)). The third class of verbs is typically transitive but may combine with a NP and a predicate to form a resultative construction (cf. (2.8)).

(2.6) Jim danced Mary tired.

(2.7)
a. He washed the soap out of his eyes.
b. He shaved his hair off.
c. They wrung a confession out of him.
d. They ate us out of house and home.
(Hoekstra 1988: 116)

(2.8)
a. They painted the door green.
b. They cooked the chicken dry.
c. They pushed him into the well.
(Hoekstra 1988: 117)

Hoekstra points out that the postverbal NPs in both (2.6) and (2.7) occur with verbs 'that do not usually take an object' and that they do not exhibit any 'sensible semantic relationship' with respect to the matrix verb (1988: 116). This leads him to conclude that the postverbal NP is not an argument of the verb and that all three types of resultatives should be analyzed along the same lines. Based on this verb classification, Hoekstra proposes the following structure for the three different kinds of resultatives in (2.6)-(2.8):

(2.9)

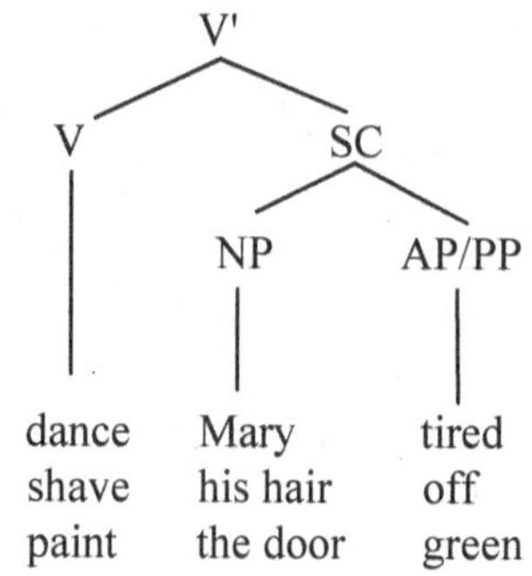

The structure in (2.9) shows that all three classes of resultatives exhibit the same syntactic structure: the postverbal NP and the resultative phrase form a Small Clause constituent which is realized as the complement of the matrix verb.[10] Note, however, in order for Hoekstra's account to work for transitive verbs such as *paint*, *cook*, and *push* in (2.8), he has to make the problematic assumption that transitive verbs get detransitivized in resultative constructions so that the postverbal NP is the subject of the Small Clause rather than the direct object of the matrix verb. Hoekstra (1988: 118) attributes interpreting the postverbal NPs of transitive verbs as direct objects of the matrix verbs to a purely pragmatic phenomenon, or so-called 'shadow interpretation'.[11] Sentences such as (2.10a-c) are taken as evidence that the two postverbal elements in (2.9) form a syntactic constituent, namely a resultative SC, which has to be theta-marked by the matrix verb:

(2.10) a. John paints the door.
b. *John paints green.
c. John paints.

According to Hoekstra, sentences such as (2.10a) do not contain a resultative predicate as part of a SC complement structure which means that they cannot be interpreted as resultatives. (2.10b) is unacceptable since the post-

[10]Stowell's (1983) account of resultatives differs from Hoekstra's (1988) analysis in that Stowell assumes that the matrix verb does select for and theta-marks the postverbal NP. Stowell's (1983: 306) approach to what he calls 'quasi causative constructions' analyzes resultatives in terms of ternary branching structures that include a SC whose subject is PRO.

[11]Wilder (1994: 222, 233-234) comes to the same preliminary conclusions as Hoekstra (with regard to the shadow interpretation of postverbal NPs in resultative constructions). Wilder's account differs from Hoekstra's, however, in that he assumes a SC adjunction analysis for only those verbs that can appear in the Middle Construction. On this view, then, not all resultative constructions are complement SCs.

verbal NP, i.e., the SC subject, is missing. Finally, (2.10c) cannot be interpreted as a resultative because it simply denotes an activity without a resultant state denoted by a resultative SC. Thus, according to Hoekstra's analysis, the sentences in (2.10a-c) cannot be interpreted as resultatives because the matrix verb cannot assign the appropriate theta-role to the resultative SC constituent.[12]

Hoekstra is also concerned with the requirements for the licensing of the result SC, specifically with the constructions that appear with verbs that are usually intransitive. After reviewing Jayaseelan's (1984) 'Small Clause Rule' and Simpson's (1983) analysis, Hoekstra turns to a semantic explanation in order to motivate the licensing of SCs. Combining Vendler's (1967), Lakoff's (1970) and Dowty's (1979) aspectual classifications of verbs, Hoekstra distinguishes two main classes of verbs, namely stative and non-stative verbs. Stative verbs such as *know* or *like* show 'no internal temporal structure, i.e., there is no clear beginning or end, and there is no internal differentiation.' (Hoekstra 1988: 128) In contrast, non-stative verbs typically denote processes or activities.[13]

With this classification of verbs at hand, Hoekstra claims to be able to account for the licensing environments of complement SCs: in his view, verbs denoting an activity or process, i.e., non-stative verbs, are able to take SCs as their complements. Stative verbs, on the other hand, take NPs as their complements, because they denote states of affairs (Hoekstra 1988: 129). This distinction allows Hoekstra to explain why verbs such as *build* can take both a result-denoting complement SC and an NP complement in Dutch as in (2.11) and (2.12): 'the state of affairs resulting from the activity can be represented by either a SC or an NP.' (1988: 129)

(2.11) Jan bouwt [de stad vol].
'John builds the city full.'

(2.12) Jan bouwt [een huis].
'John builds a house.' (Hoekstra 1988: 129/130)

---

[12]Note that Hoekstra remains vague with respect to the nature of the theta-role assigned to the resultative SC: 'The SC-complement receives a particular theta-role from the matrix verb, a role that may also be borne by a full clausal complement in the general case.' (Hoekstra 1988: 115)

[13]Hoekstra's classification differs from Vendler's (1967) classification of predicates in one important point. Vendler distinguishes between states, activities, accomplishments and achievements. Hoekstra's framework consists of two classes of verbs, namely statives and non-statives, the latter class including verbs denoting processes (which are merely happening) and activities (which are instigated by some participant).

Hoekstra is careful to point out that 'not any type of NP may be combined with an activity denoting verb to denote a resulting state.' (1988: 130) Unfortunately, he does not provide an exact classification of the class of NPs that combine with activity denoting verbs. Moreover, Hoekstra's assumption that the postverbal NP and the resultative predicate form a syntactic constituent raises the following theoretical problems.

First, for Hoekstra's detransitivization approach to work for verbs like *paint*, it must contain an additional rule that operates over the matrix verb's argument structure in the syntax. This rule must be part of a larger apparatus that has to determine first, which syntactic structure a transitive verb appears in and second, the direct object of the verb's argument list. This procedure resembles deletion operations of earlier generative accounts that have been shown to be problematic. Moreover, the existence of such detransitivization processes is not supported by any independent empirical data. Hoekstra's detransitivization rule seems therefore untenable.[14]

The second problem in Hoekstra's theory is his argument that the matrix verb's detransitivization prohibits the postverbal NP from functioning as its direct object. Recall that only the resultative predicate assigns the postverbal NP a theta-role whereas the matrix verb assigns a theta-role to the entire SC constituent. Carrier and Randall (1992) point out, however, that resultative constructions with obligatory transitive verbs semantically select for the postverbal NP:

(2.13) a. *The bears frightened the campground empty.
b. *The baby shattered the oatmeal into portions.
c. *The magician hypnotized the auditorium quiet.
(Carrier and Randall 1992: 187)

Based on these and other data (see Section 2.3.3), Carrier and Randall claim that obligatory transitive verbs exhibit the same semantic restrictions in resultative constructions as they do in non-resultative sentences. Contrary to Hoekstra (1988), who has no mechanism to rule out unattested forms like those in (2.13), Carrier and Randall (1992) conclude that the transitive verbs in resultative constructions have not become detransitivized. The fact that matrix verbs in resultative constructions differ with respect to the number of

---

[14]Note that Hoekstra (1988) is also unclear about where such detransitivization rules apply. Since he postulates such rules, he must assume that the lexical entry of such verbs is specified as transitive. This means that at some point in the syntactic derivation, Hoekstra's detransitivization rule applies in order to detransitivize the transitive verb. However, altering a verb's subcategorization frame during the syntactic derivation is a violation of the Projection Principle (cf. Chomsky 1981: 29, 38).

arguments they take therefore remains unaccounted for in Hoekstra's analysis.[15]

Finally, consider the status of the SC predicate, i.e., the resultative phrase. According to Hoekstra, the resultative phrase theta-marks the postverbal NP because the two elements are in a subject-predicate relationship. However, Hoekstra's analysis has no principled way of capturing the distribution of resultative phrases in the following sentences:

(2.14) a. John painted the house {green/*old/*expensive}.
b. The joggers ran their Nikes {threadbare/*purple/*new}.
c. The gardener watered the tulips {flat/*red/*cheap}.

The resultative predicates *old* and *expensive* in (2.14a) can be predicated of the SC subject *the house* in regular depictive sentences (*The house is old/expensive*), i.e., they are able to assign a theta-role to their subject in full-fledged clauses. However, they are not allowed as predicates of the resultative SC because they do not permit a resultative predication. Similar observations can be made about the sentences in (2.14b) and (2.14c). This problem is in part due to Hoekstra's allowing the matrix verb to assign only one theta-role to the entire SC without specifying the exact status of the theta-role.[16]

In this section I have shown that Hoekstra's theory is problematic on three levels. First, it assumes that all resultative constructions exhibit the same structural pattern which forces the theory to assume a superfluous detransitivization mechanism. Second, Hoekstra's analysis has no effective mechanism to account for the semantic selection restrictions with respect to the SC subject. Moreover, Hoekstra has no mechanism to explain the licensing of resultative SCs following intransitive verbs. Finally, Hoekstra's framework has no mechanism that adequately captures the semantic distribution of resultative predicates. Thus, Hoekstra's framework of resultative

---

[15]Den Dikken and Hoekstra (1994) defend the analysis of resultatives in terms of SCs by claiming that in intransitive resultatives, there is 'an empty resultative predicate heading the verb's SC complement' (1994: 92). On this view, there is no selection restriction that holds between the matrix verb and the postverbal NP. 'The verb s-selects a specific type of resultative phrase, and this resultative phrase in its turn predicates of a specific type of subject'. (1994: 95) However, den Dikken and Hoekstra remain unclear about the details of how the s-selection of resultative predicates works. Specifically, they do not give any criteria that help to determine how the resultative predicate selects for the postverbal NP in their account. Moreover, they give no licensing mechanisms for the fake object cases. From all this follows that their account does not offer any advantages besides being able to claim that it satisfies GB-internal requirements such as the binary branching principle or the restricted Theta Criterion.

[16]For an elaborate discussion and critique of theta-roles, see Rauh (1988).

SCs is unable to adequately capture the full range of the distribution of resultative constructions.

2.2.3 Resultatives as Verb-Preposition Constructions

Following work by Kayne (1984, 1985), Aarts' (1989) presents an analysis of resultatives that distinguishes between two classes of verbs. On the basis of coordination and stand alone tests, Aarts (1989: 280-282) suggests that so-called A-verbs such as *switch off* in (2.15a) differ from B-verbs such as *look up* in (2.15b) in that the former subcategorize for a SC whereas the latter do not. This structural difference is illustrated in (2.16)

(2.15) a. I *switched* the light *off.*
b. I *looked* the information *up*.

(Aarts 1989: 179)

(2.16) a. A-verbs: $[_{VP}$ V $[_{IP}$ NP PP]]
b. B-verbs: $[_{VP}$ V NP PP]

The distinction between the two verb classes is important because Aarts suggests that 'spatial-resultative constructions' contain A-verbs.[17] Following Stowell (1981, 1983) and Hoekstra (1991, 1992a, 1992b, 1992c), among others, Aarts claims that the SC predicate in (2.16a) theta-marks the SC subject, whereas the matrix verb assigns a theta-role to the entire SC and an accusative case to the SC subject. In structures including B-verbs, on the other hand,

> the v-node assigns a theta-role to the NP, and to the prepositional phrase. We can view this prepositional phrase as what has been called a 'quasi-argument' (see Chomsky 1981: 37, 325). Such arguments occur in theta-positions and, because of their idiomatic status, receive dummy theta-roles. (Aarts 1989: 284)

Based on the syntactic differences between A-verbs and B-verbs, Aarts (1989: 280) proposes that A-verbs subcategorize for 'spatial-resultative constructions.' For example, in (2.17), the verb *switch off* is used in a resul-

---

[17] In earlier works on this topic, A-verbs and B-verbs are classified as so-called phrasal verbs, as opposed to prepositional verbs. See Chomsky (1957), Marchand (1969), Bolinger (1971), Dixon (1982), Emonds (1976, 1985), Herslund (1984), and Kayne (1984), among many others.

tative sense in that there is a patient argument, *the light*, which undergoes an action and ends up in a specific result state as a result of that action.[18]

(2.17) a. I switched the light off.
b. I switched off the light.

Given that particle verbs with a resultative sense can be classified as A-verbs, we now turn to the question of whether Aarts' account of 'spatial-resultative constructions' in terms of properties of A-verbs succeeds on two levels. First, we examine whether Aarts' account explains the structure of verb-preposition structures that are interpreted as resultatives. Second, we examine whether it is also capable of analyzing other resultative constructions in a similar manner.

The first point is concerned with the movement of the SC subject. While Aarts (1989) assumes that the SC subject can move to the right to adjoin to VP, this does not seem to be the case with 'regular' resultatives as the following sentences illustrate:

(2.18) a. Jim painted the house red.
b. *Jim painted red the house.

Note that even if we were to assume that 'regular' resultative constructions are different from verb-preposition constructions containing A-verbs in that the former do not allow rightward movement of the postverbal NP, Aarts' analysis is unable to account for the distribution of the following sentences.

(2.19) a. Rachel drank herself silly.
b. *Rachel drank herself six feet tall.

(2.20) a. Rachel is silly.
b. Rachel is six feet tall.

Aarts' approach fails to account for the difference in acceptability between the sentences (2.19a-b) since the resultative predicates by themselves seem to behave like 'regular' predicate adjectives in full clauses in (2.20a-b), i.e.,

---

[18]For an alternative analysis, see den Dikken (1995) who analyzes particles as independent heads of complement SCs. Since particles are non-lexical elements in his framework (1995: 270), den Dikken's findings cannot be applied to resultative constructions without elaborate changes to his theory which I do not want to attempt in this work. For a complex predicate analysis of this phenomenon, see Hoeksema (1991), Neeleman and Weerman (1993), Neeleman (1995), and Neeleman and van de Koot (2001).

they theta-mark their subject with the proper theta-role. Since the 'full' clause counterparts (2.20a-b) of the resultative SCs in (2.19a-b) are acceptable, it is not clear what causes the ill-formedness of the structure in (2.19b). Another possibility for ruling out the structure in (2.19b) could be seen in the theta-marking properties of the matrix verb. Recall Aarts' suggestion that the matrix verb theta-marks the resultative SC constituent (1989: 283). While the theta-marking of the SC constituent seems to occur for theory-internal reasons, i.e., the matrix verb has to assign an internal theta-role, it is of little help in dealing with the present data. Aarts does not specify exactly what kind of theta-role the matrix verb assigns to the SC constituent, i.e., even if we were to assume with other SC adherents that the matrix verb assigns a propositional theta-role to the SC (see Hoekstra 1992a, 1992b, 1992c), we would not have any way of ruling out the sentence in (2.19b). This seems to be related to the fact that SC Theory does not give an exact description or characterization of the theta-role assigned to the SC constituent. I suspect that the difference in acceptability has to do with the fact that the semantic interpretation of the matrix verb is in some way incompatible with that of the resultative phrase. Thus, the theta-role assignment mechanism and its status as a constraint on combining different lexical items in a construction does not adequately explain the above data. A similar problem can be observed in the following sentences:

(2.21) a. Rachel drank herself silly.
b. *Rachel drank Mathias silly.

(2.22) a. Rachel is silly.
b. Mathias is silly.

Comparing the sentences in (2.21a-b) with the sentences in (2.22a-b) we again see that the SCs are exact counterparts of their fully inflected clauses such that the SC subject is a valid subject of the SC predicate. However, once the SC combines with the matrix verb, the overall structure becomes unacceptable. Again, Aarts has no principled way of ruling out (2.21b) because the matrix verb assigns the same (unspecified) theta-role to the resultative SC constituent in (2.21a-b). Moreover, Aarts' (1989) treatment does not account for the occurrence of patient NPs following lexically transitive verbs, or nonsubcategorized object NPs following lexically transitive verbs (see our discussion of Hoekstra's (1988) analysis in Section 2.2.2 above). From our discussion it must be concluded that Aarts' analysis of spatial-resultative constructions does not adequately capture the distribution of resultative constructions. What is needed is an account that explains not only the semantic selection restrictions that hold for postverbal NPs but also the differences in subcategorization restrictions of intransitive and transitive verbs in resultative constructions.

2.2.4 A Pragmatic Account Towards Resultatives

In a different analysis, Aarts (1992) proposes to analyze resultative constructions in terms of adjunction structures in which the secondary predicate is Chomsky-adjoined[19] to the maximal projection of the verb:

(2.23)

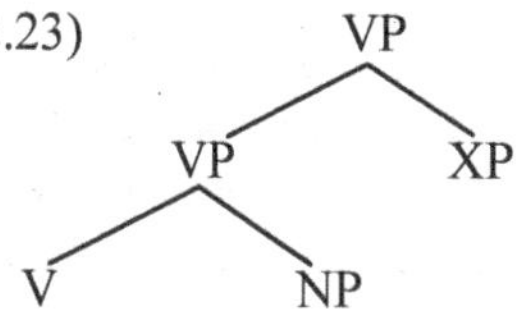

where XP is a resultative predicate phrase.

(Aarts 1992: 59)

After rejecting Rothstein's (1983) analysis which seeks to explain the distribution of resultatives in terms of lexical selection of the matrix verb, Aarts reviews proposals made by McCawley (1971) and Fabb (1984) that attempt to analyze resultative constructions in terms of semantic restrictions. Following Dowty (1976), Aarts proposes the following:

> What is clear from all this is that if we do have semantic restrictions holding between resultative predicates and their subjects they are very difficult to state. (…) This suggests that the observed restrictions should perhaps not be treated in terms of semantic principles, which belong to the grammar, but in terms of extra-grammatical principles whose application is context-driven. (Aarts 1992: 62)

To support his claims, Aarts cites the following examples as evidence:

(2.24) A I was surprised to see Clara clean the kitchen table this morning.

---

[19]See Chomsky (1986), Speas (1986), Roberts (1988), and Haegeman (1994).

B Yes, I asked her to tidy up, but she didn't do a very good job. At one point she was wiping the tables, but rather than wiping them clean she was wiping them dirty by using that filthy rag which is normally used for the loo!

(2.25) A I hear that loony shepherd was shooting at people again the other day.
B Yes, that's right, but this time things got out of hand: he shot Tom in the arm and Jeff is now lame.
A He shot Jeff lame? That man should be put behind bars!
(Aarts 1992: 63)

Note that the resultative predicates in (2.24) and (2.25) do not usually denote prototypical result states that are associated with the action denoted by their matrix verbs: *lame* is not typically expected to appear as the resultative predicate of *shoot*, whereas *dirty* is not readily associated with *wipe*. Since Aarts does not propose a semantic account of the restrictions that hold on the resultative predicate, he concludes that resultatives 'are filtered out by pragmatic principles (which I will not attempt to formulate here).' (1992: 63) However, he neither states the pragmatic principles that underlie the structure of resultative constructions nor does he have any explanation for the distribution of the SC subject in resultatives. This lack of predictability of the distribution of resultative constructions makes Aarts' account problematic. Aarts (1992) claims to have proposed an analysis of resultatives, but he does not sketch out any details (such as what exact (pragmatic or semantic) factors determine the combinatorial patterns of matrix verbs, postverbal NPs, and resultative predicates). Although his observations regarding the role of pragmatics are intuitively correct at first glance, Aarts does not develop them to explain the data. We will return to his ideas about the pragmatic licensing of resultatives in Chapter 6.

2.2.5 A Binary Branching Analysis of Resultatives

In this section, we take a closer look at some of the proposals made by Bowers (1997) regarding the analysis of resultative constructions in terms of binary branching structures within a minimalist framework (cf. Chomsky 1992, 1995).[20] The author bases his analysis on the assumption that every

[20] Chomsky (1992: 12) assumes that SCs are maximal projections of their predicates. These maximal projections are dominated by a functional category, namely AGR. This assumption relates to Abney's (1987) proposal that each lexical category is dominated by at least one functional category.

form of predication reduces to a functional head Pr(edicate) which is the head of a maximal projection PrP.[21]

(2.26)

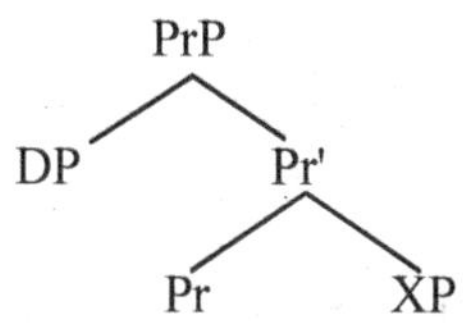

According to Bowers, there is a predication relation between the predicate XP and the structural subject which is base-generated in [DP, PrP] (Bowers 1993: 595). On this view, the verb subcategorizes for a PrP, whereas the Pr itself potentially subcategorizes for any kind of lexical category. Transitive resultatives as well as intransitive resultatives are analyzed by Bowers (1997) as binary branching structures including PrPs as in (2.27b) and (2.28b). Both types of structures are subcategorized for by the matrix verb:

(2.27) a. The gardener watered the tulips flat.
b.

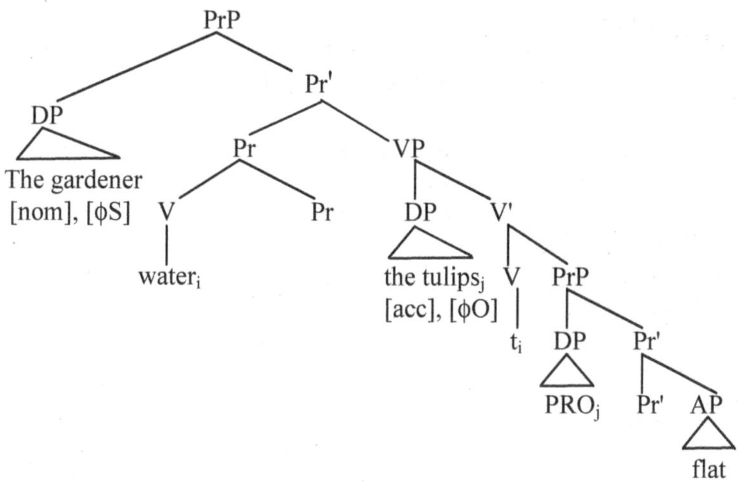

(Bowers 1997: 45)

[21] By positing a new functional category, Bowers (1993) follows numerous other authors who have proposed various functional categories within the Principles and Parameters framework. See, e.g. Pollock (1989) for an analysis of Tense, Chomsky (1995) for Agreement, Hendrick (1991) for Aspect, and Ritter (1991) for Number. Following Bresnan (1995), Ackerman and Webelhuth (1998) criticize the 'explosion' of functional categories: '(…), we posit categorial structure only when there is categorial evidence for it.' (1998: 31)

(2.28) a. The joggers ran their Nikes threadbare.

b.

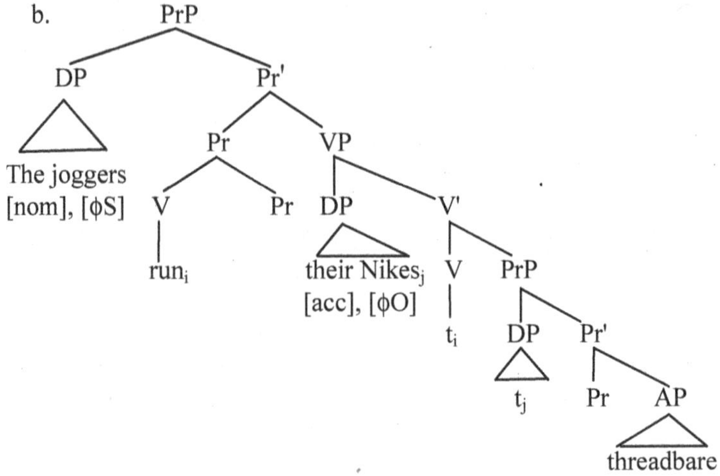

(Bowers 1997: 45)

Bowers explains that in his framework,

> Pr has strong V-features which cause the head of XP to adjoin obligatorily to Pr. I assume in addition that accusative case is strong in English and is checked in [Spec, V], while object agreement features are weak and are checked in the specifier of PrP. (…) Similarly, I assume that nominative case is strong and is checked in [Spec, Pr], while subject agreement features are checked in [Spec, T]. Crucially, I assume that case must be checked when a DP is either merged or moved into either [Spec, V] or [Spec, Pr]. (Bowers 1997: 44)

The movement operations that apply to derive the correct word order are explained as follows:

> In both cases, the strong ϕS features will ultimately force the subject DP to move overtly to [Spec, T], whereas the ϕO features (which are weak in English) will not be checked until LF. Similarly, the strong [acc] case-marked subject of the resultative PrP is forced to move overtly to [Spec, V] to check case features. (Bowers 1997: 45)

Bowers points out that the advantage of his approach is that it allows him to analyze both transitive and intransitive resultatives along the same lines. In particular, he claims that this kind of analysis is superior to other proposals that treat the sentences in (2.27a) and (2.28a) as ternary branching structures because it 'preserves both binarity and a form of the SC analysis, while at the same time preserving the isomorphism between semantic structure and argument structure, on the one hand, and D-structure, on the other.' (1997: 45) While Bowers' main motivation for a binary branching analysis of resultative constructions in terms of PrP seems to lie in his desire to adhere to theory-internal assumptions of GB and the minimalist framework such as the binary branching hypothesis, there are additional problems with his minimalist analysis.

First, consider the status of the postverbal NP. Bowers agrees with Carrier and Randall (1992) 'that the postverbal argument in transitive resultatives (…) is an argument of the verb.' (Bowers 1997: 45) His proposal differs from Carrier and Randall's (1992) account with respect to the structural position of the postverbal NP (=DP) in that he suggests 'that the D-structure position of the postverbal NP is [Spec, V], rather than the complement position.' (Bowers 1997: 45) Unfortunately, Bowers does not present any data to support his claim, nor does he mention any other reasons that could give independent empirical support to his proposal.

Next, we turn to Bowers' claim that postverbal NPs in intransitive resultatives belong to a similar binary branching structure as those in transitive resultatives (cf. (2.27a) and (2.28a)). While we have just seen that the author assumes that the postverbal NP of transitive resultatives is an argument of the matrix verb, Bowers' theory offers no explanation for how the postverbal NP of intransitive resultatives is licensed. The following sentences illustrate my point:

(2.29) a. The joggers ran their Nikes threadbare.
b. *The joggers ran threadbare.

Whereas Hoekstra (1988) assumes that all resultative constructions (both transitive and intransitives) are based on transitive verbs, Bowers' analysis does not even discuss the structural and semantic differences between the postverbal NP of transitive and intransitive verbs. Therefore, his analysis lacks an integral component to account for the occurrence of postverbal NPs with resultatives that are based on lexically intransitive verbs. In short, Bowers' analysis fails to adequately differentiate between transitive and intransitive resultatives' postverbal NPs.

Besides focusing on the status of the postverbal NP we should also take a close look at the status of the resultative predicate in Bowers' framework.

While Bowers claims that 'there can surely be no disagreement that the verb s-selects the result XP in both intransitive and transitive resultatives' (1997: 46/47), he also assumes 'that it is the PrP constituent containing the result XP as its complement that is an argument of, and hence a sister of, the verb.' (1997: 47) In other words, the matrix verb s-selects the resultative predicate by the fact that it subcategorizes for the PrP (=SC) complement. If we follow Bowers' assumption, we might also want to have an explanation for the mechanism that restricts the distribution of PrPs including resultative predicates. Bowers' framework requires not only that the PrP be a complement of the matrix verb but that 'the lexical XP' be the complement of the functional Pr (Bowers 1997: 44). Although there is no explicit mentioning of a possible restriction that holds on the resultative phrase, one might think of the Theta Criterion (Chomsky 1981: 335) which could possibly establish a restriction between the matrix verb and the occurrence of its complement PrP which contains the respective resultative XP under discussion. Consider the following sentences which contain unacceptable resultative phrases and need to be ruled out by an adequate analysis:

(2.30) a. ??The gardener watered the tulips {red/shiny/big}.
b. ??The joggers ran their Nikes {expensive/fashionable}.

In order to exclude (2.30a, b), one might invoke a restrictive mechanism involving the Theta Criterion. However, Bowers first remains 'neutral as to where θ-roles are assigned' (1997: 44) and then claims that

> [w]henever a subject and a predicate form a semantic unit, there is a corresponding constituent in the syntax, namely, PrP. This constituent in turn corresponds to a single argument position in the θ-grid of a verb (or to a single adjunct position, in the case of 'depictive' SCs).
>
> (Bowers 1997: 56)

This assertion indicates that Bowers follows Hoekstra (1988) and Aarts (1992) in claiming that the matrix verb assigns a theta-role to the PrP in order to maintain the θ-criterion in its strongest form (1997: 56) and to 'maintain a far more restrictive theory of grammar.' (1997: 57) Unfortunately, maintaining the θ-criterion in its strongest form to 'maintain a far more restrictive theory of grammar' comes with a price: because the verb theta-marks only the PrP and not its individual constituents, it is unable to account for the distribution of resultative phrases. As I have shown in the foregoing discussion and in the discussion of Hoekstra (1988) and Aarts

(1992), no theory of resultatives should exclude or ignore the distribution of resultative phrases in order to satisfy theory-internal assumptions and requirements.

Our discussion of Bowers' (1997) account shows that although the idea of analyzing both transitive and intransitive resultatives in terms of a uniform Binary Branching Analysis is appealing for theory-internal reasons particular to the Minimalist Program, it poses serious empirical problems when an attempt is made to motivate the occurrence of postverbal NPs of intransitive resultatives. Moreover, there is no mechanism that accounts for the distribution of resultative phrases in this framework. The central problem with Bowers' analysis, as with the other SC analyses presented in this chapter, is the fact that they lack an adequate analysis of the semantic relations that hold between the matrix verb, its postverbal NP, and the resultative phrase.[22]

2.2.6 Summary

Our discussion of a number of different SC analyses has shown that the analysis of resultative constructions in terms of Small Clauses is unsatisfactory for three main reasons. First, the SC analyses come to too far-reaching predictions regarding matrix verbs. Thus, they do not account for the fact that the matrix verbs are lexically different with respect to the number and types of arguments for which they subcategorize. Second, although there are striking resemblances between complement SCs and resultative constructions in terms of the status of the subject-predicate relation, resultatives do not exhibit the same behavior as complement SCs. Further, I have argued that matrix verbs show preferences with respect to the semantic range of resultative phrases. This can only be accounted for by an analysis allowing a semantic selection restriction of resultative phrases by the matrix verb. Moreover, I have presented evidence suggesting that there is indeed some restriction with respect to what kinds of postverbal NPs can appear in resultative constructions. Whereas Aarts (1995: 194) points out that 'Small Clauses will probably remain controversial for some time to come, but they are undoubtedly here to stay,' the above sections demonstrate that SC Theory is unnecessary for the analysis of resultative constructions. In the following sections, we look at alternative approaches towards resultative con-

[22]Radford's (1997: 378/379) account of resultatives within the minimalist framework (Chomsky 1995) differs from Bowers' approach in that it proposes a VP shell analysis (Larson 1988a) that makes use of an abstract tense affix.

structions within GB that differ from SC Theory in their emphasis on thematic relationships in the analysis of predication structures.

2.3 Resultatives in Predication Theory

The set of analyses discussed in the following sections is based on Williams' (1980) Predication Theory (henceforth PT) which outlines a different view of the subject-predicate relation than assumed in 'standard' GB theory (Chomsky 1981/1986). Under this alternative proposal, the problems posed by SC Theory can be avoided if one abandons the assumption that the postverbal NP and the secondary predicate form a syntactic constituent. Williams (1980, 1983) claims that predication is a more elaborate notion which cannot be captured in strictly configurational terms at the syntactic level. He therefore suggests that there is an additional level of representation in grammar that is derived from Surface Structure, namely Predicate Structure (henceforth PS). According to Rothstein (1990: 599), the level of PS should be seen as a 'mapping relation between syntactic predicates and predicates in the semantic representation.' On this view, PS is derived from Surface Structure by a set of predication rules of which are used to indicate the subject-predicate relations found in a sentence (see Williams 1980: 237).[23]

In Williams' framework, resultative constructions are analyzed as a subclass of object-related predication constructions in which there is a predication relation between a verb and the theme of the verb within a VP.[24] This is illustrated by the following diagram.[25]

---

[23]Williams' Rule of Predication (Coindex NP and X. (Williams 1980: 206)) in combination with a C-command Condition on Predication (If NP and X are coindexed, NP must c-command X or a variable bound to X. (Williams 1980: 205)) are central for deriving Predicate Structure. Following Reinhart (1976), c-command is defined by Williams (1980: 204, fn. 1) as follows: 'α c-commands β iff every branching node which dominates α dominates β.'

[24]Object-related predication constructions are also known as *thematically governed predications* (as opposed to *grammatically governed predication* where 'there is a predication relation between a matrix clause subject NP and another element' (Aarts 1992: 26)). Williams (1980: 207) defines the central notion of 'theme' rather vaguely: 'The use of the notion theme is not crucial here. In the worst possible case, it will be necessary to specify which NP a VP-dominated predicate modifies. In this worst case, *theme* is being used as a purely diacritic rule feature. In a large number of cases, though, *theme* seems to give the correct answer, at least to the extent that the notion *theme* is clear in the first place.' See also Roberts (1988), Nakajima (1990), and Winkler (1997) for a discussion of object-related predication.

[25]Although Williams (1980, 1983) does not explicitly mention resultative constructions as falling within the class of object-related predications, subsequent analyses within Predication Theory (e.g., Rothstein (1985), Napoli (1989), Carrier and Randall (1992)) have advocated this view. For expository purposes I have therefore chosen to present the analysis of resultatives in terms of object-related predicates at this point.

(2.31)

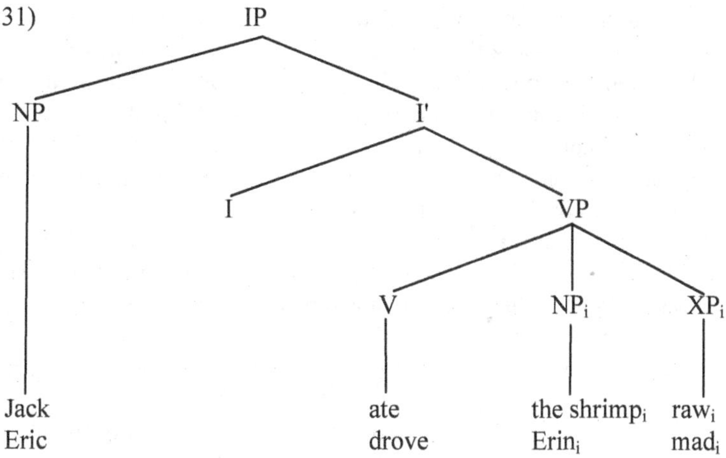

(2.31) illustrates that the secondary predicates *raw* and *mad* are sisters to the postverbal NPs *the shrimp* and *Erin*. Thus, the predication relation that holds under the condition of c-command between the secondary predicates and their respective thematic subjects is represented by coindexation between the two elements. Note that the predication relation between the postverbal NP and the secondary predicate is not reflected in terms of a clausal constituent in syntax: the two constituents are sisters to the matrix verb in a flat tree structure with VP as their mother node. Under this approach both the primary and secondary predicate can theta-mark the postverbal NP.[26]

We now turn to the question of how this approach deals with the distribution of constituents in resultative constructions. First, consider the distribution of resultative phrases in the following sentences.

(2.32) a. John painted the house$_i$ {green/*old/*expensive}$_i$.
b. The joggers ran their Nikes$_i$ {threadbare/*purple/*new}$_i$.
c. The gardener watered the tulips$_i$ {flat/*red/*cheap}$_i$.

Restricting the range of resultative predicates in sentences like (2.32a-c) necessitates a mechanism that (i) takes into account the lexical-semantic

[26]Note that Williams (1983: 300) has to assume a revised Theta Criterion which allows theta-marking under an expanded set of circumstances. For other proposals that argue for a modified version of the Theta Criterion see Schein (1995), Chomsky (1986: 96, 97), and Napoli (1989: 86), among others. For a distinction between primary and secondary theta-roles, see Nakajima (1990: 295/96).

information associated with the matrix verb as well as the resultative predicate and (ii) by using this information, has a principled way of determining which combinations of matrix verb and resultative predicate are permissible. Under Predication Theory as advocated by Williams (1980, 1983), there does not seem to be any such constraint available. Thus, Williams' approach to secondary predication does not seem to offer any compelling alternative to SC Theory in this respect.

Next, consider examples as in (2.33) where the distribution of postverbal NPs seems to be restricted to a rather narrow class of NPs seemingly closely related to the activity denoted by the matrix verb.

(2.33) a. John painted {the house/?his dog/*his beer/*the sky}$_i$ green$_i$.
b. The joggers ran {their Nikes/?their shirts/*their headbands}$_i$ threadbare$_i$.
c. The gardener watered {the tulips/?the apple tree/*the football}$_i$ flat$_i$.

John in (2.33a) can *paint* various objects like *the house* or even *his dog*. However, painting *his beer* is problematic because liquids are typically dyed rather than painted. Moreover, *the sky* sounds odd since one can hardly imagine a real life situation in which a person is able to paint *the sky*. The kind of collocational dependency that holds between the postverbal NP and its matrix verb (and the resultative phrase) in sentences like (2.33a-c) is, however, not represented in the syntactic structure under a Williams-style Predication Theory analysis. To exclude such cases, we need to (i) understand the kinds of relationships that hold between the matrix verb and the postverbal NP and (ii) find a constraint that restricts the range of permissible postverbal NPs in this environment. Thus, if Predication Theory is to fully account for the structure of resultatives, it must be enhanced by a number of semantic restrictions on the postverbal NP and the resultative phrase. We turn to a number of different approaches aimed at capturing this insight in the following sections.

2.3.1 Predicate Linking

Rothstein's (1985) analysis of predication structure differs from Williams' approach in that the former's notion of predication is a purely syntactic licensing mechanism on acceptability at S-Structure within the overarching theory of GB rather than primarily a thematic relation in terms of coindexing (see Rothstein 1985: 7).[27] In order to regulate the occurrence of non-theta-marked constituents, Rothstein proposes the rule of predicate linking in (2.34) which has the same theoretical status as the Theta Criterion (Chomsky 1981: 335) restricting the occurrence of theta-marked constituents in GB:

(2.34) *Rule of predicate Linking (for English):*
   a. Every non-theta-marked XP must be linked at S-structure to an argument which it immediately c-commands and which immediately c-commands it.
   b. Linking is from right to left (i.e., a subject precedes its predicate).

(Rothstein 1985: 11)[28]

Instead of making use of Williams' system of coindexation, Rothstein employs the new rule of predicate linking which links the subject and predicate at S-Structure. Thus, the relation between the subject and its predicate is not only defined structurally in terms of c-command. The following restrictions in combination with (2.34) allow for the licensing of constituents as predicates that would normally not be licensed as predicates under 'regular' GB licensing principles.

(2.35) X is predicated of Y (is a predicate of Y) if and only if X is linked to Y under (…)
(2.36) X is the subject of Y if and only if Y is linked to X under (…)

(Rothstein 1985: 11)

Assuming a modified version of c-command that builds on the notion of maximal projection, Rothstein points out that the distribution of object-

[27]Note that Rothstein (1985), unlike Williams, does not assume an extra level of Predication Structure that is derived from S-Structure to represent coindexing between subjects and predicates. Under her analysis, thematic relations are 'checked at the level of Semantic Representation (SR), which takes LF as its input.' (1985: 4) This view allows her to account for semantic and syntactic asymmetries between external and internal arguments.

[28]Rothstein (1985: 11) points out that '(a) may be universal, whereas (b) is language specific and may have no status in UG, but instead it may follow independently from the language specific properties.' Mallén (1992: 13) shows that Rothstein's rule of predicate linking also holds for Spanish, thus strengthening her claim that secondary predicates are licensed in purely syntactic, but not semantic terms.

related predicates differs from the distribution of resultative predicates as the following examples illustrate.[29]

(2.37) a. Jake hammered the metal flat hot.
b. *Jake hammered the metal hot flat. (Rothstein 1985: 19)

Contrasting (2.37a) and (2.37b) indicates that the resultative predicate must precede the object-related predicate, leading Rothstein to claim that …

> [r]esultative predicates, like thematic arguments of a verb, are selected by the semantic nature of the verb and are represented at S-structure as immediate sisters of the verb.
>
> (Rothstein 1985: 17)

From this observation Rothstein concludes that both types of secondary predicates are licensed by their respective subjects within the VP. The difference between the structure containing the object-related predicate and that containing the resultative predicate is that the semantic relationship between *raw* and its subject *the shrimp* in (2.31) above is not as close as that between *mad* and *Erin*. Rothstein claims that this difference is due to the fact that 'within the lexicon, selectional demands are for semantically appropriate predicates, and are stated in category-neutral terms.' (1983: 83). Therefore, the resultative predicate must be realized as a sister of the matrix verb, whereas the object-related predicate is Chomsky-adjoined (see Chomsky 1986) to a position higher up in the VP. This difference in structural position also explains the difference in linear order in (2.37a, b) above: since the resultative predicate has a closer semantic relationship than the object-related predicate, the former must also precede the latter in sentences containing both kinds of predicates.[30]

Rothstein's lexical selection approach towards resultatives is a first start for (1) representing the close semantic relationship between matrix verb and resultative phrase and (2) establishing a licensing mechanism for resultative phrases. Yet Rothstein's approach also has problems capturing the full

---

[29]Rothstein's modified version of c-command: α c-commands β if and only if every maximal projection dominating α also dominates β. (Rothstein 1985: 15)

[30]Roberts (1988) offers an analysis of resultatives based on the VP-internal subject hypothesis (see Fukui and Speas (1986), Koopman and Sportiche (1991), and Speas (1990)). Under his analysis resultative predicates and object-related predicates are located in the same structural position. For a critique of this view, see Winkler (1997: 70-73). For a modification of Rothstein's original proposal that regards predication as a satisfaction of theta-role requirements, see McNulty (1988).

range of semantic/pragmatic restrictions that hold between the two constituents. Examples (2.38a-d) illustrate my by now familiar point:

(2.38) a. *John hammered the metal {beautiful, safe, tubular}.
b. *John wiped the surface {damp, dirty, stained}.
c. *She wrenched the stick {broken, tight}.
d. *She shot him {lame, paranoid, wounded}.
(Green 1972)

Another problem inherent to Rothstein's approach is the fact that it has no semantic constraint that holds for the distribution of postverbal NPs. As we have seen in the previous section, ruling out uninterpretable sentences as in (2.39) is therefore problematic within Rothstein's analysis.

(2.39) a. John painted {the house/?his dog/*his beer/*the sky}$_i$ green$_i$.
b. The joggers ran {their Nikes/?their shirts/*their headbands}$_i$ threadbare$_i$.
c. The gardener watered {the tulips/?the apple tree/*the football}$_i$ flat$_i$.

The above examples show that Rothstein's lexical selection mechanism is insufficiently equipped to account for the entire distribution of resultative predicates and postverbal NPs. This means that Rothstein's syntactic analysis of resultatives should be supplemented by a detailed lexical semantic treatment making it possible to capture the full distribution of resultatives by also allowing contextual background information to license resultatives. The alternative analysis proposed in Chapter 6 incorporates Rothstein's initial intuition about the close semantic relation between the matrix verb and the resultative predicate.[31]

2.3.2 Resultatives as Degree Modifiers

Napoli's (1989, 1992) account of English and Italian resultatives rests on the assumption that 'there is no isomorphism between syntax and semantics.' (1989: 28)[32] Based on this claim, she adopts Levin and Rappaport's

---

[31]Emonds (1985: 36) presents a similar idea about the close semantic relation between the matrix verb and the secondary predicate. Under his analysis, the matrix verb directly theta-marks the secondary predicate. Then, the secondary predicate assigns a theta-role to its external argument NP.

[32]This observation is based on a variety of syntactic tests ('Non Theta Bearing Items', 'VPs that do not constitute or contain a semantic predicate') discussed in Napoli (1988: 337-340).

(1988) view that languages make use of the process of Lexical Subordination which allows for a semantic process that permits the extension of the basic meaning of a verb by the addition of modifier phrases such as 'a change-of-state or a change-of-location phrase.' (1992: 61) More specifically, Napoli (1992: 56) suggests that in resultative constructions the postverbal NP and the resultative predicate are interpreted as a degree modifier of the verb (see also Carrier and Randall 1988). In order to license the occurrence of the resultative predicate and the postverbal NP, she proposes an analysis that incorporates a productive mechanism called linking flexibility. Per Napoli, linking flexibility is a mechanism that accounts for the fact that postverbal NPs are licensed in a number of different environments, but only under certain conditions as the following examples illustrate.

(2.40) a. She wrapped [the baby] in [a blanket].
b. She wrapped [a blanket] around [the baby].
(Napoli 1992: 67)

Wrap in (2.40) belongs to a verb class that allows flexible linking patterns which is crucial for the analysis of resultatives because the matrix verbs of resultative constructions exhibit a comparable range of linking flexibility (see, e.g., the different linking patterns of matrix verbs mentioned in Chapter 1). Under Napoli's analysis, then, the addition of the resultative predicate *out of the room* and the addition of the postverbal NP *Ralph* in (2.41) is a manifestation of the linking flexibility of *laugh.*

(2.41) Sue laughed Ralph [out of the room]. (Napoli 1992: 66)

The concept of linking flexibility is also used to account for the distribution of fake objects (Simpson 1983). Following Jones (1988), Napoli proposes that reflexive fake objects behave like cognate objects in that they allow lexically intransitive verbs to become transitive, i.e., they act 'as degree modifiers when taken together with a resultative' (1992: 70) as in (2.42). Non-reflexive fake objects, according to Napoli, are analyzed along the same lines in (2.43).[33]

Based on these tests, the author argues that 'there cannot be a one-to-one correspondence between syntax and semantics.' (1988: 349)

[33] Napoli (1992: 71) explains the distribution of fake objects as follows: 'If the resultative is present, it licenses its subject. The resultative itself, of course, is licensed by virtue of the fact that the resultative and its subject modify the verb. And their ability to be understood as modifying the verb follows from the fact that the resultative predicate relates to the endpoint of the

(2.42) She ran herself [ragged].
(2.43) She ran her sole [thin]. (Napoli 1992: 70)

The constraint in (2.44) serves to restrict the distribution of resultatives and rests on the stipulation that 'verbs will have to be marked in the lexicon as to whether or not they allow resultatives.' (1992: 75)[34]

(2.44) *Resultative Interpretation*

> In a sentence with a resultative AP, the primary predicate must be interpreted as focusing on the endpoint of the activity denoted by that predicate. (Napoli 1992: 75)

On this view, 'resultative arguments (...) will appear in the predicate-argument structure and in the subcategorization frame of a verb.' (1992: 75) Napoli points out that her approach is 'not stated in formal terms, and, so far as I can see, is not formalizable. For that reason, it is difficult to evaluate.' (1992: 75) In this connection, Napoli criticizes Simpson's (1983) proposal that 'only appropriate and predictable results are allowed,' and suggests that 'not all semantically and pragmatically appropriate and predictable results are allowed.' (1992: 79, fn. 18) In order to support her rule of Resultative Interpretation, Napoli takes note of the relevant restrictions, albeit without providing a detailed analysis or formalization that would make it possible to characterize the distribution of resultatives. Her restrictions are concerned with the fact that (1) English resultatives which denote a point on a scale deal with an endpoint as in (2.45), (2) modification of a resultative can render it more acceptable as in (2.46), and (3) 'a clear endpoint makes a resultative sound better' (1992: 84) as can be seen in (2.47).

(2.45) a. She wrung the shirt [{dry/*damp}].
b. She watered the tulips [{flat/*droopy}].
c. We heated the coffee [{hot/*tepid}]. (Napoli 1992: 79)

---

main verb's activity. (...) But if the resultative is not present, the non-argument direct object cannot be licensed unless it is interpretable as modifying the main verb.'

[34]According to Napoli, the only constraint that is general enough to be stated in more abstract terms is that 'most AP resultatives that deal with a point on a scale, deal with the endpoint.' (Napoli 1992: 76)

(2.46) a. ??I wrote the letters [long].
b. ?I wrote the letters [long and beautiful].
c. I wrote the letters [so long no one could read them].
(Napoli 1992: 80)

(2.47) a. *That pot sure scrubbed [shiny].
b. That pot sure scrubbed up [shiny], didn't it?
c. *That type of pot scrubs [shiny] easily.
d. That type of pot always scrubs up [shiny].
(Napoli 1992: 80/81)

Napoli attributes these restrictions to an observation made by Bolinger (p.c.) who suggests that the appropriate context can render resultatives that are not endpoints on a scale more acceptable (Napoli 1992: 80). However, the fact that she gives no formalization which can be used to describe the exact distribution of resultative constructions is problematic. Moreover, her rule of Resultative Interpretation does not always seem to hold, as the following German data illustrates.

(2.48) Rotraut hustete ihren Freund krank.
'Rotraut coughed her boyfriend sick.'

The matrix verb *husten* ('to cough') in (2.48) does not necessarily have to be interpreted as focusing on the endpoint of the activity denoted by it (except for the purpose of *husten*, i.e. that something is coughed up for reasons of sickness), yet it may appear with a resultative AP. The resultative endpoint reading in (2.48), namely that *ihren Freund* ('her boyfriend') is sick, is simply a by-product of the activity of *husten* (it is probably not intended). In other words, the boyfriend does not get immediately sick after the agent *Rotraut* stops coughing but rather a few hours or days later as he must first develop a sickness. The fact that the endpoint of the activity and the result state do not always have to coincide shows that Napoli's interpretation rule is too narrow to allow for the correct interpretation of the full range of resultatives. A further problem with Napoli's interpretation rule is that it does not cover resultative phrases that are PPs:

(2.49) a. He washed the soap out of his eyes.
b. They ate us out of house and home.
(Hoekstra 1988: 116)

Napoli proposes the constraint in (2.50) to capture her observation that resultative PPs are semantically less restricted than resultative APs. Although she sees (2.50) as 'evidence that resultatives are arguments' (1992: 86), she does not give any account of the selection restrictions that hold between the matrix verb, the postverbal NP, and the resultative predicate in (2.51).

(2.50) A resultative of category XP can occur in post-direct-object position as sister to V only if other non-predicative arguments of category XP can occur in that same position.

(Napoli 1992: 86)

(2.51)
a. *John hammered the metal {beautiful, safe, tubular}.
b. *John wiped the surface {damp, dirty, stained}.
c. *She wrenched the stick {broken, tight}.
d. *She shot him {lame, paranoid, wounded}.

(Green 1972)

In summary, I have shown in this section that Napoli's constraints on resultative formation do not account for the full set of selection restrictions that hold between the matrix verb, the postverbal NP, and the resultative predicate. Although her account exhibits a number of problems that preclude it from explaining the full distribution of resultatives, it has some interesting insights to offer with respect to linking flexibility and semantic selection restrictions between matrix verbs and postverbal arguments. These will be taken up by our alternative analysis in Chapters 5 through 7.

2.3.3 Resultatives as Ternary Branching Structures

Carrier and Randall (1992) present a semantic analysis of resultative constructions which suggests that postverbal NPs of transitive verbs are internal arguments of the matrix verb. Postverbal NPs of intransitive resultative constructions, on the other hand, are not internal arguments of their matrix verbs. Carrier and Randall's first argument to distinguish transitive from intransitive resultative verbs is concerned with the selection restrictions on the postverbal NP. The following examples suggest that transitive verbs select for their postverbal NPs and that they are therefore arguments of the verb. This leads Carrier and Randall to conclude that the matrix verb and the postverbal NP are sisters.

(2.52)
a. *The bears frightened the campground empty.
b. *The baby shattered the oatmeal into portions.
c. *The magician hypnotized the auditorium quiet.

(Carrier and Randall 1992: 187)

The second point taken as evidence for the claim that the postverbal NP is the internal argument of the matrix verb is concerned with Middle Formation. Carrier and Randall propose the condition in (2.53) to explain the difference in distribution between transitive and intransitive resultatives in the process of Middle Formation (MF) as in (2.54) and (2.55):

(2.53) *Condition on MF*
MF applies to a verb only if it has an internal argument. (Carrier and Randall 1992: 189)

(2.54) *Middles from transitive resultative verbs*
NP water the new seedlings flat
-> New seedlings water t flat (easily).
NP break those cookies into pieces
-> Those cookies break t into pieces (easily).

(2.55) *Middles from intransitive resultative verbs*
NP run Competition Nikes threadbare
-> *Competition Nikes run threadbare (easily).
NP talk Phys Ed majors into a stupor
-> *Phys Ed majors talk into a stupor (easily).
(Carrier and Randall 1992: 191)

According to Carrier and Randall, 'MF requires that its inputs have a direct internal argument, and transitive resultatives meet this requirement.' (1992: 192) Under their analysis, then, the constraint in (2.53) explains why MF cannot apply to intransitive verbs: they do not have a direct internal argument. The data on Middle Formation as well as data from Adjectival Passive Formation (1992: 189-192) and Verbal Passive Formation (1992: 194-195) lead Carrier and Randall to propose a ternary branching analysis for both transitive and intransitive resultative constructions that differ with respect to theta-role assignments. The postverbal NP of transitive verbs as in (2.56a) receives two theta-roles in the resultative construction: the first theta-role from the matrix verb, the second theta-role from the resultative phrase. Resultative constructions containing intransitive verbs as in (2.56b), on the other hand, assign only one theta-role to the postverbal NP. In these structures, it is only the resultative phrase which theta-marks the postverbal NP.

(2.56) (a)

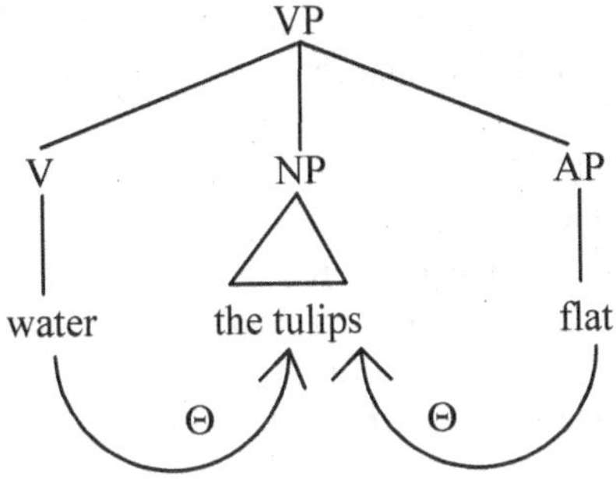

(b)

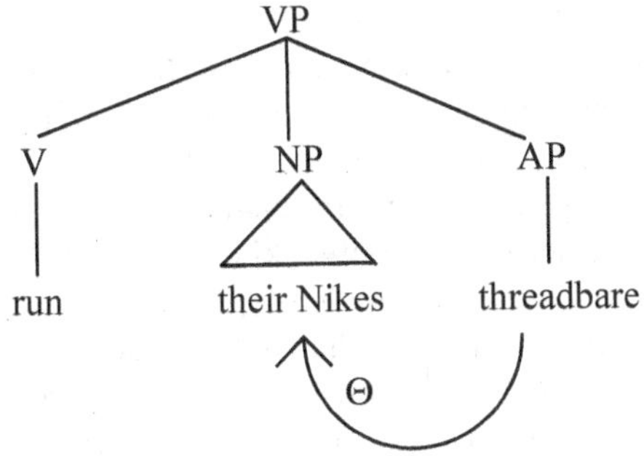

(cf. Carrier and Randall 1992: 176)[35]

Carrier and Randall's account differs from other proposals discussed so far in that it makes a distinction between resultative constructions based on transitive verbs and those based on intransitive verbs. However, it also faces a number of problems when it comes to accounting for the full distribution of resultatives. For example, Rapp (1997) shows that Carrier and Randall's claim according to which obligatory transitive verbs exhibit the same se-

[35]Den Dikken and Hoekstra (1994) claim that Carrier and Randall's theory is not tenable because it weakens the Theta Criterion, abandons the Binary Branching Principle, and does not represent the subject-predicate relation in terms of a clausal structure. Another problem with Carrier and Randall's approach is related to the claim that the postverbal NP is only selected for in transitive resultatives. Since I have already argued (and will show again), that there is a selection restriction imposed by the verb in intransitive resultative constructions as well, den Dikken and Hoekstra's counterargument does not hold water. Den Dikken's and Hoekstra's (1994) own theory, however, assumes an empty resultative predicate for intransitive resultatives which, in my view, finds no empirical data to support its existence. Rather, it seems as if the existence of the empty resultative predicate is motivated by purely SC-internal assumptions. Since their alternative explanation in terms of SCs does not explain the distribution of resultatives in detail, I do not accept it.

mantic restrictions in resultative constructions as they do in non-resultative sentences is untenable for German.[36]

(2.57) a. *Er streichelte.
'He stroked.'
b. Er streichelte die Katze/*ihre trüben Gedanken.
'He stroked the cat/*her sad thoughts.'
c. Er streichelte ihre trüben Gedanken /*die Katze weg.
'He stroked her sad thought/*the cat away.'
(Rapp 1997: 101)

The sentences in (2.57) show that the matrix verb *streicheln* ('to stroke') imposes different semantic selection restrictions on the postverbal NP depending on what kind of construction it occurs in. In other words, in (2.57b), the matrix verb imposes its 'regular' lexical selection restrictions on their postverbal NPs. In the resultative counterparts (2.57c), however, the matrix verbs s-select for different kinds of postverbal NPs. I suggest that the difference in selection restrictions is related to whether the verb occurs in a resultative or in a non-resultative construction. To put it differently, there seems to be some correlation between a change of a verb's argument structure and its occurrence in a resultative construction. Under Carrier and Randall's analysis, this change in selection restriction is not accounted for because it proposes that transitive verbs impose the same selection restrictions on their postverbal NPs in resultative constructions as they do in non-resultative constructions. I will return to the correlation between argument structure change and semantic selection restrictions in Chapters 3 and 4.

Another problem with Carrier and Randall's account is the claim that postverbal NPs of intransitive resultative verbs are not direct internal arguments of the verb. Goldberg (1995: 182-185) shows that Carrier and Randall's conclusions drawn from tests on middle formation are misdirected. For example, middles as in (2.58) are not always grammatical when they are formed from transitive verbs.

(2.58) a. *Pat kicks black and blue easily.
b. *The washer loads full easily.

[36]Note that the same observation can be made about the English counterparts. Rapp (1997: 101) also shows that Carrier and Randall's tests that are used to determine the argumenthood of the postverbal NPs do not yield the same results for German. This leads her to the conclusion that the postverbal NP should be analyzed as an internal argument of the matrix verb in both transitive and intransitive resultative constructions.

c. *His face washes shiny clean easily.
(Goldberg 1995: 182)

Based on data such as in (2.58), Goldberg suggests that one cannot take processes such as Middle Formation as clear indicators for direct internal argumenthood of a postverbal NP. In addition, she adduces the following data which show that even closely related transitive verbs differ in whether they can undergo these processes:

(2.59) a. This movie watches easily.
b. *This movie sees easily. (Goldberg 1995: 183)

Such data lead Goldberg to conclude that the restrictions on the middle construction's application (as well as adjectival passive formation and nominalization constructions) are due to factors other than the transitivity of the matrix verb. She therefore claims that there are no 'other reasons for, or benefits to, attributing a non-argument status to the postverbal NP.' (1995: 183) In this connection, notice that the conditions on Middle Formation (2.53) are ad-hoc stipulations which are stated in purely syntactic terms without covering the full range of verbs with direct internal arguments.[37]

Before closing this section, we look at another interesting claim made by Carrier and Randall about the status of postverbal NPs. The authors claim that verbs occurring in resultative constructions differ with respect to their lexically specified argument structures:

		Basic verb	Resultative verb
(2.60)	a. *water*	agent [theme]	agent [theme r-state]
	b. *run*	agent [ ]	agent [r-state]

(Carrier and Randall 1992: 179)

(2.60) shows that the resultative versions of *water* and *run* inherit the argument structure of their respective 'basic' verbs and have an added argument, namely the r(esultant)-state. They differ, however, in that only the transitive

[37]Note that even Carrier and Randall admit that the constraint on Middle Formation 'is still an arbitrary stipulation, one that we should hope to explain. In fact, though, the possible inputs to MF are limited by other subtle semantic conditions that, as far as we know, have never been adequately characterized. (…) For now, we consider ([2.53], *H.C.B.*) a descriptive statement that may ultimately follow from the right semantic characterization of the possible inputs to MF.' (Carrier and Randall 1992: 189, fn. 15) In addition to the problems noted in the preceding paragraphs, Carrier and Randall's (1992) analysis has no principled way of determining the restrictions on the range of postverbal NPs and resultative phrases as pointed out in the previous sections.

resultative verb has a 'theme' argument to which it assigns a theta-role. Although Carrier and Randall's intuition about the relation between the basic verb and the resultative verb is certainly on the right track, their analysis does not specify how and where the latter 'inherits' the argument structure of the former. Is it a productive process that applies to all verb classes in the lexicon? How is the s-selection of the resultative phrase restricted? Should this only be captured in terms of 'aspectual' clash à la Simpson (1983) (cf. Carrier and Randall 1992: 184) or are other factors involved too? The lack of any detailed mechanisms that license and restrict the occurrence of both the postverbal NP and the resultative phrase prevents Carrier and Randall from arriving at an analysis with full coverage of the distribution of resultative constructions. In Chapter 6 we will see that Carrier and Randall's basic ideas can be taken as the basis for a lexical account of resultatives which regulates semantic selection restrictions between a verb and its arguments at the lexical level. Moreover, Carrier and Randall's intuitions about the mismatch between semantics and syntax in resultative constructions seem to be headed in the right direction. I will pick up and refine these points of their analysis in Chapter 6 in order to arrive at a more complete framework for resultative constructions.

2.3.4 Summary

In the sections above, I have argued that although the predication-type analyses offer both conceptual and empirical advantages over the SC-type analyses of resultatives discussed in Section 2.2, they also exhibit a number of problems when it comes to capturing the full distribution of resultative constructions. I have shown that this shortcoming is due to the lack of a detailed study of the lexical semantic information associated with the constituents of the resultative construction. The evidence I presented suggests that verbs may exhibit different semantic selection restrictions when they occur in resultative constructions. I have argued that this change in semantic selection restrictions is triggered by a change in the verb's argument structure. In Chapter 5 we will see that this is due to the lexical-semantic information associated with different senses of verbs.

2.4 Conclusions

To summarize, this chapter has presented specific arguments against a set of syntactic analyses of resultatives developed within Small Clause Theory and Predication Theory. Our discussion has shown that both theories exhibit a number of deficiencies when it comes to accounting for the full distribution of resultative constructions. More specifically, I have argued that none of the analyses provides a detailed mechanism allowing for a proper semantic and pragmatic selection of postverbal constituents as they occur in a broader range of resultative constructions. While I have shown that Small Clause Theory and Predication Theory are not properly equipped to handle the semantic and syntactic relations holding between the constituents of the resultative construction this does not mean that the overall frameworks should be abandoned altogether. As we will see, the alternative constructional analysis of resultatives I lay out in Chapters 5 through 8 is to a large degree compatible with more syntactically oriented approaches.

3

The Role of Event Structure and Lexical Semantics

3.1 Introduction

This chapter discusses the role of event structure and lexical semantics for the licensing of resultative constructions. After introducing the notions of aspectual verb classes, it examines in detail the different ways in which authors like Tenny (1994), Winkler (1997), and Rappaport Hovav and Levin (1998, 2001) have developed the notion of event structure in order to account for the distribution of resultatives. All accounts share the understanding that resultative constructions exhibit a complex event structure consisting of a causing event and a caused event, which sets them apart from other types of events such as activities. On this view, resultative constructions are licensed in cases in which the aspectual properties of the matrix verb are compatible with both the aspectual properties of the resultative phrase and the postverbal NP such that they fit into a complex aspectual event structure template. Based on a comparison of verbs that are closely related in meaning and exhibit the same type of event structure I argue that it is extremely difficult to capture the distribution of resultatives on the basis of event structure alone. This in turn leads me to abandon event structure based analyses of resultative constructions.

3.2 From Aspectual Classes to Event Structure

Based on Aristotle's classic distinction between static and dynamic, or states and events, Vendler (1967) suggests that verbs and verb phrases can be distinguished according to the kinds of eventualities they denote in the real world. The ability of verbs and verb phrases to occur in the progressive and with different kinds of time adverbials (among others) leads Vendler to propose a classification of four distinct aspectual verb classes (or, *Aktionsarten*): activities, accomplishments, achievements, and states.[1] Verbs such as *sleep, run*, or *play* in (3.1a) are examples of activity verbs because they denote 'a sequence of events identifying the same semantic expression.' (Pustejovsky 1991: 56) As such, they typically cannot occur with a frame adverbial that refers to an explicit change of state as can be seen in (3.1b).

(3.1) a. Marge {slept/ran/played} yesterday.
b. Marge {slept/ran/played} for 20 minutes/*in 20 minutes.

Accomplishment verbs such as *build, break*, or *dry* differ from activity verbs in that they denote activities that lead to a change of state as the result of the activities. Thus, in (3.2c), the activity of *Lisa*'s drying *her blouse* causes her blouse to become *dry*.[2]

(3.2) a. Homer built a garage.
b. Bart broke his skateboard.
c. Lisa dried her blouse.

Achievement verbs are similar to accomplishment verbs in that they too denote a change of state. They differ from accomplishment verbs in two ways: (1) the change of state is instantaneous rather than gradual and (2) the verb typically does not provide any information regarding how the change

[1]Tobin (1993) explains the differences between aspect and *Aktionsart* as follows: 'There is also another widely used German term, *Aktionsart*, related to aspectuality, which generally refers to the subtle semantic distinctions related to the lexical meanings of verbs – thus creating a dichotomy between "grammatical" and "lexical" (also referred to as "subjective" and "objective", "aspect" and "character", "viewpoint" and "situation") approaches to aspectuality. More often than not, the distinction between aspect and *Aktionsart* is ignored or overlooked and different scholars have often argued either for or against the maintaining of the distinction between these two categories of aspectuality.' (1993: 1) For further discussion of the differences between aspect and *Aktionsart*, see Tobin (1993: Chapter 1), Brinton (1988: 1-11), Smith (1997: Chapter 2), Deutschbein (1939: 34-46), and Comrie (1976: 6-7). For discussion as well as different types of classifications of aspectual verb classes, see Mourelatos (1978), Dowty (1979), Brinton (1988), Moens and Steedman (1988), Smith (1997), Tenny (1992, 1994), Verkuyl (1993), and Engelberg (1998), among others. For an overview of English aspectual verb classes and their characteristics, see Wanner (1999: 24-39).

[2]Note that besides lexically encoded achievements, there are also derived achievements which consist of a regular activity verb plus a terminating phrase that indicates the termination of the activity (e.g., *run to the store*). Similar meaning shifts are possible when a transitive verb occurs with a bare plural or with a single NP. For a detailed discussion, see Heim (1982).

of state has come about. Examples of achievement verbs are *find*, *arrive*, and *die*.

(3.3) a. Jim found his book.
b. Dave arrived.
c. Joe died.

Finally, states are different from all other aspectual classes in that they denote 'a single event, which is evaluated relative to no other event.' (Pustejovsky 1991: 56) Pustejovsky characterizes states as follows:

> Following Carlson (1977) and Kratzer (1989), we can distinguish two kinds of stative predicates *individual-level* and *stage-level*. Predicates such as *tall*, *intelligent*, and *overweight* might be thought of as properties that an individual retains, more or less, throughout its lifetime, and can be identified with the individual directly. These are *individual-level predicates*. Properties such as *hungry*, *sick*, and *clean* are usually identified with non-permanent states of individuals, and have been called *stage-level predicates*. (Pustejovsky 1995: 15)

Vendler's classification of aspectual classes forms the basis for almost all subsequent work on aspectual classes and, subsequently, event structure.[3] We now turn to Tenny's (1994) framework which incorporates aspectual verb classes as an explanatory mechanism for the licensing of arguments at the syntactic level.[4]

[3]Davidson (1967), Bach (1983, 1986), and Higgenbotham (1985, 1987) are among the first works that explicitly argue for linguistic representations to include the notion of 'events'. For more recent accounts that incorporate 'event structure' as a central notion for linguistic explanation, see Pustejovsky (1991), Van Voorst (1986, 1988, 1992), Moens and Steedman (1988), Hale and Keyser (1986, 1987), Grimshaw (1990), Jackendoff (1987, 1990), and Levin and Rappaport Hovav (1999), among others.

[4]Although Vendler's (1967) aspectual classes have been taken as the basis for many subsequent analyses, there are also accounts which point out a number of shortcomings of his classification. Mori, Löbner, and Micha (1992: 259-260), e.g., show that Vendler's classification does not adequately capture the full range of Japanese verb classes. For an extensive overview and critique of Vendler's classification of verbs, see Dowty (1979: 51-59), Binnick (1991: 170-184), and Verkuyl (1993: Chapter 2).

3.3 The Aspectual Interface Hypothesis

Tenny (1994) proposes that 'the intersection between syntax and lexical semantics is basically an aspectual one. Furthermore, the interactions between the two components are highly constrained, since they are organized around a limited vocabulary of aspectual notions.' (Tenny 1994: 1) Her characterization of aspect as the central notion for linguistic theories of linking and argument realization leads her to propose the Aspectual Interface Hypothesis (AIH).

> *Aspectual Interface Hypothesis*
>
> The universal principles of mapping between thematic structure and syntactic argument structure are governed by aspectual properties. Constraints on the aspectual properties associated with direct internal arguments, indirect internal arguments, and external arguments in syntactic structure constrain the kinds of event participants that can occupy these positions. Only the aspectual part of thematic structure is visible to the universal linking principles. (Tenny 1994: 2)

Tenny posits a difference between event structure and aspectual structure in that 'event structure encompasses all the internal temporal structure of an event, while aspectual structure is a subpart of event structure, and may not be present in all event structures.' This leads her to propose that '[a]spectual structure involves decomposition into the distinct semantic and syntactic parts that make up a measuring-out and a delimiting.' (1994: 132) The mapping between syntax and semantics is sensitive to aspectual properties such as 'delimitedness' and 'measuring out.' The former term 'refers to the property of an event's having a distinct, definite and inherent endpoint in time.' (1994: 4) This term relates to Vendler's (1967) distinction between simple activities (not delimited) and complex accomplishments and achievements (delimited). 'Measuring-out' refers to the ability of a verb's direct internal argument to delimit an event.[5] On this view, it is the aspec-

---

[5]Following Williams (1981) and Rappaport and Levin (1988), Tenny distinguishes between external arguments, direct internal arguments, and indirect internal arguments. An external argument 'is the noun phrase (NP) argument of the verb which is projected in the phrase structure outside the maximal projection of the verb, and which receives a thematic role from the verb phrase via predication. This argument always becomes the syntactic subject. (…) [T]he verb's direct internal argument is that NP argument which is governed by the verb at D-structure and which receives its thematic role directly from the verb. (…) Indirect internal NP arguments are governed by a preposition (as in English) or by a case marker other than nomi-

tual role MEASURE that 'names an event participant that measures out the event, providing both the single parameter or scale along which the event transpires over time, and the endpoint on that scale.' (Tenny 1994: 94)

Based on aspectual notions such as 'delimitedness' and 'measuring out', Tenny claims that resultative constructions require a MEASURE role to be licensed because they 'serve the semantic function of introducing a temporal endpoint and measuring-out to the event.' (1994: 152) A comparison of her aspectual role-account of event structure with Levin and Rappaport's (1988) lexical subordination analysis of resultatives leads Tenny to the conclusion that resultative constructions can be accounted for in terms of 'an operation solely over aspectual structure. It is an aspectual operation in which the MEASURE aspectual role is added to an empty aspectual grid.' (1994: 200)[6] According to Tenny, then, resultative constructions are to be analyzed in terms of meaning extensions of basic verb meanings by operations over aspectual structures as is shown by the following examples.

(3.4) a. Evelyn wiped the dishes.
$wipe_1$: Aspectual structure: [ ]

b. Evelyn wiped the dishes dry.
$wipe_2$ Aspectual structure: [MEASURE]
(Tenny 1994: 200)

According to (3.4), the meaning of *wipe* is extended through an operation over the aspectual structure of the verb, in this case, by adding a MEASURE role to its aspectual structure. In other words, the resultative phrase is licensed because it is able to contribute a MEASURE role to the aspectual grid of the matrix verb. Tenny claims that an operation over aspectual structure gives her approach a significant advantage over other analyses that account for resultative constructions in terms of LCS (Lexical Conceptual Structures) (e.g., Levin and Rappaport 1988 and Jackendoff 1990) in that

---

native or accusative in some languages. Indirect NP arguments receive their thematic roles from the preposition (or case marker) or from the preposition (or case marker) in conjunction with the verb.' (1994: 9)

[6] Levin and Rappaport (1988) propose an analysis of resultatives in terms of lexical conflation of verb meanings. On this view, conflation of verb meanings is only observed with specific kinds of meaning extensions of verbs. Take, for example, verbs of sound emission that can be used in a directed motion sense (*The elevator groaned/The elevator groaned slowly upward*). The authors argue that under certain narrow semantic conditions (that are difficult to specify), verbs of sound emission can be conflated with the directed motion sense. Given this conflation sense, a change in argument structure can take place.

'aspectual roles are rigorously definable in a way that predicates of LCS are not.' (1994: 202) Note that if we followed Tenny's argument and assumed that it is really aspectual structure that determines the licensing of resultatives, we would not expect the following sentences:

(3.5) a. Evelyn wiped the crumbs off the table.
b. Evelyn wiped herself clean.

On Tenny's account, resultative phrases are licensed by adding a MEASURE role to the aspectual grid of the verb. Although the phrase *off the table* in (3.5a) is a combined PATH and TERMINUS role that fulfills the same function as a MEASURE role (Tenny 1994: 95), it is not clear how the postverbal NP *the crumbs* is licensed under Tenny's proposal. That is, *wipe* in (3.5a) has a different meaning than *wipe* in (3.4): in (3.5a) *wipe* refers to moving an object by directed surface contact motion whereas in (3.4) *wipe* means to eliminate wetness (from a surface). Thus her aspectual analysis of resultatives is problematic in terms of accounting for such a meaning change and in terms of making restrictions regarding the type of verb class to which such aspectual operations apply.[7]

Although Tenny insists that the resultative construction be only analyzed in terms of an aspectual operation over a verb's aspectual grid, she points out in a short section of her analysis that 'Lexical Conceptual Structures are necessary to fine-tune the statement of what verb classes in what languages these operations may apply to.' (1994: 202) This remark indicates that Tenny seems to accept that lexical semantic (i.e. thematic) structures influence operations over the aspectual grid of a verb. However, she does not clearly describe the way in which the two structures interact to license the distribution of resultative constructions.

(3.6) a. Evelyn wiped the dishes dry. (Tenny 1994: 200)
b. *Evelyn wiped the dishes red. (Tenny 1994: 201)
c. John painted the house red.

According to Tenny, (3.6b) is not acceptable because there are no 'conflations with elements of meaning that do not participate in aspectual structure; for example conflations with color or manner.' (1994: 201) Thus, (3.6b) is supposedly ruled out because at the level of conceptual structure, *red* is in-

[7]Notice that at a different point, Tenny (1994: 200) does indeed consider the possibility of 'narrow semantic constraints' over verb classes. However, she does not pursue this matter any further.

terpreted as '[x 'wipe' y] ['in a manner, e.g. while wearing red']' (1994: 201). Note that Tenny's interpretation of the meaning of (3.6b) presumes that the sentence is ruled out due to thematic structure. However, given the proper context (3.6b) is perfectly acceptable. For example, if the towel used to wipe off the dishes is full of red paint (3.6b) is unproblematic. Tenny's analysis, however, does not address the role of world knowledge and the influence of contextual background information.

Moreover, if Tenny's proposal regarding the semantic status of resultative phrases were correct, we would not expect sentences like (3.6c), in which *red* measures out the event denoted by *paint* and thus participates in its aspectual structure. Sentences (3.6b) and (3.6c) show that it is difficult for such an account to distinguish between conflations of elements that participate in aspectual structure and those that do not. In my opinion this is due to the heavy emphasis Tenny's analysis places on the aspectual properties of verbs while failing to account for the different senses that are inherent to a verb's lexical semantics.[8] In other words, Tenny's account of resultative constructions would be greatly improved if it included a more detailed mechanism that linked aspectual to thematic grids, thereby enabling her to make more precise predictions on aspectual grounds. The discussion in this section has shown that any account of argument structure alternations (e.g., the resultative construction) in terms of aspectual structure also needs to include a detailed analysis of how aspectual structure interfaces with thematic (lexical semantic) information. We discuss an approach that seeks to incorporate these points in the following section.

3.4 Combining Thematic Relations with Event Structure

Adopting a modified Larsonian sentence structure (Larson 1988a), Winkler (1997) offers an analysis of resultative constructions in terms of complex predicates to mirror the close semantic relationship between the matrix verb and the resultative phrase.[9] She proposes that the matrix verb and the resul-

---

[8]Filip (1996: 135) also observes that Tenny's Aspectual Interface Hypothesis does not give an adequate explanation for the fact that resultatives can be telic (*John broke the vase to pieces*) or atelic (*The horses dragged the logs smooth*). 'The compatibility of a complex verbal predicate with a resultative predicate does not provide any conclusive evidence about the telic or atelic nature of the complex predicate.' (Filip 1996: 135) For related problems with Tenny's Aspectual Interface Hypothesis, see Wanner (1999: 106-109).

[9]Winkler's complex predicate analysis of resultatives is in spirit with other proposals that suggest a complex predicate analysis for secondary predication constructions. See, e.g., Chomsky (1957, 1986), Dowty (1978), Bach (1979), Bowers (1983, 1993), Simpson (1983), DiSciullo and Williams (1987), Larson (1988a), Hoeksema (1991), Williams (1997), Neeleman and van de Koot (2001), and Müller (2002).

tative phrase form a complex predicate represented as sisters at D-structure (see (3.9) below).[10] The complex predicate formation is triggered and constrained by insights from two different frameworks, namely Pustejovsky's (1991) theory of event structure and Higgenbotham's (1985, 1989) theory of thematic relations. There are three important assumptions underlying Winkler's analysis of resultatives.

First, Winkler (1997: 336-338) adopts Pustejovsky's (1991: 55/56) proposal that resultative constructions are instances of so-called event compositions that combine an activity or process verb with a resultative phrase. This is interpreted as a delimiting expression because it denotes the final, i.e., the result state. In other words, the matrix verb needs to belong to a non-delimiting verb class.

Second, for her event composition account to work for resultatives, Winkler (1997: 337) proposes that the postverbal NP has to be 'an affected argument' which serves to measure out the event. This restriction serves to rule out sentences like (3.7a) in which *chickens* is not an affected argument of the verb.

(3.7) a. *Martha eats chickens fat. (Winkler 1997: 339)
b. Martha eats herself fat. (Winkler 1997: 338)

Third, Winkler points out that resultative predicates must be interpreted as stage-level predicates (1997: 338/339). According to this view, stage-level predicates are defined as those states 'which can be changed by being acted upon' (Pustejovsky 1991: 65), 'and are represented as functions from processes to transitions (<P, T>).' (Winkler 1997: 339)[11] This constraint on resultative predicates rules out sentences like (3.8a):

(3.8) a. *Martha owns chickens fat.
b. Martha feeds chickens fat. (Winkler 1997: 338)

Feed is a process verb consisting of two subevents, whereas *own* is a stative verb consisting of only one event. Winkler (1997: 339) claims that *fat* is able to change 'the process interpretation of the verb *feed* into a transition verb *feed fat*' in (3.8b), thereby delimiting the process and giving the sentence a resultative interpretation. In (3.8a), however, there is no event struc-

[10]Secondary predicate constructions containing depictive predicates, on the other hand, are treated as syntactic adjuncts in this framework.

[11]For a discussion of the differences between stage-level and individual-level predicates, see Milsark (1976), Carlson (1977), and Pustejovsky (1991, 1995), among others.

ture that can be delimited, since *own* is a stative verb whose event structure contains only a single event.

Based on these three points, Winkler follows Higgenbotham's (1985, 1989) assumption that the event structure of transitive resultatives is directly mapped onto syntactic D-structure as illustrated in the following diagram.

(3.9) a. The gardener watered the tulips flat.
b.

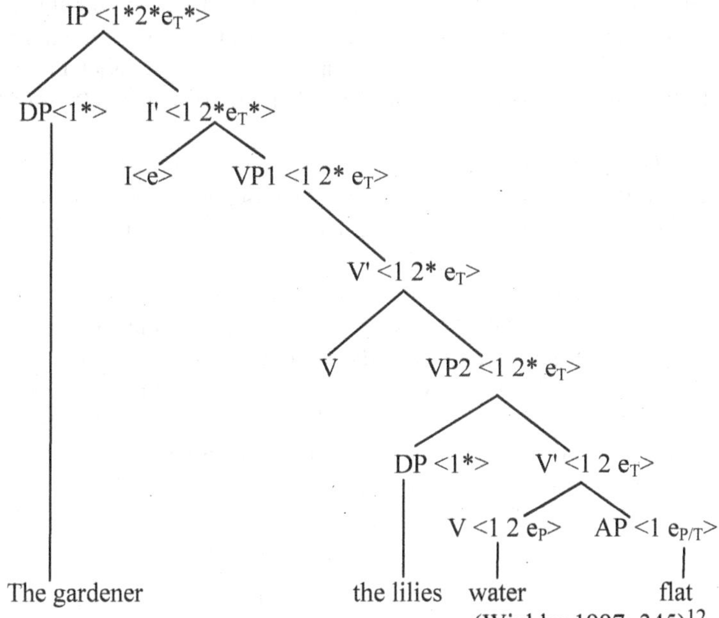

(Winkler 1997: 345)[12]

Winkler suggests that the predicates in (3.9) contain theta-grids that in turn contain so-called event positions (marked by <e>) in addition to their argument positions. The event positions reflect basic event types, namely <e_S> for states, <e_P> for processes, <e_T> for transitions, and <$e_{P,T}$> for resultative predicates. In (3.9) the process of event composition restricts the formation of resultative constructions to the combination of a verb and a resultative

---

[12]It is unclear why Winkler adapts Pustejovsky's classification of resultative predicates as events that are both processes and transitions (' <$e_{P/T}$> for resultative predicates' (1997: 345)). Although they serve to delimit the event denoted by the matrix verb, resultative predicates denote a final state or location and should therefore be characterized as states instead of processes and/or transitions (e.g., *Mary watered the lilies flat*).

predicate; the verb belongs to the process event type and the resultative predicate denotes the change from a process to a transition. Thus, the complex predicate itself (i.e., V') is of the event type transition. To guarantee proper mapping in combination with event structure composition, Winkler's analysis of resultatives incorporates an additional mechanism, namely Higgenbotham's (1985, 1989) theory of theta-saturation. This framework assumes that lexical items contain theta-grids whose open positions become saturated during the syntactic derivation. On this view, the resultative predicate 'is licensed by its subject in that it saturates an open position in the theta-grid of the predicate.' (Winkler 1997: 90). The combination of insights from Pustejovsky's constraints on resultative event composition with Higgenbotham's account of theta-saturation leads Winkler to propose the following licensing principle for R(esultative) S(econdary) P(redicates):

> *Licensing conditions for RSPs*
> A resultative secondary predicate is licensed by event composition and theta-identification at the level of D-structure. (Winkler 1997: 345)

With this overview of Winkler's treatment of resultatives in mind, let us now turn to some data that are problematic for her approach. First, consider Winkler's proposal regarding the status of stage-level predicates and her restrictions on the matrix verb. On her view, it is sufficient to require that the matrix verb belong to the general class of process verbs. The following sentences containing process verbs and resultative predicates that can be interpreted as stage-level predicates, however, suggest that this general requirement is insufficient.

(3.10) a. *Martha cooked chickens fat.
b. ??The gardener washed the lilies tall.
c. ??Mary watered the nails flat.

In (3.10a-c) the use of process verbs such as *cook*, *wash*, and *water* does not guarantee that the resultative constructions are acceptable. Although the respective verbs' event structures consist of two subevents and the postverbal NPs are affected by the activity denoted by the matrix verb, cooking chickens does not make them fat nor does washing lilies make them tall. This means that Winkler's account is unable to constrain the class of process verbs allowed as matrix verbs in a resultative construction. Any uniform treatment of process verbs that is not sensitive to the semantics of the elements involved is unable to describe why (and how) certain process verbs can appear in resultative constructions while others cannot.

A second problem with Winkler's approach has to do with her theta-identification mechanism which allows the open theta-position of the resultative phrase <1> to be identified with the open position <2> in the theta-grid of the verbal head (see (3.9) above). Winkler proposes that this mechanism allows the resultative phrase to take the postverbal NP as an argument and to assign a theta-role to it. She goes on to point out that '... the underlying process of complex predicate formation is nothing else but event composition.' (1997: 346). We have just seen in the previous paragraph that event composition by itself is not able to rule out unacceptable sentences like those in (3.10a-c) because it refers to a too general class of process verbs. Once theta-identification rules out uninterpretable combinations of matrix verbs and resultative predicates, we are left with the observation that the resultative phrase takes the postverbal NP as an argument without specifying what kind of argument is required by the resultative phrase. In particular, Winkler does not offer an explanation of how theta-role assignment might be used to rule out uninterpretable combinations of postverbal NPs and/or resultative phrases, nor does she sketch out a theory of theta-roles that could be employed to impose rudimentary selection restrictions on postverbal elements. In other words, Winkler's implementation of Higgenbotham's (1985, 1989) theory of theta-identification is not very efficient when it comes to constraining the range of permissible process verbs. It is obvious that Winkler's licensing condition on resultative predicates to rule out uninterpretable resultative constructions needs to be modified in order to capture the full distribution of resultative constructions.

Similar observations can be made about the licensing of the resultative phrase. In Winkler's analysis, the only restriction that holds for such predicates is that they be interpreted as stage level predicates (see Winkler 1997: 339).

(3.11) a. *The gardener watered the tulips black.
b. *John cooked the chicken new.
c. *Mary hammered the nail big.

The examples in (3.11a-c) all include process verbs that denote non-delimited events. While the sentences all share the property of entailing two subevents (thereby fulfilling the event composition requirement of the Licensing Condition for RSPs), they are nevertheless uninterpretable because the semantics of the resultative phrases seem to be incompatible with the semantics of the respective matrix verbs. Winkler avoids this issue by not discussing relevant aspects of the lexical semantic structure associated with either the resultative phrase or the matrix verb she is attempting to account for in terms of her licensing condition.[13]

Another problem with Winkler's account concerns the licensing of postverbal NPs. She does not explain how theta-roles can be used to rule out postverbal NPs which render resultative sentences unacceptable. Compare, for example, the postverbal NP *the lilies* in (3.12a) with the postverbal NPs *the old oak* in (3.12b) and *the fence* in (3.12c).

(3.12) a. The gardener watered the lilies flat.
b. *The gardener watered the old oak flat.
c. *The gardener watered the fence flat.

The examples in (3.12) illustrate that there are certain pragmatic restrictions at work which restrict NPs such as *the old oak* and *the fence* from being properly interpreted in a resultative construction containing the matrix verb *water* and the resultative predicate *flat*. According to Winkler, postverbal elements are required to be 'totally affected' arguments (Winkler 1997: 340), i.e., they need to 'be construed as the theme of a become relation expressed in the second subevent' (1997: 340), and they must measure out the event. The two postverbal NPs *the old oak* and *the fence* can be interpreted to be totally affected by the event of watering, i.e., it is possible to construe a situation in which the gardener holds a water hose and sprinkles water on them.

The crucial points that are of importance to our present discussion, however, are the last two requirements. With respect to them, Winkler suggests that the 'NP *lilies* is essential for the process of event composition since this NP is involved in the predicate opposition at event structure and measures out the event in Tenny's terminology.' (1997: 346) On this account, all postverbal NPs can be construed as measuring out an event because they can be predicated of the resultative predicate and can therefore measure out the event. The point missing in Winkler's analysis is that the matrix verb and the resultative predicate seem to have one single semantic selection restriction with respect to the postverbal NP. In other words, any attempt that relies solely on event composition (the notion of 'totally af-

[13] Neeleman and Weerman (1993) offer an analysis of Dutch and English resultatives in terms of complex predicates that exhibits some of the same mechanisms used by Winkler (1997). They argue that 'resultatives are base generated in a position adjoined to the verb' (1993: 433) and that resultatives are adjoined to the verb at D-Structure. However, their account (as well as Neeleman and van de Koot 2001) exhibits the same problems as Winkler's analysis in that it does not provide a semantic mechanism that would rule out unattested examples such as (3.11) and (3.12b,c).

fected argument') and the ability to measure out the event misses the crucial point that there are probably no separate assignments of theta-roles to the postverbal NP by the matrix verb and the resultative predicate, but only the assignment of one theta-role, namely the theta-role of the matrix verb.[14] Thus, Winkler's account is not very effective in regulating the semantic range of postverbal NPs in resultative constructions.[15] This problem is partly due to the fact that she takes into account neither a more fine-grained semantics nor context and world knowledge. An analysis that takes a step towards such a type of semantics is offered by Rappaport Hovav and Levin (1998, 2001).

3.5 Building Verb Meanings Through Event Structure Augmentation

On the template-based view of event structure as proposed by Rappaport Hovav and Levin (1998, 2001) (henceforth: R H and L), event structure plays a central role as the interface between lexicon and syntax. The framework laid out by R H and L seeks to explain why verbs such as *sweep* in (3.13) show variation with respect to their meanings and the number of arguments for which they subcategorize.

(3.13) a. Terry swept.
b. Terry swept the floor.
c. Terry swept the crumbs into the corner.
d. Terry swept the leaves off the sidewalk.

---

[14]Another problem for Winkler's account is the licensing of fake objects with intransitive verbs (1997: 347-349) (cf. *Sue danced Pat tired* vs. **Sue danced her shoes tired*). Since neither event composition nor theta-role assignment by the resultative phrase are powerful enough to determine which NP should appear in postverbal position, she has no principled way of determining under what exact circumstances the licensing of a 'fake object' takes place.

[15]By giving intransitive (cf. *Amanda ran the pavement thin*) and pseudotransitive (cf. *Gerald drank the pub dry*) resultatives a unified treatment, Winkler (1997: 349) does not take into account the fact that with intransitive verbs there is an addition of a postverbal NP to the verb's subcategorization frame. With pseudotransitive resultatives, however, the 'original' lexical postverbal NP of the transitive gets demoted from the verb's argument structure and a new postverbal NP is added onto the verb's argument structure. By not discussing the exact nature of the verb's different argument structure alternations, Winkler does not address the fact that the two verb classes 'enter' the resultative construction under different circumstances. The distinction is also relevant to the licensing of the resultative phrase: If Winkler assumes that the resultative phrase introduces the internal argument into the theta-structure of the matrix verb, then there should be some explanation of how the resultative phrase gets initially licensed to appear with an intransitive verb, thereby overriding its lexical default subcategorization frame.

e. Terry swept the floor clean.
f. Terry swept the leaves into a pile.

(R H and L 1998: 97/98)

Building on earlier works by Levin (1993), Levin and Rappaport (1995), and Pinker (1989) who assume 'that the lexical property of a verb that is taken to determine its syntactic behavior is its meaning' R H and L (1998: 97) argue that verbs can be divided into two distinct classes, namely manner verbs like *sweep* in (3.13) and result verbs like *break* and *open*.[16] According to the authors, the two verb classes differ from each other in that result verbs are much more restricted in their range of possible meanings and syntactic contexts than manner verbs. For example, (3.14) shows that two-argument result verbs do not allow the omission of the direct object as freely as manner verbs in (3.15).[17]

(3.14) a. Tracy broke the dishes.
b. *Tracy broke. (R H and L 1998: 117)

(3.15) a. Phil swept the floor.
b. Phil swept. (R H and L 1998: 115)

R H and L propose that the dissimilar syntactic behavior of manner and result verbs is due to their 'different aspectual classifications' (1998: 103) which they describe by using the mechanisms of predicate decomposition (see Dowty 1979, Parsons 1990, Pustejovsky 1991/1995, and Van Valin 1993, among others). It is assumed that Universal Grammar contains a certain number of so-called 'event structure templates' which represent different combinations of primitive predicates (1998: 107).[18] On this view, result

[16] R H and L point out that the class of result verbs consists of two subclasses: The members of the first subclass, such as *break*, *dry* or *widen*, 'lexicalize a particular achieved state, and the verb denotes the bringing about of this state.' (1998: 104) The members of the second subclass, such as *come*, *go*, and *arrive* 'lexicalize an achieved location (and usually also a direction), but not a manner of motion.' (1998: 105) Miyata (2000) offers a similar analysis in terms of 'object-oriented' and 'event-oriented' modifiers.

[17] Another difference is that 'these two types of verbs differ in the range of objects that they can take: verbs of surface contact and motion may take other than "normal" objects, but change of state verbs cannot.' (R H and L 2001: 779) Compare the following examples.

(i) Leslie scrubbed her knees sore.
(meaning 'Leslie's scrubbing the floor made her knees sore')
(ii) *The clumsy child broke his parents to distraction.

(R H and L 2001: 780)

[18] The event structure templates proposed by R H and L (1998: 108) are:

(i) [x ACT $_{<MANNER>}$] (activity)

verbs such as *break* are accomplishments that exhibit a complex event structure consisting of a causing event (typically an activity) and the change of state it brings about (typically an achievement). The variation among the different syntactic realizations of *break* in (3.14) is due to the fact that 'verb meaning is built up incrementally' (1998: 105) and 'verbs of change of state are expected to always be transitive, while verbs of surface contact and motion are not' (R H and L 2001: 779). Since the template for *break* has 'a fully lexically-specified representation', it 'cannot take on activity readings without eliminating a lexically-specified component of verb meaning (the result state).' In this way R H and L (1998: 105) try to explain the unacceptability of (3.14b).

3.5.1 Event Structure Template Augmentations

Based on the idea that verb meanings are built up incrementally, R H and L develop an analysis which 'proposes that the event structure-to-syntax mapping is governed by several well-formedness conditions on argument realization, some of which are sensitive to event complexity.' (R H and L 2001: 779). The first well-formedness condition in (3.16) ensures that complex event structure templates be only built on simpler ones which 'are consistent with the basic inventory of lexical event structure templates.' (1998: 111)

(3.16) Template Augmentation:
Event structure templates may be freely augmented up to other templates in the basic inventory of event structure templates.
(R H and L 1998: 111)

This condition ensures that the basic activity template of *sweep* can enter into other possible event structure templates, e.g., that of an accomplishment 'as long as the resulting complex event structure meets the well-formedness conditions on syntactic realization' (1998: 118) (see the examples in (3.13)). The second well-formedness condition is based on the idea that a verb's meaning consists of two parts: (1) a structural part (the primi-

---

(ii) [x <STATE>] (state)
(iii) [BECOME [x <STATE>]] (achievement)
(iv) [[x ACT <*MANNER*>] CAUSE [BECOME [y <STATE>]]] (accomplishment)
(v) [x CAUSE [BECOME [y <STATE>]]] (accomplishment)

tive predicate) which identifies the verb's semantic/aspectual class and therefore represents the grammatically relevant information of a verb's meaning and (2) an idiosyncratic part (the constant) which includes idiosyncratic information that distinguishes the verb in question from other members belonging to the same verb class rather than any information relevant to grammatical behavior. The Argument Realization Condition in (3.17) forces both structure participants of each individual subevent of an externally caused change of state verb to be realized overtly, namely as subject and object (see also Brisson 1994, Grimshaw and Vikner 1993, and Wunderlich 1997).[19]

(3.17) Argument Realization Condition:
   a. There must be an argument XP in the syntax for each structure participant in the event structure.
   b. Each argument XP in the syntax must be associated with an identified subevent in the event structure.

(R H and L 1998: 113)

The constraints in (3.16) and (3.17) allow R H and L to account for the differences observed between *break* in (3.14) and *sweep* in (3.15) as follows. *Sweep* is a manner verb which is associated with two participants: a sweeper and a surface. It is an activity verb in that it is associated with an activity event structure template whose single variable is matched up with the sweeper participant (thereby becoming a structure participant). The second participant, i.e., the surface, is licensed by the constant.[20] *Break*, on the other hand, is associated with the event structure of an externally caused change of state verb, consisting of an activity and a resulting state. Both participants of *break* need to be realized obligatorily because the two participants each realize the structure participant of one of the subevents. R H and L therefore suggest that 'the sharp difference between *break* and *sweep* with respect to the obligatoriness of the direct object arises from the difference in their event structures.' (1998: 117)

---

[19]Another constraint proposed to regulate template augmentations is the 'Subevent Identification Condition: Each subevent in the event structure must be identified by a lexical head (e.g., a V, an A, or a P) in the syntax.' (R H and L 1998: 112) Also, a number of canonical realization rules (*manner, instrument, place, externally caused event*, etc.) are used to relate the underlying minimal elements of meaning of a constant to their syntactic counterparts, thereby creating 'event structure' (for more details, see R H and L 1998: 109-110).

[20]A so-called 'recoverability condition' requires the realization of constant participants which can be left unexpressed if they are understood as 'prototypical' (1998: 113, 115).

Differences in event structure are also claimed to be responsible for the amount of meaning variation between manner verbs such as *wipe* and result verbs such as *break*. The authors propose that accomplishment verbs like *break* cannot be found in sentences with the same form as (3.18b) 'in which the direct object does not correspond to the "normal" direct object of the verb; that is, they cannot take nonsubcategorized objects' (1998: 121). On this view, the ungrammaticality of (3.18a) is due to the fact that it cannot have the reading 'Kelly broke the table and as a result the dishes went off the table' which would be parallel to the interpretation of (3.18b) in which *wipe* does not subcategorize for the direct object *the crumbs* as an argument of the causing subevent.

(3.18) a. *Kelly broke the dishes off the table.
b. Kelly wiped the crumbs off the table.
(R H and L 1998: 126)

R H and L summarize the role of event structure and event structure augmentation in the licensing of resultative constructions as follows.

> [B]ecause the template associated with a verb like *break* cannot be augmented further, no other achieved state or location can be added to a sentence with *break*, even with the normal direct object. (…) Thus, the properties that distinguish the verb *break* from the verb *sweep* can be accounted for through the interaction of their event structure representation, the operation of Template Augmentation, and the well-formedness conditions.
>
> (R H and L 1998: 122-23)

3.5.2 On the Relation Between Event Structure and Word Meaning

Despite R H and L's detailed event structure analysis, the following data suggest that the unacceptability of *break* may in certain cases not be caused by the fact that it exhibits a different event structure than *sweep*.

(3.19) a. ??Nicole broke the dishes valueless.
b. *Nicole broke the dishes off the table.
c. *Nicole broke the dishes onto the table.
d. Nicole broke the dishes into pieces.

(3.20) a. Sascha wiped the table clean.
b. Sascha wiped the crumbs off the table.
c. Sascha wiped the crumbs into the trash.
d. Sascha wiped the crumbs into pieces.
e. ?Sascha wiped the crumbs black.
f. ??Sascha wiped the crumbs to death. (resultative reading)

The data in (3.19) – (3.20) show that *break* forces the secondary predicate to denote a part-of type, whereas *sweep* allows a broader range of secondary predicates. This suggests that in the lexicon there are more meanings associated with *wipe* than with *break*. The fact that *wipe* is more flexible than *break* with respect to what kind of resultative predicate it can occur with is thus not primarily related to a verb's event structure *per se*, but seems to be intimately related to the idiosyncratic part (what R H and L call the constant) of a verb's meaning. It follows that although event structure is involved in licensing the occurrence of resultative phrases, its power to license a resultative phrase crucially depends on the verb's lexical semantics. I propose that the idiosyncratic part of a verb's lexical semantics determines the range of resultative phrases it can occur with while event structure only 'helps' in licensing the resultative phrase. In this connection, consider the following examples in light of R H and L's claim that *break* can only occur with a very small set of resultative phrases because of its 'special' event structure.

(3.21) a. Dawn broke the egg into the bowl.
b. Christian broke the branch off the tree.
c. Johannes broke the door open.
d. Claire broke a hole through the wall.
e. Stefan broke the leg away from his old desk.

The sentences in (3.21a-e) illustrate that *break* can occur with a much wider range of resultative phrases than assumed by R H and L.[21] The data suggest that the occurrence of the wider range of resultative phrases is not limited by the event structure associated with the verb ([[x ACT <MANNER>] CAUSE [BECOME [y <*BROKEN*>]]] (1998: 116)) as proposed by R H and L, but that it is the lexical semantic information of the verb that dictates with what kinds of resultative phrases it can occur. On this view, *break* must be associated with at least two more distinct meanings in the lexi-

[21]Note that *break* in (3.21b) also has a distinct meaning. It does not imply that the branch is actually broken, but that it is not part of the tree anymore.

con.[22] The sentences in (3.21) show that R H and L's claim that the event structure template of *break* cannot be further augmented to include a different achieved state or location is false.[23] It is clear that *break* does not behave very differently from simple activity verbs (R H and L's manner verbs) such as *sweep* when occurring in a resultative construction after all. That is, although result verbs seem to enter the stage with a different event structure than manner verbs, they show the same kind of effects with respect to which resultative phrases they combine with as do manner verbs. This means that the difference in the distribution of resultative phrases is not primarily due to the event structure templates associated with a verb but rather to its lexical semantics.[24] We now turn to a discussion of the notions of word meaning and verb class as employed by R H and L to account for the distribution of resultatives.

---

[22]Similar observations can be made about other result verbs such as *melt* and *dry*. According to R H and L (1998), these result verbs should also be accounted for in terms of accomplishment event structure templates that lexically specify for a specific state. On this view, the resultative phrases in sentences such as *Sue dried her hair crisp* and *Joe melted the butter to liquid* serve as modifiers to the lexicalized resultant state of the result verbs. However, sentences such as *Sue dried her hair around her ears* and *Joe melted the butter onto the stove* show that we must assume at least a second 'basic' verb meaning for *dry* and *melt*. That is, *around my ear* and *onto the stove* do not serve to modify a property of the postverbal NPs, but rather give information about their locations. These sentences suggest that we cannot assume a fixed 'basic' verb meaning for all result verbs.

[23]Even if the authors decided to hold on to their 'fixed lexical template' augmentation for result verbs like *break*, they would be forced to introduce template changing rules in order to explain the different occurrences of resultative phrases in (3.21a-e). This step, however, would raise the question of how such template changing rules could be constrained in a way so they do not overgenerate unwanted verb meanings (see Pustejovsky 1995 for a discussion of this question). The discussion illustrates an inherent problem with R H and L's approach to verb meaning. By claiming that there are basic verb meanings and derived verb meanings they first have to decide on a basic verb meaning. Then, they are forced to assume sets of rules to derive other verb meanings. The data in (3.21a-e) show that this approach is very problematic, because its analysis of structured polysemy cannot account for the many idiosyncrasies that many verbs exhibit.

[24]Another problem with R H and L's analysis is their assumption of a zero morpheme in the case of the intransitive use of *break* (cf. *The dishes broke*. (1998: 117)) in order to satisfy the Argument Realization Condition. Based on data from Romance and Slavic languages (cf. Nedjalkov 1969 and Haspelmath 1993) which have overt morphemes marking the intransitive use of complex event verbs like *break*, they claim that English possesses a zero morpheme which is part of the event structure of complex events. However, no empirical evidence is cited to support the existence of a zero morpheme for English.

3.5.3 'Basic' Word Meanings and Verb Classes

Recall that by constructing 'a generative theory of verb meaning' (1998: 126), R H and L wish to avoid the claim that 'the lexicon must contain a vast number of verbs with multiple lexical entries' which in their view is 'undesirable' and 'counterintuitive' (1998: 98) (for similar views, see, e.g., Grimshaw (1990) and Pustejovsky 1995).

Recent work on polysemy (e.g., Kilgarriff 1992, 1997, Gibbs and Matlock 1997, Fillmore and Atkins 2000, and Klein and Murphy 2001) has tackled the question of how different meanings of words are related to each other and whether they need to be represented in the lexicon individually. Based on vast amounts of corpus material as well as data from psycholinguistic experiments, Baker (1999), for example, argues for 19 distinct senses of the verb *see*: 'The psycholinguistic evidence suggests that speakers have mental representations (or processing strategies) that are at least partially separated for at least a dozen senses.' (1999: 186) This leads him to conclude that ...

> although models of the lexicon which minimize the number of senses have a certain theoretical appeal, the preponderance of evidence suggests that people do store quite a number of relatively specific senses for highly polysemous words. (Baker 1999: 186)

The findings of Baker's work indicate that any theory dealing with lexical semantic representations cannot ignore the fact that speakers potentially have a multitude of distinct mental representations associated with a lexical item.[25] On this view, positing a generative theory of word meaning which takes a certain meaning as 'basic' in order to derive other related meanings seems highly questionable, especially when the main motivation lies in reducing the amount of information stored in the mental lexicon.[26] To this end, Langacker (1987: 41) observes that 'the principle of economy must be interpreted in relation to other considerations, in particular the requirement of factuality: true simplicity is not achieved just by omitting relevant facts.'

---

[25]Fillmore and Atkins (1992: 76) observe that 'a verb's meaning can be understood only with reference to a structured background of experience, beliefs, or practices, constituting a kind of conceptual prerequisite for understanding the meaning.'

[26]Dan Slobin (p.c.) notes: 'The brain is great at storing millions and millions of irrelevant details, so why should it have trouble with a few verb meanings? And why should every lexical item have just one central meaning? I think this is a sort of 19th-century bookkeeping, in which we try to keep the brain as simple as something we can think about and write down on a sheet of paper.'

These observations also form the basis of Slobin's work (1997). He points out that

> [w]e have really no way of knowing how many false hypotheses it takes to overburden the vastly complex human brain, or how quickly and efficiently they can be revised or dismissed. It is unsettling to realize how many of our theories are aimed at the simplistic criterion of 'economy' when we have no rational measure of that economy.
>
> (Slobin 1997: 310-11)

That is, the brain seems to be able to store a vast amount of information with respect to linguistic items. Regarding the question of how to deal with great numbers of related word meanings, Fillmore and Atkins (2000: 100) point out that

> [l]exical semantics is in a poor position to solve the problem of polysemy. To the lexical semanticist, polysemy is a prototype concept, in which the paradigm case is quite clear, but departures from the prototype provide us with all sorts of unsolvable problems. (...) The prototype for a situation of polysemy can be thought of as having the following features:
>
> (1) the multiple senses of the word can each be clearly traced back to the same word (this is the polysemy/homonymy distinction);
> (2) the set of senses permits a network-like description in which pairs of adjacent senses in the network are related by motivated linguistic processes (such as one or another type of metaphoric mapping) that recur across the lexicon; and
> (3) in all such links there is a cognitive asymmetry in that the understanding of each derivate sense is aided by knowledge of the sense from which it is derived.

Baker (1999) and Fillmore and Atkins (2000) both suggest that deriving multiple word senses from a single lexical entry is problematic. Similarly, I have argued above that R H and L's treatment of multiple word meanings in terms of 'a generative theory of word meaning' (1998: 126) has certain drawbacks that preclude reaching an analysis covering the full range of resultatives.[27]

---

[27]In Levin and Rappaport Hovav (1996), the authors take a different approach to verb meaning in terms of unaccusativity (which is claimed to be semantically based). Based on their discussion of multiple meanings of verbs of sound, they claim 'that verbs of sound have two different

With respect to the notion of 'verb class' and its influence on the licensing of resultatives, R H and L observe that 'the variation in syntactic context correlates with variation in meaning' (1998: 98).[28] This leads them to propose that the variation found within verbs of surface contact through motion 'is not associated with individual verbs, but rather with entire semantic classes of verbs' (1998: 99). Consider the following sentences.

(3.22) a. Terry swept the crumbs into a pile.
b. Terry wiped the crumbs into a pile.
c. ??Terry rubbed the crumbs into a pile.
d. *Terry polished the crumbs into a pile.
e. *Terry sandpapered the crumbs into a pile.
(R H and L 1998: 97)

Note that although *sweep*, *wipe*, *rub*, *polish*, and *sandpaper* involve a surface contact through motion, they do not participate in the same syntactic pattern as predicted by R H and L. Next, consider R H and L's claim that 'the verb *run* shows a pattern of behavior characteristic of all verbs of manner of motion.' (1998: 99)

(3.23) a. The coach ran the athletes around the track. (1998: 98)
b. ?The coach jogged the athletes around the track.
c. ??The coach crawled the athletes around the track.
d. ??The coach tiptoed the athletes around the track.
e. ??The coach promenaded the athletes around the track.

Although the verbs *run*, *jog*, *crawl*, *tiptoe*, and *promenade* are members of the manner of motion verb class (cf. Levin 1993: 264, 266), they typically cannot all occur in the same context as predicted by R H and L.[29] The same shortcoming holds for another class of verbs discussed by R H and L, namely verbs of sound emission (Levin 1993: 234/235). They do not behave uniformly with respect to their syntactic surface patterns as the following examples illustrate.

---

but related meanings, each correlated with a different classification' (cf. .... *the elevator wheezed upward*) (1996: 495).

[28] This proposal relates to Levin's (1993: 5) suggestion '(...) that general principles of grammar are at work allowing the syntactic behavior of a verb to be predicted from its meaning. Their existence should explain a speaker's ability to make the judgments (...).'

[29] Note, however, that under proper contextual background conditions, some of these verbs may occur in the same usage pattern as *run* (e.g., *The mother promenaded her family around the park.*) which shows that verb behavior is subject to variability.

(3.24) a. Kim whistled her appreciation. (R H and L 1998: 98)
b. ?Kim gurgled her appreciation.
c. *Kim whined her appreciation.
d. *Kim boomed her appreciation.
e. *Kim plopped her appreciation.

The data in (3.22)-(3.24) show that although all of the verbs belong to certain broad semantic verb classes, there is something about their inherent lexical semantics that distinguishes almost every member of a verb class from other members of the same class.[30] I would like to claim that it is this tiny difference in meaning between individual members of a semantic verb class that determines whether a verb can occur in a certain context. This means that although it seems as if one can make a limited number of predictions about a verb's syntactic behavior based on its membership in a broader semantic verb class (which R H and L seem to equate with a certain 'basic' event structure template), these predictions do not take us very far when it comes to determining the range of resultative constructions in which a given verb may occur, even if R H and L's (2001) claim suggests the opposite: [31]

> In our semantic account the explanatory burden is borne by event structure representations, well-formedness conditions on these representations, and principles of mapping from event structure to syntactic structure.
>
> (R H and L 2001: 766)

However, I have argued above for the importance of paying special attention to the interrelated senses of a verb and the way in which these varying senses differ from those of other verbs.[32] In R H and L's terms, we need to

[30]R H and L (1998: 99) seem to have the intuition that 'verbs naming similar concepts appear in the same range of syntactic contexts, with verbs in each class showing a unique pattern of behavior.' They also state that 'not all English verbs allow the same range of flexibility in meaning and argument expression, and again this property is correlated with a verb's semantic class.' However, the authors do not discuss the problematic cases of the members of a single semantic class not being able to occur in the same syntactic environment and thus avoid accounting for the – in my view – most important part of a verb's meaning, namely its idiosyncratic part.

[31]Regarding the relationship between basic and augmented meanings, and verbs and their semantic class membership, R H and L (1998: 101) make the following suggestion: '... we assign this verb a basic classification as an activity verb because all its uses entail an activity involving a particular manner of surface contact.'

[32]To this end, Pinker (1989: 108) observes: '[I]t's not what possibly or typically goes on in an event that matters; it's what the verb's semantic representation is choosy about in that event

come up with a more detailed description of a verb's constant (the idiosyncratic part), i.e., we need to describe what it means to *run*, to *whistle*, or to *break*, and what it means to arrive at a final state where an object is *broken*. It follows from my arguments that an adequate theory of the distribution of resultative constructions necessitates better understanding what interplay of factors determines the structure of word meanings and how they are related to each other.[33] In Chapter 6 we will return to the question of how to account for different senses of words in order to adequately capture the distribution of resultative constructions.[34]

In summary, the problems with R H and L's (1998, 2001) event structure account of resultatives can be attributed to the following factors: (1) their assumption that verb meanings can be derived by augmentation of 'basic' event structure templates with other event structure templates; (2) their proposal that there are basic and derived word meanings, and (3) their suggestion that 'verbs naming similar concepts appear in the same range of syntactic contexts, with verbs in each class showing a unique pattern of behavior' (1998: 99).[35] However, despite my criticisms of R H and L's ac-

---

that matters.' Engelberg (1998: 33) suggests listing individual meanings of verbs with their respective individual event structure representations in the lexicon. These basic event structures are then subject to further event structure 'operations.' Nakamura's (1997) account of resultative constructions using predicate decomposition structures faces similar problems as R H and L's (1998) analysis when it comes to restricting the range of resultative constructions, because he assumes that 'the resultative construction is a productive process because semantic conflation is involved.' (1997: 506)

[33]Ritter and Rosen (1998) take a different view on the relation between the lexicon and event structure. They propose that 'syntactic structure plays a role in determining the realization of arguments and the interpretation of the sentence. (...) We conclude that the origin of sentences is not in the lexical representation of verbs, but rather in the syntactic representation of event structure.' (1998: 136) For different accounts that regard event structure as the central interface between syntax and semantics, see Arad (1998), Borer (1998), Erteschik-Shir and Rapoport (1997), Slabakova (1997), Ramchand (1997), and van Hout (1996).

[34]Levin and Rappaport Hovav's (1995) syntactic account of resultatives is faced with similar problems, because it does not fully take into account the lexical semantic information associated with the individual constituents of the resultative construction. That is, based on the Direct Object Restriction (1995: 34) and the Change-of-State Linking Rule (1995: 151), Levin and Rappaport Hovav's analysis is problematic when it comes to determining the semantic range of postverbal arguments (cf. *She drove {me/*the car} crazy, They ran themselves {to exhaustion/*smart}*) as well as determining the syntactic range of the resultative phrase (cf., e.g., *They killed the thief {dead/*to death}, They tortured us {to death/*dead}, It amazes me to think that clubs still run themselves {into financial ruin/*ruined}*.) Verspoor (1997: 112) points out similar observations, namely that Levin and Rappaport Hovav's (1995) syntactic account of resultatives does not capture the fact that the causativization process exhibited by resultatives is only semi-productive.

[35]Although the accounts by Kaufmann (1995), Stiebels (1996), and Kaufmann and Wunderlich (1998) pay closer attention to the individual semantics associated with the constituents of

count, their intuition that certain senses of a word are related in one way or the other is certainly on the right track. In addition, the authors have convincingly pointed out that event structure does play an important role in understanding how resultative constructions are distributed.[36]

3.6 Conclusions

In this chapter I have argued that the notion of event structure has been overemphasized as an explanatory factor in the licensing and distribution of resultative constructions. In particular, we have seen that those accounts which primarily rely on aspectual classes (à la Vendler 1967) and their combinatorial possibilities in terms of event structure refer to general semantic classes of verbs in order to restrict event structure composition. I have shown that the well-formedness conditions imposed on the composition of event structures by Tenny (1994), Winkler (1997), and Rappaport Hovav and Levin (1998, 2001) are not powerful enough to restrict the range of unattested resultative constructions. These shortcomings can be attributed to the defining criteria used to establish groups of semantic classes by such accounts as Tenny (1994) or Rappaport Hovav and Levin (1998, 2001).[37] I have argued that any theory which seeks to employ the notion of semantic class in order to refer to specific syntactic properties of the members of such a class needs to present a more detailed description of a verb's idiosyncratic meaning.

Our discussion has also shed some light on whether event structure templates can be recruited to derive extended verb meanings from basic verb meanings. Approaches such as Rappaport Hovav and Levin (1998, 2001) and Tenny (1994) are certainly on the right track in suggesting that

---

the resultative construction, their predicate decomposition analyses of resultative constructions face the same problems as R H and L's (1998, 2001) account. In particular, the restrictions regulating the augmentation of different types of predicates are not sufficient to capture the full range of attested resultative constructions, because they do not take into account the multiple senses associated with verbs.

[36]Rapp's (1997) event structure account of German resultative constructions faces similar problems as R H and L's analysis. This is because Rapp primarily relies on event structure composition to explain the distribution of resultatives without addressing the influence of the idiosyncratic lexical semantics of the individual constituents participating in the construction. For more details, see Boas (2000b).

[37]Based on their analysis of lexical reflexives and reciprocals in Kannada, Hebrew, and Malay, Mohanan and Mohanan (1998) make a similar proposal. They suggest that '[l]exical semantics is composed of semantic content which expresses the meaning differences between lexical items, and semantic structure which expresses those meanings that interact with the grammatical system.' (1998: 191) For similar proposals, see Mohanan and Mohanan (1999).

event structure plays a role in determining whether a given activity verb can be interpreted as an accomplishment verb. However, I have shown that only a detailed lexical semantic description of a verb's meaning will reveal whether its meaning can be potentially 'expanded' so that it can occur in a resultative construction.

4

The Role of Argument Structure Constructions

> To adopt a constructional approach is to undertake a commitment in principle to account for the entirety of each language. (Kay and Fillmore 1999: 1)

4.1 Introduction

In this chapter we turn to the role of argument structure constructions in explaining the distribution of resultatives. Working within the framework of Construction Grammar (Fillmore and Kay 1993, Fillmore, Kay and O'Connor 1988, Kay and Fillmore 1999, and Lakoff 1987, among others), Goldberg (1995) presents a semantic account emphasizing the role of independently existing meaningful constructions in licensing the postverbal elements in resultative constructions. In contrast to other frameworks underlying the analyses discussed in the previous two chapters, Construction Grammar integrates different kinds of linguistic information - semantic, pragmatic, and syntactic information, among others - in such a way that allows us to determine the extent to which the different kinds of information are related to and influence each other.

Section 4.2 gives an overview of the main principles of Construction Grammar. Goldberg's (1995) Construction Grammar approach to resultative (and caused-motion) constructions is discussed in Section 4.3. In Section 4.4 I provide a variety of empirical data demonstrating that Goldberg's proposal regarding the status of an independently existing argument structure construction that licenses resultatives cannot be maintained in this form. This insight leads me to adopt a number of important points from Goldberg's analysis and to sketch out the cornerstones of an alternative approach to resultative constructions within Construction Grammar.

4.2 Construction Grammar

The main idea behind Construction Grammar (henceforth CxG) is that a linguistic model should be able to account for all facets of a speaker's knowledge about her language. Unlike many other theories of grammar, CxG does not make any theoretical distinctions between different areas of grammar such as core and periphery (cf. Chomsky 1965, 1981) and therefore aims to achieve full coverage of the relevant facts of a language. CxG does not limit itself to analyzing a slice of interesting data representing regular processes in the grammar of a language (e.g., subject-predicate constructions, relative clause constructions, wh-question constructions). Rather, CxG is also concerned with accounting for semi-productive processes (e.g., *Way-constructions* (Goldberg 1995, Israel 1996), *What's X doing Y?* (Kay and Fillmore 1999), *Ditransitive* (Goldberg 1995), *let alone* (Fillmore et al. 1988) and idiomatic constructions (e.g., *kick the bucket; the Xer, the Yer*)) by using the same kinds of descriptive and explanatory principles used to account for more regular processes. Regarding the much debated question of how to account for idiosyncrasy in language, Goldberg (1997) summarizes the view commonly held by most construction grammarians as follows:

> Although most of the aspects of language are highly motivated, in the sense that they are related to other aspects of the grammar and are nonarbitrary, Construction Grammar holds the view that much of language is idiosyncratic to varying degrees and must therefore be learned.

Another way in which CxG differs from approaches nested within the generative transformational tradition is that it is non-derivational, non-modular, and flexible enough in its notation to allow for the introduction of new constructions and features when motivated by empirical facts that indicate that a satisfactory analysis of a set of given data cannot be arrived at without attributing the observed patterns to an already existing construction or feature thereof. This means, for example, that in CxG there is no strict separation between lexicon and grammar. Furthermore, all form-meaning pairs are given the same theoretical status as constructions, or 'constructs' (Kay and Fillmore 1999: 2). Lexical entries of individual words differ from phrases and sentences in that their information may contain more specific information. For example, a verb will contain information about its semantic frames and its syntactic valence whereas a verb phrase construction will contain more general information about what kinds of constituents contribute to its formation.

Rather than positing distinct modules of grammar that interact with each other, Construction Grammar takes the notion of the linguistic sign (Saussure 1916) as central and posits that each particular form is associated with a specific meaning that licenses as well as constrains it. Goldberg (1995) gives the following definition of a construction.

> C is a CONSTRUCTION iff_{def} C is a form-meaning pair <F_i, S_i> such that some aspect of F_i or some aspect of S_i is not strictly predictable from C's component parts or from other previously established constructions.
>
> (Goldberg 1995: 4)

The form of a construction can be associated with different kinds of grammatically relevant information that can be semantic, pragmatic, syntactic, morphological, phonological, or lexical in nature. The CxG approach towards a formal description and subsequent explanation of language facilitates accounting for so-called interface phenomena that have posed problems to analyses nested in other frameworks (largely due to the idea that language can be neatly separated into different modules). Thus, besides being concerned with what has traditionally been called the 'syntax-semantics interface' (e.g., Ackerman and Webelhuth 1998, Croft 2001, Fillmore and Kay 1993, Goldberg 1995, Kay 2002a, Kay and Fillmore 1999), CxG accounts range from dealing with phenomena traditionally attributed to the interface between morphology and syntax (e.g., Koenig 1999) and the interface between phonology and morphology (e.g., Orgun 1996, Boas 2002e) to analyzing pragmatic (e.g., Fillmore 1985, Kay and Fillmore 1999, Lambrecht 1994) as well as intonation phenomena (e.g., Lambrecht and Michaelis 1998).

CxG architecture uses the same representations for displaying information about words, phrases, and sentences. Further, it employs inheritance hierarchies to capture generalizations across constructions. The use of inheritance hierarchies makes it possible to state relevant information only once and then have other constructions inherit it if needed. Information about constructions is often represented in terms of Attribute-Value Matrices (AVMs) which make it easy to account for the licensing of expressions in terms of unification of constructions. Thus, only when two AVMs contain non-conflicting information may they unify to form a particular expression.

Before closing this section it is important to note that CxG is not a framework with a predefined set of notations whose use implies a specific commitment to theory-internal principles and parameters as in other frameworks (see, e.g., Chomsky 1981, 1995). Instead, CxG analyses typically make use of feature-based formalisms in many different ways to ensure theoretical compatibility between different CxG approaches. For CxG approaches using different kinds of notations see Ackerman and Webelhuth (1998), Croft (2001), Goldberg (1995), Kay and Fillmore (1999), Koenig (1999), and Lakoff (1987), among others. The use of feature-based formalisms makes it relatively easy to convert CxG notation into Head-Driven Phrase Structure Grammar notation and vice versa (see, e.g., Koenig 1999, Kathol 2000, Davis 2001, and Kay 2002a). With this short introduction to Construction Grammar, we now turn to Goldberg's (1995) analysis of caused-motion and resultative constructions.[1]

4.3 Caused-Motion and Resultative Constructions

Goldberg's CxG analysis regards the notion of 'meaningful constructions' (1995: 224) as central to any theory of language. On her view, constructions 'are taken to be the basic units of language' (1995: 4) and 'can be viewed as free-standing entities, stored within the lexicon alongside lexical items, idioms, and other constructions that may or may not be partially lexically filled.' (1995: 221). More specifically, constructions can be characterized as 'pairings of syntax and semantics that can impose particular interpretations on expressions containing verbs which do not themselves lexically entail the given interpretation.' (1995: 220) One of Goldberg's central arguments for positing constructions that exist independently of the words which instantiate them has to do with her wish to 'avoid the claim that the syntax and semantics of the clause is projected exclusively from the specifications of the main verb.' (1995: 224) Thus, Goldberg's Construction Grammar view of language has the advantage of not being forced to posit implausible verb senses for cases in which verbs occur in an unusual environment such as *sneeze* and *talk* in the following examples.

(4.1) a. He sneezed the napkin off the table.
b. Dan talked himself blue in the face.

(Goldberg 1995: 224)

[1] A number of ideas presented in this chapter have formed the basis for Boas (2000a, 2002a, 2002b, 2002c, 2002d, 2002f).

According to Goldberg, the verbs in (4.1) are associated with specific lexical semantic information that allows them to integrate (or 'fuse') with the semantics of the argument structure constructions. This in turn licenses the direct object. Goldberg points out that contrary to DiSciullo and Williams (1987) and Jurafsky (1992), a set of constructions does not consist of independent entities that exhibit irregular organizational patterns, but is instead a 'highly structured lattice of interrelated information' (1995: 5) that 'display prototype structures and form networks of associations.' (1995: 5)[2]

4.3.1 Caused-Motion Constructions

On Goldberg's CxG analysis, the existence of an independent and distinct caused-motion construction is based on the observation that the common range of syntactic realizations that the verbs in (4.2) can occur in cannot possibly be attributed to the meanings of the verbs, but rather to a free-standing caused-motion construction which contributes additional arguments to the semantics of the verbs. The sentences cannot be explained compositionally because verbs like *laugh*, *sneeze*, or *urge* do not independently have the meaning they exhibit in the caused-motion construction.

(4.2) a. They laughed the poor guy out of the room.
b. Frank sneezed the tissue off the table.
c. Mary urged Bill into the house.
(Goldberg 1995: 152)

Although the verbs in (4.2a)-(4.2c) contribute their basic meanings, it is the caused-motion construction 'that is itself associated with meaning' (1995: 10) and therefore contributes the additional arguments providing the final interpretation of caused-motion. The representations in (4.3a-c) illustrate how the constructional semantics (constructional roles) of the caused-motion construction and the verbal semantics (participant roles) of an intransitive matrix verb are fused in Goldberg's framework in order to form the caused-motion interpretation (4.3c).

[2]Based on research in language acquisition (Clark 1978, Slobin 1985, and Bowerman 1989), Goldberg (1995: 5) proposes that 'simple clause constructions are associated directly with semantic structures which reflect scenes basic to human experience.'

(4.3)a. Caused-Motion Construction

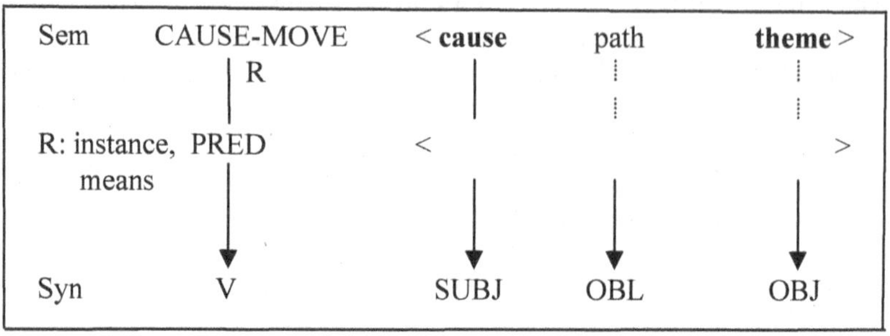

(cf. Goldberg 1995: 163)

b. sneeze: < **sneezer** >

c. Mary sneezed the napkin off the table.

The boxed diagram in (4.3a) represents the caused-motion construction and consists of three different layers. In the top line of the box we find the construction's own meaning (Sem). It contains the semantic arguments of the construction (the constructional roles) and represents their semantic relations with respect to each other. Thus, the caused-motion construction is associated with the semantics 'X CAUSES Y TO MOVE Z.' Solid lines between the semantic roles and roles in the predicate's role array indicate that the semantic role must be fused with an independently existing verbal participant role. Dotted lines indicate that the construction is able to provide additional participant roles. The middle line of the construction contains open slots into which the verb's participant roles fuse and in the bottom line we find the overt syntactic realizations of the semantic arguments (OBL stands for oblique) of the combined verb-construction semantics. Roles represented in bold are 'profiled' arguments, i.e., entities in a verb's semantics that are 'obligatorily accessed and function as focal points within the scene, achieving a special degree of prominence (Langacker 1987).' (Goldberg 1995: 44)

(4.3b) is a representation of the lexical entry for *sneeze* in Goldberg's framework. The representation shows that the verb is associated with a single participant argument role, in this case the sneezer. The participant role is represented in bold print to reflect the observation that the sneezer role is lexically 'profiled.' Under Goldberg's analysis, verbs are associated with specific semantic frames. The term 'frame' is borrowed from Fillmore's (1982, 1985) theory of Frame Semantics. Frame semantic information captures the richness of the various meanings associated with a lexical item, such as references to world and cultural knowledge, experiences, and beliefs (see Petruck 1996). Since the semantics of verbs are modeled in terms of frame semantic knowledge in Goldberg's analysis, the lexical entries for any given verb contain participant roles representing the frame semantic information. This means that when *sneeze* fuses with the caused-motion construction in (4.3a), the verb *sneeze* contributes the *sneezer* role (sneeze: <**sneezer**>), whereas the construction contributes both a theme and a goal role to the verb's semantics.[3] In other words, *sneeze* specifies the means by which the CAUSE-MOVE relation is achieved whereas the construction provides the rest of the semantics which then in (4.3c) yields the interpretation of *Mary caused the napkin to move off the table by sneezing.* [4]

4.3.2 Relationship Between Caused-Motion and Resultative Constructions

Contrary to other approaches that treat resultative constructions as a uniform phenomenon (Jackendoff 1990, Wechsler 1997, Verspoor 1997), Goldberg aims for a distinct treatment of caused-motion and resultative constructions due to the differing meanings of the two constructions. Her approach is exemplified by the following paraphrases.

---

[3]When a verb is lexically associated with two participant roles (e.g., in the case of *push*: <**push**, **pushee**>), the caused-motion construction only contributes one argument role, namely the goal role. In cases in which a verb is lexically associated with three participant roles (e.g., put: < **putter**, **put.place**, **puttee** > (cf. 1995: 52)), 'the constructional meaning is entirely redundant with the verb's meaning and the verb merely adds information to the event designated by the construction.' (1995: 51)

[4]Besides a number of constraints specific to the caused-motion construction 'to avoid arbitrary lexical stipulations on each verb that could potentially occur in the construction' (Goldberg 1995: 165, 174), the following two constraints generally regulate the fusion of verbal and constructional semantics. '*The Semantic Coherence Principle:* Only roles which are semantically compatible can be fused. Two roles r_1 and r_2 are semantically compatible if either r_1 can be construed as an instance of r_2, or r_2 can be construed as an instance of r_1. For example, the kicker participant of the *kick* frame may be fused with the agent role of the ditransitive construction because the kicker role can be construed as an instance of the agent role. Whether a role can be construed as an instance of another role is determined by general categorization principles.' (1995: 50) '*The Correspondence Principle:* Each participant role that is lexically profiled and expressed must be fused with a profiled argument role of the construction. (...) If a verb has three profiled participant roles, then one of them may be fused with a nonprofiled argument role of a construction. (...)' (1995: 50)

(4.4) a.	Caused-Motion	X CAUSES Y TO MOVE Z	Sub V Obj Obl Pat sneezed the napkin off the table.
b.	Resultative	X CAUSES Y TO BECOME Z	Sub V Obj XComp She kissed him unconscious.

(1995: 3)

Goldberg's second argument in support of a distinct treatment of caused-motion and resultative constructions is based on the claim that the two constructions are related by a metaphorical mapping by which the 'dominating construction's semantics is mapped to the dominated construction's semantics.' (1995: 81) As a consequence of this mapping mechanism, resultative constructions are analyzed as a metaphorical extension of the central sense of caused-motion constructions and therefore crucially involve 'a metaphorical interpretation of the result phrase as a metaphorical type of goal.' (1995: 81)[5] Claiming that resultative constructions are metaphorical extensions of the central caused-motion sense allows Goldberg to account for the 'syntactic specifications of the metaphorical extensions' that 'are inherited from the caused-motion construction.' (1995: 89) It also allows her to state the Unique Path Constraint in (4.6) in order to explain why the resultatives in (4.5a) exhibit the same co-occurrence restrictions as the caused-motion construction in (4.5b) and (4.5c).

(4.5) (a) *Sam kicked Bill black and blue out of the room.
(b) *Sam kicked Bill out of the room black and blue.
(Goldberg 1995: 81)
(c) *Shirley sailed into the kitchen into the garden.
(Goldberg 1995: 82)

(4.6) *Unique Path (UP) Constraint*: If an argument X refers to a physical object, then no more than one distinct path can be predicated of X within a single clause. The notion of a single path entails two things: (1) X cannot be predicated to move to two distinct locations at any given time t, and (2) the motion

---

[5]The metaphor which accounts for 'the relation between the semantics of the two constructions' – according to Goldberg – is 'Change of State as Change of Location.' (1995: 88-89)

must trace a path within a single landscape.

(Goldberg 1995: 82)

4.3.3 Resultative Constructions

Goldberg motivates the existence of resultative constructions as independently existing meaningful constructions on the basis of data which show that the interpretation of a sentence cannot be derived compositionally from the meanings of its individual constituents. As with the caused-motion construction, the resultative construction shown in (4.7) is associated with a particular argument structure configuration and has its own constructional semantics 'X CAUSES Y TO BECOME Z' independently of the verbs which instantiate it. When a verb fuses with the resultative construction, the construction can add either a result-goal argument in the case of transitive verbs like *wipe* in (4.8a) or both a result-goal and a patient argument in the case of intransitive verbs like *talk* in (4.8b). When *wipe* fuses with the resultative construction, it provides the means by which the CAUSE-BECOME relation is achieved whereas the construction provides the result-goal argument denoting the activity's outcome. The semantics resulting from the fusion of *wipe* with the construction can be paraphrased as *He caused the table to become clean by means of wiping.*

(4.7) Resultative-Construction

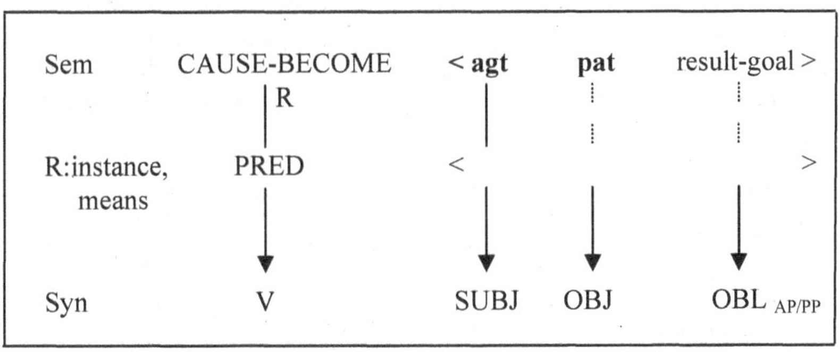

(1995: 189)

(4.8) a. wipe < **wiper** wiped>
He wiped the table clean.

b. talk < **talker** >
He talked himself blue in the face. (1995: 189)

Another property of this analysis is that so-called fake objects (cf. *himself* in (4.8b)) are analyzed as semantic arguments provided by the construction rather than as arguments motivated on syntactic grounds (cf. Simpson 1983, Carrier and Randall 1992).[6] Thus, when *talk* (4.8b) fuses with the resultative construction (4.7), it is the construction that provides the semantic patient argument *himself* to the verb's semantics.[7] By proposing this solution, Goldberg is able to account for the fact that fake and regular non-reflexive objects exhibit the same semantic relation to the matrix verb in that both are interpreted as patient arguments.[8] Having reviewed the main points of Goldberg's approach, we now turn to data which show that Goldberg's analysis is problematic when it comes to constraining the constructions' application and explaining the full distribution of resultative and caused-motion constructions.

4.4 Towards an Integrated Account of Caused-Motion and Resultative Constructions

4.4.1 Metaphorical Extension Revisited

One of Goldberg's motivations for positing an architecture in which resultatives are regarded as metaphorical extensions of caused-motion constructions has to do with the fact that neither construction allows the postverbal NP to be predicated of two phrases that denote two distinct locations (cf. the Unique Path Constraint in (4.6)). According to Goldberg, this is naturally explained when one assumes that resultatives are metaphorical extensions

[6]By critically analyzing the arguments put forward by other researchers in favor of a syntactic analysis of fake objects (Adjectival Passive Formation, Nominalizations, Middle Formation), Goldberg (1995: 182-185) convincingly shows that fake objects show properties typical of internal arguments.

[7]The following constraints restrict the application of resultative constructions to a verb's semantics in Goldberg's framework: '(a) The two-argument resultative construction must have an (animate) instigator argument. (b) The action denoted by the verb must be interpreted as directly causing the change of state: no intermediary time intervals are possible. (c) The resultative adjective must denote the endpoint of a scale. (d) Resultative phrases cannot be headed by deverbal adjectives (Green 1972; Carrier and Randall 1992).' (Goldberg 1995: 193)

[8]For determining whether a given constituent shows the properties of a patient argument, Goldberg (1995: 180) adopts Lakoff's (1976) tests for patienthood ('(a) What X did to <patient> was, ... (b) What happened to <patient> was, ...') Note that other semantic and syntactic properties of fake objects differ from those of regular direct objects. Thus, fake objects typically fail to passivize (Cf. **Himself was talked hoarse*).

of caused-motion constructions. However, the following sentences show that the constraint on multiple predication over the postverbal NP of caused-motion and resultative constructions is due to a more general constraint that holds for predication structures in general. That is, each subject only allows one semantically coherent predicate.[9]

(4.9) a. *Della ran crawled home.
b. *Melissa talked laughed with Julie.
c. *Julie considers Pat smart cool.
d. *Eric finds warm beer unbearable great.

The restriction on double predication structures of the kind in (4.9) by more general constraints of English suggests that the analysis of resultatives in terms of metaphorical extensions from caused-motion is not necessary to explain the fact that resultatives exhibit the same types of constraints with respect to their secondary predicates as caused-motion constructions.[10]

Next, consider another set of data adduced by Goldberg as support for her claim that caused-motion constructions should be distinguished from resultative constructions. On her view, the fact that 'resultatives can only apply to arguments which can be categorized as *patient* arguments (...) alone serves to distinguish resultatives from caused-motion expressions.' (1995: 87)

(4.10) a. Joe moved it onto the table.
b. Joe ran out of the room.

(4.11) a. ??What Joe did to it was he moved it.
b. ?*What happened to Joe was he ran.

(Goldberg 1995: 88)

[9]Of course, things are different in coordination structures in which the predicates are conjoined by *and*, cf. *Melissa talked and laughed with Julie*, and *Jenny considers Pat smart and cool.* Again, this general option of coordination structure also licenses double predications with resultative and caused-motion constructions as the following sentences illustrate. *The boom swings over Joe and slams into Patricia, knocking her unconscious and into the raging sea* (J.P. Shanley, *Joe versus the Volcano*) (cited in Morita 1998: 138).

[10]This does not necessarily mean that most resultative phrases cannot be interpreted as metaphorical movements to a new location. What it does suggest, however, is that the metaphorical interpretation does not automatically have to be represented in terms of a metaphorical link between the two constructions, but that the metaphorical interpretation can also be arrived at in terms of more general metaphorical mapping principles that hold for the language in general, and are able to map linguistic structures from source to target domains across the entire language. On this view, metaphorical extensions fall out naturally.

Goldberg proposes that '[d]irectionals do not require that the argument which they predicate be a patient, only that they be a theme.' (1995: 87) On her account, this distinction explains the unacceptability of (4.11a, b) which are patient-test paraphrases of the preceding examples (4.10a, b). Since *it* and *Joe* do not pass the tests for patienthood in (4.11), Goldberg concludes they must be themes of a caused-motion construction rather than patients of a resultative construction. In other words, the difference in distribution of patient and theme arguments is one of the crucial points that Goldberg takes as justification for her distinct treatment of caused-motion and resultative constructions.

The evidence from (4.10) and (4.11), however, is problematic because Goldberg's comparison is based on two syntactically and semantically distinct verbs. That is, whereas (4.10a) includes a postverbal NP *it* and means *Joe caused it to be on the table by moving it there*, there is no such postverbal NP or causal interpretation available in *Joe ran out of the room* in (4.10b) that could serve as the basis for a patient-test paraphrase. This difference explains the unacceptability of (4.11b): since (4.10b) is not even a regular transitive caused-motion construction in comparison to (4.10a), it also cannot serve as a basis for the patient test. To this end, notice that once we start out with a postverbal NP such as *himself* in (4.12), we may get both caused-motion and resultative constructions.

(4.12) a. Joe ran himself out of the room.
b. Joe ran himself to exhaustion.

Once the postverbal NP is present as the basis for a patient test, we may apply the test and get the following acceptable results.

(4.13) a. What happened to Joe was he ran himself out of the room.
b. What happened to Joe was he ran himself to exhaustion.

This comparison shows that *run* is conventionally associated with both the caused-motion and resultative pattern. Moreover, there is no strict difference between a theme and a patient interpretation of the postverbal NP that would provide for a categorial distinction between caused-motion and resultative constructions. In addition, note that the acceptability of Goldberg's data in (4.11a) also increases once *it* is replaced by a regular r(eferring)-expression such as *the bottle* as in (4.14a) which then yields an appropriate patient interpretation of the postverbal NP in (4.14b).

(4.14) a. Joe moved the bottle onto the table.
b. What Joe did to the bottle was he moved it onto the table.

The examples in (4.14) indicate that it is possible to have arguments that can be interpreted as patients in caused-motion constructions. Further, when patient arguments do occur in caused-motion constructions, Goldberg's categorial distinction between caused-motion and resultative constructions based on the patient-test are superfluous. Moreover, it is not even necessary to posit the existence of two distinct constructions. Instead, I propose that a verb's ability to occur with a caused-motion and/or resultative pattern is a property that is lexically associated with each individual verb without a construction adding additional arguments to it. This bottom-up view allows specific occurrence restrictions to be placed on the verb itself and eliminates the need to constrain the application of different constructions in a top down fashion by motivating a metaphorical extension analysis of one construction in terms of another. The discussion in this section has pointed to another interesting component of Goldberg's theory, namely constructional polysemy, an issue to which we turn next.

4.4.2 Constructional Polysemy

Based on sentences such as (4.15a-d), Goldberg proposes that the central sense 'X CAUSES Y TO MOVE Z' of the caused-motion construction extends to four systematically related yet distinct senses that should be analyzed as constructional polysemy.[11] On this view, the central sense motivates each of the extended senses which by themselves each constitute a minimally different construction in terms of their meanings yet inherit the same syntactic specification of the core construction. The individual sense extensions of the caused-motion construction include (1) verbs of communication as in (4.15a),[12] (2) 'force dynamic verbs that encode the removal of a barrier,' as in (4.15b),[13] (3) verbs that encode the concept of '"X PREVENTS Y FROM MOVING Comp(Z)"' as in (4.15c), and (4) verbs that mean '"X HELPS Y TO MOVE Z"' (1995: 162) as in (4.15d).

[11]Parts of this section formed the basis for Boas (2002b).

[12]These have specific force-dynamics such that if 'the conditions of satisfaction associated with the act denoted by the predicate entail: "X causes Y to move Z".' (1995: 161)

[13]When used in a caused-motion construction, these verbs roughly mean '"X ENABLES Y TO MOVE Z"' (1995: 161).

(4.15) a. Sam ordered him out of the house.
b. Sam allowed Bob out of the room. (Goldberg 1995: 161)
c. Harry locked Joe into the bathroom.
d. Sam helped him into the car. (Goldberg 1995: 162)

Positing constructional polysemy has the theoretical advantage of not necessitating lexical rules in order to account for sense extensions of verbs (see Pinker 1989, Rappaport Hovav and Levin 1996, Wechsler 1997) 'whose various senses are not predictable and must be conventionally associated with the construction.' (Goldberg (1995: 34)) More specifically, Goldberg points out the following:

> It might be tempting to think that by positing constructional polysemy, we are simply adding complexity to the construction which would otherwise be attributed to the verb. That is, it might be thought that while we avoid polysemy of lexical items by not postulating separate input and output senses of verbs that undergo lexical rules, we create polysemy of the construction instead. However, this is emphatically not the case. The polysemy attributed to the constructions is polysemy that exists independently of our decision as to how verb meanings should be represented, since it corresponds to polysemy across *outputs* of what is generally taken to be a single lexical rule on traditional accounts. (...) We may conclude that irrespective of whether we posit distinct verb senses or whether we attribute the resulting semantics to an interaction of verb and construction, it is necessary to account somehow for the observed differences in the resulting semantics. (Goldberg 1995: 37-39)

Note that the alternative proposal in favor of stating the relevant occurrence restrictions in the verb's semantics put forward in the last section argues neither for an analysis of caused-motion and resultative constructions in terms of lexical rules nor in terms of an abstractionist approach. What it does argue for, however, is that each verb has its own lexical semantic polysemy network which contains information about the range of possible constructions that the verb may occur in. That is, on this alternative view, the different meaning patterns that Goldberg describes as constructional polysemy fall out naturally from the rich lexical-semantic information associated with individual verbs rather than being attributed to distinct but related constructions (for similar arguments, see Nemoto 1998, Boas 2002a, Boas 2002c, Iwata 2002, Kay 1996, Kay 2002b).

The alternative proposal is thus different from (yet still compatible with) Goldberg's analysis in that it assumes that the crucial information determining whether a verb can occur in a given syntactic frame is already contained in the verb's lexical semantic information and does not stem from the construction's contributing specific meanings to the verb. Note that on the verb-centered polysemy view, there is no need to assume there are related but distinct constructions contributing different kinds of meanings to verbs so that positing an elaborate system of constructional polysemy is unnecessary.

By pushing the explanatory burden to the verbal level, we avoid another methodological problem of Goldberg's analysis that has to do with the motivation of her constructional polysemy classes. Note, for example, that some of the extended meaning classes of the caused-motion construction (1995: 163) only reflect that part of verb meaning they have been set up to account for. For instance, 'X ENABLES Y to MOVE Z' (1995: 161) reflects only the meaning inherent to the part of expressions containing verbs like *allow* or *let* that encode motion. In other words, by postulating these extended constructional senses, Goldberg's analysis seems to duplicate (at the constructional level) some of the senses that are already inherent to the conventionalized usage of these verbs.

At the same time, Goldberg's definition of verb classes which occur in some of her polysemous constructional variants is not precise enough to explain why the meaning of certain verbs is not 'affected' by the meaning of a construction. Take for instance the verb *open* which denotes the removal of a barrier and should therefore be able to occur with the 'X ENABLES Y to MOVE Z' extended sense of the caused-motion construction. Although *open* involves an 'active removal of a barrier' (1995: 161-62) and the enabler is typically an agent, sentences like **Steve opened Melissa into the room* are ruled out because of some verb specific requirements to which the construction has no direct access.[14] By giving more detailed lexical semantic descriptions of verbs like *open*, we may be able to avoid problems having to do with a verb's individual semantic requirements. With these problems regarding the nature of constructional polysemy in mind, we now turn to a more detailed discussion of the interaction of constructional and verbal semantics in Goldberg's framework.

[14]The sentences in (i) – (iv) also show that a construction does not have enough information to discriminate between two given transitive verbs such as *sweep* and *open*. The different distribution suggests that the verbs somehow lexically determine whether they can occur in a resultative pattern or not. Note that outside of resultative constructions they show identical distribution: *Pat swept the floor/ Pat opened the door*, and *Pat swept the floor with a broom/Pat opened the door with a key*. This shows that it is also hard to predict the distribution of resultatives based on a verb's behavior outside of resultative constructions.

(i) Pat swept the floor clean.
(ii) Pat swept the broom to pieces.
(iii) Pat opened the door (wide open).
(iv) *Pat opened the key to pieces.

4.4.3 The Role of Semantic Constraints

Recall that on Goldberg's constructional approach, a verb can only fuse with a construction when the semantics of the two are compatible by meeting both general as well as construction-specific constraints. For example, the constraint on resultatives which requires them to code an end of a scale captures the observation that 'most of the adjectives which can occur in the construction can be independently classified as having a clearly delimited lower bound and are therefore typically nongradable.' (1995: 195) On this analysis, there are two main exceptions to the constraint, namely causative verbs which 'are much freer in the semantic and syntactic type of resultative phrase they may occur in' (1995: 196) and other exceptional cases that 'tend to be from the same semantic domain as more conventionalized cases, and can be seen as one-shot novel extensions from a grammaticalized pattern.' (1995: 197) Note that there are additional exceptions to Goldberg's analyses. According to Goldberg (1995: 195), sentences such as **He wiped it dirty* and **He hammered the metal safe* are judged unacceptable. Given the appropriate contextual background information, however, these sentences become acceptable for most speakers of English as the following examples illustrate.

(4.16) a. Having spent all night working at the restaurant, Matt had gotten really tired. After he had wiped some ketchup and mayonnaise off a table, he forgot to clean his sponge before wiping the next table. Thus, *he wiped it dirty*.

b. When Marc got out of Martin's old Cadillac, he cut himself on a piece of metal that stuck out from the door. Since he started bleeding really badly, he had to go to the hospital to get stitches. The next day, Martin got a hammer and went back to his car. *He hammered the metal safe*.

Under Goldberg's analysis, such data as in (4.16) should be ruled out (1) due to her stipulation that *dirty* and *safe* cannot occur in resultative constructions and (2) because 'profiling is lexically determined and highly conventionalized – it cannot be altered by context.' (1995: 44) This means that under Goldberg's uniform constructional constraint on resultatives the possibility that certain interpretations can be licensed by the lexical semantics of the verb in combination with contextual information is not fully accounted for. Although she regularly mentions that 'there is a great deal of idiosyncrasy involved' (1995: 192) and that pragmatics plays a certain role in the interpretation of constructions (cf. 1995: 173, 175), her framework does not provide a detailed description of the exact mechanisms that determine the interaction between verbal, constructional, and contextual information. What is needed, then, is an approach towards resultatives that allows lexically profiled default information to be overridden under appropriate contextual conditions.[15] I suggest that once more attention is paid to the lexical semantic information associated with the constituents of the construction, especially the verb, a better understanding of the relevant constraints and their exceptions will follow.[16]

In this connection notice that Goldberg remains silent about what exact factors decide over the semantic and/or syntactic range of resultative phrases that may occur with a verb. If we assume that the resultative construction adds additional arguments to a verb's arguments, how are they to be expressed? Take, for example, the difference between *kill* and *strangle*. Whereas the former prefers *dead* as its resultative phrase, the latter requires *to death*. In Goldberg's approach, it is unclear where such collocational

---

[15]Note that Goldberg's assumption that 'nongradable adjectives are said to be unable to appear (ceteris paribus) with quantifying phrases' (1995: 195) is only a lexical default constraint that can be overruled given the proper contextual conditions. One of the adjectives that is not supposed to be gradable is *sober* (cf. ?*a little sober*). In the following context, however, *sober* is gradable: *After drinking all night, Chris woke up with a terrible headache and decided to go for a long run in order to run himself sober. However, after running for half a mile, Chris all of a sudden felt considerably better and decided that he could bear the remaining pain for the rest of the day. He was so glad that he had run himself a little sober.*

[16]Within the framework of Head-Driven Phrase Structure Grammar (HPSG) (Pollard and Sag 1994), Wechsler (1997) offers an analysis of resultatives that is based on the distinction between control and ECM-resultatives. On his view, the former include resultative phrases 'whose predication subject is a semantic argument of the matrix verb,' (cf. *John hammered the metal flat*) whereas the latter include resultatives phrases 'whose predication subject is NOT a semantic argument of the matrix verb.' (cf. *The dog barked itself hoarse*) (1997: 309) Wechsler claims that control resultatives place semantic restrictions on their resultative phrases whereas ECM-resultatives do not. On this view, a verb's lexical entry determines whether a given verb may occur with a resultative phrase of a certain semantic type or not. While Wechsler's account comes close to capturing most of the relevant properties of resultative constructions, there are, however, two main problems for his analysis. First, his distinction between control and ECM-resultatives is questionable. As we have seen in Chapter 2, even the class of resultatives that Wechsler categorizes as ECM-resultatives places semantic restrictions on their resultative phrases (cf. **She ran her Nikes blue/new/to death*). In this connection note that Wechsler's approach is also problematic when it comes to determining the exact syntactic category of the resultative phrase (cf. *They tortured him to death/*dead*). The second problem with Wechsler's account has to do with the status of ECM-resultatives which are licensed by a lexical rule adding additional arguments to the verb's basic syntactic argument structure. Since the application of this rule relies primarily on syntactic criteria ('Since there is no thematic control, any resultative PP or AP on the ARG-S list would trigger rule (33), ...' (1997: 318)), it is difficult to constrain and thus leads to overgeneration of resultative constructions (cf. **Mary ran herself threadbare*/ **Mary ran her Nikes exhausted*).

restrictions on the occurrence of resultative phrases are to be stated.[17] Next, we turn to Goldberg's constraints on the caused-motion construction.

Goldberg proposes that the causer argument of the caused-motion construction must be an agent or a natural force but cannot be an instrument. Based on the sentences below, she claims the following: 'the choice of argument encoded as a subject plays a role in the acceptability of caused-motion expressions demonstrates that the semantics of the construction must make reference to that argument, and that it cannot be stated as a VP construction.' (1995: 165)

(4.17) a. *The hammer broke the vase into pieces.
b. *The hammer broke the vase onto the floor.
c. (The hammer broke the vase.)

(4.18) a. *His cane helped him into the car.
b. (His cane helped him get around.) (Goldberg 1995: 165)

When checking with a group of fifteen native speakers, all speakers found (4.17c), and subsequently (4.17a) acceptable. In contrast, (4.18a) was judged 'weird' or 'not immediately acceptable' by eleven native speakers. When asked why they thought that the sentence was 'weird', the eleven speakers all responded that they had never heard such a sentence before or that they had difficulties imagining such a scene.[18] The different judgments on the acceptability of (4.17a-c) and (4.18a-b) indicate that Goldberg's Causer Argument Constraint does not seem to hold up uniformly. Furthermore, note that there are other contexts in which the acceptability of an instrument as the causer argument is greatly improved as in (4.19) – (4.21).

---

[17]Morita (1998: 329) makes a similar observation with respect to prepositional resultative constructions containing *to death*. Compare the following sentences:

(i) Women should worry. All they have to do is starve themselves half to death and they get thin. (WordBank)

(ii) Lenard Clar, 13, was nearly beaten to death 13 months ago in a mostly white Chicago neighborhood, the apparent victim of a brutal racial attack. (WordBank) (1998: 328)

He points out that 'the end-of-scale constraint, if at all, is restricted to adjectival resultatives, since they do not designate a transition to the resultant state expressed, which adverbial expressions of this kind would modify. By contrast, since prepositional resultative *to death* has the preposition that expresses a transition to the resultant state, they can have these adverbial expressions representing that such a transition has not been achieved or has done halfway through.' (Morita 1998: 328)

[18]The same observation holds for Goldberg's constraints on resultative constructions. Thus, of the 15 informants asked, twelve found *The hammer pounded the metal flat* acceptable, whereas nine found *The feather tickled her silly* acceptable.

(4.21) shows that *pound* can take a subject which is typically classified as an instrument. In this case the instrument is licensed because it is construed as a causer due to contextual background information (cf. Dowty's 1991 proto-agent properties).

(4.19) a. The computer locked Stefan out of the database.
b. The wheelchair helped her into the house.
c. The GPS system guided Christian through the city.
d. The alarm clock rang Claire out of bed.
e. The espresso maker blew steam into the milk.

(4.20) a. Four mighty steam-hammers pounded iron at Parkhead. (BNC)
b. The feather excited her into a frenzy.
c. The work pushed him to the brink of insanity.
(Verspoor 1997: 134)

(4.21) The impact knocked the bus off its frame and into two pieces. (San Francisco Examiner, 3/28/2000)

(4.21) shows that under certain contextual background conditions even an abstract event or entity can occur as the subject if it can be construed as a force-emitting causer argument which acts upon an undergoer. A different treatment of caused-motion and resultative constructions may not require the construction to be responsible for selecting the causer argument in terms of notions such as agent or natural force. Rather, an alternative analysis may emphasize the subject's force-emitting properties that - given the proper contextual background information - make it possible to construe it as a causer. Based on a list of features, it would then be possible to construe agents or natural forces not only as causers but also as instruments and possibly other types of event participants (cf. 4.21).

Our discussion has shown that the problems with Goldberg's constraints are partly due to the heavy emphasis she places on the meaning component of caused-motion and resultative constructions. Since she proposes that the construction has the capability of imposing arguments 'on the semantics directly associated with the predicates' (1995: 221), Goldberg has to state her constraints at the constructional level which sometimes turns out to be a level of abstraction that is too general. In the following section we will therefore investigate Goldberg's treatment of the status of lexical semantic information and its relation to constructional and contextual background information.[19]

4.4.4 Lexical-Semantic Information and the Role of Frame Semantics

Instead of positing verb sense shifts in terms of lexical rules (cf. Pinker 1989, Rappaport Hovav and Levin 1988, 1995, 1996, among others), Goldberg assumes a 'rich frame-semantic knowledge associated with verbs' (1995: 31) in order to 'allow for the possibility of meaningful interpretation and translation, and to predict correct inferences.' (1995: 29) To this end, she is integrating an approach towards semantic description labeled 'Frame Semantics,' 'a research program in empirical semantics which emphasizes the continuities between language and experience.' (Petruck 1996: 1) The main idea behind Frame Semantics as developed by Fillmore (1976, 1982, 1985) lies in the assumption that words have to be understood in context in order to arrive at a complete semantic description. On this view, a word's semantic description should therefore include information about how speakers apply their lexical knowledge in interpreting and producing real discourse. Fillmore proposes that in order to understand the meanings of the words in a language we must first have knowledge of the conceptual structures, or semantic frames that underlie the meanings of words. Semantic frames contain frame elements, i.e., descriptions of the meanings of the frame's participants in terms of situational roles.[20] Adopting these ideas, Goldberg suggests a frame-semantic analysis of verbs whose 'designation must include reference to a background frame rich with world and cultural

[19]Verspoor (1997) presents an HPSG-style analysis of resultative constructions in terms of lexical rules operating over lexical entries of verbs. Although her approach is able to account for a broad variety of resultative constructions by taking contextual background information and pragmatic reasoning into account as well as pointing out the important role of a number of lexicalized idiomatic resultative constructions, her analysis is problematic because 'a use of the verb in a particular syntactic frame triggers the application of a rule which specifies the appropriate meaning of that use.' (1997: 144) On this view, 'the verb itself does not undergo a meaning shift or acquire a permanent additional sense encoded in the lexicon' (1997: 144) which means that verbs are interpreted according to the resultative phrases they occur with. Note that this type of explanation is faced with problems when it comes to explaining the full distribution of resultatives from the perspective of language production, because it is difficult to describe under which circumstances a given verb may occur with a certain semantic and/or syntactic type of resultative phrase. That is, the range of application of lexical rules deriving resultatives is not entirely clear in Verspoor's analysis (for a more general critique of lexical rules and their range of application, see Koenig (1999: 29-49)).

[20]See Chapter 6 for a more detailed discussion of Frame Semantics.

knowledge.' (1995: 27) Admitting that 'it is typically difficult to capture frame-semantic knowledge in concise paraphrase' (1995: 27), she proposes that by 'distinguishing verbal semantics from constructional semantics, we can predict an observation noted by Pinker (1989) as to the nature of "syntactically relevant aspects of verb meaning," or what is here claimed to be constructional meaning.' (1995: 28) Compare, for example, how the participant roles of the verbs *wipe* (4.8a) and *talk* (4.8b) fuse with the resultative construction (here repeated for convenience as (4.22a) and (4.22b)).

(4.22) a. wipe < **wiper** wiped >
He wiped the table clean.
b. talk < **talker** >
He talked himself blue in the face. (Goldberg 1995: 189)

The integration process is described by Goldberg as follows: 'To see how the construction is able to add arguments, consider the following cases. Verbs such as *wipe* and *talk* can integrate into the resultative construction because they have compatible roles.' (1995: 189) While the integration of verbal and constructional semantics looks intuitively correct at first sight, questions arise when comparing the attested sentences in (4.22a,b) with the following examples.

(4.23) a. ?He wiped the table dirty.
b. *He spoke himself blue in the face.
c. *He whispered himself blue in the face.
d. *He grumbled himself blue in the face.
e. *He grouched himself blue in the face.

The sentences in (4.23) show that substitution of one verb or resultative phrase of a resultative construction by another verb or resultative phrase renders the construction unacceptable. Sentences such as (4.23a) are typically judged unacceptable without the proper contextual information because wiping usually refers to the removal rather than the addition of an unwanted object or substance. Recall that in order to 'avoid arbitrary lexical stipulations on each verb that could potentially occur in a construction' (1995: 164) Goldberg proposes that the semantics of both the verb and the construction are integrated to yield the semantics of the particular expression. Since the construction used to provide the additional arguments in (4.22) is the same as in (4.23), we are left with the frame semantic information associated with the verb as the deciding factor. Next, consider the following examples.

(4.24) a. wipe < **wiper** wiped >
b. speak < **speaker** >
c. whisper < **whisperer** >
d. grumble < **grumbler** >
e. grouch < **groucher** >

The lexical entries in (4.24) exhibit the same architecture as Goldberg's original lexical entries for *wipe* and *talk*. Note that besides the fact that the frame roles are labeled differently, there is no difference in the architecture of the lexical entries of the verbs *wipe*, *speak*, *whisper*, *grumble*, and *grouch* that would allow a construction to decide – based on the information contained in the lexical entry – whether it can add additional roles to the verb's semantics or not.

This problem shows two things. First, that the architecture of lexical entries presented by Goldberg does not have any features that may block a verb's integration into a construction on formal grounds.[21] Second, because there is no such mechanism available, there is (as far as I can see) no principled way by which the integration of the verbs in (4.24) into a construction may be straightforwardly blocked. What is needed, then, is some way of encoding information in a verb's lexical entry that can block its integration into the construction, thereby licensing attested cases and ruling out unattested cases.[22] Another way of dealing with the problem is to directly en-

[21] A similar observation can be made for the verb *wipe*. Its frame-semantic information includes the two frame elements *wiper* and *wiped*. However, it does not include any information about a possible resultant state of the verbal activity that could serve as the basis for a constraint that evaluates whether one resultative phrase is more acceptable than another one. Thus, when the resultative construction integrates *clean* in (4.22a) and *dirty* in (4.23a), it (or its respective constraints) does not have enough frame semantic information associated with *wipe* upon which it is able to discriminate against one semantic class of resultative phrases, but not against other semantic classes of resultative phrases. One could argue that the fusion of the participant and argument roles in (4.23) is prohibited because of more general semantic constraints, such as Goldberg's Semantic Coherence Principle. But notice that this constraint, too, crucially relies on the notion of construal and semantic compatibility. In other words, without having access to more detailed semantic information about the frame elements of the verb (in particular the kinds of properties of the frame element that can be changed and therefore affected) as well as the resultative phrase, even such a general constraint has problems evaluating the acceptability of a resultative construction, because it does not have the necessary information upon which it can make the decision about which roles to fuse and which roles not to fuse.

[22] Another example is the verb *bark*. Based on such frame semantic information as < barker > a construction would not have any way to determine the distribution of postverbal arguments. Compare the following sentences which illustrate that the lexical entry for *bark* must somehow allow elaborate world knowledge and its linguistic relevance to play a role in this account (for a more detailed discussion of the data, see Boas (2000a), (2002d)).

code in a verb's lexical entry whether it occurs with the resultative pattern or not, thereby eliminating the problem of having to state semantic constraints that restrict the application of constructions.[23]

In this section I have argued that Goldberg's amount of frame semantic information is not sufficient to describe the full range of attested resultative constructions while ruling out unattested resultative constructions. The discussion has shown that there is a need for a richer, more detailed collection of frame-semantic information. Moreover, it is worth taking another look at Goldberg's account of verbal and constructional polysemy.

4.4.5 Constructional Polysemy and Verbal Polysemy Revisited

Based on 'several observations in the literature' that 'lead to the conclusion that the verb in isolation does not inherently encode the caused-motion semantics,' (1995: 153) Goldberg claims that *hit* in (4.25a) does not have a caused-motion interpretation, whereas in (4.25b) *hit* does have a caused-motion interpretation.

(4.25) a. Joe hit the table.
b. Joe hit the ball across the field. (Goldberg 1995: 153)

While her observation that *hit* has different interpretations is certainly true for (4.25a) and (4.25b), I would like to claim that the difference in interpre-

---

(i) The dog barked itself hoarse.
(ii) *The dog barked the postman hoarse.
(iii) ?The dog barked itself off the property.
(iv) The dog barked the postman off the property.

[23]It could be argued that Goldberg's notion of lexical profiling (1995: 43-48) plays a role in determining the semantic compatibility requirements in (4.24a-e) and other comparable sentences. On her account, 'verbs lexically determine which aspects of their frame-semantic knowledge are obligatorily profiled. Lexically profiled roles are entities in the frame semantics associated with the verb that are obligatorily accessed and function as focal points within the scene.' (1995: 44) In her discussion of *rob* and *steal*, Goldberg points out that 'the differences in the expressions of their arguments can be accounted for by a semantic difference in profiling.' (1995: 45) However, since she categorically rejects the possibility of verbs lexically specifying particular senses that occur only in one constructional pattern, the notion of profiling would probably not help Goldberg to rule out sentences like (4.24a-e). In addition, there is a systematic problem with accounting for the sentences in (4.24a-e) in terms of profiling in Goldberg's framework. On her view, 'profiling is lexically determined and highly conventionalized – it cannot be altered by context.' (1995: 44) In section 4.4.3, however, we have seen that the lexical semantic information associated with a verb is defeasible given the proper contextual background information. All in all, then, the notion of profiling as characterized by Goldberg is not sufficient for ruling out the sentences in (4.24a-e).

tation is not due to the caused-motion construction which on Goldberg's view takes the basic verb *hit* in order to supply it with a caused-motion interpretation by providing a goal phrase.[24] Instead, I propose that the different interpretations are due to a separate sense of *hit* that has to be encoded in the lexicon. Compare the following sentences.

(4.26) a. Joe hit the ball.
b. *Joe hit the table across the field.

Sentence (4.26a) is formed in analogy to sentence (4.25a) above. It differs from sentence (4.25a) in that it contains a different postverbal NP as its patient argument. Note that in this case *hit* automatically receives a different interpretation. Typically a hand or some instrument is used to hit a table and a ball. However, when *hit* occurs with *the ball* as its postverbal patient as in (4.26a) it has a particular default interpretation, namely that the ball is hit with the express intention of making it move. Thus, *Joe hit the ball* inherently encodes a caused-motion sense of *hit.* The fact that the ball flew somewhere is in this particular context unimportant. However, if the speaker wishes to convey additional information about the direction in which the ball flew as the result of Joe's hitting it, a resultative phrase may be added. The crucial point here is that whereas the same sense of *hit* (let us call it the sports sense of *hit*) is represented in (4.26a) and (4.25b), the pure physical impact sense of *hit* is represented in (4.25a).[25]

Our examples illustrate that the different interpretations of *hit* in (4.25a,b) above do not have to be attributed to the caused-motion construction contributing a separate goal phrase to the verb's participant roles, as Goldberg claims. Rather, the different senses result from two distinct conventionalized senses of the same verb which have to be distinguished at the lexical semantic level. These sentences also suggest that speakers associate (at the lexical/pragmatic level) specific senses of a verb with specific result states or locations. Thus, the sports sense of *hit* (but not the pure physical impact sense of *hit*) seems to lexically pre-specify a location for the postverbal NP (compare (4.25b) vs. (4.26b) above). Note that the distinct distribution of the sports sense of *hit* is also documented by corpus data.

---

[24]Thus, on Goldberg's account, the caused-motion construction would take the verb *hit* <hitter hittee > and add a goal phrase, such that the argument frame of the whole expression would look as follows: < hitter hittee goal >.

[25]In this connection, compare the difference between *She hit the table hard* and *She hit the ball hard.*

(4.27)
a. Kelly broke down the left, hit the ball from 30 yards out into the corner. (COBUILD)
b. The problem is that unlike in golf, where you look at a guy and he can still hit the ball 250 yards ... (COBUILD)
c. He has every shot in the book and loves to hit the ball over the top. (COBUILD)
d. At Broadmoor, 6,000 feet above sea level, she will hit the ball over 300 yards. (COBUILD)
e. I can hit the ball across more than a 2-inch span of the club face with little loss of distance. (Message-ID: 19990108052045.21602.00008999@ng-fp1.aol.com)
f. This is true if you opt for stroke and distance – that is, go back to where you hit the ball into the bunker. (Message-ID: 36a01496.0@newsfeed1.cybertours.com>)
g. In fact if you are drawn wide off the court you can hit the ball around the side of the net post. (Message-ID: 19990802084241.14794.00001171@ng-cj1.aol.com)
h. Although Van de Velde was laying two in the rough a long way from the hole, it was still possible for him to hit the ball onto the green and hole a putt for par. (Message-ID: 7n0th6$9p9$1@nntp3.atl.mindspring.net)
i. Of course it was an accident, you weren't trying to hit the ball through the plate glass window! (Message-ID: 331ee191.2258314@news.m.iinet.net.au)

Further evidence for speakers' abilities to lexically distinguish between separate word senses when given the relevant contextual background information comes from psycholinguistic research such as Gibbs and Matlock (1997), Bybee (1998), Harris (1998), and Frisson and Pickering (2001). For example, with respect to the ability of a speaker to distinguish between related, yet distinct senses given contextual information, Harris points out that

> the question of how polysemous words are interpreted in context becomes easier, since many polysemous words may be stored with both their contexts and the unique meaning for that context. This means that on hearing an expression like *cut down*, listeners don't have to compute a meaning based on the intersection of a set of meanings for *cut* and the set of meanings for *down*. Instead, the conventional meaning for cut down, **reduce**, is immediately available.
>
> (Harris 1998: 68-69)

In the case of the different senses of *hit*, this would mean that speakers have distinct mental images connected with the lexical item *hit*.[26] Thus, when listeners hear *hit* in combination with *the ball*, they automatically conjure a mental image of the ball being hit with the intention of changing the location of the ball (typically a sports scene) and subsequently expect to hear some information regarding where the ball has moved to as a result of being hit. In the case where no information is provided about the ball's location (*John hit the ball*), it is typically understood that the ball has moved somewhere (unless contextual background information overrules this default interpretation by providing information about a ball of unusual size or a hitter handicapped in some way).[27]

Our discussion so far has shown that there are at least two distinct senses of *hit,* each with different implications with respect to the object that is being hit. In contrast to Goldberg, whose framework proposes that the sports sense of *hit* is a product of the fusion of the pure physical force sense of *hit* with the caused-motion construction, we have seen that there are good reasons for listing two distinct (yet related) senses of *hit* in the lexicon (physical impact and sport sense). Furthermore, I have proposed that the sports, but not the pure physical impact sense of *hit* lexically subcategorizes for a location.[28] Thus, by listing the different senses that a verb is conventionally associated with in the lexicon, it is possible to make predictions as to what kinds of resultative phrases can occur with a given verb. On this view, there is no need for a construction to add information to a verb's semantics because this information is already contained in the form of a different sense.

---

[26]Similar observations are reported by Frisson and Pickering (2001) who used eye-tracking experiments to measure differences in processing of polysemous word senses with and without supportive context. Going a step further than Harris (1998) and Frisson and Pickering (2001), Gibbs and Matlock (1997: 221) point out that words derive their meanings via their interactions with entire sentence contexts, and not just from their interaction with certain words.

[27]Goldberg (2001) presents a detailed analysis of the interactions between constructions, lexical semantic factors, and contextual background information as they relate to cases in which patient arguments of causative verbs can be omitted.

[28]Note that there are many more senses attributed to *hit* which one would have difficulties accounting for using Goldberg's frame semantic information < hitter hittee >. Jackendoff (1990) identifies three distinct senses of *hit,* whereas Iwata (1998) identifies 11 distinct, but systematically related, senses for *hit.* Also note, that there are many idiomatic expressions associated with *hit* that need to be listed as separate, yet related senses. Take, e.g., the phrase *hit the wall,* which can either have a literal interpretation as in *He hit the wall with a hammer*, or it can have an idiomatic interpretation as in *It was America where Lyle's career hit the wall, and it is there that he will seek to revive it* (COBUILD) (meaning he was unsuccessful). Other idiomatic usages include *hit the roof, hit the bars, hit the jackpot, hit the island* (traveling to a location), among many others.

Similar objections apply to Goldberg's treatment of caused-motion senses of intransitive verbs such as *laugh* and *sneeze* in (4.28) and (4.29) which has the advantage of not having to 'attribute the meanings of entire expressions of caused motion to the meanings of individual lexical items.' (1995: 159) [29]

(4.28) The audience laughed the poor guy off of the stage.
(4.29) Frank sneezed the napkin off the table. (Goldberg 1995: 154)

Although Goldberg's constructional analysis of the caused-motion senses of *laugh* and *sneeze* seems attractive at first sight, it is not without its problems. Compare the following sentences showing that not all intransitive verbs can receive additional argument roles from the caused-motion construction given conventional contextual background information, even when they share certain elements of meaning.

(4.30) a. The audience laughed the poor guy off of the stage.
b. ?The audience giggled the poor guy off of the stage.
c. ??The audience smiled the poor guy off of the stage.
d. ??The audience pouted the poor guy off of the stage.
e. ??The audience grinned the poor guy off of the stage.

(4.31) a. Frank sneezed the napkin off the table.
b. ?Frank breathed the napkin off the table.
c. ??Frank wheezed the napkin off the table.
d. ??Frank belched the napkin off the table.
e. ??Frank yawned the napkin off the table.

It could be argued that the unacceptable sentences are ruled out by Goldberg's constraints on the caused-motion construction, e.g., her constraint 'The path of motion must be completely determined by the action denoted by the verb.' (1995: 174) But note that in order for the construction to be able to determine whether the path of motion can be determined in a certain way, it must first have information about the possible force-dynamic implications that are associated with the action denoted by the verb. As Goldberg puts it: 'The semantics associated with the construction defines a semantic

[29] As such, Goldberg's analysis differs from Gawron (1985, 1986), Rappaport Hovav and Levin (1991), Pustejovsky (1991, 1995), and Hoekstra (1992c), who argue in favor of accounting for the different verb senses in terms of a compositional account (positing one basic verb sense and deriving other verb senses by composing the verb's basic meaning with the meanings of the other constituents of the sentence).

frame, and the verb must inherently designate a particular salient aspect of that frame.' (1995: 65). However, Goldberg's interpretation and use of frame semantics in terms of listing a single set of semantic roles for a given verb does not provide enough information to decide whether a verb may occur in a caused-motion construction (cf. sneeze: <sneezer>, wheeze: <wheezer>, belch: <belcher>). This means that we cannot exactly describe under what circumstances a verb may occur in the caused-motion construction.

If, on the other hand, we were to list more lexical semantic information in the lexical entry of the verb itself, we would have sufficient data which – in combination with the respective contextual background information – could be used to determine whether the verb can take on a caused-motion interpretation. Note that on this view intransitive verbs are treated differently from transitive verbs. Whereas specific senses of transitive verbs seem to lexically predetermine what kinds of resultative phrase they occur with, intransitive verbs do not. However, even intransitive verbs like *laugh*, *sneeze*, *bark*, and *cough* occur in other constructions that denote some kind of directed force:

(4.32)
a. Like not being able to sneeze on the cheese. (BNC)
b. Parry complained that someone coughed on his backswing and another dropped a chair a few holes later. (COBUILD)
c. She and her husband and children laughed at me a great deal, but it was all good natured. (COBUILD)
d. Sneezing in his fucking beer. (BNC)
e. All I'll say is that only a foolish dog barks at a flying bird. (BNC)

The sentences in (4.32a-e) show that verbs which Goldberg claims do not have an independent motion sense outside of the caused-motion construction do in fact have motion senses in other contexts. All of the verbs in (4.32a-e) denote the flow of some sort of force (air stream or sound) from the emitter into a certain direction. The usage of the verbs in (4.32a-e) differs from their usage in the caused-motion construction, however, in that in (4.32a-e) there is no object that is in the way of the directed force emitted by the agent of the action. Note, however, that if there were any situations in which there were objects in the way of the directed force (air, stream or sound), then we would want to express the situation in terms of a caused-motion construction as in (4.32a-e). These data suggest that intransitive verbs like *sneeze*, *laugh*, and *cough* do indeed have some sort of lexical semantic information attached to them that independently informs us about their inherent force-dynamics. I propose that the reason why these verbs do not occur in a motion sense that frequently is to be attributed to conventionalization. In other words, when using these verbs in everyday discourse, we usually want to convey a specific kind of information, thereby profiling our attention on the activity of laughing, sneezing, or coughing, for example. However, if we do not want to focus our attention primarily on the activity itself, but rather want to express other events that can be intimately related to this activity as well, then – based on the lexical semantic information available to us as well as our world knowledge (e.g., when we sneeze we emit a more forceful stream of air than when we breathe, elephants are bigger than babies, etc.) – we employ the kinds of sentence patterns encountered in (4.32a-e) above. The caused-motion usage of these verbs is arrived at by similar means, i.e., a combination of lexical semantic information with contextual background information. The crucial point here is that we need a more detailed lexical semantic representation of individual verb senses. I will present a more detailed proposal in the following chapters.[30]

4.4.6 Non-canonical Resultative Constructions

Another set of data that is problematic for Goldberg's approach has to do with resultative constructions in which the postverbal NP is a non-prototypical patient argument. Compare the following sentences.

(4.33) a. Stefan ate his food up.
b. Stefan ate his plate clean.

(4.34) a. Christian drank his beer up.
b. Christian drank his glass dry.

(4.35) a. Bernie fried his steak black.
b. Bernie fried the pan black.

---

[30]Note that the alternative proposal with regard to extending the amount of lexical semantic information associated with verbs does not directly conflict with Goldberg's view on verbal polysemy. Thus, she notes that 'occasionally verbs have distinct senses which are systematically related by a difference as to which participant roles are profiled.' (1995: 56) In contrast to Goldberg, however, I suggest that it is not necessarily the difference as to which participant roles are profiled which groups related senses of a given verb together. Rather, a lexical entry of a verb may contain many distinct, yet somehow related, information structures that all share a common feature (sometimes, this might reduce to the phonological string of the word in the case of idiomatized expressions (e.g., *run a business, hit the bar, kick the bucket*)).

In each of the sentence pairs, the patient argument in the (b) sentences is a non-prototypical patient argument of the verb, as the following sentences show:

(4.36) a. ?Stefan ate his plate.
b. *Christian drank his glass.
c. *Bernie fried the pan.

Although Goldberg does not discuss the case of non-canonical transitive resultative constructions in detail, it is reasonable to assume that in her framework *eat*, *drink* and *fry* contain frame semantic information regarding the participant roles of the eating, drinking, and frying events (eat: <eater eaten>, drink: <drinker drinkee>, fry: <fryer fryee>). Note that this frame semantic information does not provide the necessary information for the resultative construction to license the postverbal NPs in (4.33b-4.35b) as related to the respective events because of a semantic/pragmatic violation of the frame semantic selection restrictions of the respective verbs. Thus, the construction does not have sufficient frame semantic information in order to provide additional argument roles to the verb's participant roles. It also does not 'know' what kinds of combinations of patient arguments and resultative phrases to contribute to the verb's semantics. Moreover, it is not clear how a construction would be able to distinguish between those verbs receiving additional non-prototypical argument roles and those left alone as the following examples show.

(4.37) a. Stefan chewed his food up.
b. *Stefan chewed his plate clean.

(4.38) a. *Stefan devoured his food up.
b. *Stefan devoured his plate up.

(4.39) a. Christian swallowed his beer down.
b. ?Christian swallowed his glass empty.

Given the structure of frame semantic information associated with *chew* (<chewer, chewed>), *devour* (<devourer, devouree>), and *swallow* (<swallower, swallowed>), it is difficult to determine the range of circumstances under which the construction may provide a non-prototypical argument to the verb's semantics. A possible solution to this problem would be to lexically encode whether a given transitive verb as in (4.37)-(4.39) exhibits a distinct meaning that sets it apart from other meanings. It would then also be possible to specify whether a given sense of a verb can occur with a resultative phrase (and what kind of resultative phrase).

Recall that under Goldberg's approach, such a move is generally inappropriate because she does not want to stipulate senses of verbs that are unique to specific constructions in order to 'avoid the problem of positing implausible verb senses.' (1995: 225) However, contrary to her general tendency to attribute related verb senses to meaningful constructions, she does not categorically deny the possibility of attributing certain instances of related meanings to verbal polysemy. Throughout her work Goldberg considers circumstances under which she assumes verbal polysemy to represent distinct senses of a word instead of attributing a resultative or caused-motion interpretation to the semantics of a construction. One such case involves differences in the profiling of participant roles.[31] Goldberg (1995: 56) observes that

> [a]lthough I have generally tried to avoid positing additional verb senses to account for each possible syntactic pattern, I do not rule out the possibility that *some* alternations must be accounted for by postulating distinct but related verb senses.

With respect to the different senses of *eat*, *drink*, and *fry* in (4.37)-(4.39), an alternative analysis in terms of distinct senses for these verbs is thus not contrary to Goldberg's assumptions regarding the nature of verbal polysemy.[32] In contrast, verbs like *devour*, *chew*, and *swallow* would be marked in the lexicon as not allowing any additional senses besides their prototypical sense. We will return to a detailed treatment of these problems in the next chapters.

The discussion in this section has shown that it is difficult to account for non-canonical transitive resultative constructions without lexically marking the respective verbs with a feature or a specific sense indicating whether such a non-prototypical patient may appear in the construction. I suggest that a richer frame semantic polysemy network which captures the individual senses attributed to a verb at the verbal level instead of the con-

[31]The other case involves the metaphorical extension of *drive* to mean *drive-crazy*. Compare Goldberg (1995: 99).

[32]In a different place Goldberg points out that '[w]e know from extensive studies of polysemy that lexical items are typically associated with a set of related meanings rather than a single abstract sense (...) Therefore the existence of two, three, or more distinct but related verb senses is expected. These polysemous senses can be explicitly related by appealing to the frame semantics associated with each of them.' (1995: 44)

structional level may be able to capture the distribution of resultatives in greater detail.[33]

4.5 Conclusions

In spite of my criticisms of Goldberg's constructional account towards caused-motion and resultative constructions, her claims with respect to the semantic distribution of most of the verbs in these constructions achieve by far a greater explanatory power than any of the other accounts presented so far. However, I have pointed out a number of problems in her analyses.

First, I have shown that there is no need for a metaphorical extension analysis of the caused-motion to the resultative construction in order to account for the data. Furthermore, we have seen that Goldberg's constructional polysemy analysis paired with her semantic constraints is sometimes too general when it comes to determining whether a given verb can fuse with a construction. Based on this observation, I have argued that a detailed lexical-semantic description of the polysemy of verbs is potentially more precise when it comes to describing a verb's distribution in resultative and caused-motion constructions. My proposal is based on the insight that various senses of polysemous verbs can occur in resultative constructions, whereby each sense lexically determines the semantics of the resultative phrase. On this view, Goldberg's proposal to include an elaborate constructional polysemy network consisting of various constructions that all share a

---

[33] Jackendoff (1997) presents an analysis of resultative constructions in terms of constructional idioms that resembles in large parts the proposals put forward by Goldberg (1995). On his view, 'the construction is listed in the lexicon just like an ordinary idiom, except that it happens to have no phonological structure.' (1997: 172) Jackendoff proposes that the syntactic structure '[$_{VP}$ V NP PP/AP'] is paired with an interpretation represented by conceptual structure as "cause NP to go PP/to become AP, by V-ing (NP)"' (1997: 171) which leads him to propose that 'the construction is productive' while 'it differs from ordinary idioms, whose terminal elements are fixed.' (1997: 172) Note, however, that Jackendoff (1997) does not specify any particular semantic and/or syntactic restrictions that limit the productivity of the construction. Kageyama's (1996) mechanism of resultative formation exhibits similar problems. In a different analysis, Jackendoff (1990) offers a detailed analysis of three different classes of resultative constructions (grammatical Patient, discourse Patient, no Patient at all) which differ with respect to the relations between the matrix verb and the postverbal NP on the action tier. Although his account gives a detailed analysis of the different structural relations that exist between the matrix verb and the other constituents of the construction, it runs into difficulties when it comes to predicting the full distribution of resultative constructions. In particular, it is not clear how Jackendoff's different adjunct rules are capable of deciding when and how to apply to different types of verbs, thereby determining whether a given verb occurs with a PP or an AP (e.g., *kill dead/*to death, torture to death/*dead*). In addition, Goldberg (1995: 186), contrary to Jackendoff's (1990) proposal that non-subcategorized NPs are licensed by an adjunct rule, points out that postverbal NPs show argument properties.

certain core sense is unnecessary. That is, by capturing the relevant lexical-semantic properties of verbs in more detail at the lexical level, Goldberg's description of what she labels constructional polysemy naturally falls out from the individual verbs that show specific semantic properties depending on one of their individual conventionalized senses.

In the case of intransitive verbs like *sneeze*, *talk*, *cough*, or *laugh*, I have presented data which indicate that these verbs denote motion when occurring outside of the caused-motion construction. Goldberg's proposal to attribute the motion sense of these verbs to an independently existing meaningful caused-motion construction which contributes both a patient and a goal argument to their semantics is therefore superfluous.

In summary, then, the data and discussion suggest that a more detailed lexical semantic description and analysis of the different senses of a verb may enable us to arrive at a more fine-grained system that makes it possible to account for the distribution of resultative constructions. My view is also compatible with Goldberg's (1995: 192) observations with respect to resultative constructions and their being lexically encoded: 'What needs to be noted is that there are grammaticalized instances of the construction which are partially lexically filled.' The data surveyed so far suggest that the number of 'grammaticalized instances of the construction which are partially lexically filled' constitutes, in fact, the majority of resultative constructions. In other words, we have seen that resultatives are to a large degree lexically specified which explains the difficulty that top-down approaches face when trying to account for the distribution of resultative constructions.

5

Towards a Usage-Based Analysis of Resultatives

> So strong are the co-occurrence tendencies of words, word classes, meanings and attitudes that we must widen our horizons and expect the units of meaning to be much more extensive and varied than is seen in a single word. (Sinclair 1996)

5.1 Introduction

In this chapter I outline the cornerstones of a usage-based analysis that regards the lexical semantic information associated with verbs as central to the licensing of resultative constructions.[1] More specifically, the account I present in this and the following chapters aims to capture the distribution of resultatives as illustrated in (5.1) – (5.8), a summary of the relevant data discussed in the last three chapters. It includes the licensing of resultative phrases (cf. (5.1) and (5.2)), the licensing of nonsubcategorized postverbal NPs (cf. (5.3)-(5.5)), the semantic and pragmatic restrictions on resultative phrases and nonsubcategorized NPs (cf. (5.6) and (5.7)), and the question of why only certain verbs allow resultatives (cf. (5.8)).

(5.1) Licensing of optional resultative phrase
  a. Jonathan painted the house red.
  b. Ed shot the deer dead.
  c. Lida broke the vase to pieces.

[1]Based on the arguments made in the last chapter, I regard what Goldberg (1995) calls caused-motion construction and resultative construction as one unified phenomenon. Throughout the rest of this work, I will refer to these as resultatives or resultative constructions.

(5.2) Licensing of required resultative phrase
  a. Dawn wiped the crumbs off the table.
  b. Christian washed the soap out of his eyes.
  c. Johannes ran his shoes threadbare.

(5.3) Licensing of reflexive objects
  a. Jack drank himself sleepy.
  b. Flora talked herself hoarse.
  c. Jackie walked herself to the store.

(5.4) Licensing of nonsubcategorized objects with transitive verbs
  a. Beryl painted the brush to pieces.
  b. John hammered a hole through the wall.

(5.5) Licensing of nonsubcategorized objects with intransitive verbs
  a. Melissa ran her feet sore.
  b. Donna sneezed the napkin off the table.
  c. Pat laughed his head off.

(5.6) Semantic and pragmatic selection restrictions on the resultative phrase
  a. Jonathan painted the house {red/*rusty/*expensive}.
  b. Melissa ran her feet {sore/*clean/*rested}.
  c. Jack drank himself {sleepy/*mad/*smart}.
  d. Kristin painted the brush {to pieces/*to exhaustion/*cheap}.
  e. Pat laughed his head {off/*away/*on/*under}.

(5.7) Semantic and pragmatic selection restrictions of the postverbal NP
  a. Pam sneezed {the napkin/*the book/*the monitor} off the table.
  b. Troy hammered {a hole/*a dent} through the wall.
  c. Erin talked {herself/*Dave} hoarse.
  d. Eric ran {his feet/*his hands/*his jaw} sore.
  e. Dave hit {the ball/*the table/*his book} across the field.

(5.8) Only certain verbs 'allow' resultatives

a. Evin {talked/*whispered/*giggled} herself hoarse.
b. Pam {sneezed/*exhaled/*snorted/*wheezed} the napkin off the table.
c. Beryl {painted/?colored/*stained/*dyed} the brush to pieces.
d. The audience {laughed/?giggled/*pouted} the poor guy off the stage.

In this chapter, I will present my arguments in favor of a usage-based analysis of the data in (5.1) – (5.8) by discussing the following topics: (1) the role of conventionalization in language use, (2) the importance of corpus data in developing a descriptively adequate account of resultatives, and (3) the different communicative functions of resultative constructions. Based on corpus data I show that the lexical-semantic information associated with a word is to a very large degree conventionalized and can therefore not be predicted on general grounds. This problem in turn calls for a detailed lexical-semantic description of each verb, the verb's respective arguments, and the relationship between verbs and arguments.[2]

5.2 Usage-Based Models of Language

When we look at the underlying principles that guide communication, i.e., the production and interpretation of utterances, it is obvious that when new information is conveyed in discourse, it is always interpreted with respect to already existing world knowledge, or old information (see Levelt 1989). Communicative acts can therefore be regarded as a constant updating of information as the following sentences illustrate.[3]

---

[2] I adopt Lewis' (1969) definition of convention as agreement on the part of members of a group about the accepted meanings of particular form-meaning pairs, words or expressions. On this view, conventions about the use of words can be compared with the conventions about the information conveyed by traffic signs. Each sign carries its own meaning and depending on which country one reads traffic signs, they will look differently and mean different things (e.g., in the U.S. the speed limit is written out as 'SPEED LIMIT' accompanied by the respective miles per hour, whereas in Europe the speed limit sign is a white, circular sign with a red circle surrounding the km/h limitation).

[3] Prince (1981: 224) calls the discrepancy between old information and new information informational asymmetry. To this end she points out that 'the crucial factor appears to be the tailoring of an utterance by a sender to meet the particular assumed needs of the intended receiver. That is, information-packaging in natural language reflects the sender's hypotheses about the receiver's assumptions, beliefs and strategies.'

(5.9) Would you like some *baked bread*?
(5.10) Last night *a two-legged person* came into the bar!
(5.11) Did you know that *the week has seven days*?

The examples sound odd to native speakers of English because the information conveyed is redundant to members of speech communities in the western world. That is, among native speakers of English it is generally assumed that bread is baked and that a week has seven days.[4] Moreover, these types of specific assumptions, beliefs, and strategies associated with a particular word are to a large degree conventionalized according to the norms and experiences of a speech community.

The role of conventionalization in language becomes even more apparent when it comes to examining speech communities wherein they employ words in unusual ways by attributing new meanings and presuppositions to them. . For example, in areas such as sports, law, medicine, and technology, words can denote different concepts than in 'ordinary' English. This phenomenon can lead to confusion if someone is unfamiliar with the conventionalized meanings and presuppositions a speech community attaches to specific words. The following example illustrates how standard conventionalized meanings of words can change when used in a specific context, in this case 'computerese.'

(5.12) Not so long ago... An *application* was for employment, a *program* was a TV show, a *cursor* used profanity, a *keyboard* was a piano! *Memory* was something that you lost with age, a *CD* was a bank account. And if you had a 3 1/2-inch *floppy* you hoped nobody found out! *Compress* was something you did to garbage not something you did to a file. And if you *unzipped* anything in public you'd be in jail for a while! *Log on* was adding wood to a fire. *Hard drive* was a long trip on the road. A *mouse pad* was where a mouse lived, and a *backup* happened to your commode! *Cut* - you did with a pocketknife, *paste* you did with glue. A *web* was a spider's home, and a *virus* was the flu![5]

[4]Speech communities are groups of speakers that share the same language conventions. Speech communities are defined by various factors such as region, ethnicity, social standing, age, sex, religion, technical expertise, etc. For a detailed discussion of the notion of 'speech community,' see Labov (1972), Wolfram (1991), and Milroy and Milroy (1997).

[5]Thanks to Christian Ohlendorf for providing this example.

Each of the italicized words is associated with different kinds of meanings and presuppositions depending on whether they are used in a technical or non-technical sense. When encountering objects and relations that lack established words or phrases to denote them, members of a speech community invent new words, borrow words, or extend the meanings of already existing words (see Hock (1986) and Jackson and Amvela (2000) for an overview). The italicized words in (5.12) illustrate how important it is to interpret words with respect to the context in which they occur. In contrast, the following sentences lack contextual background information and are therefore extremely difficult to interpret.

(5.13) a. Guess what, I got a new *application*!
b. Where is your *keyboard*?
c. Then I *unzipped* it.
d. Whatever happened to your *backup*?
e. Help, I've got a *virus*!

Sentences grounded in very specific contexts that rely on specialized world knowledge are similarly problematic.

(5.14) Joyce hung on and broke himself decisively in the ninth game - though Wilko missed four points to defend his serve. (COBUILD)

(5.15) But when Dr. Evil froze himself so he could return years later, Austin bravely volunteered to do the same. (COBUILD)

The sentences in (5.14)-(5.15) include the verbs *break* and *freeze* which are used in a rather non-conventional way. Without knowing that (5.14) is uttered in a sports context to describe a tennis player's attempt to win a match, it is difficult to interpret the meaning of *broke*. This problem is due to a violation of Grice's (1975) co-operative principle which underlies conversational interactions: 'Make your contribution such as is required, at the stage at which it occurs, by the accepted purpose and direction of the talk exchange in which you are engaged.' (Grice 1975: 45) The co-operative principle is linked to a number of maxims that speakers typically adhere to in order to communicate effectively, according to Grice. The relevant maxim here is the maxim of relation: 'Be relevant.'[6]

---

[6]For more detailed, yet somewhat different, views on the notion of 'relevance,' see Sperber and Wilson's (1986) Relevance Theory.

The meaning of *freeze* in (5.15) is similarly dependent on very specific world knowledge, in this case the story behind the Austin Powers' movies. Had (5.15) been uttered before the creation of the Austin Powers storyline, an elaborate description of a machine enabling humans to travel through time through some type of freezing mechanism would have been necessary for the sentence to be understood.

Without providing the proper contextual background information needed to interpret the meaning of *freeze* in (5.15), the speaker does not adhere to a number of principles pointed out by Clark and Clark (1979) for the use of verbs. On this view, whenever a speaker uses a verb, he assumes that he is denoting '(a) the kind of situation (b) that he has good reason to believe (c) that on this occasion the listener can readily compute (d) uniquely (e) on the basis of their mutual knowledge.' (Clark and Clark 1979: 787)

The examples above show that the meanings and forms of both words and utterances are to a large degree conventionalized within a given speech community. Thus, the analysis of language must focus not only on the structural relations and interdependencies between words in a sentence but also on the way in which words are used in different contexts. Following Langacker (2000: 22), who points out that '[n]ovel expressions are not created by the linguistic system *per se*, but rather by the speaker, drawing on all available resources,' I adopt a usage-based approach to the analysis of language. Applying this approach to the analysis of resultatives entails that we do not limit ourselves to a small slice of resultative data. Rather, we need to cover the full range of attested resultatives and examine the conditions under which they are produced. As Fillmore (1989) argues:

> Any aspect of the study of usage which requires mention of particular linguistic forms - as opposed to merely mentioning meaning - belongs properly to the study of grammar. (Fillmore 1989: 35)

In what follows I extend the usage-based approach to resultatives to show that the conditions under which verbs may be used in resultative patterns are to a large degree conventionalized and thus require a much more detailed lexical-semantic description than previously assumed.

5.3 Resultatives and Conventionalization

5.3.1 Different Degrees of Conventionalization

The broad range of resultative constructions surveyed so far has shown that English allows packaging of a causing event and a caused event within a single sentence by using a verb in combination with a resultative phrase, thereby creating what Talmy (1996) calls a causal sequence, or a causal chain. By adding a resultative phrase, it is thus possible to conflate information which can be conveyed by two separate sentences (cf. (5.16a)) into a single sentence (cf. (5.16b)). Diagram (5.17) illustrates that the information conveyed by the verb in combination with a resultative phrase may refer to both the causing event and the caused event within the same sentence, cf. (5.16b).

(5.16) a. Jack ate his food. As a result of his eating the food, the plate became clean.
b. Jack ate his plate clean.

(5.17) <u>Causal Chain</u>

Information conveyed by the verb in combination with the resultative phrase

causing event caused event

Note, however, that this conflation pattern is not always available.

(5.18) a. Claire opened the door. As a result of her opening the door, the key broke.
b. *Claire opened the key to pieces.

(5.19) a. Brigid loaded the table with food. As a result of her loading the table with food, the table's legs became bent.
b. *Brigid loaded the table's legs bent.

The sentence pairs illustrate that a causal chain can be set up by using two sentences describing the causing event and the caused event, respectively. However, *open* and *load* do not allow the same kind of event conflation as *eat* in (5.16) although the caused event is a direct result of the causing event.[7] Note that outside of the resultative construction, *eat*, *open*, and *load*

---

[7]English is relatively flexible with respect to this restriction as all of the attested resultative constructions in this work show. Other languages like Kalam, however, have a general restriction against using a single verb to refer to an entire causal chain (for more details, see Pawley 1987: 350-55).

show otherwise similar properties with respect to the range of postverbal arguments with which they may occur.

(5.20) a. Jack ate his food.
b. Claire opened the door.
c. Brigid loaded the table.

Since the three verbs show similar syntactic properties outside of the resultative construction but different properties when combined with a resultative phrase, it is not clear on what syntactic or semantic grounds any general predictions can be made about a verb's ability to occur with a resultative. The data thus suggest that a verb's ability to occur in resultative constructions is a matter of conventionalization, i.e. it cannot be explained by more general constraints. In other words, most verbs seem to have their own lexical specifications with respect to their ability to occur with a resultative phrase: while some verbs only exhibit very general specifications with respect to their ability to occur with resultatives (such as *open* and *load* vs. *eat*), other verbs exhibit very specific requirements when it comes to the type of resultative phrase with which they occur. The following data from Verspoor (1997) is further evidence for the proposal that the distribution of resultatives is to a very large degree idiosyncratic. The examples illustrate that resultative phrases which are very closely related in meaning cannot be substituted for each other in resultative constructions

(5.21) a. i. He laughed himself to death.
ii. *He laughed himself dead.
b. i. He laughed himself to sleep.
ii. *He laughed himself sleepy/asleep.
c. i. He laughed himself out of a job.
ii. *He laughed himself jobless/unemployed.
iii. *He laughed himself out of the room/down the hall.
d. i. He laughed himself silly.
ii. He laughed himself faint/dizzy.
iii. ?He laughed himself tired.
e. i. They laughed John out of the room.
ii. #They tittered John out of the room.
iii. #They laughed John into the room/down the hall.
iv. #They insulted John out of the room.
f. i. He danced himself to fame.
ii. *He danced himself famous.

g. i. He danced his feet sore.
ii. *He danced his feet to soreness.
iii. ?He danced himself sore.
iv. *He danced himself crippled. (Verspoor 1997: 119)

While at first sight the data in (5.21) may look like an isolated pattern that only holds for a few verbs in combination with their resultative phrases, these types of idiosyncratic patterns can be found throughout the language as the following distribution of APs and their respective PP counterparts in corpus data illustrate.[8]

(5.22) a. And it seemed he was intent on driving her *crazy/*to craziness.* (BNC)
b. It was supposed to drive you *wild/*to wildness* with desire. (BNC)
c. Perhaps they'll run themselves *dry/*to dryness* and we can have a decent drive. (Message-ID:xIy6FCADBdt 2Ew$c@islander1.demon.co.uk)
d. Nomo walks himself *to death/*dead.* (Message-ID: 74nejs$7dc$1@winter.news. rcn.net)
e. It's true that we didn't get much sleep the night before, and we had danced ourselves *silly/*to silliness*, so … (Message-ID: 19981111165541.14994.00000135@ ngo108.alo.com)
f. They outdid themselves tonight with the music they played and I danced myself *sore/*to soreness* and sang and yelled till I was *hoarse/*to hoarseness*. (Message-ID: 20000101054007.00367. 0000239@ng-ck1.aol.com)
g. … we basically danced ourselves *to exhaustion/ *exhausted*. (Message-ID: 40rahl$2kl@newsbf02.news. aol.com)
h. And I recall a certain ship, in a certain time, that we were supposed to go down with, as the strings played 'Autumn' and we danced ourselves *to dust/*dusty*. (Message-ID: 19980918191301.PAA27679@ladder01.news.aol.com)
i. Albert had spoken so calmly that it made her *calm/*to calmness* too. (BNC)

[8]The starred sequence represents the unattested syntactic counterpart of the respective attested resultative phrase. Besides searching the British National Corpus and Internet sites for both the attested and unattested counterparts, I have consulted with 15 native speakers in order to verify the acceptability of the judgments.

j. Hargreave wiped his plate *clean/*to cleanliness* with a piece of garlic bread. (BNC)
k. He cried so hard that he rained himself *empty/*to emptiness*. (BNC)
l. Denny Butler nearly crushed you *flat/*to flatness*. (BNC)
m. You've screamed yourself *hoarse/*to hoarseness*. (BNC)
n. Supermodels can make you *sick/*to sickness*. (BNC)
o. This will make you *sleepy/*asleep/*to sleep*. (BNC)
p. But their comparative softness made it a simple matter to rub them *smooth/*to smoothness* and set them en cabochon. (BNC)
q. Congratulations to your golf score, but we don't have to run ourselves *into extinction/*extinct*. (Message-ID: 85i2m4rj1@nnrp1.deja.com)
r. He's put away the wild times, joined a twelve-step programme and willed himself *sober/*to soberness*. (BNC)
s. I never knew she was going to fall through the bloody ceiling and get knocked *soft/*to softness*. (BNC)

The corpus data show that certain verbs semantically and syntactically only allow for a specific type of resultative phrase. While some verbs are very strict about the syntactic category of the resultative phrase (e.g. *make* only allows APs, but not PPs), other verbs are less strict but show clear tendencies nevertheless. Take, e.g., one of the meanings of *drive* when it is used to denote a person's (typically negative) change of mental state. In this particular use, *drive* occurs 329 times in the British National Corpus. Out of those 329 times, *drive* occurs with an AP 253 times and with PPs 76 times. Compare the following table which lists the resultative phrases occurring with the 'drive-crazy' sense of *drive*.

(5.23) Total distribution of resultative phrases occurring with the 'drive-crazy' sense of *drive* in the BNC[9]

Resultative Phrase	No. of occur.
mad/to madness	108/5
crazy	70
to distraction	27
insane	23
wild	22
nuts	18
up the wall	13
to suicide	9
to despair	8
to desperation	7
batty	4
dotty	4
crackers	4
into a frenzy	3
over the edge	3
to insanity	1

The table shows that 'drive-crazy' occurs only with resultative phrases that belong to a semantically very homogenous group denoting a (typically) negative mental state. While in some cases it does allow alternation between APs and PPs (*mad/to madness*), it usually picks one syntactic phrase type or the other. Although there are no clear boundaries that one could draw in order to predict exactly whether the 'drive-crazy' sense of *drive* selects for APs or PPs, one can nevertheless show that there is a clear preference for APs (253 out of 329) over PPs (76 out of 329). The fact that there are no clear boundaries with respect to what type of syntactic category appears with 'drive-crazy' is in fact expected if one subscribes to the notion of fuzzy boundaries and prototype-effects in language (cf. Wittgenstein 1953, Rosch 1973, Lakoff 1987, among others).

Besides the syntactic preferences of 'drive-crazy' with respect to its choice of resultative phrases, there is another interesting observation about the conventionalized usage of this particular sense of *drive*. Although it

---

[9]For the full list of corpus examples, see Appendix B.1. Note that the search for resultative phrases was limited to phrases no longer than three words.

lexically subcategorizes for only a specific semantic type of resultative phrase, the semantic limitations set no limits to a speaker's creativity with respect to the types of resultative phrases, as long as they adhere to the semantic specifications imposed by 'drive-crazy.' To this end, compare the following sentences.

(5.24) a. Their own 'family disease' can drive them *to distraction and despair.* (BNC)

b. While making Mutiny on the bounty in Tahiti, the megrims of working with Marlon Brando drove him *to drink more than usual*. (BNC)

c. His lifelong ambitions thwarted again and again, driving him *to drink and gambling and unreasoning rage*. (BNC)

d. Stephen Thomas says the ordeal has driven him *to the brink of suicide*. (BNC)

The sentences in (5.24) show that although 'drive-crazy' imposes semantic restrictions with respect to the types of resultative phrases with which it may occur, there is great productivity and creativity within these boundaries. Next, let us turn to additional data supporting the view that resultatives are to a large degree conventionalized. The following tables representing the exhaustive distribution of *dead* and *to death* in resultative constructions found in the BNC illustrate that verbs exhibit specific requirements with respect to the types of resultative phrases with which they may occur.

(5.25) Distribution of *dead* in resultative constructions in the BNC. (Total number of occurrences in BNC: 11644. In resultative constructions: 434)[10]

Verb	No. of occur.
shoot	408
cut	11
kill	9
strike	8
stop	6
make , knock	3
make the ball	2
flatten, kick, smite	1

[10] For the full list of corpus examples, see Appendix A.7.

(5.26) Distribution of *to death* in resultative constructions in the BNC. (Total number of occurrences in BNC: 1766. In resultative constructions: 592)[11]

Verb	No. of occur.
stab	114
beat	74
put	44
batter	39
frighten	34
crush	25
scare	24
burn	18
torture	16
drink, starve	15
bludgeon, hack	12
shoot, kick	11
club	9
bore, knife, choke	8
blast, trample, work, worry	7
love	6
strangle	4
dash, poison, kiss	3
ax, bayonet, boil, bring, clap, suffocate, kick, freeze, spear, spray, stone, suck, gun, hammer, hug, knock, nag, peck, play, rape, shag, sting	2
annoy, eat, bleed, blend, bug, bully, stab, flog, frit, cudgel, curse, dance, feed, gas, flog, jog, laugh, pitchfork pound, run, schmaltz, scorch, scratch, seduce, shock, sing, smother, squash, squeeze, stamp, strike, sweat, whip	1

The tables list the verbs that occur with the phrases *dead* and *to death* in resultative constructions. Note that certain verbs are very particular about what type of resultative phrases they occur with. Thus, *stab, beat, put, batter, frighten, crush, scare, burn,* etc. only occur with *to death* and never with *dead. Shoot,* on the other hand, occurs overwhelmingly with *dead* (408

[11]For the full list of corpus examples, see Appendix A.43.

times), and only in a few instances with *to death* (11 times). The distribution of *dead* versus *to death* clearly shows that particular types of verbs are conventionally associated with specific types of resultative phrases.[12]

Note that for illustrative purposes, I included a few idiomatic phrases such as *cut dead* or *stop dead* in the tables summarizing the results of corpus searches in the BNC. The idiomatic phrases were chosen on the basis of the high frequency with which they occur in the BNC. They are listed to demonstrate that there is not always a one-to-one relationship between form and meaning. That is, in a sentence such as *It has stopped him dead* (BNC) the syntactic frame [NP V NP AP] occurring with *stop* does not reflect a canonical resultative semantics. More specifically, the sentence shows that combinations of verbs and APs or PPs occurring in a syntactic frame that is identical to that of resultative constructions exhibit different degrees of idiomaticity.[13] Next, compare the distribution of *to sleep* and *sleepy*.

(5.27) Distribution of *to sleep* in resultative constructions in the BNC. (Total number of occurrences in BNC: 2264. Number of occurrences in resultative constructions: 109)[14]

Verb	No. of occur.
put	63
cry	24
sing	5
rock, soothe	3
drink, send	2
chant, drive, eat, murmur, mutter, nurse, sob, talk, teach	1

[12]There seems to be a strong tendency for verbs denoting punctual events to occur with adjectival resultative phrases (e.g., *Kim shot Pat dead*). In contrast, verbs denoting an iterative process overwhelmingly prefer prepositional resultative phrases (e.g., *Kim stabbed Pat to death*). While these are strong tendencies, they are not exact predictions about the type(s) of resultative phrase(s) that will occur with a verb. See Section 5.3.2 for details.

[13]For a detailed classification of idioms in terms of different types of syntactic constructions, see Riehemann (2001: 230 – 243).

[14]For the full list of corpus examples, see Appendix A.48.

(5.28) Distribution of *sleepy* in resultative constructions in the BNC. (Total number of occurrences in BNC: 401. Number of occurrences in resultative constructions: 19)[15]

Verb	No. of occur.
make	19

The data in (5.27) and (5.28) illustrate that there are clear tendencies with respect to the distribution of the two phrases *sleepy* and *to sleep*. Whereas the former exclusively occurs with the lexical causative *make*, the latter exhibits a much higher frequency in resultative constructions and also a broader distribution across verbs. The fact that *sleepy* only occurs with *make* in the resultative pattern [NP V NP AP] also shows that verbs which are lexically causative independently of the resultative construction, i.e., whose basic sense entail a change of state, exhibit weaker semantic and syntactic restrictions with respect to the types of resultative phrases with which they co-occur (see Goldberg 1995: 193, 196). It is interesting to note that the flexibility of lexically causative verbs such as *make* is not limited to cases in which they occur in the resultative [NP V NP AP] pattern. Based on corpus data Stefanowitsch (2001: 85) argues that '*make* is the most productive, semantically least constrained causation verb in English: it is a hypernym of almost all other causation verbs.' This claim leads Stefanowitsch to conclude that it is 'intuitively plausible to assume that *make* is as close as possible in meaning to the type of causation expressed by analytic causatives in general, i.e., that it adds little or no additional semantic content beyond this.' (2001: 86) The fact that *make* is the only verb occurring with *sleepy* in (5.28) is thus not due to the restrictions exhibited by *make* in the resultative [NP V NP AP] pattern. Instead, it is due to more general restrictions exhibited by *make* outside of resultatives, e.g., in analytic causative constructions such as $[_{VP}\ V_{caus}\ NP_{obj}\ VP_{infinitive}]$ (see Stefanowitsch 2001: 172-187).

We have so far considered the selection restrictions exhibited by the verbs in (5.21) – (5.28) to be due to conventionalization. In other words, we have not been able to identify any factors above the level of lexical semantics of individual verbs or verb senses to be responsible for the restrictions on the postverbal elements. In the following section we thus turn to the question of whether there are more general semantic factors involved in an explanation of the distribution of resultatives.

[15] For the full list of corpus examples, see Appendix A.33.

5.3.2 Abstract Semantic Constraints and Compositionality

Based on corpus data from Boas (2000b), Wechsler (2001) argues for a number of more general semantic constraints determining the range of possible adjectives in resultatives. He proposes that resultative constructions fall into two classes. The first class, also known as control resultatives (see Carrier and Randall 1992, Simpson 1983, Wechsler 1997), includes cases in which the predication subject of the resultative phrase is a semantic argument of the matrix verb (see (5.29)). The second class, also known as ECM ('exceptional case-marking') resultatives, includes cases in which the predication subject of the resultative phrase is not a semantic argument of the matrix verb (see (5.30)).

(5.29) a. He wiped the table *clean*. => He wiped the table.
b. The water froze *solid*. => The water froze.

(5.30) a. The dog barked itself *hoarse*. ≠> *The dog barked itself.
b. Mary ran the soles *off her shoes*. ≠> *Mary ran the shoes.
(Wechsler 2001: 3)

Wechsler's semantic explanation for the restrictions holding for adjectives used as resultative predicates is based on two claims. The first is the uncontroversial assumption that resultatives are telic, i.e., they describe events with a definite endpoint (see Dowty 1979, Pustejovsky 1991, Rappaport-Hovav and Levin 1998, 2001). The necessary parts of a telic event are defined as

> an affected theme, a property scale, and a bound, related as follows (cp. Krifka 1998): some property of the affected theme argument changes by degrees along a scale due to the action described by the verb, until it reaches a bound. (Wechsler 2001: 6)

According to Wechsler, there 'are two further requirements that must be met in order for telicity to result:

1. The telic event and the path must be (a) homomorphic (parts of the event must correspond to parts of the path and vice versa) and (b) co-extensive (the event must begin when the affected theme is at the start of the path and end when the affected theme reaches the end of the path).

2. The affected theme must be an argument of the event-denoting predicate.'

(Wechsler 2001: 6)

The second claim concerns the division of adjectives into two semantic classes, namely gradable (e.g., *long*, *flat*, *straight*) and non-gradable (e.g., *dead*, *invited*, *sold*) adjectives. Following Klein (1980) and Kennedy (1999), Wechsler points out that the class of gradable adjectives contains both closed-scale and open-scale adjectives. The former 'further divide into maximal endpoint and minimal endpoint adjectives. Because the endpoint is infinitesimally low for minimal endpoint adjectives, they behave in many respects as de facto open scale adjectives.' (Wechsler 2001: 9)[16]

Combining the claims about the nature of telicity and the semantic classification of adjectives, Wechsler argues that 'because of the homomorphism between the property scale and the event, the telicity of the event directly depends on the scalar structure of the adjective – that is, whether it is closed- or open-scale.' (2001: 9) This observation leads him to conclude that 'because of the coextension requirement, the duration of the event must be appropriate to the scale as well.' (2001: 9) Wechsler suggests the following 'possible situations that are predicted to yield a telic sentence' (2001: 9) in order to explain the different distribution of resultative phrases with varying verbs occurring in control resultatives:

(5.31) <u>Type I. Verb is durative, resultative is a gradable, closed-scale adjective.</u>
Mary hammered the metal flat. (Wechsler 2001: 10)

(5.32) <u>Type II. Verb is punctual, resultative is a non-gradable adjective.</u>
At another mill, the Fox mill, he and a confederate shot the miller dead, ...(Wechsler 2001: 11)

(5.33) <u>Type III. Verb is durative, resultative is a path PP whose object NP specifies the bound.</u>
The rabbits had apparently been battered {*dead/to death}.
(Wechsler 2001: 12)

Wechsler's classification of verbs and adjectives into different semantic classes as well as his conditions on how they may combine is certainly an important step toward accounting for resultatives in terms of general seman-

---

[16]Examples of closed-scale adjectives with maximal endpoints are *full*, *empty*, and *dry*. Examples of closed-scale adjectives with minimal endpoints are *wet* and *dirty*. The latter differ from the former in that even the presence of the smallest entity returns a positive value for *wet* or *dirty*.

tic constraints. In particular, his generalizations about the combinatorial restrictions placed on adjectives by a verb's event structure utilize more abstract semantic factors and as such are able to go much further than the idiosyncratic lexical semantic restrictions that were attributed to conventionalization of individual verb senses in Section 5.3.1 above.

However, the problem with Wechsler's proposal is that while it lists the *necessary* conditions, it does not list all of the *sufficient* conditions involved in licensing the full distribution of resultatives. As such, his proposal offers only weak predictions. Compare, for example, the contrast in the following sentence cited by Wechsler (2001: 10).

(5.34) He wiped it clean/dry/smooth/*damp/*dirty/*stained/*wet. (Green 1972, ex. 6b, 7b)

According to Wechsler (2001: 10), '[t]he adjectives *clean*, *dry*, and *smooth* are all maximal endpoint closed-scale adjectives, which thus provide suitable bounds for the event. In contrast, the adjectives *damp*, *dirty*, *stained*, and *wet* are minimal endpoint adjectives – what I have called de facto open-scale adjectives.' This observation leads him to the conclusion that '[t]heir inherent standards are too low to be useful, so contextual standards normally prevail. But inherent standards are needed in order to serve as suitable telic bounds. Since resultative constructions must be telic, these sentences fail.' (2001: 10) While Wechsler's claim seems to naturally fall out from examples like (5.34), note that his abstract semantic restrictions do not always hold as the following sentences illustrate.

(5.35) a. I used to make mine by soaking the paper, blotting it *damp*, stacking the papers together between two blotters, and sealing them in plastic. (1995/03/08, Newsgroups: rec.arts.fine)
b. Cool to room temperature. Dip a soft cloth in the solution, wring it *damp* and wipe furniture with it. (1998/12/31, Newsgroups: rec.antiques)
c. Should a rather large speck show, I take the brush and swipe it *damp*, then gently pick up the speck with the tip of the brush. (2000/02/22, Newsgroups: rec.models.scale)

(5.36) a. The simplest approach is to require the application to mark it *dirty* after making any changes and before dropping its strong references. (2000/1/18, Newsgroups: comp.lang.java. programmer)
b. Actually, if you're trying for a Vietnam-look, the best way to do it would just color it *dirty* (2001/3/4, Newsgroups: rec. models.scale)

(5.37) a. Everyday I wipe it *wet* with WD-40 before I ride and then wipe it *dry* after my ride. (2002/4/19, Newsgroups: rec.bicycles.misc)

b. He found his lips *dry* and licked them *wet* again before taking a sip from the already sweating beer can. (2002/6/20, Newsgroups: alt.sex.stories.moderated)

The examples demonstrate that adjectives like *damp*, *dirty*, and *wet* may indeed provide the telic bounds on events expressed by matrix verbs although under Wechsler's classification they should not. This means that their inherent standards are not too low to be useful and can therefore serve as appropriate resultative predicates. The unacceptability of *damp*, *dirty*, and *wet* in (5.34) is thus not due to the fact that they do not belong to a certain class of adjectives. Instead, a comparison of (5.34) with (5.35) – (5.37) strongly suggests that the incompatibility of these adjectives with certain resultatives is due not to their semantic classification but to the inherent lexical semantics of the matrix verb(s). Another problem with Wechsler's account is his claim that in his Type II resultatives ((5.32) above) 'the verb in a resultative construction with a non-gradable adjective must be punctual.' (2001: 12) This observation does not explain why some punctual verbs occur in resultative constructions but others do not. Compare, e.g., the punctual verbs *strike*, *hit*, and *injure* in the following examples.

(5.38) a. The soldier struck the civilian dead.

b.??The soldier hit the civilian dead.

c. *The soldier injured the civilian dead.

The three verbs share a bodily injury sense in which *the soldier* (the agent) inflicts harm on *the civilian* (the patient). Although all three verbs denote a punctual event and should therefore be capable of occurring with *dead* in a resultative construction according to Wechsler's generalization, there is some difference that allows *strike* but disallows *hit* and *injure* to occur in the resultative pattern. I suggest that the difference in the verbs' behavior is due to lexical-semantic differences between them. In other words, although there is a considerable overlap in meaning between the three verbs, they each individually encode slightly different types of events at the lexical semantic level. It is this difference that precludes *hit* and *injure* from occurring in the same configuration as *strike* in (5.38).

There is a more serious problem with Wechsler's analysis. He proposes that Type II resultatives crucially differ from Type III resultatives in that the former combine punctual verbs with non-gradable adjectives whereas the latter combine durative verbs with resultative path PPs. While Wechsler's generalization regarding the differences observed in the corpus data correctly captures the strong tendency of verbs to fall naturally into separate classes, it does not explain the underlying factors responsible for this grouping. On Wechsler's account, we would expect punctual verbs such as *explode* and *detonate* to occur in resultative constructions with non-gradable adjectives (Type II). However, this is not the case as the following examples illustrate.

(5.39) a. The terrorist exploded the bomb (??to pieces).
b. The soldier detonated the mine (??to pieces).

Note that *explode* and *detonate* do not readily occur in resultative constructions. When they do occur (given the proper contextual background information), they may occur with PPs as resultative phrases and not with non-gradable adjectives as expected under Wechsler's punctual vs. durative verb classification. In order to deal with this issue, one could take into account Wechsler's comment on the ability of some punctual verbs (e.g., *shoot*) to also occur with path PPs in resultatives. He points out that '[t]here is nothing to rule this out, since a path can be very short. Perhaps for markedness reasons, there is a tendency to select *dead* over *to death* when possible.' (Wechsler 2001: 12) While Wechsler's proposal is on the right track regarding situations in which punctual verbs show a strong tendency to occur with non-gradable adjectives as opposed to path PPs, it cannot be applied to our examples in (5.39) because there is no corresponding non-gradable adjective to the resultative phrase *to pieces*. Cases such as (5.39) therefore run counter to Wechsler's predictions regarding the strong tendency of punctual verbs to occur with non-gradable adjectives.

The problems with Wechsler's general semantic constraints on the distribution of resultative phrases are partly due to the fact that for him, as for nearly all other researchers (Dowty 1979, Gazdar et al. 1985, Shieber 1986, and many others), most of syntax and semantics are the result of compositional processes. Consider Wechsler's own words:

> Our starting point is that telicity is a constructional feature of resultatives. It is a requirement placed on the output of the semantic composition of the sentence. From this simple assumption, all else follows as a deduction.
>
> (Wechsler 2001: 5)

Wechsler's claim illustrates his belief that the compositional process by which verbs and postverbal elements combine into a resultative construction is restricted by general semantic constraints. The central idea here is that the semantics of the resultative construction is compositional, i.e., its meaning must be a function of the meanings of its immediate constituents and the syntactic rule(s) used to combine them (Goldberg 1995: 13).[17] And this is exactly where the problem lies with Wechsler's analysis. Once he assumes that there is a process of semantic composition that is responsible for creating resultative constructions, he has to state general principles describing which elements may combine to form resultatives. In his case, these principles involve classifications of verbs, adjectives, and path PPs into different classes and constraints on how to combine them. The empirical data he adduces strongly support his proposal. However, as we have seen, there are a number of counterexamples that do not fit Wechsler's generalizations and thus run counter to his predictions. This means that as long as one cannot explain the exceptions above in terms of general principles, it is highly questionable whether abstract mechanisms can be claimed to underlie the compositional process by which verbs and postverbal elements are combined to form resultatives. Thus, the main question to which we seek an answer is: to what degree can the co-occurrence of specific matrix verbs with particular resultative phrases and postverbal NPs be explained in terms of compositionality?

Looking at the role of compositionality and the influence of abstract semantic constraints in more detail, one might then also ask why the overwhelming majority of analyses have repeatedly invoked these two notions in order to explain the distribution of resultatives. As we have seen in previous chapters, resultative constructions seem to be – at first glance – a coherent phenomenon explainable in terms of compositional syntactic mechanisms. However, once more attention is paid to the semantics of elements that combine in the construction it becomes clear that other factors of a more general nature are at play. In the case of Wechsler's (2001) analysis, we have seen that the general semantic constraints do not offer strong predictions once we start looking at more verbs. Consider the following diagram.

[17]The standard notion of compositionality is reflected by the following quote: 'A semantic theory of a natural language (…) should reflect the fact that, except for idioms, phrases and sentences are compositional – in other words, that the meaning of a syntactically complex expression is determined by the meaning of its constituents plus their grammatical relations.' (Akmajian et al. 1995: 233)

(5.40)

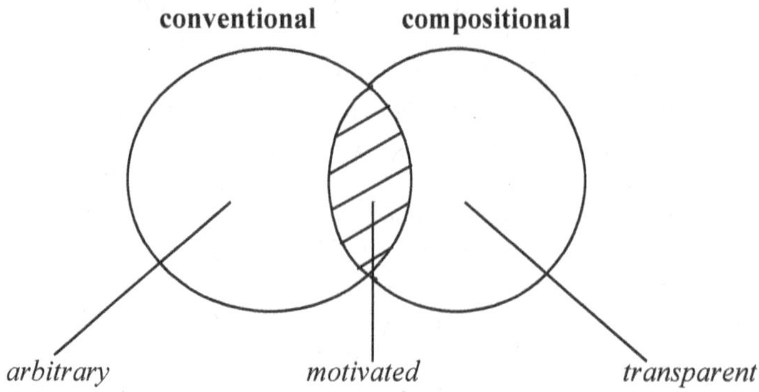

The diagram illustrates the relationship between conventional and compositional constructions. Whereas the distribution of the former is arbitrary and typically cannot be accounted for in terms of more general principles of a language (such as already existing constructions or compositional mechanisms), the distribution of the latter is transparent and therefore predictable from other more general aspects of the grammar. The distinction drawn between conventional and compositional constructions is comparable to the traditional distinction between 'lexicon' and 'grammar'. On this view, lexical items are taken to be conventionalized units whose distribution is typically not explainable in terms of abstract principles found in the language. In other words, something is conventionalized if we do not find ordinary compositional processes that give us the meaning of a construction. For example, (5.41) is Clark's (1996) definition of a convention that is used to explain the relation between arbitrariness and the use of linguistic signs in speech communities.

(5.41) Definition of a convention

1. a regularity in behavior (e.g. producing the string of sounds *butterfly*)
2. that is partly arbitrary (we could have used *Schmetterling* instead; that's what the German speech community did)
3. that is common ground in a community (we in the English language community all know we use *butterfly* ...)
4. as a coordination device
5. for a recurrent coordination problem (talking about butterflies). (Clark 1996:71)

While the notion of convention certainly applies to lexical items, it is unclear how it may be extended to cover chunks of language that cannot definitively be identified as belonging to the purely lexical domain. Note, however, that there is an important intersection between conventional and compositional constructions that is often overlooked. This intersection (indicated by the shaded area in (5.40)) includes cases in which a given construction is both compositional (i.e. transparent) and conventional (i.e. arbitrary) at the same time. In other words, it is motivated to some degree. For example, Sinclair (1996: 84) points out that the phrase *naked eye* is not entirely semantically transparent as it could denote 'without spectacles' or 'with unprotected eyes' in addition to its conventionalized meaning, 'without the use of telescope, microscope, etc.' This example shows that although the phrase *naked eye* is in part compositional and semantically transparent, it is also (to some degree) conventionalized at the semantic level.

The data reviewed so far strongly suggests that resultatives are similar to phrases such as *naked eye* and therefore belong to the intersection between conventional and compositional constructions indicated in (5.41). We have seen that the dual status of resultative constructions is challenging from an empirical point of view because the fact that they exhibit great regularity and therefore appear transparent (i.e. compositional) has led researchers to account for their distribution in terms of general constraints. However, once close attention is paid to the distribution of these constructions, it becomes clear that for each member belonging to the intersection between conventional and compositional the speaker needs to know specific (i.e. non-general) information in order to form a resultative. This means that although resultatives are transparent in meaning and pose no problem for decoding, they do pose a problem for encoding (see Fillmore et al.'s (1988: 504-505) distinction between idioms of decoding and encoding).[18]

In other words, although there is a reason for the distribution of resultative constructions in the sense that they are motivated (there are semantic differences between verbs and resultative phrases), our discussion of Wechsler's (2001) analysis has shown that it is extremely difficult to predict this distribution in terms of abstract semantic constraints. We have seen that once we find counterexamples to Wechsler's semantic restrictions, his account loses its ability to capture the full distribution of resultatives. This means that in the case of resultatives it is possible to observe great regular-

[18]Resultative constructions typically do not pose a problem for decoding when a hearer knows the meanings of the individual constituents of the construction. That is, it is possible to decode a resultative even in cases when one has never heard this particular combination before. However, resultatives pose a problem for encoding because the speaker has to know the conventional way of how to encode the resultative (as our discussion has shown, there are typically no general principles in the language that tell the speaker the types of postverbal NPs and resultative phrases that go with a particular matrix verb).

ity (in the types of resultative phrases that go with certain types of verbs) that is conventionalized in a specific way (i.e., individual verbs determining the types of postverbal constituents they combine with in resultatives). Since the distribution of resultative phrases is at least partially arbitrary and cannot be predicted on general grounds, it must be conventionalized information associated with matrix verbs.[19] As Stubbs (2001: 58) puts it: 'Many other perfectly grammatical ways of saying the same things are conceivable: but people just don't say them.'

A further example illustrating my point regarding the role of conventionalization is a difference between British and American English. Whereas both varieties have a specific sense of *drive* that describes a (typically negative) change of mental state as in *This problem drives me mad*, only British English *send* exhibits a similar sense as in *This problem sends me mad*. This example shows two things. First, British English *send* differs from American English *send* in that it has an additional sense. Since it does not seem to be possible to explain this difference in terms of general principles of the language, this sense of *send* must be conventionalized. Second, the interpretation of the two sentences requires the presence of both the matrix verb and the resultative phrase. Only when both elements are present is it possible to interpret the sentence appropriately. More importantly, the British English example illustrates that it is only possible to interpret the combination of *send* and *mad* when one is familiar with this combination (as a speaker of British English). For most speakers of American English, this unfamiliar combination of *send* and *mad* is difficult to interpret.[20] Examples like this suggest that certain combinations are conventionalized in British English but not in American English.[21]

---

[19]Another problem with Wechsler's (1997, 2001) analysis is his classification of resultatives into control resultatives and ECM resultatives. Whereas in the former, the postverbal NP is an argument of the matrix verb, 'in ECM resultatives *the predication subject is not an argument of the verb*.' (Wechsler 2001: 13) He claims that 'the fact that the predication subject for ECM resultatives is not part of the argument structure of the verb means that no homomorphism or coextensiveness requirement obtains.' (2001: 13) However, applying Lakoff's 1976 test for patienthood shows that the postverbal NP in a sentence such as *We laughed the speaker off the stage* (Wechsler 2001: 13) is a patient and should thus be regarded as an argument of the matrix verb (although in a somewhat specialized conventionalized sense (cf. the unacceptability of **We sighed the speaker off the stage*)): a. What we did to the speaker was … b. What happened to the speaker was …

[20]Seventeen out of twenty speakers of American English had difficulties coming up with an explanation for what *This problem sends me mad* meant.

[21]Similar observations regarding the nature of conventionalization can be made about path PPs like *to death*. Sentences like *I prefer life to death, She fell to her death, He shot him to death,* and **Let's go to death* illustrate that *to death* is not an ordinary transparent PP that is interpreted according to general principles of compositionality (e.g. as a comparable PP headed by

To summarize, our discussion has shown that the combination of verbs and resultative phrases cannot be solely predicted on the basis of compositional mechanisms or general semantic constraints (they cannot be derived 'computationally'). Therefore, the distribution of resultatives must be stated as part of the construction, in this case as part of the information associated with the verb which tells us not only something about the type of activity, but also something about what type of resultative phrase may be used to express the telic bounds of the event. This means that to the extent that Wechsler's generalizations hold, they are epiphenomenal in that they are a side effect of only a certain number of verbs conforming to them.[22] In the following section we turn to an alternative method of accounting for the motivated yet conventionalized restrictions holding between verbs and postverbal constituents in resultative constructions in terms of collocational restrictions.

5.3.3 Collocations as Units of Meaning

Collocations are multiword expressions that frequently occur in combination with each other. This often makes it difficult to distinguish between collocations and pure idioms (see Palmer 1933, Cowie 1988, 1994, Hausmann 1989, Sinclair 1991, Nunberg et al. 1994), both of which are characterized by Firth's (1957: 11) famous remark that '[y]ou shall know a word by the company it keeps.' Idioms such as *kick the bucket* are entirely or partially fixed so that there is a 'central internal stability' (Wray 2002: 51). This has lead researchers to describe idioms 'as semantically opaque word-combinations – that is, combinations whose global meaning is different from the sum of the individual meanings of the constituent parts.' (Fontenelle 1998: 191)[23]

---

to in *They walked to the store*). The examples illustrate that each of the verbs exhibit different requirements as to whether they may occur with *to death*. In cases in which verbs do pattern with *to death*, the prepositional phrases are interpreted differently in each case. This strongly suggests that there are no general compositional principles at work here, but rather conventionalization because the meaning of the utterances cannot be predicted on the basis of their component parts.

[22] I would like to thank Charles Fillmore for stimulating discussions about questions having to do with compositionality and conventionalization.

[23] Fontenelle (1998: 191) also points out that '[o]ther authors (Fraser 1970, Michiels 1975) lay stress, in defining idiomaticity, on an expression's resistance to a number of syntactic manipulations (passivization, pronominalization, fronting, clefting, insertion of material, etc.). Carter (1988) gives various examples of idioms, including *it's raining cats and dogs*, which is immutable in so far as it cannot be passivized, does not allow insertion, and has a fixed order (cf. **it's raining dogs and cats*). *To drop a brick* (meaning 'to commit a blunder') is an idiom of another structural type, which is resistant to other classes of manipulations. Insertions of mate-

In contrast, collocations do not exhibit the same degree of frozenness as idioms. Rather, collocations are 'combinations of words that are preferred over other combinations which otherwise appear to be semantically equivalent.' (Croft 2001: 180)[24] In other words, 'collocation is an aspect of lexical cohesion which embraces a "relationship" between lexical items that regularly co-occur.' (Carter 1988: 163) An example of a collocation is the lexical relation between the words *bitter* and *cold* as in *bitter cold.* It is part of a speaker's knowledge that these two words co-occur in order to denote an extremely cold temperature. In addition, a speaker knows that *sour* or *salty* are not usually elements that are free to combine with *cold* to form a similar type of collocation. Furthermore, it is an essential aspect of linguistic competence to know that *bitter* combines with *cold,* and not with *hot* to form expressions denoting extreme hot temperatures. This example shows that when expressions in which two or more words occur within a stated distance of each other more frequently than chance would predict, they may be characterized as collocations (see Sinclair 1991: 109-116).

One of the reasons collocations are often overlooked by many analyses is the fact that while the meaning of a collocation can be computed by combining the meanings of the component parts, it is usually problematic to predict which elements will form a collocation. That is, from the perspective of language production, it is difficult if not impossible to predict which words will collocate with *cold* to express an extremely cold temperature. For our example of *bitter cold* this means that although its meaning can be computed compositionally, it is part of the linguistic competence of speakers of English that they prefer *bitter* to collocate with *cold* instead of *sour* or *salty.* Since this knowledge cannot be predicted on the basis of other more general aspects of the language, it must be part of the speaker's conventionalized knowledge about how to use the words *bitter* and *cold.*

Examples of idioms such as *kick the bucket* and collocations such as *bitter cold* illustrate that not all of language is naturally innovative as Chomsky (1959) claims: 'It is easy to show that the new events that we accept and understand as sentences are not related to those with which we are familiar by any simple notion of formal (or semantic or statistical) similarity

---

rial and passivization are permitted but pronominalization is not (**John dropped a brick yesterday and Tom dropped one too* is unacceptable).' See Riehemann (2001) for an in-depth study of idioms in Head-Driven Phrase Structure Grammar.

[24]Early work by Palmer (1933) recognized the importance of studying collocational patterns. Based on more than 6000 English collocations, Palmer emphasized the need for a more in-depth study of collocational patterns in order to better understand how the lexicon is structured. To this end, he concluded that collocations 'exceed by far the popular estimate of the number of simple words contained in our everyday vocabulary.' (Palmer 1933: 7)

or identity of grammatical frame.' (Chomsky 1959: 57) Since there are language patterns that are much less rule-governed than Chomsky would like to admit, the question is how to bridge this gap between regularity and idiosyncrasy. Following research by Pawley and Syder (1983) who show that there is a 'novelty scale' against which utterances can be measured and that lexicalization and productivity are matters of degree rather than a clear-cut dichotomy, Sinclair (1991) proposes two complementary principles to classify rule-governed and prefabricated use of language. The open-choice principle describes an 'analytical process which goes on in principle all the time, but whose results are only intermittently called for.' (Sinclair 1991: 114) It involves language use in which abstract grammatical rules are employed to create novel utterances in a purely compositional manner. In contrast, the idiom principle states that particular lexical items commonly occur together in terms of 'a large number of semi-preconstructed phrases that constitute single choices, even though they might appear to be analyzable into segments.' (Sinclair 1991: 110) It is important to keep in mind that the idiom principle and the open-choice principle constitute separate ends of a continuum that ranges from 'totally free combinations of words to completely frozen, fixed multiword units. Collocations will be found in the fuzzy area half-way between free combinations and idioms.' (Fontenelle 1998: 191)

The data we have reviewed on the distribution of resultatives in the sections above provide strong evidence for characterizing the relation between matrix verbs and postverbal elements as collocational dependencies. First, matrix verbs and their postverbal constituents are combinations of words that are preferred over other combinations which otherwise appear to be semantically equivalent. The corpus data cited in Sections 5.3.1 and 5.3.2 illustrate that verbs exhibit strong preferences for particular types of resultative phrases while at the same time disfavoring near-synonyms. Second, I have argued that the distribution of resultatives is difficult to explain based on general semantic principles. This means that matrix verbs and postverbal constituents must be learned together, and usually cannot be pieced together from their component parts to predict their distribution.

5.4 The Communicative Functions of Resultative Constructions

To account for the collocational restrictions holding between verbs and their postverbal constituents in resultative constructions, we first turn to an analysis of the different communicative functions of resultatives. I will argue that resultative constructions are employed to point out a special perspective of the outcome of an event. Then, I will show that depending on the perspective, verbs exhibit different types of collocational restrictions. These restrictions reflect the degree of conventionality that is associated with the activity denoted by the verb as well as the (possible) final state resulting from that activity.

5.4.1 Perspectivizing the Outcome of an Event: Resultative Constructions

The examples in (5.42) illustrate the main function of resultative constructions. (5.42a) conveys information about a painting event from a general perspective, namely that there are two event participants *Melissa* and *the house* and that *the house* was in some way affected by Melissa's painting activity. This interpretation is possible because of the information associated with the verb *paint*, i.e. in the prototypical case, painting is associated with an agent applying a liquid to a surface in order to cover that surface.[25] Based on the information in (5.42a), although it is possible to infer that *the house* is in some way affected by Melissa's painting activity the exact outcome of the event is not clear. That is, without other contextual background information, the color of the house resulting from Melissa's painting activity is uncertain.

(5.42) a. Melissa painted the house.
b. Melissa painted the house pink, green and black.

In (5.42b), the resultative phrase *pink, green and black* conveys a more specific viewpoint of the painting event by specifying a particular outcome of Melissa's painting activity. The difference between (5.42a) and (5.42b), then, is that the resultative phrase contained in the latter specifies the exact outcome of the activity denoted by the verb *paint*, whereas the former does not. In other words, the resultative phrase serves to highlight the outcome of the painting event, thereby conveying a more specific viewpoint of the event denoted by the verb *paint*. The following diagram illustrates the function of the resultative phrase in (5.42b).

---

[25] In this connection, see Lakoff's (1987) concept of 'idealized cognitive models.' Lakoff proposes that expressions refer to a set of interrelated complex models that are represented as radial categories, i.e., categories with a central subcategory which combines all of the interrelated models (cf. in particular his discussion of the concept of *mother*). With respect to the verb *paint*, this means that one typically associates a prototypical painting event (and its related concepts) with specific event participants upon hearing the verb *paint* (depending on the kinds of contextual background information).

(5.43) Resultative Construction

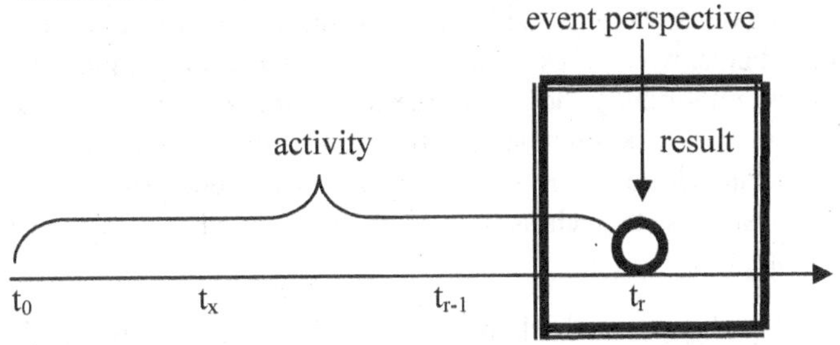

The diagram illustrates the progression of an event over a period of time from its beginning at t_0 to its end-result state at t_r.[26] Verbs like *paint* may be used to convey information about the entire extent of a painting event from t_0 to t_r. In (5.42b), *paint* is employed to convey a specific viewpoint of the outcome of an event, namely, that the prototypical patient has undergone a specific change of state. The box in (5.43) represents the specific resultative viewpoint of a painting event that is conveyed by the resultative phrase in combination with the verb *paint* in (5.42b). In other words, the resultative phrase serves to convey a specific perspective of the outcome of the painting event, while the painting activity that has preceded the end result state is entailed by the information associated with *paint*. The close semantic relationship between the matrix verb and its resultative phrase is reflected by the fact that there is a collocational dependency between the two: it is normally not possible to substitute non-color denoting phrases for the APs in (5.42b) (cf. **Melissa painted the house intelligent*). Based on these observations, I propose that the resultative construction is a semantic/pragmatic mechanism serving to convey a specific perspective of an event, namely the result state of the patient participant.

5.4.2 Looking at Events from Different Perspectives: 'Cookbook Sentences and Resultative Constructions'

The function of resultative constructions contrasts with the function of other kinds of what I would like to call communicatively motivated constructions, i.e., conventionalized speech patterns used to convey a specific type of in-

---

[26]Note that on this view, a change of state is represented similarly to a change of location because both kinds of events proceed along the same time axis and are perceived similarly (cf. also Lakoff and Johnson's (1999: 180-193) discussion of the 'States are Locations' metaphor). Furthermore, both kinds of changes describe a change of a property of an event participant (location is an external property because it is perceived as a figure against a ground; property *per se* is an internal property because it is a property of the object itself).

formation about events. Take, for example, instructions that are used in cookbooks. They typically serve to inform the reader on how to handle ingredients, what types of utensils to use, what temperature setting to use and, most importantly, how long the food should be cooked, baked, boiled, etc. The primary communicative function of these kinds of sentences is thus to indicate for how long something should be cooked so that it won't reach an undesired state such as being too soft, burned, etc. Consider the following sentences.

(5.44)
a. Cook the onion until soft but not brown. (COBUILD)
b. Heat the butter in a sauté pan and cook the onion until soft but not brown. (COBUILD)
c. Cook the rigatoni until just tender. (COBUILD)
d. Cook the penne until tender. (COBUILD)
e. ... put the lid on and cook the fish for five to eight minutes. (COBUILD)
f. Heat the oil and cook the onion until softened. (COBUILD)

The examples in (5.44a)-(5.44f) illustrate an important difference between resultative constructions as in (5.42b) above and cookbook instruction sentences of a specific type. Whereas the former focus the hearer's attention on a specific outcome of an event by perspectivizing that outcome, the latter are not primarily interested in perspectivizing the outcome of the cooking event, but rather the time span that it takes to reach that outcome. The difference is illustrated in the following diagrams.

(5.45) Resultative Constructions as in (5.42b)

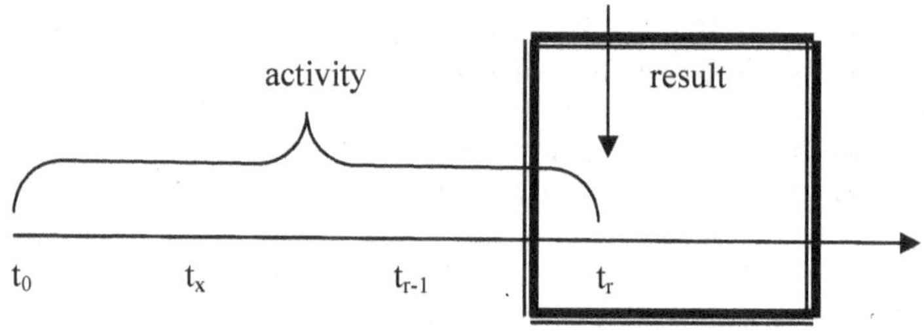

(5.46) Cookbook Sentences as in (5.44a)- (5.44f)

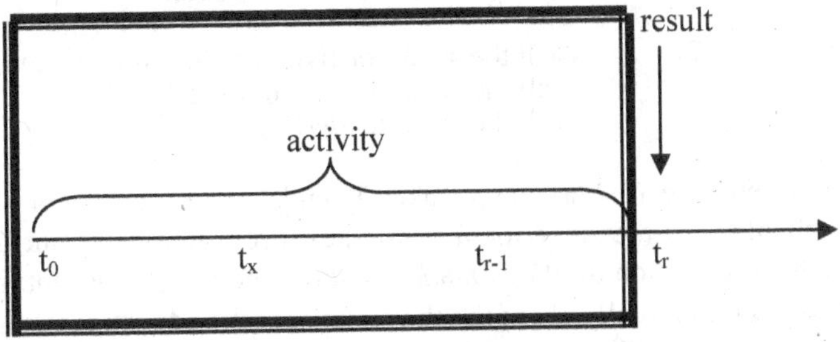

The two diagrams each represent a simplified description of an event over a certain time span. The events described by the respective verbs range from their beginning at t_0 over a subsequent series of time intervals t_x and t_{r-1} to the final stage of the events at t_r. The sentences illustrated by the two diagrams differ in the kinds of perspectives they give of the respective events. The perspectives are indicated by boxes which can be regarded as windows through which one can look at an event.[27] Whereas the resultative construction perspectivizes the final outcome of the event (indicated by the box containing the arrow), i.e., the result state of one of the event participants, 'cookbook sentences' place a different emphasis on the perspective taken of events.

Although cookbook sentences also contain information about the outcome of the event (*tender*, *not brown*, etc.), they highlight a different part of the event, thereby giving the hearer the kind of perspective that is relevant for the cooking instruction discourse function (indicated by the box). Thus, they inform the hearer of the requisite *duration* the activity must have to prevent the food from being under- or overcooked. Information regarding the activity's *outcome* is not necessarily provided (although that is ultimately important as well). The kind of information conveyed by cookbook sentences as in (5.44a)-(5.44g) and resultatives as in (5.42b) is not as differ-

[27]Talmy (1996) refers to different parts of an event being highlighted as 'windowing.' On his view, our cognitive ability to direct our attention in different ways, different aspects of an event may be highlighted which in turn leads to different linguistic expressions. In this connection, Arnold et al. (2000) claim that different structures of linguistic expressions should be explained in terms of grammatical complexity (heaviness) and discourse status (newness). Based on corpus studies and psycholinguistic experiments, they show that 'postponing heavy and new information facilitates processes of planning and production.' (2000: 28) Note that in most resultative constructions, the resultative phrase typically comes at the end of the utterance, i.e., it is placed at the end of the sentence because it is the heaviest and most relevant piece of information of the utterance.

ent as one might think. The following sentences illustrate that it is possible to convey different perspectives of the same event.

(5.47) a. Grill the steak for five minutes until it is tender!
b. Grill the steak for five minutes!
c. Grill the steak tender!

In sentence (5.47a) the speaker intends to let the hearer know that she should grill the steak for five minutes. From the viewpoint of the speaker, the information *until it is tender* is not immediately relevant; it could be left out without really changing the communicative function of the sentence, as shown in (5.47b). Under this circumstance, the hearer would typically grill the steak for five minutes and then take the steak off the grill to avoid further grilling of the steak. The sentences in (5.47a) and (5.47b) thus take the same perspective of the grilling event which is represented by diagram (5.46) above.

In contrast, sentence (5.47c) serves to inform the hearer to grill the steak until it is tender. While both the speaker and the hearer are probably aware of the fact that it might take some time for the steak to become tender as the result of grilling (world knowledge), this information is irrelevant under the present circumstances. In this case, the speaker uses the resultative construction to express that perspective of the grilling event. This perspectivization is illustrated by diagram (5.45) above.

Having contrasted the communicative function of resultative constructions with those of other types of closely related perspectivizing constructions such as 'cookbook sentences,' we now turn to a more fine-grained analysis of the different communicative functions that resultative constructions exhibit. I will show that in each case, the occurrence of the resultative is motivated by the speaker's intention to provide a specific viewpoint of the event's outcome. The resultative is licensed by the lexical semantic information associated with the individual verbs.

5.4.3 Different Kinds of Discourse Information Provided by English Resultatives

5.4.3.1 Emphasizing the Endpoint of an Event

One type of communicative function of resultatives is concerned with emphasizing the change of state of an event participant as the result of some previous activity. Such resultatives occur with a special class of verbs whose members have been characterized by other researchers as externally caused change of state verbs (Dowty 1979, Parsons 1990, Pustejovsky

1995, Levin and Rappaport Hovav 1995) and result verbs (Rappaport Hovav and Levin 1998, 2001). Consider the following sentences.

(5.48) a. She shattered the vase.
b. They melted the butter.
c. Jill suffocated Kim.
d. The fridge froze the water.

Given 'normal' contextual background information, the verbs *shatter*, *melt*, *suffocate*, and *freeze* convey information about the change of state of the event participants. This means that there is normally no need to mention any additional information with respect to the change of state of the event participants because the verbs are conventionally associated with a specific result state and, if no other conflicting information is given, will be interpreted to denote exactly that kind of result state. If, however, one intends to point out something special about the result state of the event participants, it is possible to highlight the outcome of the event by providing additional information. In this case, the resultative phrase serves to highlight that part of the event that is particularly worth mentioning from the speaker's point of view. Compare the following sentences.

(5.49) a. She shattered the vase to pieces.
b. They melted the butter to liquid.
c. Jill suffocated Kim to death.
d. The fridge froze the water solid.

A comparison between (5.48) and (5.49) shows that the occurrence of the resultative phrase conveys more specific information. The licensing of the resultative phrase, in turn, depends on the semantic and syntactic specifications of the respective verbs that relate information about the event. In Section 5.3 we have seen that a verb's ability to occur with resultatives is not predictable on general grounds and should therefore be captured in terms of conventionalized collocational restrictions holding between the verb and the resultative phrase. This means that when a speaker chooses to highlight the change of state of an event participant, she makes use of the conventionalized usage patterns associated with a verb. When a verb is not associated with a resultative pattern, the speaker has to find a different way of perspectivizing the outcome of an event (see our discussion of *eat*, *open*, and *load* in Section 5.3.1). This shows that although the resultative is motivated by the speaker's intention to highlight the outcome of an event, it is restricted by the lexical specifications of individual verbs (i.e., their collocational restrictions) that may be used to describe events.

5.4.3.2 Being Less Vague About the Endpoint of an Event

We now turn to the second function of resultative constructions. Instead of simply emphasizing the outcome of an event as in (5.49), resultatives may be employed to specify the result state of an event participant by providing information about the exact outcome of an event participant. Compare the following sentences.

(5.50) a. Jack painted the house.
b. Flora washed her sweater.
c. Dave hammered the metal.
d. Jackie cut the bread.
e. Tom broke the vase.
f. John strangled Kim.

The sentences in (5.50a)-(5.50f) contain information about the change of state of an event participant, in this case the postverbal NP.[28] In all of these cases, it is possible to infer from the information conveyed by the verb that the postverbal NP underwent some change of state. However, the exact outcome of the change of state is left vague. That is, given regular contextual background assumptions and world knowledge, one may infer that, e.g., in (5.50a), the house underwent some change of state as the result of the painting activity, most probably a change in color.[29] However, without any other information, the exact outcome remains vague. Although one can infer from (5.50b) that the sweater was washed whether or not it was really cleaned is left unclear. Similarly, although one can infer that the metal in (5.50c) underwent some change of state as the result of being hammered, it is not clear what kind of change of state occurred. The following sentences illustrate that resultative phrases may be employed to convey information that reduces the vagueness of the outcome, in this case the postverbal event participant's change of state.

(5.51) a. Jack painted the house red.
b. Flora washed her sweater clean.
c. Dave hammered the metal flat.

---

[28]Using different classification criteria, these resultatives have been classified by other researchers as weak resultatives (Washio 1997), control resultatives (Wechsler 1997, 2001), and resultatives with manner verbs (Rappaport Hovav and Levin 1998, 2001).

[29]Other possible end result states associated with painting could be waterproof, bug-proof, etc. In all of those cases it is not necessarily the case that a surface changes color. In cases in which transparent liquid is applied to wood, e.g., there is no obvious change in color. In this case the goal of the painting activity is to change a different property of the wood than what is entailed by a prototypical painting event, i.e., changing the color of the surface.

d. Jackie cut the bread to pieces.
e. Tom broke the vase to pieces.
f. John strangled Kim to death.

Whereas in the last section, the resultative phrase served to emphasize the (implied) result state, in (5.51a)-(5.51f) it serves to reduce the vagueness in interpretation associated with the verb. In some cases, information conveyed by a resultative phrase about the exact outcome of an event can be 'a matter of life and death.' That is, in sentences such as *he starved himself* it is not clear whether the person actually died. Compare the following sentence pairs.

(5.52) a. There was an old woman who starved herself to give what she had to her little girl. (COBUILD)
b. A tragic loner who starved himself to death was cremated yesterday. (COBUILD)

(5.53) a. Sergey Dmitriyev poisoned himself very badly, but still had the heart to appear as sub on 76 min. (www.quark.lu.se/~oxana/reports/day25.html)
b. At 4:00 p.m. on July 23, he poisoned himself to death. (www.yad-vashem.org.il/holocaust/chronology/4245right.html)

(5.54) a. After a chilling silence she volunteered, 'I burned myself. With some oven cleaner.' (COBUILD)
b. A battered wife who burned her brutal husband to death was freed from jail yesterday. (BNC)

(5.55) a. A man who accidentally shot himself in the penis was discharged in the Southern Districts Court yesterday on three firearms offenses. (COBUILD)
b. In a bizarre incident on April 29, Nodar Imiadze, the Vice-President of the Adzhar autonomous republic (ASSR) in south-west Georgia, attempted to assassinate the acting President, Aslan Abashidze, and was himself shot dead by security guards. (BNC)

The sentences illustrate that the verbs *starve, poison,* and *burn* are vague with respect to the exact result state of the person undergoing the event. The resultative phrase is thus employed to reduce the vagueness associated with the outcome of the event denoted by the verb. The data show that the resultative fulfills the communicative function of conveying special information about the outcome of an event which may not be inferred from the information conveyed by the verb alone. That is, the resultative is motivated by the speaker's intention to provide additional information. It is licensed by the individual verbs which determine whether they allow resultative modification (cf. *She painted the brush to pieces* vs. **She dyed the brush to pieces*). In other words, the restrictions holding between verb and resultative phrase are of a collocational nature.

5.4.3.3 Perspectivizing a Participant Different from the Prototypical Patient Participant

In this section we discuss a perspectivizing function of resultatives that differs from those reviewed in the last two sections. It is the ability of a resultative to perspectivize the end result state of an event participant that is different from the prototypical patient argument of the event described by the verb. These types of resultatives have been analyzed by other researchers in terms of ECM resultatives (Wechsler 1997, 2001) and resultatives based on manner verbs (Rappaport Hovav and Levin 1998, 2001). This class of resultatives includes sentences such as the following.

(5.56) a. Erin painted the brush to pieces.
b. Pam ran her feet sore.
c. Eric swept the broom to pieces.
d. Troy ran the pavement thin.
e. Flora talked herself hoarse.

In each of these sentences, the postverbal NP is what is typically called a fake object (Simpson 1983) of the matrix verb. Previous analyses have accounted for the licensing of the postverbal NPs in terms of transitivizing operations over intransitive variants of the respective verbs (Hoekstra 1988), event structure augmentations (Rappaport Hovav and Levin 1998, 2001), lexical rules that add additional arguments (Wechsler 1997, Verspoor 1997), or grammatical constructions that supply constructional arguments to a verb's subcategorization frame (Goldberg 1995). In contrast, I propose a much simpler way of accounting for the occurrence of both the fake object and the resultative phrase. Following our observations above, I suggest that the two postverbal elements are licensed by the verbs, thereby allowing the speaker to express a different perspective of an event than what is conventionally associated with the respective verbs. The speaker takes this specific perspective of the event because she wants to convey an unconventional viewpoint of the event's outcome. Thus, when a speaker chooses to convey information about an event as in (5.56a)-(5.56e), she intends to convey information that is outside of the regular scenario associated with those verbs or is usually not considered worthy of mention.

This point becomes clear when we look at what types of information the verbs in (5.56a)-(5.56e) typically convey in discourse. The prototypical goal of painting in (5.56a) is to change the color of a surface. People usually run in order to change their location, not to change the condition of their feet or the pavement, cf. (5.56b) and (5.56d). When a person sweeps, the prototypical goal is to remove an unwanted substance from a surface, not to destroy the instrument used to achieve that goal, cf. (5.56c). The same is true of talking which is typically intended to pass on information to a hearer, not to change the condition of the speaker's voice, cf. (5.56e). What all of the sentences in (5.56a)-(5.56e) have in common then, is that they denote a result state of an event participant which is outside of the conventionalized scenario typically associated with the respective verbs when they are uttered without any additional background information. This is not to say that the postverbal event participants in (5.56a)-(5.56e) do not play a role in the regular conventionalized usage of these verbs. Rather, their involvement or their potential change of state within the prototypical event is relatively unimportant with respect to the intended goal conventionally associated with the semantics of the verb (one paints to change the color of a surface, etc.). That is, the postverbal event participants in (5.56a)-(5.56e) are implicitly understood when the verbs are employed in their prototypical conventionalized usage even though they are not part of the verb's core focus in conventionalized discourse. Rather, these event participants belong to what I would like to call off-stage information, or world knowledge.[30]

However, if the speaker intends to convey some special information about an event participant which is not part of the normal conventionalized core usage of the verb, she may 'recruit' her world knowledge, i.e. relevant peripheral meanings of the verb, to give the hearer a special perspective of the event. In order for the hearer to understand the unconventional usage of the respective verbs, she must share the same relevant world knowledge as the speaker. That is, a speaker would have difficulty understanding sentences such as (5.56c) if she were part of a speech community in which there are no brooms and sweeping is accomplished with a vacuum cleaner. On this view, then, the speaker only applies the event participant perspective shift if she wants to report an event's outcome from an unconventional point of view. However, it is not always possible to change the perspective

[30]According to Jackendoff's (1990) analysis, the postverbal NPs in (5.56) are discourse patients (as opposed to grammatical patients which are subcategorized for by the verb), i.e., they 'are Patients by virtue of discourse or pragmatics: a story is generated in which the Actor somehow adversely affects the Patient.' (1990: 230)

of event participants. That is, some verbs allow a perspective shift of event participants whereas other verbs do not. Compare the following sentences.[31]

(5.57) a. Erin swept the floor (with a broom).
b. Erin swept the broom to pieces.

(5.58) a. Tom unlocked the door (with a key).
b.*Tom unlocked the key to pieces.

Both sentence pairs contain events in which the agent utilizes an instrument to achieve a certain result state of the conventionalized patient argument as can be seen in (5.57a) and (5.58a). However, only in (5.57b) is it possible to convey information about the result state of an event participant that differs from the conventionalized prototypical patient event participant without changing the verb (*sweep*). In contrast, *unlock* in (5.58b) does not allow this option; in order to convey information about the effect of an opening event on the instrument event participant, a new verb must be utilized as the following sentence illustrates.

(5.59) Tom broke the key (when unlocking the door).

Examples such as these suggest that not every verb allows the speaker to simply switch perspectives with respect to the change of state of an event participant. Expressing some special outcome of an event (brooms and keys don't break that frequently) may require the use of a completely different verb. Our analyses show that the meanings of verbs and the perspectives that can be taken on the events they describe are highly conventionalized. This conventionalization is reflected by the fact that the verbs and their postverbal arguments discussed in this section exhibit stricter collocational dependency relations than those discussed in the previous section. These restrictions do not seem to be predictable based on more general patterns found in the language. Instead, they seem to be dependent on the lexical-semantic information associated with the individual verbs. I will return to the link between the degree of conventionalization and of collocational restriction in the following two chapters.

---

[31]Note that the (b) sentences describe results that may happen during the activity that leads to the prototypical result of the respective activities in the (a) sentences. Thus, under normal circumstances one needs a broom in order to sweep the floor, or a key in order to unlock a door.

5.4.3.4 Perspectivizing a Participant Outside of the Conventionalized Event-Scene

The last communicative function of resultatives to be discussed deals with yet another instance of what we have called shift of perspective. In this case, the resultative is used to report an unconventional scenario that falls outside of the class of event perspectives conventionally described by a single verb. This type of perspective shift is exemplified by sentences such as the following.

(5.60) a. Stefan sneezed the napkin off the table.
b. ??Stefan wheezed the napkin off the table.
c. *Stefan exhaled the napkin off the table.

(5.60a) illustrates a creative use of *sneeze*. On witnessing a scene in which *Stefan* sneezes and as a result the napkin flies off the table, one does not have any readily available verb to describe this cause and effect relation effectively within one sentence. Instead of packaging the two events into two separate sentences (cf. *Stefan sneezed. As a result of his sneezing, the napkin flew off the table*), the speaker wishes to express this rather unconventional scenario in one sentence in order to highlight the immediate cause and effect relation between the two events. In this case, the meaning of *sneeze* is creatively expanded to highlight a specific perspective of the event. That is, the perspective shift is concerned neither with highlighting or disambiguating a prototypical event participant's change of state nor with perspectivizing the change of state of a nonconventionalized undergoer event participant.

This means that the two postverbal constituents in (5.60a) are motivated by the speaker's intention to convey information about an event participant's special unconventional result state which is caused by a conventional causing event. They are licensed by the lexical semantics associated with the verb that makes it possible to use the verb in a non-conventional usage pattern. This is achieved by extending the meanings of verbs in a creative way. The unacceptability of (5.60b) and (5.60c) shows that the extension in (5.60a) is limited to only a few verbs that are associated with lexical-semantic information which serves as the basis for a creative extension given the proper context. We return to a more detailed discussion of this proposal (and how to formally represent it) in the following two chapters.

5.5 Conclusions

In this chapter I have outlined the cornerstones of a usage-based approach to the analysis of resultative constructions. I have argued that the distribution of resultatives is not strictly predictable from a verb's distributional patterns outside of resultative constructions. Based on distributional corpus data we have seen that individual verbs lexically subcategorize for specific semantic and syntactic types of resultative phrases. These observations have led me to propose that the distribution of resultative constructions is to a large degree conventionalized in terms of collocational dependencies. On this view, each verb is conventionally associated with a resultative usage pattern that specifies the semantic and/or syntactic type of its resultative phrase (and nonsubcategorized postverbal NP). Furthermore, I have argued that the distribution of resultatives is not strictly predictable in terms of general semantic constraints à la Wechsler (2001).

In the last part of this chapter I have identified four different communicative functions of resultative constructions, each of which portrays the change of state of an event participant from a specific viewpoint: (1) emphasizing the endpoint of an event, (2) reducing the vagueness in interpretation associated with the endpoint of an event, (3) perspectivizing a different event participant than the prototypical patient, and (4) perspectivizing a participant outside of the conventionalized event-scene. In each case I have argued that there are two factors that play a role in motivating and licensing the resultative phrase (and, in some cases the nonsubcategorized postverbal NP). First, the speaker's intention to convey some special information about the outcome of an event motivates the use of a resultative construction. Second, the lexical semantics and the conventionalized collocational patterns associated with the individual verbs and types of events they may describe license the linguistic realization of resultatives. In the following chapter, we turn our attention to the structure of lexical semantic information associated with verbs. In Chapter 7, we will see how this conventionalized lexical semantic information serves to license the four different types of resultatives surveyed in this chapter.

6

Event Based Frame Semantics

> Wie verhält sich nun die Sprachwissenschaft angesichts der ungeheuren Wichtigkeit des Wortes? Wir verfügen über eine hochgezüchtete Lautlehre, über eine raffinierte Satz- und Formenlehre. Aber eine Wortlehre als klare und eindeutige Disziplin existiert nicht, lediglich einige spezielle, an sich hochinteressante Forschungszweige, von denen noch zu sprechen sein wird. Der Grund für das Fehlen einer allgemeinen Wortlehre liegt, wie schon mehrfach bemerkt worden ist, offenbar darin, daß man sich nicht im klaren ist, was eigentlich am Wort erforscht werden soll. Es fehlen uns die Begriffe, die Kategorien, mit denen wir operieren könnten.
>
> (Leisi 1954: 8)[1]

6.1 Introduction

This chapter is concerned with the structure and content of lexical semantic information needed to account for the distribution of resultatives. Section 6.2 argues for a splitting approach towards the description of verbal semantics. On this view, each sense of a verb is represented by its own rich idiosyncratic 'packet of semantic information' (an event-frame). It includes information about event participants, force-dynamic relations that hold between the event participants, temporal information, world knowledge, and collocational specifications with respect to the types of resultative phrases that may occur with a given sense of a verb. Section 6.3 deals with differ-

[1]Translation: What does linguistics have to say when faced with the immense importance of the word? We have a sophisticated theory of sounds, a well-thought out theory of sentences and forms. But a theory of words does not exist as a clear and independent discipline, only some specialized fields of study concerned with very interesting problems that we will come back to. The reason for this lack of a general theory of words is, as has been said before, due to the fact that one is not exactly sure about what it is that could be investigated in this field. The terms and categories used to describe words are lacking.

ences between senses that are associated with the same verb as well as questions of possible generalizations across different verb classes.

6.2 Information Contained in a Verb's Lexical Entry

6.2.1 The Role of the Lexicon

One of the basic issues in linguistic theory regarding the role of the lexicon is the type of information that should be included in a word's lexical entry. This issue is important to linguists from a wide range of theoretical traditions because lexical information has a determining role in the structuring of sentences. That is, the different types of mechanisms used to piece together phrases and sentences in various linguistic theories crucially depend on the information contained in a lexical entry. Characterizing different approaches towards the structure of the lexicon, Jackendoff (1997: 123) distinguishes between two types of approaches, namely the *impoverished entry theory* and the *full entry theory*.

The origins of the *impoverished entry theory* can be traced back to Bloomfield's (1933) characterization of the lexicon as 'an appendix of the grammar, a list of basic irregularities' (1933: 274). This view of the lexicon has been extremely influential as it forms the theoretical basis for a large number of current accounts of the lexicon that aim at reducing the amount of information contained in a verb's lexical entry (see, e.g., Pinker 1989, Levin 1993, Pustejovsky 1995, 2000, Mohanan and Mohanan 1998, Rappaport Hovav and Levin 1998, 2001). For example, Levin (1993: 11) points out that 'the ideal lexical entry for a word should minimize the information provided for that word. This goal can be achieved by factoring predictable information out of lexical entries, leaving only idiosyncratic information.' For linguists advocating the impoverished entry theory, the motivation behind keeping the information contained in the lexicon to a minimum finds further support by the theoretical assumption that the 'language faculty is nonredundant and that the lexicon appears in terms of an "optimal coding".' (Jackendoff 1997: 124) Jackendoff summarizes the reasons for why 'optimal coding' is so appealing to a number of linguists as follows:

> If there is a generalization among a number of items, it takes fewer bits to store them than if they were unrelated (and therefore in the traditional view of memory as a filing system, less 'space'). In principle, then, this is a nice way to conceptualize matters. (Jackendoff 1997: 124)

Note, however, that the simplistic view of the lexicon in terms of a filing system has serious shortcomings. As we have already seen in our discussion of Rappaport Hovav and Levin (1998, 2001) in Chapter 3, postulating a minimal lexical entry and deriving extended word senses by applying generative mechanisms to it creates both theoretical and empirical problems. It ignores to a large degree the multiple facets of related, yet distinctly different word meanings that have been pointed out by analyses concerned with the nature of word meanings, polysemy, and lexical fields.[2] Although the results of reductionist approaches seem to be promising at first sight when it comes to arriving at broad-scale generalizations about a certain segment of natural language, the data and discussion in Chapters 2-5 have shown that there are gaps, unpredictable senses, and conventionalized usages of lexical items. Based on corpus data, I have argued that their distribution does not adhere to the general principles applied to generate extended word senses on the basis of 'basic' word senses. The same point is made by Cruse (2000) who claims that

> attempts to model word meaning and semantic composition in terms of unitary, sparse, lexical representations and compositional principles (*à la* Pustejovsky) are doomed, except as first approximations (...). If the picture presented here is correct, there is no such thing as 'the meaning of a word' in isolation from particular contexts: decontextualization of meaning is variable, and in principle, always incomplete. In other words, lexical meanings are irreducibly complex.
>
> (Cruse 2000: 51)

In contrast to the *impoverished entry theory*, the *full entry theory* of lexical listing maintains that it is necessary for a lexical entry to contain the information necessary to account for all of a word's attested usages (see, e.g., Fillmore and Atkins 2000, Langacker 2000, Croft 2001, Boas 2002a, Iwata 2002). This does not mean that there are no systematic generalizations to be observed (see Section 6.3.3). However, the most efficient (although time consuming) means of arriving at a theory of full coverage is to first gather and describe a complete inventory of the attested distribution of lexical items under investigation. Only then is it possible to finally arrive at precise and efficient generalizations over the full amount of empirical data. By fol-

---

[2]See, e.g., Trier (1931), Weisgerber (1951), Leisi (1955), Mel'čuk (1974, 1998), Fillmore (1968, 1978, 1985), Apresjan (1974), Nunberg (1978), Cruse (1986), Sweetser (1990), Lakoff (1987), Brugmann (1988), Deane (1988), Jackendoff (1990), Lehrer (1990), Fillmore and Atkins (1992, 2000), Faber and Usón (1999), Levin (1993), and Iwata (1998, 2002).

lowing the bottom-up approach, the full entry theory of lexical listing has the further advantage that there 'is no need for a process of Lexical Assembly' (Jackendoff 1997: 129) That is, in contrast to the impoverished entry theory, there 'is no problem of integrating idiosyncratic information in a composed lexical entry with predictable information' as Jackendoff (1997: 129) points out.[3] This step also allows us to state very clearly which verbs closely related in meaning may occur in the resultative construction and which may not. This procedure will help us to account for the idiosyncratic distribution of resultatives as in the following examples.

(6.1) a. Flora ran Jack off the street.
b. ?Flora jogged Jack off the street.
c. ?Flora walked Jack off the street.
d. *Flora crawled Jack off the street.

(6.2) a. Tom drank himself to sleep.
b. ?Tom sipped himself to sleep.
c. *Tom slurped himself to sleep.
d. *Tom gulped himself to sleep.

(6.3) a. Erin ate her plate empty.
b. ?Erin swallowed her plate empty.
c. *Erin devoured her plate empty.

Positing full entries for individual verb senses also eliminates the problem of having to decide on a 'basic' verb sense. On this view, each entry lists information that makes it possible to explain under which circumstances a specific sense of a verb will be able to occur in the resultative pattern (given the 'proper' contextual background information). For the reasons discussed in this section as well as in the preceding chapters, I adopt the full entry theory in order to keep generative mechanisms that derive new and extended verb senses to a bare minimum (see Section 7.3). This step will allow us to account for the full range of corpus-attested data without having to worry about theoretical assumptions such as 'conceptual necessity' that are difficult to verify or falsify on the basis of empirical data currently

[3]With respect to the 'informational cost' associated with the lexicon under a full entry theory Jackendoff (1997: 129) points out the following: '[L]exical entries are fully listed, but (...) lexical rules render parts of these entries redundant, so the "cost" of learning them and listing them is less. On the other hand, idiosyncratic content not predicted by a lexical rule costs "full price".' As we will see in Section 6.3.3, the 'informational cost' of the full entry theory becomes less once one follows through with the bottom-up approach by making appropriate generalizations at empirically verifiable levels of abstraction.

available. Adopting the full entry theory also has the advantage of allowing us to capture the fact that 'native speakers can make extremely subtle judgments concerning the occurrence of verbs with a range of possible combinations of arguments and adjuncts in various syntactic expressions.' (Levin 1993: 2) Levin's observation suggests that any theory of language claiming to be descriptively and explanatorily adequate must capture the native speaker's knowledge about the wide range of different idiosyncratic distributions of verbs and the collocational restrictions they impose on resultative constructions. The data reviewed throughout this monograph strongly suggest that the full entry theory offers significant advantages over the impoverished entry theory in accounting for the distribution of resultatives.

In the remainder of this chapter, I will lay out the architecture of such a theory of resultatives by discussing in detail the types of semantic information necessary for their licensing. This discussion will then serve as the foundation for accounting for the distribution of resultative constructions in Chapter 7.

6.2.2 Frame Semantics

Examining the meanings of words brings us to the question of how to account for the semantics of the constituents occurring in the resultative construction. In light of all that has been said so far in previous chapters, it is not surprising that linguists have used a wide variety of theoretical concepts in order to formally represent the meanings of words. One of the main problems in representing the meanings of words has to do with what Peirce (1932) calls the 'irreducibility of the sign.' Peirce pointed out that it is difficult to describe and analyze the meanings of words in terms of a metalanguage. In his view, it is impossible to account for linguistic signs in terms of elements that are not themselves signs.

Nevertheless, besides Rappaport Hovav and Levin (1998, 2001), a number of theories have emerged, each taking a different strategy and employing a unique metalanguage to analyze the meanings of words.[4] For example, Jackendoff (1990, 1997) employs an abstract semantic metalanguage that partly resembles that of Rappaport Hovav and Levin (1998, 2001) in that it uses semantic decomposition mechanisms in order to ac-

---

[4]Since Rappaport Hovav and Levin's (1998, 2001) approach towards word meaning has been discussed at length in Chapter 3, it is not necessary to review it again at this point. Note that Rappaport Hovav and Levin's analysis of word meaning represents in some sense a continuation of the lexical decomposition approach introduced to generative linguistics by Katz and Fodor (1963).

count for meaning. However, Jackendoff differs from Rappaport Hovav and Levin in that he assumes representational modularity that regards words and phrases as fixed matchings of phonological, syntactic, and conceptual structure (<PS, SS, CS>). Combining PS, SS, and CS makes it possible not only to account for properties of words but also for idiomatic constructions much like Construction Grammar does (see Jackendoff (1997: 171-77)). Furthermore, employing abstract conceptual functions such as ELT (Element of), COMP (Composed of), or CONT (containing) allows Jackendoff (1990) to represent complex semantic relations in terms of simpler ones. However, as discussed in Chapter 4, Jackendoff's approach faces a number of problems when it comes to accounting for the distribution of resultatives. Our discussion in Chapter 4 showed that Jackendoff's framework is problematic because in its present form it has no mechanism to systematically account for the collocational restrictions between verbs and their postverbal constituents in resultative constructions.

As a basis for our analysis, I adopt the principles of a usage-based approach to language analysis as it is laid out in Fillmore's (1982, 1985) theory of Frame Semantics.[5] This approach to semantic description differs from other theories such as Rappaport Hovav and Levin (1998, 2001), Jackendoff (1990, 1997), Pustejovsky (1995), and Wierzbicka (1992, 1996) in that it refers to a common background of knowledge (a 'frame') against which the meaning of each word is interpreted.[6] Frame Semantics does not rely on a narrow inventory of semantic predicates or semantic universals that form the basis for compositionally deriving larger chunks of meaning. That is, the Frame Semantic approach to semantic description differs from 'checklist theories of meaning' (Fillmore 1975: 128) which consist of a checklist of conditions that have to be satisfied in order for the word to be appropriately or truthfully used. Fillmore and Atkins (1992) summarize the core principles of Frame Semantics as follows.

---

[5]The term 'frame' has also been used in work on artificial intelligence. To this end, Minsky (1975: 212) describes a frame as 'a data-structure representing a stereotypical situation.' Work in psychology employs a similar concept which refers to knowledge structures for sequences of events, cf. Schank and Abelson's (1975) 'restaurant script.'

[6]Pustejovsky's (1995) Generative Lexicon distinguishes between at least four basic levels of linguistic representation (argument structure, event structure, qualia structure, and lexical inheritance structure). Using generative devices such as type coercion, subselection, and co-composition, Pustejovsky 'connects these four levels, providing for the compositional interpretation of words in context.' (Pustejovsky 2000: 71) While Pustejovsky's approach is extremely successful at accounting for the flexibility of word senses, it encounters similar problems as Rappaport Hovav and Levin's (1998, 2001) analysis (with respect to overgeneration of unattested word senses, among others (see Nirenburg and Raskin 1996)).

> A word's meaning can be understood only with reference to a structured background of experience, beliefs, or practices, constituting a kind of conceptual prerequisite for understanding the meaning. Speakers can be said to know the meaning of the word only by first understanding the background frames that motivate the concept that the word encodes. Within such an approach, words or word senses are not related to each other directly, word to word, but only by way of their links to common background frames and indications of the manner in which their meanings highlight particular elements of such frames.
>
> (Fillmore and Atkins 1992: 76-77)

It is important to keep in mind that in Frame Semantics a word is defined not in relation to other words but in relation to its background frame.[7] As Petruck (1996: 2) puts it, 'a frame is used as a cognitive structuring device, parts of which are indexed by words associated with it and used in the service of understanding.' Fillmore's core ideas about understanding the meaning of a word against a background frame can be exemplified by the commercial transaction frame which involves several semantically related verbs with different valence requirements such as *buy*, *sell*, *cost*, *spend*, and *charge*.[8] The commercial transaction frame represents a scenario with different frame elements such as buyer, seller, goods, and money that participate in a commercial transaction in which 'one person acquires control or possession of something from a second person, by agreement, as a result of surrendering to that person a sum of money. The needed background requires an understanding of property ownership, a money economy, implicit contract, and a great deal more.' (Fillmore and Atkins 1992: 78) The following diagram gives a rough sketch of the commercial transaction frame.

[7]For approaches that employ the notion of semantic fields in order to define words in relation to other words, see, e.g., Trier (1931) and Weisgerber (1951).

[8]Our discussion focuses on verbs, but a complete description of the words representing the relationships between the frame elements in the commercial transaction frame would also include nouns such as *sum*, *price*, or adjectives such as *cheap*, *expensive*, etc. Note that the commercial transaction frame is a specific subframe of a more abstract money-transferring frame which includes verbs such as *exchange* or *give to*, and nouns such as *tip*, *ransom*, *allowance*, *refund*, *tuition*, *rent*, *child support*, and *salary*.

(6.4) Commercial Transaction Frame

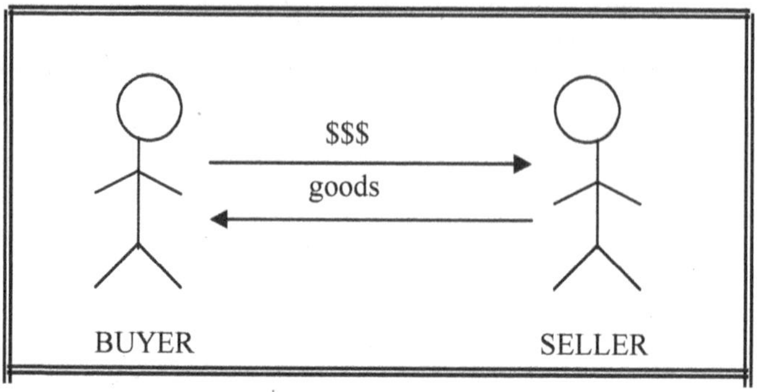

With such a frame-semantic description it is possible to describe the meanings of the individual verbs in relation to this frame, i.e., which frame elements are profiled and which frame elements are backgrounded. Compare the following sentences.

(6.5) a. **Margaret** *bought* **a book** from Collin for 20 dollars.
b. **Collin** *sold* **a book** to Margaret for 20 dollars.
c. **Collin** *charged* Margaret **20 dollars** for the book.
d. **Margaret** *spent* **20 dollars** on the book.
e. **The book** *cost* **20 dollars.**

The verbs in (6.5a)-(6.5e) describe an event which takes place within the same commercial transaction frame. However, the frame elements are all realized differently at the linguistic level. The frame elements in bold are said to be profiled, whereas other frame elements are backgrounded. The difference between profiled and backgrounded frame elements has to do with the kind of perspective that a verb takes of an event. Depending on the perspective, frame elements differ with respect to the obligatoriness of their realization at the linguistic level. Whereas some verbs like *buy*, *sell* and *cost* describe a specific perspective of the commercial transaction event and obligatorily profile the goods, verbs like *charge* and *spend* do not exhibit this requirement because they describe a different viewpoint of the event. *Cost*, on the other hand, takes yet again a different perspective and therefore requires the money to be profiled, whereas verbs like *sell* and *buy* background this frame element. Since all of the verbs convey a different perspective of the same scene, 'understanding the choice of words for talking about that scene requires appealing to the history of events leading up to it.' (Petruck 1996: 5) For example, whereas *buy* and *sell* describe a commercial transaction event from beginning to end, a verb like *cost* only profiles a specific time slot of the event, i.e., typically the phase in which the buyer is informed of the goods' price. In Frame Semantics, a complete description of a verb not only includes reference to its background frame but also a set of valence descriptions which covers the syntactic range in which a verb may express its frame elements.[9]

Applying Frame Semantics to cross-linguistic data allows us to find a common reference frame for the semantic description of verbs across different languages (see Chapter 8 for an analysis of German resultatives). Of particular interest is the question of how verbs differ when it comes to realizing the frame elements of the commercial transaction frame. Compare, e.g., the German counterparts of (6.5a)-(6.5e) above.

(6.6)
a. **Margaret** *kaufte* **ein Buch** von Collin für 20 Dollar.
'Margaret bought a book from Collin for 20 dollars.'
b. **Collin** *verkaufte* Margaret **ein Buch** für 20 Dollar.
'Collin sold a book to Margaret for 20 dollars.'
c. **Collin** *berechnete* Margaret **20 Dollar** für das Buch.
'Collin charged Margaret 20 dollars for the book.'
d. **Margaret** *bezahlte* **20 Dollar** für das Buch.
'Margaret paid 20 dollars for the book.'
e. **Das Buch** *kostete* **20 Dollar**.
'The book cost 20 dollars.'

The comparison between the English data in (6.5) and the German data in (6.6) shows that the five verbs under investigation profile their frame elements identically in the two languages. Note, however, that there is a difference of how the perspectives of the commercial transaction frame are expressed by the verbs in the two languages. Whereas English denotes the different perspectives of the primary transaction scene with the two verbs *buy* and *sell*, German signals the perspective shift by prefixing a *ver-* onto *kaufen* ('buy'), thereby yielding *verkaufen* ('sell'). By overtly signaling the perspective shift from the perspective of the person who acquires something to the person who gives monetary compensation in return, German exhibits a morphologically expressed perspective shift. Changing the perspective by

[9]This theoretical approach has been successfully implemented in a computational lexicography environment to produce the basic information structures for a machine-readable dictionary on semantic grounds (the FrameNet project at the International Computer Science Institute in Berkeley, California). See, e.g., Lowe, Baker and Fillmore (1997), Baker, Fillmore and Lowe (1998), and Baker and Ruppenhofer (2003).

prefixing *ver-* is not limited to *kaufen* and *verkaufen* but is also exhibited by verbs of the more general exchange frame which describe an exchange event from different perspectives.

(6.7) a. *mieten* ('to rent'), *vermieten* ('to rent out')
b. *pachten* ('to lease from'), *verpachten* ('to lease to')

In order to account for the distribution of resultatives, we adopt the core ideas of Fillmore's Frame Semantics as outlined in this section. However, we will extend the term frame to the term *event-frame* because temporal and spatial information play an important role in the construal of events.[10] That is, except for states, other event types (see the overview of Vendler's aspectual classes in Chapter 3) evolve along a time and space axis. For the same reason, we will label what we have so far called frame elements as event participants. We now turn to a discussion of how to encode different types of frame semantic information in the lexicon.

6.2.3 Structure and Content of Event-Frames

In Chapters 3-5, we discussed speakers' knowledge about the fact that certain actions have conventionally expected results. Since this knowledge has been incorporated in different accounts such as Washio (1997) and Wechsler (1997) to explain the distribution of resultatives, it is important to consider it in our discussion of what types of information to encode in a verb's lexical entry.

6.2.3.1 On-Stage and Off-Stage Information

The question of whether a distinction can be drawn between linguistic knowledge (knowledge of a language) and encyclopedic knowledge ('real-world' knowledge) has been hotly debated by linguists, anthropologists, psychologists, and philosophers for as long as language has been studied.[11] Some linguists argue that what we know about the meanings of words such

[10]Our use of the term 'event-frame' or 'event' differs from Talmy's (1996) use of 'event-frame.' Talmy characterizes event-frames as 'including certain kinds of conceptual material but not other kinds.' (1996: 285) and identifies different types of event-frames such as a path, a causal chain, a cycle, a participant interaction and an interrelationship. I use the term 'event-frame' to denote an abstract event or scene from the beginning to its end. That is, the verb *run* refers to the running event-frame and can be used to describe any time interval of a running event as we will see below.

[11]For a detailed overview of the lexicon-encyclopedia debate, see Inchaurralde (2000), Larrivée (2000), Peeters (2000), and Taylor (2000).

as *car*, *beer*, and *football* should in principle be distinguishable from our factual knowledge about cars, beer, and footballs (see, e.g., Katz and Fodor 1963, Bierwisch 1983, Raskin 1985, Marantz 1997, Goddard 1998). This approach – let us call it the dividing approach - is usually based on the argument that linguistic knowledge is shared between all the speakers of a language. For example, by hearing a word such as *car*, a speaker of English will typically understand that it is a count noun that describes a four-wheeled vehicle with a steering wheel. However, car mechanics, beer connoisseurs, and professional athletes may know a great deal more about cars, beer, and footballs than the average speaker. This specialized knowledge differs from lexical knowledge because it is supposedly encyclopedic in nature. Separating lexical from encyclopedic knowledge is appealing to linguists who subscribe to the theoretical assumption that the 'language faculty is nonredundant and that the lexicon appears in terms of an "optimal coding".' (Jackendoff 1997: 124) That is, the exclusion of encyclopedic information from the lexicon makes it possible to minimize the amount of lexical information, thereby creating a lexicon of an economical size that looks descriptively elegant.

An alternative approach to lexical semantics – let us call it the unified approach - holds that it is impossible to partition linguistic and encyclopedic knowledge into two distinct realms (see, e.g., Fillmore 1982, 1985, Langacker 1987, 1988, Lakoff 1987, Fauconnier 1994, Geeraerts 1994, Bergenholtz and Kaufmann 1996, Croft 2000). The quote from Fillmore and Atkins (1992) in Section 6.2.2 exemplifies this alternative view. Langacker (1987) illustrates the inseparability of lexical and encyclopedic information by discussing the relation of a profile to a base, both of which are relevant to the meaning of a word. The profile is the entity designated by the word whereas the base is the context necessary for the conceptualization of the profile. For example, the two words *radius* and *hypotenuse* are not synonymous, yet they both designate a line segment. According to Langacker, the two words can only be appropriately interpreted when they are understood as profiles against a base. In the case of *radius* (the profile), the concept of a circle (the base) is necessary to interpret the meaning of radius. Similarly, *hypotenuse* (as a profile) presupposes the concept of a right-angled triangle (as a base).

In trying to come to a decision about whether to employ the dividing or the unified approach towards encoding lexical and encyclopedic information about resultatives, we first need to take a closer look at the empirical facts. In Chapter 5, I have shown that those verbs capable of appearing with resultatives lexically determine the types of conventionally expected results (*wipe clean*, *stab to death*, etc.) (see also Wechsler 1997 and Washio 1997). Furthermore, I have argued that outside of resultative constructions, knowledge about conventionally expected results associated with the activities that are denoted by verbs is typically irrelevant and therefore not mentioned. In other words, this knowledge only becomes relevant once the speaker decides to point out a special perspective of the event's outcome. In these cases, the speaker employs the same verb that in turn imposes collocational restrictions on its postverbal constituents.

Clearly, the empirical facts are not as simple as they seemed to be at first sight. However, they help us to decide between the dividing and the unified approach in two important ways. First, the data suggest that it is possible to apply the dividing approach to the description of a verb's (lexical) meaning in order to describe its syntactic subcategorization frame and semantic selection restrictions outside of resultatives (*Kim stabbed Pat, Joe ran*). In this case, there does not seem to be a need for elaborate encyclopedic information about conventionally expected results. This means that the somewhat narrow lexical meaning available under the dividing approach might suffice to describe verb meaning in this context. Second, the data show that once the verb occurs in a resultative construction, it imposes collocational restrictions on its postverbal elements that are typically not present outside of resultatives (*Kim stabbed Pat to death, Joe ran his shoes threadbare*). This poses a problem for the dividing approach since it relegates information about conventionally expected results of the activity denoted by the verb to the encyclopedia. However, since under the dividing approach encyclopedic knowledge does not play any significant role in describing meaning, it appears difficult if not impossible to account for a verb's collocational restrictions solely in terms of limited lexical meaning under the dividing approach.

In order to overcome these problems, I propose a modified version of the unified approach. Following ideas by Bolinger (1965), Klinkenberg (1983), Eco (1984), and Pustejovsky (1995), I suggest that there are indeed different types of meaning that crucially depend on each other when it comes to interpreting a word. My proposal differs from others in that I maintain that it is not always possible to clearly identify whether a meaning component of a word belongs to the lexical or the encyclopedic realm.[12] Rather, each meaning component of a word is located somewhere along a

---

[12]Another point in which the account presented here is similar to Pustejovsky (1995) is that it differentiates in principle between different types of meaning components. However, my proposal crucially differs from generative accounts such as Pustejovsky (1995) in that it does not exploit encyclopedic knowledge (Pustejovsky's *qualia structure*) to generate new meanings. Instead, each individual sense of a verb is represented in terms of an event-frame associated with different meaning components. These meaning components are only employed to contribute to the interpretation of event-frames in different contexts, not to generate extended verbs senses on the basis of existing verb senses.

continuum ranging from lexical to encyclopedic meaning. I propose that the meaning of a word consists of (at least) two components, one tending towards the lexical, the other towards the encyclopedic pole of the continuum. Each of the (at least) two meaning components crucially depends on the other when it comes to determining the meaning of a word. Moreover, these two meaning components cannot always be neatly separated into distinct categories depending on whether or not they are required for the interpretation of a word (see Inchaurralde's (2000) notion of 'Lexicopedia').

My main point is that the relative degree to which each meaning component is needed for the interpretation of a word crucially depends on the context in which the word is used. For example, in the case of a verb occurring outside of the resultative construction almost no knowledge about conventionally expected results is required (e.g., *Joe ran*, *Kim stabbed Pat*). That is, the meaning component tending towards the lexical end of the continuum in combination with very little encyclopedic information seems to be all that is needed to interpret the meaning of the verb in this context. The situation is different when the same verb occurs in a resultative construction. In this case a great deal more 'encyclopedic' information is needed on top of the 'lexical' information in order to predict the conventionally expected result. As we have seen in Chapter 5, this (encyclopedic) information is necessary in order to determine the collocational restrictions reflecting the different types of conventionally expected results associated with a given verb.[13] The alternative advocated here is compatible with Inchaurralde's connectionist model of a 'lexicopedia' incorporating different types of semantic information.

> But meaning is a complex reality, with pointers to events and entities in the external world that build up complex associative networks of concepts with different degrees of concreteness or abstraction, and also of judgments and impressions. Our store of words is fundamentally based on experience and, as a result, it has a strong encyclopedic nature, with a strong distributed structure in terms of what individual items refer to.
>
> (Inchaurralde 2000: 109)

Returning to the main question of how to encode different types of word meaning, I follow conventional wisdom in that I assume that verbs are associated with distinct senses. Each sense of a verb is represented in terms of

[13]Note that in the case of results that are not conventionally expected (e.g., *Joe ran his shoes threadbare*), even more off-stage information has to be recruited. See Chapter 7.2 for details about fake objects.

an event-frame containing frame semantic information of two types.[14] The first type of information is what has traditionally been called lexical meaning and what has been identified above as the meaning component tending towards the lexical end of the meaning continuum. This information is conceptually relevant information about an event that is immediately linguistically relevant for the interpretation of the meaning denoted by an event-frame. Let us call this meaning component 'on-stage' information. It includes information about the prototypical event participants of an event-frame. For example, when the verb *run* is used in its prototypical sense under normal contextual background conditions, it is associated with a prototypical scene (even if somewhat less specified) that includes 'on-stage' information about (1) a runner, and (2) an energetic movement from point A to point B. Note my caution used in pointing out that this lexical semantic information only denotes *one set* of on-stage lexical semantic information associated with the verb *run*. That is, this type of conceptually relevant information may be relevant only for one particular sense of *run*. Since *run* is a highly polysemous word in English, it is associated with a broad variety of different senses (semantic concepts), each of which are represented by a discrete event-frame.[15]

In contrast to 'on-stage' information, 'off-stage' information is not immediately relevant for the present construal of an utterance because it is part of world knowledge.[16] That is, although one is subconsciously aware

---

[14]For the purpose of the present discussion it is not necessary to identify all of the senses associated with a given verb. Instead, we will point to a number of distinct conventionalized verb senses that give rise to different types of resultative interpretations and which in turn select for specific types of resultative phrases. Each of these distinct senses associated with a verb is described in terms of an event-frame which represents all of the on-stage and off-stage information of that particular sense of a verb. For an overview of tests that may be employed to distinguish different verb senses from each other, see Cruse (1986), and ten Hacken (1990). For a critical review of these tests see Geeraerts (1993), and Kilgarriff (1992, 1997).

[15]Take, for example., the different uses of *run* as in *run a business* or *run a show*. In these cases the relevant on-stage information does not include information about a conceptually relevant event participant that energetically moves from point A to point B (a prototypical runner), but rather about a person who operates a business or supervises a show.

[16]Off-stage information is what has traditionally been called encyclopedic knowledge and what has been identified above as the meaning component tending towards the encyclopedic end of the meaning continuum. In Section 5.2 we referred to this type of information as 'periphery meaning.' Off-stage information as it is used here is similar to the information contained in Pustejovsky's (1995) *qualia structure* (which he uses for type coercion) in that it can be recruited to give information about a word's usage in specific contexts (e.g., resultative vs. non-resultative). It is different from Pustejovsky's *qualia structure* in that it is relevant for determining the collocational restrictions (semantically represented as conventionally expected results) exhibited by the main verb. This off-stage information serves as the basis for lexical licensing of post-verbal constituents in resultatives.

of the off-stage information associated with a word when encountering it in discourse it does not bear mention because it is by default associated with the word by the rest of the speech community (see Johnson-Laird (1983: 370-1), (1988: 245)). In the case of the prototypical sense of *run*, this includes information such as: running necessitates the use of legs and feet, westerners typically wear shoes to run, and energy is expended when running. Although this type of information about the usage conditions of words and the types of event relations it describes is typically conceptually irrelevant, one nevertheless has passive or off-stage knowledge of it. This information is connected with the on-stage information related to a specific sense of a lexical item and is thus stored in connection with the conceptually relevant 'on-stage' information in memory.[17] The interplay between on-stage and off-stage information is best characterized by Allan's characterization of the interplay between what has traditionally been called 'lexicon' and 'encyclopedia':

> The lexicon entry is one access point into the isomorphic set of encyclopedia entries, all of which are activated by recognition of the listeme. If the encyclopedia is a data-base, then the lexicon forms an integral component of the encyclopedia. (Allan 1995: 294)

To summarize, the intertwined collection of on-stage and off-stage information about a specific sense of a verb is called an event-frame. With this sketch of how on-stage and off-stage information is organized in the event representation of a verb, let us now turn to the content of event-frames.

6.2.3.2 Event Participants

The first type of information contained in an event-frame is concerned with the number and semantic types of event participants. In order to capture the necessary information for resultatives we will focus on the roles of the two most salient event participants, namely agents and patients. The minimal lexical semantic information contained in one-participant event-frames representing the prototypical senses of verbs like *sing*, *run*, or *sneeze* includes

---

[17]The proposal that meanings of words are stored in combination with their meanings in context has been recently confirmed by a number of psycholinguistic studies, most notably Harris (1997), Klein (2000), and Klein and Murphy (2001). Based on a study of common word combinations and multi-word idioms, Harris (1997) shows that 'many polysemous words may be stored with both their contexts and the unique meaning for that context. This means that on hearing an expression like *cut down*, listeners don't have to compute a meaning based on the intersection of a set of meanings for *cut* and the set of meanings for *down*. Instead, the conventional meaning for *cut down*, **reduce**, is immediately available.'

information about the agent of a singing, running, or sneezing event, cf. (6.8). Two-participant event-frames representing senses of verbs like *break*, *shoot*, or *paint* contain information about both the agent and the patient of a breaking, shooting, or painting event, cf. (6.9). Compare the following 'minimal' lexical semantic information that specifies information for only one sense (to be represented by a single event frame) of the verb, the prototypical sense.

(6.8) sing: AGENT
run: AGENT
sneeze: AGENT

(6.9) break: AGENT, PATIENT
shoot: AGENT, PATIENT
paint: AGENT, PATIENT

If nothing more were said about the minimal lexical semantic information specified for these event-frames, it would not be possible to distinguish one verb from the other when encountering the 'semantic' information AGENT or PATIENT in a linguistic description (see my critique of Goldberg (1995) in Chapter 4). In order to avoid the problem of employing notions like agent and patient as pure diacritics without any meaning for our analysis of resultative constructions, it would be helpful to have a collection of meaning representations for each of the respective event participants of the verbs in (6.8) and (6.9). By meaning representations I mean a collection of semantic information that captures all of the conceptually relevant information about what a runner is (as opposed to a walker or a sneezer) or what a painter is (as opposed to a colorer, a breaker, or a shooter). Taking the prototypical sense of runner as an example, this would include information such as: running necessitates the use of legs and feet, westerners typically wear shoes to run, running can be tiresome, and running involves rapid and energetic movement from point A to point B.

However, we do not yet have such powerful representational means available which would allow us to cover all of the necessary information about what a 'runner' is. The present account differs from other accounts in that it always employs and defines the terms agent and patient in relation to each other for each individual sense (event-frame) associated with a given verb. Whereas analyses such as Pustejovsky (1995) and Rappaport Hovav and Levin (1998, 2001) aim at deriving verb meanings in terms of one lexical entry (with basic specifications for agents and patients) per verb in combination with some mechanism, thereby deriving other meanings associated with the same verb, the splitting approach proposed here views each conventionalized sense as a basic sense.[18] This view makes it possible to define agents and patients in relation to each other (and in relation to other possible event participants) for each individual event-frame. That is, the semantic properties of a prototypical breaking event's patient are different from those of a patient of a different event-frame associated with *break*, such as *break X off*, etc. This allows us to make the relevant distinctions between different types of agents and patients more precise than in other accounts of resultatives. The following simplified examples illustrate how information of an event-frame's prototypical event participants is encoded in a simplified event-frame. The box represents the event-frame including the on-stage event-participants. The semantic specifications for the event participants are given (in a somewhat rough version) to the right of the event-frames.

(6.10) Simplified event-frame representation of the prototypical sense of *run*

Ag	Ag: animate object moving legs quickly on a surface

(6.11) Simplified event-frame representation of the prototypical sense of *paint*

Ag	Ag: object covering a surface with paint
Pt	Pt: surface or object exhibiting a surface

The two examples illustrate the basic architecture of event-frames. In this case, they only contain on-stage information about their respective proto-

[18] One of the main problems in lexical semantics is to determine how different senses of a word are related to each other. The level of lumping and splitting (Evens 1988), i.e. where the cut-off point is determined between fine-grained and coarse-grained sense distinctions, is strongly influenced by the goals of an analysis. The advantage of a splitting approach is that it results in a great number of detailed sense descriptions. However, it is very labor intensive to arrive at such a detailed inventory, and it may take up a lot of space (in the view of people promoting 'optimal coding' this is a disadvantage). The advantage of a lumping approach is that it takes up less space and therefore adheres to the premise of 'optimal coding' (Jackendoff 1997: 124). A disadvantage of the lumping approach is that it may miss a number of distinct senses that are relevant for the description of a word (see my critique of Rappaport Hovav and Levin (1998, 2001) in Chapter 3). See Kilgarriff (1992) and Baker and Ruppenhofer (2003) for more details.

typical event-participants, i.e., agents and patients. Note that each prototypical event participant is identified by a very coarse semantic description to the right of the event-frame.[19] The semantic descriptions of event-participants capture the conceptual on-stage information necessary to distinguish between different types of objects and relations and thereby allow the differentiation of different verb senses from one another. We now turn to different types of off-stage information associated with event-frames.

6.2.3.3 Temporal, Spatial, and Force-Dynamic Relations

In order to describe the distribution of resultatives it is necessary to incorporate information about the different types of temporal sequences that can be denoted by an event frame as well as the force-dynamic relations that hold between event-participants over the course of an event. This off-stage information is crucial in determining which verbs can be employed to present a specific perspective of the event to which they refer and the way in which this viewpoint may be perspectivized by using a resultative phrase. Compare the following pairs of sentences containing the air emission verbs *blow* and *exhale*.

(6.12) a. Monica blew the air into his face.
b. Joe exhaled the air into her face.

(6.13) a. Monica blew the napkin off the table.
b. *Joe exhaled the napkin off the table.

The examples show that although *blow* and *exhale* may sometimes be employed to describe roughly similar caused-motion events, this is not always the case. The difference in acceptability is caused by a dissimilarity in the underlying semantics of the respective verbs. Whereas *blow* can be used to describe situations in which the movement of the postverbal NP originates either inside the body (typically the lungs) or outside of the body (the table), the caused-motion usage of *exhale* is conventionally associated with a situation in which the object that is being moved by air emission originates inside the body. This means that without any context that may give rise to an acceptable interpretation, (6.13b) is ruled out since under normal condi-

[19]The relevant point is that the event-participants have to be construed as matching these requirements, i.e., context plays a crucial role, as we will see in Section 7.2.2. The broad semantic descriptions do typically not cover metaphor and metonymy. In Chapter 7, we briefly address the question of how metaphors may be licensed on the basis of the basic semantic specifications of event-frames in combination with extensional mechanisms that allow extensions of an event-frame, given the proper contextual background conditions.

tions one does not have napkins in one's lungs or mouth. In order to be able to capture the distribution of sentence pairs such as in (6.12) and (6.13) and to account for the full distribution of resultatives in Chapter 7, it is necessary to encode temporal information about different sequences of complex events such as caused-motion and resultative constructions. In this connection, it is also important to encode information about the force-dynamic relations that hold between the individual event-participants of a complex event-frame over the period of an event. To this end, I adapt Talmy's (1988) theory of force dynamics which proposes that events can be viewed as interactions of two opposed force entities, namely an agonist (which I will call here patient, cf. *the napkin* in (6.13)) and an antagonist (which I will call here agent, cf. *Monica* and *Joe* in (6.12)). While the patient has an inherent tendency toward either action or rest, the agent works to oppose this tendency. In a prototypical causation event, the agent is stronger than the patient, meaning that the latter will either move or rest as a result of the interaction. The following event-frames are extensions of the simple event-frames introduced above. In addition to containing information about event-participants, they include temporal information (cf. the different time slots labeled SOURCE, PATH, and GOAL) and force-dynamic information (the arrows). We first look at simplified versions of the event-frames for caused-motion *blow* and prototypical *paint* before turning to the event-frame of caused-motion *exhale*.

(6.14) Simplified event-based frame semantic representation of caused-motion *blow*

Ag: entity that makes air move
Pt: object that may be moved by air stream emitted by Ag

SOURCE	Path	Path	Path	GOAL
↓ Ag ⇣	Ag	Ag	Ag	Ag
Pt	Pt	Pt ⇣	Pt	Pt

(6.15) Simplified event-based frame semantic representation of prototypical *paint*

Ag: entity applying paint to a surface
Pt: surface or object that exhibits a surface

SOURCE	Path	Path	Path	GOAL
Ag	Ag	Ag	Ag	Ag
↓	↓	↓	↓	
Pt	Pt	Pt	Pt	Pt

The event-based frame semantic representations of the caused-motion sense of *blow* and the prototypical sense of *paint* contain two event participants, namely an agent and a patient. The representations in (6.14) and (6.15) differ from those in (6.10) and (6.11) in that they have been expanded in order to cover different time intervals of an event. They show that events can be divided into their beginning (the SOURCE), their end result (the GOAL), and several time intervals in between (the PATH), as indicated by the top line representing the time/space axis along which events can be classified.[20] The source is that point in time at which an event begins. For example, in the case of painting, it includes the point at which an agent starts applying paint to a surface and in the case of blowing it includes the time span during which air is emitted. The path time slot denotes all the event's temporal subintervals that have to be fulfilled before the end result state (denoted by the event-frame) is reached. For example, in the case of painting, the path includes the continuous application of paint to a surface. The GOAL time slot denotes the event's end result state after no more activities take place. Again using our example of painting, the GOAL time slot is after the agent has stopped applying paint to the surface (the patient). At each of these time intervals, different relations hold between the respective event participants. For example, in the case of painting the surface is not covered with the paint that is applied by the agent at the beginning of the painting event. During the painting event, the surface subsequently gets covered more and more with paint, until it is completely covered. The end result state after all painting has ceased is such that the surface is completely covered with paint (i.e., it has a color).[21]

[20]The path of an event denotes all of the activities and relations between event participants that take place between the beginning of an event and the final result state of an event (i.e., its GOAL). The beginning of an event, its SOURCE is t_o. The end state of an event in which event participants have changed their states and/or locations is the GOAL of the event, or t_r. The intervening time intervals $t_1 - t_{r-1}$ constitute the path of an event.

[21]Note that this type of event-semantic representation also allows for a representation of information about the states of the individual event participants over the course of an event. That

Let us now turn to the force-dynamic relations indicated by the arrow notations in (6.14) and (6.15). The arrow signals the energy emitted by the agent during an activity. In prototypical one-participant event-frames (running, singing, etc.), the energy is simply emitted without any specific direction or intention with respect to another event participant. In the case of two-participant event-frames, however, the energy emitted by the agent is directed towards a prototypical patient in order to affect this patient in such a way that it will undergo a change of state towards the prototypical end result state of the event. In the case of a prototypical painting event, the energy emitted by the agent is necessary in order to apply paint with a brush to the surface. In this case, energy (represented by arrows going from the agent to the patient) is emitted from the source of the event throughout the entire path of the event. At the end of the path when no more energy is emitted, the event is terminated.

In the case of the caused-motion frame of *blow*, however, things are different because the agent emits energy only once (indicated by the arrows) in the form of an air stream at the event's source. This event-frame covers two different conceptualization options. First, the patient is immediately affected by the air stream as in *Monica blew the air into his face*. In this case, the left hand arrow indicates that *the air* (the patient) that is moved due to the agent's activity is affected at the same point in time at which Monica blows (since the air is in her body).

The second option described by the caused-motion frame of *blow* covers cases in which the patient is not immediately affected at the same point

---

is, an event-frame of a verb may be employed to convey a certain perspective of an event by only offering a small amount of on-stage information. At the same time, however, a great deal of off-stage information is encoded in the message that is decodable due to the usage conventions of the speech community. Compare, e.g., the amount of off-stage information with respect to the patient participants (given in parentheses) with the on-stage information conveyed by the verb *wipe* in the following sentences that describe a wiping event from its beginning to its end.

(i) Keith began to wipe the table. (There was a certain amount of unwanted substances.)

(ii) Keith was wiping the table. (The unwanted substances were in the process of being removed.)

(iii) Keith was halfway done with wiping the table. (The unwanted substances were removed halfway.)

(iv) Keith wiped the crumbs off the table. (A specific set of unwanted substances, namely the crumbs, have been successfully removed.)

(v) Keith was almost done with wiping the table. (Most of the unwanted substances have been removed.)

(vi) Keith wiped the table clean. (All of the unwanted substances have been successfully removed.)

in time at which the energy is emitted by the agent, such as in *Joe blew the napkin off the table*. This option is indicated by the dotted arrow to the right of the agent in (6.14) above. In this case, although the agent emits the air stream at the beginning (the source) of the event, the patient argument is not affected until the air stream covers the distance between the agent and the patient. The temporal split that exists between the emission of air by the agent and its effect on the patient is indicated by the two dotted arrows in (6.14) above. The first dotted arrow to the right of the agent in the source slot (it is shorter than the straight arrow to the left which signals that the patient gets immediately affected) signals that there is only air emission without any immediate effect on any patient. The second dotted arrow in the middle path slot indicates that some time after the agent's air emission (at the beginning of the event) the air actually affects the patient (note that the arrow points into the direction of the patient). As a result the patient is moved by the air and ends up in a new location. Our short discussion of the event-frame of caused-motion *blow* has shown that it is conventionally associated with two different types of interpretations. Compare this state of affairs with the simplified event-frame of the caused-motion sense of *exhale*.

(6.16) Simplified event-based frame semantic representation of caused-motion *exhale*

Ag: entity breathing
Pt: object (or gas) originating inside the body of the agent that is moved by air stream emitted by Ag

SOURCE	Path	Path	Path	GOAL
↓ Ag	Ag	Ag	Ag	Ag
Pt	Pt	Pt	Pt	Pt

The event-frame of caused-motion *exhale* is similar to that of caused-motion *blow* in that an agent emits air which immediately causes a patient to be moved (cf. the arrow leading from the 'Ag' to the 'Pt' in the source slot of (6.16)).[22] However, it differs from that of caused-motion *blow* in that it can only denote one type of caused-motion event, namely, cases in which the object to be moved originates from within the body of the agent. This is indicated by the force-dynamic information contained in (6.16) which lacks a second option of event-realization in the same way as the frame of *blow* in

[22] In this connection, note that the semantic event participant specifications are different for the two event-frames.

(6.14) above (cf. the missing dotted arrow to the right of 'Ag' in (6.16)). In other words, although the caused-motion event-frames of *blow* and *exhale* share certain conventionalized usage patterns (with similar inferences), there is no complete overlap between them.

So far, we have seen that there are subtle semantic differences between event-frames of verbs that are closely related in meaning such as those observed for *blow* and *exhale* in (6.12) and (6.13). Since these differences are related to force-dynamic and temporal relations that hold between prototypical event participants of the respective events, this information must be encoded in the semantic descriptions of event frames. In Section 7.3 we will see that the temporal and force-dynamic relations encoded in event-frames is crucial for the licensing of nonconventionalized resultatives. Until then, we will focus primarily on information contained in the goal slot of event-frames which is necessary for the licensing of resultative phrases and non-subcategorized postverbal NPs as we will see in the next section.

6.2.3.4 Off-Stage Knowledge, World Knowledge and Prototypical Outcomes of Events

In addition to the off-stage information discussed in the last section, event-frames are associated with other types of off-stage information about the respective contexts and circumstances of the individual events they denote. The reason for associating more information with an event-frame is due to the fact that speakers associate a great deal of information with a word that although not immediately linguistically relevant is conceptually necessary in order to understand the meaning of that word (and its related concepts and backgrounds). This is essentially as Fillmore (1968) puts it in his discussion of case roles:

> The case notions comprise a set of universal, presumably innate, concepts which identify certain types of judgments human beings are capable of making about the events that are going on around them, judgments about such matters as who did it, who it happened to, and what got changed.
> (Fillmore 1968: 24)[23]

For example, general world knowledge about what it means to run, paint, etc., is off-stage information which is typically not immediately linguistically relevant in resultative constructions (cf. *She ran home*/ *She painted the house*). The 'W' in the following simplified event-frame of *run* and *paint*

[23]Similar proposals have been put forward by Lakoff (1987) in terms of idealized cognitive models and Langacker's (1991) conceptual archetypes.

represents all of the general world knowledge a speaker associates with running and painting events. This knowledge represented by 'W' can be made linguistically relevant under certain circumstances (similar to Pustejovsky's (1995) *qualia structure*). The parentheses around the 'W' indicate that world knowledge may optionally be realized at the linguistic level. While every verb is associated with world knowledge that is linguistically not immediately relevant, verbs differ with respect to whether they allow recruitment of world knowledge in order to convey a certain perspective of an event, as we will see in Chapter 7 in our discussion of fake objects. Thus, when verbs optionally allow recruitment of world knowledge, their respective event-frames contain '(W)'. Verbs that do not allow for this option are not associated with event-frames containing this feature.[24] Compare the following simplified event-frames of *run* and *paint*.[25]

(6.17) Simplified event-frame of the prototypical sense of *run* including world knowledge 'W'

GOAL
Ag (W)

(6.18) Simplified event-frame of the prototypical sense of *paint* including world knowledge 'W'

GOAL
Ag (W) Pt

[24]This does not mean that there is no world knowledge associated with these types of verbs. What it does mean, however, is that these verbs simply do not allow overt linguistic realization of world knowledge and/or conceptually relevant information. In other words, event-frames are used to relate linguistic information about events in the real world. While some event-frames allow the speaker to convey a specific perspective of an event by linguistically realizing conceptual information, other verbs do not allow for this option. This means that event-frames function as filters that determine what types of conceptual information may be realized linguistically.

[25]Recall that we are only dealing with the GOAL slot at this point. The full event-frame semantic representation including other time/space slots of an event will be dealt with again in our discussion of non-conventionalized resultatives in Section 7.3.

In Chapter 7 we will see how general world knowledge associated with *run* and *paint* is recruited and subsequently made linguistically relevant in order to license non-prototypical event-participants such as those in (6.19b)-(6.19e) and (6.20b)-(6.20c).[26]

(6.19) a. Jim ran.
b. Jim ran himself exhausted.
c. Jim ran his feet sore.
d. Jim ran his shoes threadbare.
e. Jim ran the pavement thin.

(6.20) a. Carol painted the house.
b. Carol painted herself to exhaustion.
c. Carol painted the brush to pieces.

Besides general world knowledge 'W' associated with an event-frame, each event-frame includes information about the prototypical end result states or locations for each of its prototypical and non-prototypical event-participants. To this end, we have seen in Section 5.3 that the semantic and syntactic types of resultative phrases that may occur with certain meanings of verbs are very limited in their distribution. This observation has led us to the conclusion that they are conventionalized collocational patterns. A comparison between verbs closely related in meaning has shown that they frequently cannot be substituted for each other. The same is true for resultatives closely related in meaning. This means that each event-frame lexically subcategorizes for the types of end-result states that its event-participants end up in as a result of the prototypical event denoted by that frame.

In the case of the event-frame representing the prototypical sense of *wipe*, e.g., it must include world knowledge about the fact that the prototypical end result state of wiping is getting a surface clean (see Wechsler's (1997) notion of conventionally expected result). As a consequence, the event-frame representation of prototypical *wipe* lexically requires a resultative phrase belonging to a specific semantic class of expressions denoting cleanliness.[27] A corpus search in the BNC for the occurrences of the verb

[26]The postverbal event-participants in (6.20b)-(6.20c) are non-prototypical event-participants because it is not the prototypical goal of painting to affect the instrument (*the brush*) or the agent (*Carol*) during a painting event, but rather to change the state of the patient argument (*the house*). The postverbal NPs in (6.19b)-(6.19d) are non-prototypical event-participants because there are usually no other event participants involved in running besides the agent.

[27]The specification of the prototypical end result state in a verb's lexical entry is only default information, i.e., given the proper contextual background information, this default information may be overridden. Compare, e.g., *Keith wiped the table clean* vs. *Keith wiped the table moist.* In the former case, the resultative phrase belongs to the semantic class of prototypical result

wipe in resultative patterns supports this proposal. *Wipe* occurs 2295 times in the BNC; out of those 2295 times it is used 315 times in a resultative sense. In these 315 resultative uses, *wipe* occurs 164 times with *out* to yield the sense 'to eliminate,' 145 times with other resultative phrases to yield the 'removal of an undesired object' sense, and 6 times in other resultative uses.[28] In the 145 times *wipe* is used in the 'removal of an undesired object' sense, it occurs 53 times with the following types of adjectival phrases.[29]

(6.21) Total distribution of adjectives in the resultative sense of *wipe* denoting the 'removing of an undesired object sense.'[30]

Adjective	No. of occurrences
clean	41
dry	6
free	3
clear	2
moist	1

The table shows that except for one case, the adjectives occurring with *wipe* in its prototypical 'removal of an unwanted substance' sense form a coherent semantic class denoting a state of cleanliness. This clearly illustrates that a verb like *wipe* exhibits collocational restrictions that determine the semantic type of resultative phrase that can occur with *wipe* in this particular event-frame. Interestingly, the most prototypical member of this semantic class, *clean*, also occurs with other types of verbs which exhibit the same 'removal of an unwanted substance' sense. That is, *clean* occurs 6092 times in the BNC but is only used resultatively 109 times. The distribution among verbs looks as follows.

states of *wipe*, whereas in the latter this is not the case. As we will see in Chapter 7, default information may be overridden only under a proper set of contextual background information.

[28]For a complete listing of the distribution of *wipe* in resultative patterns in the BNC, see Appendix B.3.

[29]The fact that the respective adjectival phrases serve the same function as the particles *away*, *off*, *from*, and *up* in the 'removal of an unwanted object sense' of *wipe* indicates that they might be employed by the speaker to be more specific with respect to the end result state that she conveys information about. That is, comparing the distribution of verb-particle combinations, it becomes obvious that out of the 120 times *wipe* is used in the 'removal' sense, it is only used 37 times to perspectivize the surface, but 83 times to perspectivize the undesired objects that are removed.

[30]See Appendix B.3 for the full sentences.

(6.22) Total distribution of *clean* in resultative usages in the BNC[31]

Verb	No. of occur.
wipe	41
wash	11
sweep	10
scrub	9
rub, make, lick	6
scrape	5
rinse, suck	3
scour, pare	2
whip, wag, swab, polish, pick	1

The corpus data in (6.21) and (6.22) support the proposal made above that verbs like *wipe* lexically subcategorize for a specific semantic type of resultative phrase for their prototypical patient participants (i.e., a surface). On this view, then, the prototypical sense of *wipe* (i.e., its event-frame) lexically determines what types of resultatives may denote the outcome of a prototypical patient of a wiping event.

A similar state of affairs holds for the class of verbs which require *to death* as their resultative phrase, as opposed to those which prefer *dead* as their resultative phrase (see our discussion in Section 5.3). There we have seen that verbs show strong preferences with respect to whether they take *dead* or *to death* as their resultative phrases. This suggests that first, speakers must have off-stage knowledge about what types of resultative phrases may occur with a given verb and second, this information needs to be included in the event-frames associated with verbs.

In this connection, note that a specific sense of *drive*, the 'drive-crazy' sense of *drive*, also shows very clear semantic selection restrictions with respect to the type of resultative phrases that may follow the postverbal NP. This suggests that 'drive-crazy' lexically subcategorizes for a particular semantic class of resultative predicates which denote a (typically) negative change in the mental state of the patient.

---

[31] See Appendix A.5 for the full sentences.

(6.23) Total distribution of resultative phrases of the 'drive-crazy' sense of *drive* in the BNC[32]

Resultative Phrase	No. of occur.
mad / to madness	108 / 5
crazy	70
to distraction	27
insane	23
wild	22
nuts	18
up the wall	13
to suicide	9
to despair	8
to desperation	7
batty	4
dotty	4
crackers	4
into a frenzy	3
over the edge	3
to insanity	1

Whereas many verbs such as *wipe*, *kill*, and *drive* optionally subcategorize for a specific semantic type of resultative phrase, other types of verbs require a resultative phrase in order to form an acceptable sentence. The prototypical example is the lexically causative verb *make* in the following sentences.

(6.24) a. *It is the fat in your diet that makes you.
b. It is the fat in your diet that makes you fat. (BNC)

(6.25) a. *Super-sexy models make us.
b. Super-sexy models make us ill. (BNC)

The examples illustrate that *make* requires a resultative phrase in order to yield an acceptable sentence. This suggests that *make* lexically subcategorizes for specific semantic types of adjectives to denote the outcome of an event. It comes as no surprise, then, that the adjectives in (6.24)-(6.25) above occur almost exclusively as resultative phrases with *make* when they are used to denote the result state of an event participant. The following tables extracted from data from the BNC list the total number of occur-

[32]The length of resultative phrases occurring with this sense of *drive* has been limited to three words. See Appendix B.1 for the full sentences.

rences of the adjectives in their resultative use and the types of verbs they occur with in resultative constructions.

(6.26) Distribution of *fat* in the BNC according to verbs. Total number of occurrences: 4137 times. Occurrences in resultative constructions: 5 times.[33]

Verb	No. of occur.
make	5

(6.27) Distribution of *ill* in the BNC according to verbs. Total number of occurrences: 4808 times. Number of occurrences in resultative constructions: 66.[34]

Verb	No. of occur.
make	66

The data in (6.26)-(6.27) illustrate that *make* lexically subcategorizes for specific types of resultative phrases and that those resultative phrases occur to a large degree with *make*.[35] This indicates that the combinations are collocations that have been conventionalized through continuous use and thus come as 'pre-arranged' combinations that are marked as such in the lexicon (comparable to Erman and Warren's (2000) notion of 'prefabs', Hunston and Francis' (2000: 215) notion of 'pattern strings', or Biber et al.'s (1999: 993) notion of 'lexical bundles)). The distribution of *make* with its obligatory resultative phrase differs from verb-particle collocations that do not allow further specification by any other resultative phrases. Compare the following, by now familiar, sentences which show that conventionalized collocations denoting a specific semantic concept cannot be broken up without losing their meanings.[36]

[33]See Appendix A.13 for the corpus examples.

[34]See Appendix A.17 for the corpus examples.

[35]For other resultative collocational usages of *make* in the BNC, see Appendix A.12, A. 29, and A.31 for occurrences with *famous, safe*, and *sick*. The high degree of matching indicates that *make* is grammaticalized with those adjectives and forms regular lexicalized collocations.

[36]Most verb-particle combinations are conventionalized collocations associated with specific semantic concepts and interpretations which means that they have to be individually listed in the lexicon and cannot be derived compositionally by taking the bare verb form and then generatively producing new verb meanings by adding different types of particles. The following data containing verbs that are closely related in meaning illustrate that such a generative process is problematic.

(i) They beat each other up. / *They hit each other up.

(ii) The terrorists wiped the city out. / *The terrorists swept the city out.

(iii) They blew the candle out. / *They exhaled the candle out.

(6.28) a. *Rachel wiped the dust off clean.
b. *Dave swept the crumbs away shiny.
c. *They beat each other up bloody.
d. *The terrorists wiped the city out off the map.
e. *They blew the candle out extinguished.
f. *It broke me up down when I learned about Bernadette's baby.
g. *Jim hammered the dent out flat.

Thus far we have compared three different levels of collocational restrictions between verbs and their resultative phrases. The first type of verb-resultative phrase combination is the most restricted. It consists of conventionalized collocations denoting specific semantic concepts, such as *wipe X out* or *break X up*. These types of event-frames do not allow any further semantic or syntactic specification that would result in a different result interpretation of the postverbal NP and are therefore marked for this feature in the lexicon. In other words, although there is a complete restriction on the choice of resultative phrases, there is some flexibility when it comes to the choice of the postverbal NP.

The second type differs from the first in that it exhibits more freedom with respect to the choice of resultative phrases. It is exemplified by *make* which lexically requires a specific semantic type of resultative (adjectival) phrase. Since the *make*-resultative phrase combination is almost unique to the resultative uses of the respective adjectives I propose to treat these as collocations in the lexicon.

The third type differs from the other two in that it allows more freedom with respect to the choice of postverbal NPs and resultative phrases. The data on verbs such as *wipe*, *run*, and *paint* suggest that their event frames have access to off-stage information about conventionally expected results. This means that whenever these verbs are employed to perspectivize a specific outcome of an event participant, they lexically subcategorize for the semantic type of resultative phrase denoting the result state of their prototypical event participants. These verbs differ from the other two classes of verbs in that the realization of their resultative phrases is optional. They are also less restricted because by recruiting different types of off-stage information for the licensing of postverbal elements, it is possible to describe a broader range of situations (compare the range of fake objects discussed in Chapter 1).

(iv) It broke me up. / *It shattered me up.

(v) Jim hammered the dent out. / ??Jim pounded the dent out.

The comparison between the different levels of collocational restrictions holding between verbs and their postverbal constituents in resultative constructions reveals another interesting property of resultatives. That is, there is a link between conventionally expected result states and collocational restrictions. The degree to which an event-frame allows off-stage information to be recruited for the resultative influences the degree of collocational restrictions the verb imposes on its postverbal elements. For example, in restricted cases such as *wipe X out,* the conventionally expected result state is already known since it is encoded by *out* in combination with *wipe.* In this case the resultative pattern is extremely restricted and allows very little off-stage information to be recruited because there is no need for it. On the other end of the spectrum there are event-frames encoding the prototypical usages of verbs such as *wipe* or *paint*. In order to determine the resultative phrase, the event-frame has to allow access to off-stage information. In cases in which non-prototypical event participants (fake objects) occur with this event frame, even more off-stage information is needed about what types of participants and their possible result states are involved in the prototypical event denoted by the verb. In other words, in cases in which resultative constructions are employed to express results that are not conventionally expected, more off-stage information is required. The important point here is that there is a direct correlation between the degree to which off-stage information is involved in determining postverbal constituents in resultatives and the degree of collocational restrictions that the verb imposes on these constituents.

In order to be able to describe which senses of a verb may occur with a specific semantic and/or syntactic type of resultative phrase, we must therefore encode off-stage information used to determine collocational restrictions in the event-frames representing the individual senses of verbs. The following event-frames exhibit the same architecture as the reduced (i.e., only containing the GOAL slot) event-frames discussed in (6.17) and (6.18). They are extended by a diacritic 'p' (for property or location) representing the semantic and/or syntactic specifications for the resultative phrase denoting the end result state of each event participant.[37]

[37]For a list of 51 phrases and the types of verbs they are found with when used resultatively in the BNC, see Appendix A.

(6.29) Simplified event-frame of the prototypical sense of *run*

GOAL
Ag (p1) (W p2)

Ag: animate object moving legs quickly
p1: directional PP

The event-frame for prototypical *run* is specified for its prototypical event-participant, the agent 'Ag.' The 'p1' notation in parentheses following the 'Ag' notation denotes the prototypical end result state of a runner at the end of her running event, in this case a directional PP. The parentheses around 'p1' indicate that the syntactic realization of the phrase denoting the prototypical end result state of the agent is optional.

The line below 'Ag' and '(p1)' in (6.29) contains information about the fact that *run* optionally allows recruitment of off-stage non-prototypical event-participants from world knowledge that is associated with the event-frame of prototypical *run*. The 'W' stands for world knowledge, whereas 'p2' denotes the end result state of the recruited non-prototypical event participant from world knowledge. The parentheses surrounding both 'W' and 'p2' indicate that whenever a non-prototypical event-participant is recruited from world knowledge, there has to be some information about the end result state of that event-participant. At this point, the information accessed by 'W' and 'p2' is not relevant.[38] We will return to a more detailed discussion of these features in Section 7.2.2 (fake objects). The following linking rules regulate the linking from the event-frame of prototypical *run* to the syntactic level for the two types of sentences in (6.31):

(6.30) Linking Rules
(1) Prototypical agents are mapped as NPs to the subject position.
(2) Prototypical patients are mapped as NPs to the postverbal position.
(3) Resultative phrases specifying the prototypical end result state of the prototypical agent are linked to immediate post-verbal position.
(4) Resultative phrases specifying the prototypical end result state of the patient are linked to immediate post-patient position.

[38] In our discussion of fake objects in Section 7.2.2, we will see that non-subcategorized objects as well as their resultative phrases are licensed by world knowledge.

(6.31) Linking from the prototypical event-frame of *run* to syntax

a) Chris ran.
Su V
NP V

b) Chris ran home.
Su V ResP
NP V XP

Due to the licensing rules in (6.30), the prototypical agent of *run* is linked to subject position in both (6.31a) and (6.31b). However, the optional prototypical resultative phrase is realized in (6.31b) but not in (6.31a). Let us now turn to the representation of world knowledge and prototypical end result states with two event-participant frames such as prototypical *paint*.

(6.32) Simplified event-frame of the prototypical sense of *paint* including world knowledge 'W'

GOAL
Ag (W p2) Pt (p3)

Ag: object covering a surface with paint
Pt: surface or object exhibiting a surface
p3: AP or NP denoting a color or a property associated with the prototypical intended end result of applying paint to a surface

Besides being specified for a patient participant, the architecture of (6.32) differs from the event-frame in (6.31) in two more respects. First, it does not have any optional prototypical end result specification 'p1' for the agent of the painting event because the goal of prototypical painting events is not to change the state of the agent but that of the patient.[39] Second, it has an optional end result specification 'p3' that denotes the end result state of the prototypical patient of a painting event. The linking to syntax follows the linking rules in (6.30) and looks as follows.

[39]This captures the fact that sentences such as **Claire painted red* or **Claire painted to campus* are ruled out.

(6.33) Linking to syntax from the event-frame of prototypical *paint*

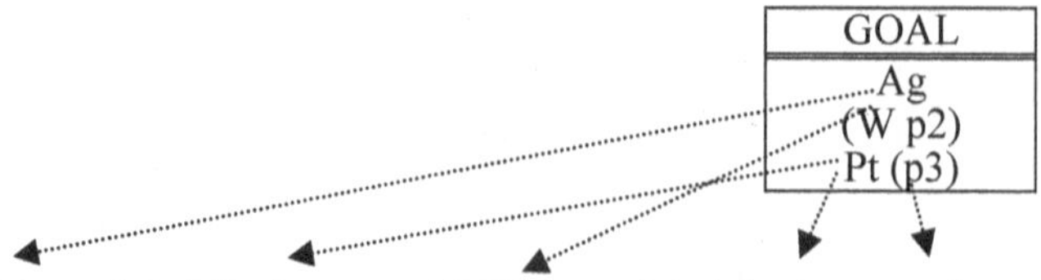

a) Claire painted the house.			b) Claire painted the house red.			
Su	V	DO	Su	V	DO	ResP
NP	V	NP	NP	V	NP	XP

In this section we discussed the basic architecture of one-participant and two-participant event-frames with their relevant on-stage and off-stage information and the way in which this frame-semantic information is linked to the syntactic level. We now turn to the question of how event-frames belonging to the same verb or verbs of the same verb class are related to each other.

6.3 Different Event-Frames, Different Result States

Mention of verb classes and different senses of verbs brings us to the problem of polysemy, or 'of the "multiplicity of meanings" of words.' (Ravin and Laecock 2000: 1).[40] According to Ravin and Laecock (2000: 6-7), there are at least three major approaches to polysemy: the classical approach, the prototypical approach, and the relational approach. While the three major approaches differ with respect to how polysemous relations should be classified, analyzed, and predicted, they all agree on the fact that different meanings of a word are somehow related to each other (for an overview, see Kilgarriff (1992, 1997), Lehrer (1992), Pustejovsky (1995), Ravin and Laecock (2000)). Note, however, that our analysis of resultatives is not primarily concerned with how different senses of words are related to each other. Instead, I concentrate on identifying a number of semantically distinct event-frames that are associated with a verb and which show distinct subcategorization patterns with respect to the kinds of resultatives they subcategorize for.

[40]Polysemy is often distinguished from homonymy. The former 'designates a situation in which a single word has a set of related meanings.' (Goddard 1998: 19). The latter 'designates a situation in which different words (homonyms) happen accidentally to have the same form; as for instance, $bank_1$ (as in *She robbed the bank*) and $bank_2$ (as in *We walked along the bank*).' (Goddard 1998: 18)

Finally, I am not immediately concerned here with either the regularity of the semantic relationships between multiple senses of a word or the productivity of the principles and rules for producing polysemy.[41] The production and interpretation of novel verb uses will be discussed in Section 7.3. In the remainder of this chapter, we are thus primarily concerned with identifying a number of different conventionalized senses of verbs that can be represented in terms of event-frames which differ in the types of resultatives they license because they denote different semantic concepts.

6.3.1 One Verb, Different Semantic Event-Frames

Whereas Pustejovsky (1995) and Rappaport Hovav and Levin (1998, 2001) pursue a generative approach towards deriving extended verb meanings based on 'basic' verb meanings (thereby claiming to be able to describe the range of resultatives that can appear with the derived senses, see Chapter 3), I suggest that an enumerative approach in terms of a lexical semantic network of interrelated yet distinct senses achieves more adequate results when it comes to describing the distribution of resultative constructions. As we have seen in Section 5.3 and Section 6.2, each of the individual senses of a verb is conventionalized.

Under my alternative proposal a phonological string (representing a morphological paradigm) commonly identified as 'the verb' serves as an identificational device that allows reference to a multitude of different events and perspectives thereof. One of the reasons that traditional approaches tie information related to a verb into tight semantic bundles is due to the fact that a given phonological string is employed in many different ways to refer to events. Compare, e.g., the different semantic event-frames that may be evoked by the conventionalized usages of a verb like *break* in combination with other words in a sentence.

(6.34)
a. Now *break* it up as it is cut along the dotted lines. (BNC)
b. Oh you cook and then you *break* them off the rest of them. (BNC)
c. It *broke* me up when I learned about Bernadette's baby. (BNC)
d. Te Clar almost *broke* himself up laughing at this idea. (COBUILD)

---

[41]For different views on the regularity of polysemy and its predictability, see Apresjan (1974), Baker (1999), Clark and Clark (1979), Cruse (1986), Deane (1988), Fillmore and Atkins (2000), Iwata (1998), Kilgarriff (1992), Lakoff (1987), Lehrer (1990), Levin (1993), Lyons (1977), Nunberg (1978), and Wierzbicka (1985), among many others.

e. Which if you *break* it down is only about a pound and three quarters a week. (BNC)
f. That's when I *broke* things off with David. (BNC)
g. They *broke* them in like a horse. (BNC)

Note that in most cases the combination of the phonological string *break* and its resultative/particle phrase denotes a particular semantic event-frame that exhibits conventionalized syntactic properties that are not predictable on semantic or syntactic grounds or features of the 'basic' sense of the verb *break* alone. To this end, consider verbs like *shatter* and *smash* that are closely related in meaning to the 'basic' sense of *break* and thus show the same basic semantic and syntactic properties outside of verb-particle/resultative phrase combinations.

(6.35) a. *Kara {broke/shattered/smashed}.
b. Kara {broke/shattered/smashed}the vase.
c. Kara {broke/shattered/smashed}the vase to pieces.

The sentences illustrate that the 'basic' senses of *break*, *shatter*, and *smash* exhibit not only closely related meanings but also similar syntactic realization patterns in their prototypical senses. Let us now turn to the question of whether *shatter* and *smash* may be substituted for *break* in some of the sentences in (6.34a)-(6.34g) above.

(6.36) a. Now {break/*shatter/*smash} it up.
b. You {break/*shatter/*smash} them off the rest of them.
c. It {broke/*shattered/*smashed} me up.
d. Te Clar almost {broke/*shattered/*smashed} himself up.
e. If you {break/*shatter/*smash} it down is only about a pound and three quarters.
f. That's when I {broke/*shattered/*smashed} things off with David.
g. They {broke/*shattered/*smashed} them in like a horse.

The unacceptability of verb-particle/resultative phrases with 'basic' senses of verbs that are closely related in meaning to the 'basic' sense of *break* illustrates that it is very difficult, if not even impossible, to make any general predictions about how the basic sense of a verb may combine with a potential resultative/particle phrase. This is not surprising if one compares the different semantic concepts that are denoted by the individual verb-particle combinations.

(6.37) a. break X up-1: to open
b. break X off-1: to forcefully remove a smaller object from a larger object to which it is attached
c. break X up-2: to lose control of one's emotions

d. break X up-3: not able to believe
e. break X down: to divide
f. break things off-2: to end a relationship
g. break X in: to get X accustomed to

The paraphrases for the verb-particle/resultative phrase combinations in (6.37a)-(6.37g) show that the semantic concepts denoted by them differ to such a degree that it is very problematic to relate them to each other by means of derivational rules from a basic sense that are able to describe the distribution of particle/resultative phrases. Instead, the data suggest that the form-meaning pairings are conventionalized idiomatic phrase combinations and to a large degree unpredictable (cf. our comparison with *shatter* and *smash* above) on general grounds. The data also show that there is a varying degree of flexibility in the combinatorial possibilities. The comparison between the individual semantic concepts denoted by the verb-particle/resultative phrase and verb-NP combinations suggests that it is necessary to encode each individual semantic concept referred to by *break* in (6.37) by a separate semantic event-frame. The semantic (and syntactic) information is then encoded in the frame-semantic event frame which denotes relevant properties for each individual semantic concept.[42]

We now turn to the discussion of some of the event-frames associated with *break* in (6.37a)-(6.37g). The following two-participant event-frame represents the frame-semantic information associated with the *break X off* sense of *break*.

[42]Note that the list of conventionalized phrase combinations in (6.37a)-(6.37g) above is not exhaustive which means that there are many other conventionalized idiomatic phrase patterns associated with *break* which are not discussed here. Cf., e.g., *Once he broke free of his trance ...* (www.gurlpages.com/obsess/edge_mystic/paige.html), *It was at this point that Cain completely and totally broke himself off from God.* (www.fortunecity.com/ millennium/ tinky-winky/ 316/faithand1.htm), and *He dumped the sedatives in the toilet and broke himself out of the hospital.* (www. 7parabians.com/indigo/nevertoolate.html)

(6.38) Reduced event-based frame semantic representation of *break X off*

SOURCE	Path	Path	Path	GOAL
↓ Ag Pt	↓ Ag Pt	↓ Ag Pt	↓ Ag Pt	Ag Pt p3

Ag: entity exerting force against an object
Pt: object that is part of and/or attached to another object
p3: *off* (plus phrase denoting the end location of the patient as a result of the agent's exertion of physical force against the patient)

The event participants' semantic description and the end result state show that *break X off* denotes an event in which an agent exerts force on a patient which detaches the latter from the object it was initially attached to.[43] The following diagram illustrates the end result state of the event participants of (6.38).

(6.39) Image of *break X off*

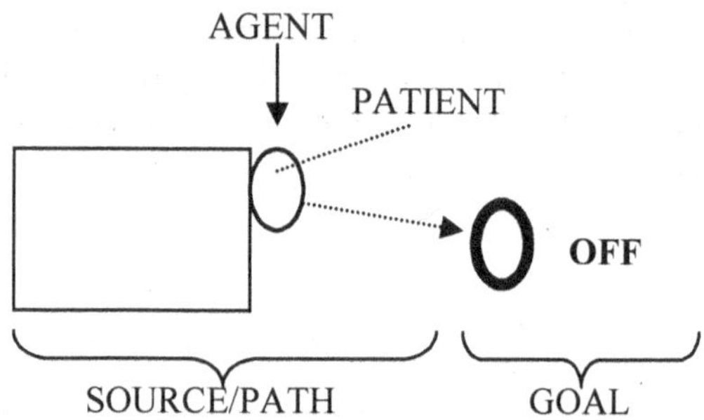

The event-semantic representation in (6.38) shows that *break X off* does not permit any further semantic specification of the patient's end result state which is not semantically compatible with *off*, nor does it allow a different resultative phrase instead of *off*. Consider the following examples.

(6.40)
a. Stevin broke the branch off.
b. Stevin broke the branch off the tree.
c. *Stevin broke the branch off away.
d. *Stevin broke off.

---

[43] Recall that the conceptual information about which objects may function as agents and patients of such an event is part of world knowledge (or, in an applied sense, may be plugged into our linguistic representation from a conceptual ontology).

(6.40a) and (6.40b) are licensed by the event-semantic representation of *break X off*. As discussed in Section 6.2.3, the canonical linking pattern applies: the agent is linked to subject position followed by the verb, the patient argument, and the resultative phrase *off*. Since *the tree* in (6.40b) serves as a modification of *off*, it is not prohibited by the event-frame requirements in (6.38). In contrast, (6.40c) is ruled out because *away* is not semantically compatible with *off* in this context. Similarly, (6.40d) is ruled out by the requirement that the patient argument of *break X off* be overtly realized. The sentences show that the event-frame in (6.38) accounts for the proper licensing conditions of the frame-semantic event participants of *break X off*. The event frames of other verb-particle combinations such as *break X up, break X away*, or *break X down* exhibit a similar architecture as that of *break X off*, except that they denote different semantic concepts containing different end result states. This means that for each of the other events, there is an event-frame exhibiting the same architecture as that of (6.38), but with different conventionalized senses of the verb *break*. We now turn to a discussion of other types of event-frames associated with *break*. The following event frame represents the frame-semantic information associated with the idiomatic 'end a situation' sense of *break*.

(6.41) Event-based frame semantic information representing *break things off*.

GOAL
Ag
Pt p3

Ag: human that makes a decision to end a situation
Pt: human relationship
p3: *off*

(6.41) differs from the event-frame of *break X off* in (6.38) in that it not only prescribes the type of resultative phrase, namely *off*, but it also regulates the type of postverbal NP that has to occur when this event-frame is employed, due to its idiomatic sense. This event frame thus pre-selects both the postverbal NP as well as the resultative phrase to yield the following distribution.[44]

[44] This event-frame contains various options for the realization of the postverbal NP. Thus, instead of *things*, *it* may occur in postverbal position as the following corpus data illustrate.

(i) Has she intimated she wants to break it off? (BNC)

(ii) That's when I broke it off with David. (BNC)

(6.42) a. *He broke.
b. *He broke things. (on the 'ending the relationship reading')
c. He broke things off.
d. *He broke things off away.
e. *He broke to exhaustion.
f. *He broke off.

So far, we have only discussed event-frames denoting idiomatic phrases associated with a verb which requires either a specific type of resultative phrase or both a specific type of resultative phrase and a specific type of postverbal NP.

We now turn to the prototypical event-frame of *break*, namely that type of event frame which denotes an event in which an object falls apart as the result of force that is applied to it by an agent. We will see that its specific collocational restrictions exhibit similar idiosyncratic properties as those of *break-off* and *break-things-off*, but within much broader borders.

(6.43) Event-based frame semantic information representing the prototypical sense of *break*[45]

GOAL
Ag Pt (p3)

Ag: entity exerting physical force against an object
Pt: object that looses its structural integrity
p3: PP which denotes structural disintegration

Note that the event-frame in (6.43) is labeled as the 'prototypical' sense of *break*. This is because upon hearing sentences like *Kara broke the vase*, one automatically infers that the structural integrity of the vase has collapsed (conventionally expected result). The general semantic restriction 'p3' in parenthesis following the patient argument in the goal slot indicates that the result phrase is optional because this event-frame does not require the overt realization of a resultative phrase in order to be acceptable. Instead, it only lexically pre-selects for a specific semantic type of resultative phrase which may be optionally realized.

(iii) They'd been engaged twice but she kept breaking it off because he couldn't hold a job down. (BNC)

[45] In Section 7.2 we will expand the event-frame for prototypical *break* to also cover the intransitive use of this event-frame.

The event-frame in (6.43) illustrates that there is no need for a lexical rule, syntactic transformation, or construction adding a constructional argument role to the verb's participant roles in order for the resultative phrase to be licensed at the syntactic level. On this view, the prototypical event-frame of *break* lexically determines the type of semantic resultative phrase which occurs with this specific event-frame. Since it already contains this information and the realization of the resultative phrase is optional, it is up to the speaker to decide whether the resultative phrase should be overtly realized or not (see our discussion of the different communicative functions of resultatives in Section 5.3). (6.43) differs from other event-frames of *break*, such as *break X off/away/up/down*, in that the resultative phrase need not be overtly realized, but is optional. Whereas one might argue that the event-frame denoted by prototypical *break* is essentially the same as that of the other *break* event-frames, this is not the case. Compare the following image representation of the prototypical sense of *break* with the image representation of *break X off* in (6.39) above.

(6.44) Image representation of prototypical event frame of *break*

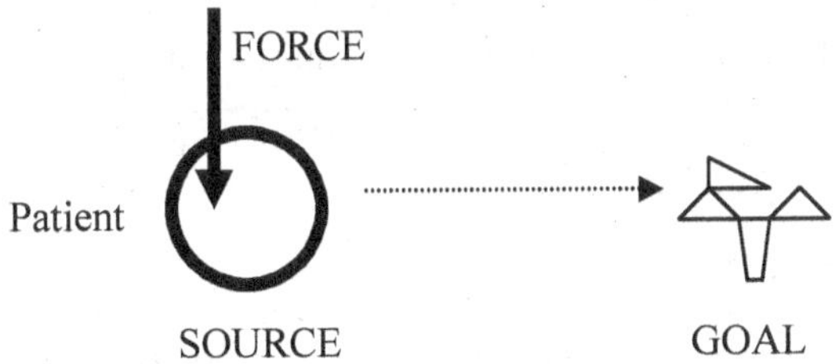

The image to the left of the horizontal arrow shows how force is applied (by the agent that is not relevant for the sake of the present discussion) to an object. The image to the right of the arrow illustrates the result state of the object after it has lost its structural integrity. In contrast to *break X off*, there is no detachment of a smaller object (the patient) from a larger object that it was attached to. Rather, the object to which force is applied is destroyed. This shows that prototypical *break* denotes a conceptually different frame semantic event frame than *break X off*.

In discussing different event-frames of *break*, we have so far seen that event-frames differ not only with respect to the types of semantic concepts they denote, but also in the way in which this event-semantic information is realized syntactically and semantically. All of the collocational restrictions are included in the lexical representation of event-frames in terms of on-stage and off-stage information. The following section looks at more data showing that splitting a verb into different event frames is more the rule than the exception when it comes to the distribution of resultatives.

6.3.2 Verbs and Different Types of Event-Frames

In what follows, a 'primary' verb is listed followed by other verbs that are closely related in meaning yet cannot be substituted for the respective 'primary' verbs in the combinations below.[46] A somewhat rough definition is followed by attested corpus examples containing different usages of the respective verbs in combination with other words that indicate the existence of separate event frames denoting distinct semantic concepts (an asterisk indicates that the closely related verbs may not be substituted and a question mark indicates that in some select cases, substitution is possible).

(6.45) *Drive* (**walk*/*?bicycle*/*?fly*)

a. *drive X 'crazy'* (change the mental state of X (typically in a negative way)). I'm fond of her, but sometimes she drives me crazy. (BNC)

b. *drive X location-1* (change the location of person or vehicle by operating a vehicle). Marler had driven his second-hand red Porsche to Dartmoor. (BNC)

c. *drive X location-2* (forcefully pushing s.b./s.th. away from agent). Swiftly they overran the island, driving their dark kinsfolk into the sea. (BNC)

d. *drive X location-3* (forcefully pushing an object into another object, with physical impact of the two as a result). He then picked me up and drove his knee straight into my balls. (BNC)

(6.46) *Beat* (**hit*/**strike*)

a. *beat X-person up* (hit somebody with the intention of physically hurting them): We'll bring our friends and they'll beat them up. (BNC)

b. *beat X-person to* (arrive at a certain goal before somebody else): I think I actually beat the police to the scene. (BNC)

c. *beat X-idea into Y-person* (activity aimed at making s.b. believe s.th.): They beat religion into you there all night. (BNC)

d. *beat the X out of Y-person* (physically hurt someone very badly): I'm surprised the guy didn't beat the shit out of me, rightfully so. (BNC)[47]

---

[46] As in the section above, the lists do not claim to cover all possible senses of the respective verbs, nor are they concerned with the question of the diachronic and semantic motivation for meaning extensions. Rather, the lists are intended to illustrate a few instances of the different distributional patterns of the respective verbs which need to be accounted for and whose occurrences with specific resultative phrases and postverbal NPs need to be explained by an account of resultatives.

[47] Other BNC-attested postverbal NPs include: *the daylights*, *bloody hell*, *the fuck*, *the crap*, and *the pulp*.

e. *beat a path to X* (free a path by shoveling people aside): All our agents beat a path to our door. (BNC)

(6.47) *Hammer* (*?pound*)

a. *hammer X property* (changing the physical property of X by using physical force). So I cut out a straight section of wire coat hanger, heated one end until it was cherry red, hammered it flat, ... (BNC)

b. *hammer X out* (create a solution to a problem) It was social laughter, an attempt to hammer out a common weapon against despair. (BNC)

c. *hammer X down* (to prevent X from moving). I was told to hammer them down and not give in until I had a sale. (BNC)

d. *hammer X direction-1* (physically forcing X to become part of another object): They can tell us what tool to use to hammer upholstery nails into a chair. (BNC)

e. *hammer X direction-2* (changing an inherent property of an object by crating or altering X by means of physical force). She seemed intent on hammering holes in the paper. (BNC)

(6.48) *Paint* (*?color/*dye/*stain*)

a. *paint X location* (creation of an object by painting). The visitors painted their symbolic image on galleries and rocky caves. (BNC)

b. *paint X color-1* (depict X). If ministers spend this week in Blackpool trying to paint the Labour Party red again ... (BNC)

c. *paint X color-2* (change the color of an object): She'd painted her toenails red. (BNC)

d. *paint the town red* (to cause noise, to party): Tonight we're going to paint the town red. (BNC)

The fact that in almost all instances the 'primary' verb may not be replaced by other verbs which are closely related in meaning suggests that the combination of verb and particle/resultative phrase forms a collocational pattern that denotes a specific semantic concept. This means that each of the examples in (6.45)-(6.48) above is licensed by a separate event-semantic frame which has its own semantic and pragmatic specifications for its event-participants, force dynamics, temporal relations, world knowledge, and resultative phrases.

6.3.3 Verb Classes and Generalizations

So far, I have followed the bottom-up method of linguistic analysis by sketching out an architecture of lexical entries that aims to capture the full distribution of usages that a given verb may be employed for in the resultative pattern. Thus far, the possibility of arriving at generalizations over semantically related verbs and verb classes has not been considered. Before turning to a more detailed analysis of different types of resultatives in the next chapter, it is necessary to address the question of possible generalizations across various event-frames and to briefly discuss the term 'verb class.'

6.3.3.1 Verb Classes

We have seen that the bottom-up approach of describing each event-frame associated with a particular verb in terms of its idiosyncratic properties (event participants, time/space axis, force dynamics, world knowledge) is more precise than accounts which aim at reducing the amount of lexical semantic information associated with a basic verb sense (see our discussions in Chapters 3-5, as well as Taylor (2000)). If the notion of 'verb class' as employed by other analyses of resultatives does not help in accounting for and capturing the full range of resultative constructions, does that mean that it is not helpful for linguistic descriptions? Not at all. Works on diathesis alternations, most notably Levin (1993), have shown that broader-scale generalizations are possible based on semantic similarities among verbs: 'The differences in verb behavior can be explained if the diathesis alternations are sensitive to particular components of verb meaning.' (Levin 1993: 7) However, my results indicate that this method of linguistic analysis is difficult to apply to the analysis of resultatives. This state of affairs is also noted by Levin (1993) who observes that '[a] wide range of verbs is found in the resultative construction, so no specific classes of verbs are identified here.' (Levin 1993: 101) The question, then, is whether any generalizations in terms of 'verb classes' are viable for a framework employed for analyzing resultatives. The next section therefore briefly addresses the question of how generalizations about the distribution of resultatives might be attainable.

6.3.3.2 Generalizations Across Verbs

We first survey a set of data in order to establish what types of event-semantic frames are denoted by verbs. Then we will attempt to arrive at some preliminary generalizations that show how broader-scale generalizations may be achieved. In dealing with the attested verb patterns, we will only be concerned with a small slice of the broad distribution since a full investigation is beyond the scope of this work (see Levin (1993) for a broad scale analysis of verb alternations and Baker and Ruppenhofer (2003) for a critical review of this approach).

6.3.3.2.1 'Paint'-Verbs

The following set of data represents a slice of attested examples containing 'verbs of coloring' (Levin 1993: 168), namely *paint*, *color*, *dye*, and *stain*.

Coloring-sense

(6.49) a. Phyllis dyed the dress. (Levin 1993: 168)
b. ??Phyllis painted the dress.
c. ??Phyllis colored the dress.
d. Phyllis stained the dress.

(6.50) a. Phyllis dyed the dress blue/a very pale shade of blue. (Levin 1993: 168)
b. Phyllis painted the dress blue.
c. Phyllis colored the dress blue.
d. ?Phyllis stained the dress blue.

Image-impression sense (cf. Levin 1993: 169)

(6.51) a. Joe painted a cross onto the wall.
b. *Joe dyed a cross onto the wall.
c. *Joe colored a cross onto the wall.
d. *Joe stained a cross onto the wall.

Characterize sense (cf. Levin 1993: 181)

(6.52) a. If ministers spend this week in Blackpool trying to paint the Labour-Party red. (BNC)
b. *If ministers spend this week in Blackpool trying to dye the Labour-Party red.
c. *If ministers spend this week in Blackpool trying to color the Labour-Party red.
d. *If ministers spend this week in Blackpool trying to stain the Labour-Party red.

'Party'-sense

(6.53) a. Tonight we're going to paint the town red! (BNC)
b. *Tonight we're going to dye the town red!
c. *Tonight we're going to color the town red!
d. *Tonight we're going to stain the town red!

The distribution of verbs in (6.49)-(6.53) shows that not every verb may be substituted by another verb that is closely related in meaning to yield a closely related interpretation. The oddity of some of the above substitutions show that specific verbs semantically subcategorize for certain objects that can undergo the 'change of color' activity. That is, dresses are typically dyed, not colored or painted. The following set of sentences suggests that these semantic restrictions exhibit collocation-like features that mirror conventionally expected results associated with the respective verbs.

(6.54) a. She'd painted her toenails red. (BNC)
b. ?She'd colored her toenails red.
c. *She'd stained her toenails red.
d. *She'd dyed her toenails red.

(6.55) a. But then he noticed her hair, she'd dyed it black. (BNC)
b. ?But then he noticed her hair, she'd colored it black.
c. ?But then he noticed her hair, she'd painted it black.
d. * But then he noticed her hair, she'd stained it black.

The above sentences illustrate that certain verbs semantically subcategorize for specific types of arguments and sound 'odd' to native speakers when replaced by other closely semantically related verbs. This indicates that an event frame needs to contain very specific semantic specifications with respect to what types of patient arguments may occur with a given verb.

Having reviewed the different senses of 'paint'-verbs, let us now return to our main line of discussion. The different senses and postverbal NPs that the above verbs of coloring appear with suggest that we have to specify the relevant descriptions about a verb's ability to occur in a certain type of resultative construction at the level of semantic event-frames denoting individual senses of a verb. On this view, each individual event-frame comes with its set of verb-specific event-frame information such as event participants, temporal relations, force dynamics, and world knowledge including the types of possible end result states for each prototypical event participant. I now address the question of how generalizations can be captured on the basis of the individual senses of verbs in order to make linguistic descriptions more general. The following diagram illustrates the very bottom of a multiple inheritance model (cf., e.g., Davis (2001)) in which distinct event-frames are shared by different types of verbs.

(6.56) Frame-generalizations across some 'verbs of coloring' and other related verbs

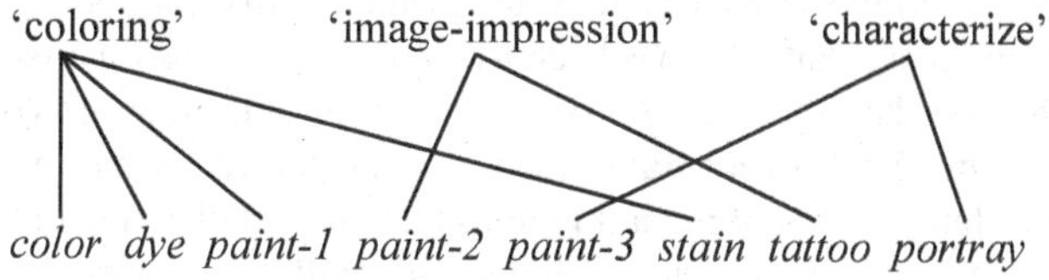

(6.56) illustrates the semantic overlap of certain verbs of coloring with each other as well as with other verbs that belong to other semantic classes. It shows that although it is possible to state an individual event-frame for each type of event that a verb may refer to, some generalizations are possible. That is, it is possible to extract the general information that the verbs *color*, *dye*, *paint*, and *stain* share with respect to the coloring event-frame. A possible generalization, for example, would involve the force dynamics, the type of liquid, and the type of agents involved in these different yet closely related coloring events. On this view, the color event-frames of *color*, *dye*, *paint*, and *stain* inherit information from a more abstract coloring frame, thereby keeping the amount of information specified in the individual frames as minimal as possible. While such generalizations are possible, each verb would have to individually list the rest of its idiosyncratic information with respect to that event-frame, just like *paint* has its own separate event frame-denotation for its 'party-sense' in (6.53) above. Such a hierarchy of event-frames also allows us to state generalizations across different event-frames as the image-impression and characterize event-frames of *paint* that overlap with *tattoo* and *portray* show. Following this procedure for verbs which share certain components of meaning would ultimately give us what Lang-acker (2000: 21) calls schematized expressions, i.e., 'templates abstracted from a set of complex expressions to embody whatever commonality is inherent in them.'

(6.56) only represents the lowest part of a large inheritance hierarchy of highly structured conceptual-semantic concepts that may be employed to capture frame-semantic information at different levels of abstraction of such a hierarchy. At higher levels, it will then be possible to reach abstractions over simple force dynamic relations such as those outlined by Talmy (1988) and Croft (1991). Since this is beyond the scope of the present work, we do not pursue this train of thought here.

6.3.3.2.2 'Removal of an Unwanted Substance' Verbs

In this section we discuss the frame-semantic distribution of 'removal of an unwanted substance' verbs such as *wipe, sweep, wash, polish*, and *rub*. The following data illustrate the types of event-frames that the verbs are associated with. Each event-frame (sense) is portrayed by an image to illustrate the different types of mental images that are associated with them (not all of the event participants are included, nor will we discuss the world knowledge details or the types of substances that may be affected by the individual frames).

(6.57) Funnel-sense (Levin 1993: 113)

a. He wiped the imaginary mess on his trousers. (BNC)
b. A couple of inmates were picking up leaves from around the graves, sweeping them into a large black sack. (BNC).
c. Kim washed the dirt into the sink.
d. *Kim polished the dust into the basket.
e. Kim rubbed the dust into the basket.

(6.58) Schematic representation of funnel-sense

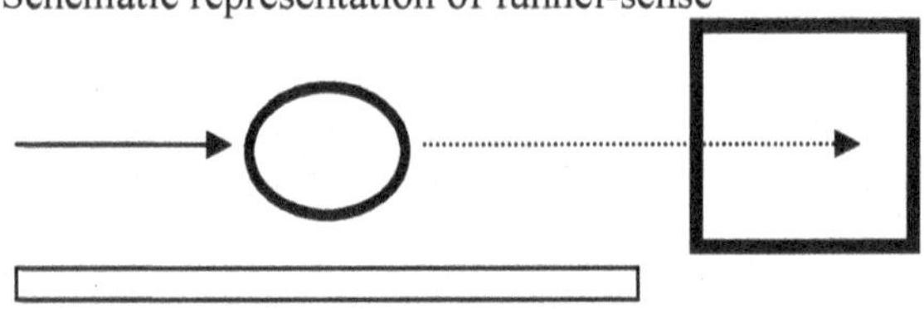

The funnel event-frame captures activities which include a substance (the circle) that is moved by the agent (to the left of the left arrow but not pictured here) into a new direction (the box). The force dynamics are indicated by the arrows. In this case, both the substance and the direction into which it is moved are profiled, as indicated by the thick lines, whereas the surface on which the substance is located (box with thin lines) is backgrounded, i.e., it does not have to be mentioned. This frame-semantic information may be captured in terms of a simplified event-semantic representation which only represents the goal of the funnel-event-frame.[48]

[48]Recall that the type of frame-semantic event representation is lexical default information, i.e., it must be embedded in discourse and made sensitive to contextual background information. Given specific contextual background information, the lexical default information may then be overridden. In metaphorical mapping, e.g., there is a mapping construction which relates features from different domains to each other in order to produce a mapping. For this type

(6.59) Simplified event-semantic representation of the funnel-event frame

GOAL
Ag
Pt p3

Ag: entity exerting force
Pt: substance
p3: directional PP with a surface or container as its end location

(6.60) Removal-sense-1 (cf. Levin 1993: 122-132)

a. Hargreave wiped his plate clean with a piece of garlic bread. (BNC)
b. Tom had swept the room clean and had fixed a lamp. (BNC)
c. It had stopped bleeding and the rain had washed it clean. (BNC)
d. He took them off, breathed on them and polished them clean with his handkerchief. (BNC)
e. Rubbing his glasses clean, he peered intently over at me through the thin rain. (BNC)

(6.61) Schematic representation of removal-sense-1

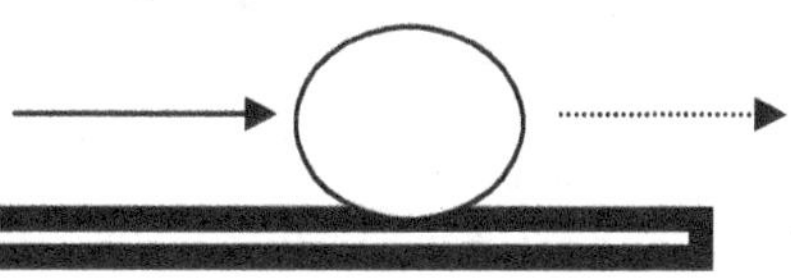

The removal-sense-1 event-frame profiles the patient (the surface). It describes the removal of an unwanted substance from the surface by the agent.

---

of operation to work, a metaphorical mapping construction takes the semantic default specification of the event participants and maps it into a different domain which means that the lexical default specifications will not be realized according to the semantic specifications of the event participants, but according to the metaphorical mapping mechanisms.

(6.62) Simplified event-semantic representation of removal-sense-1

GOAL
Ag Pt (p3)

Ag: entity exerting force
Pt: surface, or any object that has a surface
p3: property of surface that holds of the surface after unwanted substances have been removed

(6.63) *Removal-sense-2*

a. There are tears on his face and I wipe them away. (BNC)
b. Heavy flooding swept it away. (BNC)
c. Can I just rub the lipstick off the end of your nose? (BNC)
d. I would wait as long as it took to wash the mess off the roof. (BNC)
e. Every time I visited him he made me polish the dust off the bottle. (BNC)

(6.64) Schematic representation of removal-sense-2

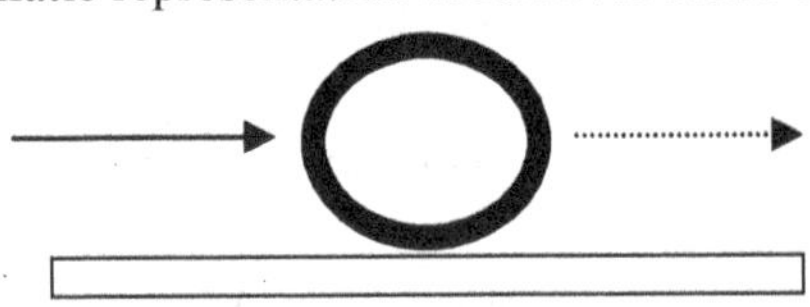

In contrast to the removal-sense-1 event frame, the removal-sense-2 event frame does not profile the surface which is being affected by the activity, but rather the substance which is removed. This is indicated by the thick circle. The difference between the two removal senses is thus a difference of profiling of event participants, similar to the difference in profiling between *buy* and *sell* in the commercial transaction frame surveyed in Section 7.2.2 above. This is represented in the event-semantic frame for removal-sense-2.

(6.65) Simplified event-semantic representation of removal-sense-2

GOAL
Ag Pt p3

Ag: entity exerting force
Pt: object or substance that may be removed from a surface by employing force to it.
p3: location that an object or subject may end up in as a result of being removed from a surface.

(6.66) Creation-sense

a. The hairdresser had swept her blonde hair into two glossy wings. (BNC)
b. With the heel of her hand, she wiped a circular space to see her face. (BNC)
c. *Claire washed the dirt into a pile.
d. *Jenn polished the dust into a pile.
e. Julio rubbed the dirt into a pile.

(6.67) Schematic representation of creation sense

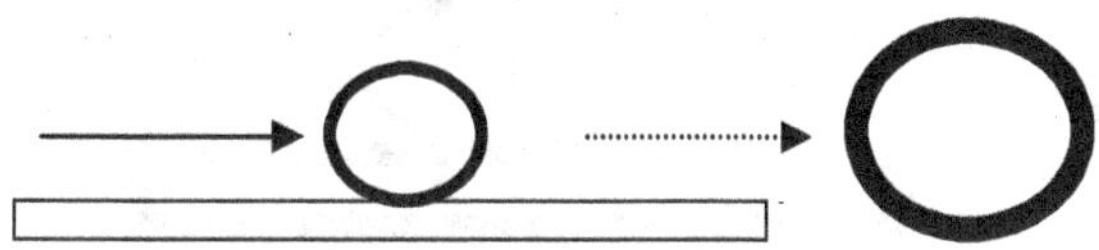

The creation-frame describes the creation of something new which was non-existing at the beginning of the event (its source). The thing created is indicated by the thick circle to the right of the dotted arrow. A simplified event-semantic representation capturing this information looks as follows.

(6.68) Simplified event-semantic representation of creation-sense

GOAL
Ag
Pt p3

Ag: entity exerting force
Pt: object affected by force emitted by the agent and which subsequently becomes part of a larger entity that contains it
p3: entity that comes into existence as the result of the activity performed by the actor upon the patient

(6.69) Absorption-sense
a. Tom rubbed the massage oil into Jackie's back.
b. *Tom swept the crumbs into the floor.
c. Tom wiped the mayonnaise into his shirt.
d. *Tom polished the dust into his shoes.
e. *Tom washed the dirt into his shirt.

(6.70) Schematic representation of absorption sense

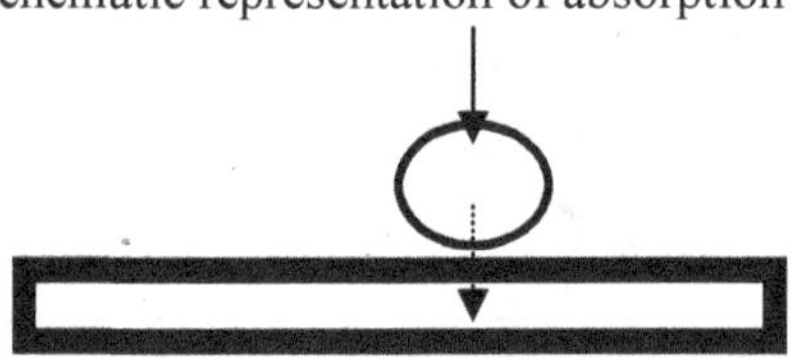

The absorption frame describes situations in which a substance is absorbed by a surface because of some external force exerting energy onto the substance, thereby forcing the substance to become a part of the surface. In this case, both the substance and the surface are profiled. Note that this frame differs crucially from the frames above which all describe events in which an undesired substance is to be removed from the surface. The simplified frame-semantic information associated with the event frame looks as follows:

(6.71) Simplified event-semantic representation of absorption-sense

GOAL
Ag Pt p3

Ag: entity exerting force
Pt: any substance that is forced to be absorbed by a surface
p3: directional PP that specifies a surface as its endpoint

The data shows that *wipe*, *sweep*, *polish*, *rub*, and *wash* have different distributions with respect to the event-frames they denote. Although all of the event frames involve some general notion of moving a substance along a surface, they each denote event-frames with their own specific outcomes, end results, and inferences that are drawn from world knowledge associated with the event frames. An implementation of event-frames into a multiple inheritance hierarchy of semantic relations could lead to a highly structured and interrelated system of conceptual-semantic information which would allow us to arrive at different levels of abstractions across different event-frames and event-frame classes. Structuring conceptual-semantic relations into different levels opens the ground for arriving at generalizations about the distribution of resultatives by only referring to a specific semantic-conceptual feature structure that is found at some level within the hierarchy. In this section we have seen that it is necessary to encode the relevant information needed to capture the distribution of different resultative phrases and postverbal NPs with the same verb and/or with different verbs for each individual event-frame of a given verb.

6.4 Conclusions

Instead of reducing lexical-semantic information to a single set of relational information about 'the verb', I have argued in this chapter to expand the amount of information associated with a verb's lexical entry to cover all of its relevant senses in terms of event-frames. On this view, a verb's lexical entry consists of a pairing between a phonological string representing a paradigm of morphological forms ('the verb') and a set of different, sometimes closely related event-frames, which capture information about the scenes that a verb may refer to. Event-frames are collections of grammatically immediately relevant on-stage information such as event participants, and grammatically not immediately relevant off-stage information such as temporal relations, force dynamics, end result states of event participants, and general world knowledge. The two types of information are highly intertwined and are both implicitly activated (to different degrees) when the verb that is associated with the event-frame appears in an utterance. We have seen that whenever a verb is used, the event participants of the respective event-frames have to be understood with respect to a common background frame. The crucial point is that off-stage information may be recruited and subsequently made grammatically relevant in order to convey more information about the event that the event-frame refers to. I have shown that since off-stage information includes information about conventionally expected results, it plays an important role in determining the collocational restrictions exhibited by the verb with respect to its postverbal constituents.

The corpus data surveyed in this chapter demonstrate that the event-frames of the verbs under discussion lexically predetermine the semantic type of resultative phrase for each event participant. However, event-frames differ with respect to the types and realization requirements of resultative phrases. Some event-frames are somewhat inflexible and require the overt realization of a specific resultative phrase such as *off* as in *break X off*. In contrast, other event-frames such as that of the prototypical sense of *break* or *wipe* do not require overt realization of a resultative phrase. They semantically predetermine the types of resultative phrases by recruiting off-stage information about conventionally expected results that is used to impose collocational restrictions on postverbal elements.

With respect to linking to the syntactic level we have seen that there is no need for complicated linking mechanisms. Each semantic event-frame lexically determines the types of event participants and their possible end result states which are automatically linked to the respective 'surface' positions. That is, in both active resultative and non-resultative expressions, agents are linked to subject position, followed by the verb and, in the case of two-participant events, by the patient argument and possibly a resultative phrase, depending on the lexical specifications of the event-frame.

Finally, we discussed the issue of possible generalizations across verb classes. Our discussion of 'coloring verbs' and 'wiping verbs' has shown that generalizations about semantic regularities must be stated at the level of event-frames in order to capture the full distribution of resultatives that may occur with different senses.

In the next chapter we will see that the architecture of semantic event-frames presented in this chapter is a step in the direction of accounting for the full distribution of resultatives on the basis of rich lexical semantic information. To this end, we will see whether event-frames and their implementation hold up to Levin's (1993: 1) call for linguistically motivated lexi-

lexical entries: 'Ideally, such a theory must provide linguistically motivated lexical entries for verbs which incorporate a representation of verb meaning and which allow the meanings of verbs to be properly associated with the syntactic expressions of their arguments.'

7

Lexical Licensing of Resultatives

> More syntactic properties of sentences than usually thought depend on the main verb. (...) The systematic description of French verbs (or simple sentences) has shown that no two verbs have the same syntactic properties. (...) As a consequence, verbs have to be described individually, and not in terms of intentional classes. The proportion of the lexicon of idiomatic sentences, of metaphorical and technical sentences with no compositional meaning, is very high. All these sentences or sentence types have anecdotal origins. Hence, they have to be described individually, that is, without reference to classes of lexical combinations or of interpretation patterns.
>
> (Gross 1994: 214)

7.1 Introduction

In this chapter we turn our attention to the architecture of individual types of event-frames necessary to license the four types of resultatives discussed in Chapter 5. There are two large classes of resultative constructions: conventionalized resultatives and nonconventionalized resultatives. In Section 7.2 we discuss conventionalized resultatives which consist of two subclasses, those which perspectivize the prototypical patient argument of the event-frame and those which perspectivize a non-prototypical patient argument. The former either highlights or specifies the end result state of a prototypical patient participant. The latter covers fake objects. In Section 7.3 we look at nonconventionalized resultatives that are licensed by analogy based on existing conventionalized resultatives. Besides overlap of conventionalized frame semantic information between a target verb and a source verb, we will see that contextual background information is crucial in licensing and restricting resultatives that are based on analogy.

7.2 Conventionalized Resultatives

7.2.1 Perspectivizing the Prototypical Patient Participant

7.2.1.1 Emphasizing the Outcome of an Event

Recall from Chapter 5 that the first class of resultatives highlights the outcome of an event in order to point out that some part of the event is exceptional. Consider the following sentences.

(7.1) a. She shattered the vase (into pieces).
b. They melted the butter (to liquid).
c. A soldier bayoneted him (to death). (BNC)
d. The fridge froze the water (solid).
e. Kenny is now in a position to kill the rest of us (dead). (BNC)

The event-frames representing the prototypical senses of the verbs *shatter*, *melt*, *bayonet*, *freeze*, and *kill* exhibit the same general architecture except for the individual on-stage information (event participants) and off-stage information (force dynamics, temporal information, general and specific world knowledge). In what follows we discuss each individual event-frame and the types of resultatives (and non-resultatives) licensed by it. In our discussion of event-frames, we will focus on the GOAL slot of the respective event frames.[1] In what follows, we assume the linking principles laid out in Chapter 6. Also, recall that the semantic description of the event participants is kept as general as possible in order to have specific objects provided by a conceptual ontology (cf. our discussion in Section 6.2.3.2).[2] We now turn to a discussion of the individual event-frames and the types of resultative constructions licensed by them. We begin with the event-frame of the prototypical sense of *shatter*.

---

[1]Note that the following discussion assumes 'normal' contextual background information. That is, most of the lexical-semantic specifications discussed in this section are default specifications. E.g., *We melted ourselves to liquid* is typically pragmatically bizarre. However, given a science-fiction context, e.g., in which a machine is created to assist in suicide by using microwaves, this context will override the lexical event-frame specifications for *melt*.

[2]Throughout our discussion I do not address the question of how metaphorical mappings may be predicted. For a possible solution of how this may be achieved, compare our discussion of analogy in Section 7.3 which deals with mapping between semantic information of source and target verbs in order for target verbs to acquire the syntactic frame of a source verb. In principle, a similar mapping process is possible to model metaphorical mappings based on lexical semantic information contained in event-frames.

7.2.1.1.1 Shatter

The simplified event-frame in (7.2) contains information about the agent ('Ag'), the patient ('Pt'), and the resultative phrase denoting the end result state of the patient ('p3') of the prototypical sense of *shatter*. Recall that parentheses indicate that event-frame information does not have to be linguistically realized. The specifications for each type of information are given below the event-frame. The specifications for the resultative phrase are split into two different parts, namely a syntactic part (SYN) and a semantic part (SEM).

(7.2) Event-based frame semantic representation of the prototypical sense of *shatter*

GOAL
(Ag) Pt (p3)

Ag: Entity exerting force[3]
Pt: Object that looses its structural integrity
p3: SYN: PP
SEM: denoting the end result state of physical disintegration

(7.3)
a. *She shattered.
b. She shattered the vase.
c. She shattered the vase into pieces.
d. She shattered the vase all over the table.
e. *She shattered the vase broken.
f. *She shattered the vase yellow.
g. *She shattered herself into pieces.
h. *She shattered herself over the table/to exhaustion.
i. The vase shattered (into pieces).

[3] Note that the event-frames in this section do not allow recruitment of any off-stage information to license fake objects. This is due to the fact that the event-frames denote a very specific outcome of an event that is conventionally associated with the respective verbs (as opposed to the event-frames to be discussed in the next section). This also explains why the resultative phrases associated with the event-frames of this section only serve to highlight the outcome of an event, instead of clearing up the vagueness with respect to the outcome of an event as in the next section.

Sentence (7.3a) is ruled out since the event-frame for the prototypical sense of *shatter* requires that the patient argument be realized. (7.3b) is licensed because both the agent and the patient participant are overtly realized. (7.3c) and (7.3d) are allowed by the event-frame specifications in (7.2) since they both denote the end result state of physical disintegration. That is, shattering involves not only a loss of the object's physical integrity (it is *in pieces*), but also a change of location (*all over the table*) of its pieces. In other words, the phrase *all over the table* in (7.3d) is construed as the end result state of physical disintegration in a context in which, e.g., a vase on top of a table disintegrates. Note that such a construal is not possible when the resultative PP denotes locations other than the surface on which the vase is located prior to its disintegration (cf. **She shattered the vase all over the fence/under the table*). The following diagram illustrates the linking of event-participants to the syntactic level according to our general linking conditions (cf. Section 6.2.3.4).

(7.4) Linking of event-participants to the syntactic level

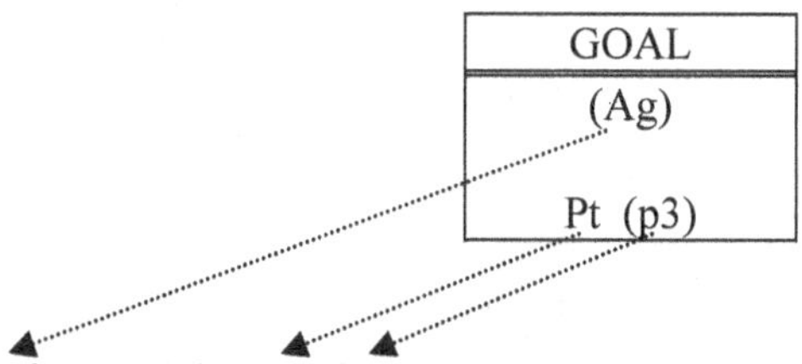

She shattered the vase into pieces.
NP V NP XP

(7.3e) and (7.3f) are disallowed by the event frame because *broken* and *yellow* are not PPs. (7.3g) and (7.3h) are not licensed by (7.2) because the event-frame does not allow recruitment of off-stage information in order to overtly realize other event participants besides the prototypical agent and the prototypical patient of a shattering event.

Finally, consider the intransitive use of *shatter* in (7.3i), in which the agent of the shattering activity is backgrounded and the patient is foregrounded. This is possible since the event-frame specifies that the agent of the shattering activity is optional and does not have to be overtly realized (the parentheses around 'Ag' indicate that it may be optionally realized). In this case, the force exerted by the agent is implicitly understood. Since the event is portrayed from a different viewpoint and the agent is backgrounded, the patient argument is automatically linked to subject position. As we will see, event-frames differ from each other with respect to whether they allow the portrayal of events from different perspectives. The difference between event-frames that allow backgrounding of the prototypical agent participant and those that do not lies in the linguistic realization allowed by the event-frames. At a conceptual level, however, there is no difference between event-frames that allow backgrounding and those that do not. By capturing both the transitive and the intransitive variant of *shatter* in one lexical entry, we do not need two separate lexical entries or any lexical rules that derive additional lexical entries on the basis of existing lexical entries.

(7.5) Linking to syntax triggered by different profiling of event participants

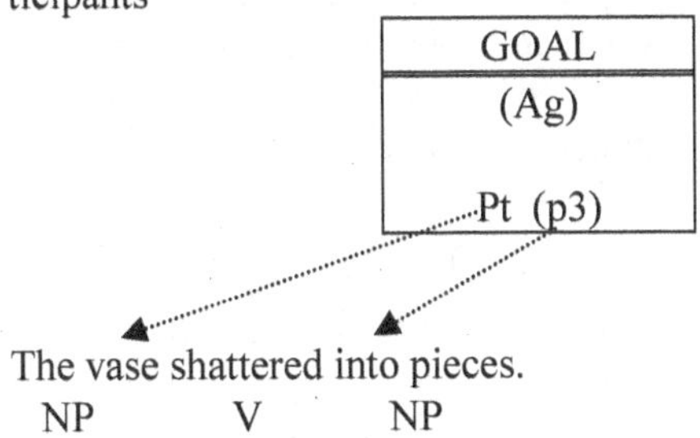

Let us now turn to the event-frames for the prototypical senses of *melt* and *freeze* which exhibit similar restrictions as the event-frame of *shatter*. Since the general observations with respect to syntactic linking made in connection with *shatter* also hold for other event-frames in this subsection and the types of sentences licensed by them, we will not discuss the linking patterns for each example individually unless there is a difference in event-frame architecture that has consequences for the syntactic realization of the verb's arguments. In other words, the linking of event participants can be straightforwardly deduced from the organization of the frame-semantic event-frames.

7.2.1.1.2 Melt

(7.6) Event-based frame semantic representation of the prototypical sense of *melt*

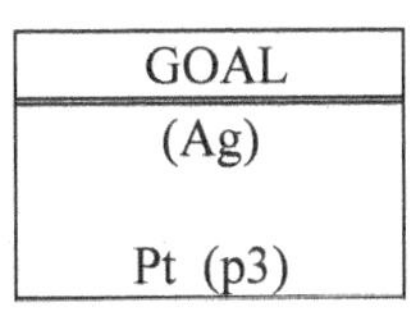

Ag: Entity exerting energy that can lead objects to liquefy
Pt: Object that warms up and/or liquefies as the result of energy being applied to it
p3: SYN: PP
SEM: denoting the end result state (or end location of a path) of a mass that has been liquefied by heat

(7.7)
a. They melted the butter.
b. They melted the butter to liquid.
c. They melted the butter over the fish.
d. *They melted the butter liquid.
e. *They melted the butter green.
f. *They melted themselves over the table/to exhaustion.
g. The butter melted (to liquid).

7.2.1.1.3 Freeze

(7.8) Event-based frame semantic representation of the prototypical sense of *freeze*[4]

GOAL
(Ag) Pt (p3)

Ag: Entity that lowers the temperature by exerting energy
Pt: Object whose physical state changes as the result of a surroundings
p3: SYN: AP or PP (headed by *to* or *into*)
SEM: denoting the result state of a liquid that is frozen

(7.9)
a. They froze the water.
b. They froze the water solid.
c. *They froze the water over the car.
d. They froze the water to ice.
e. *They froze the ice purple.

[4]Other event-frames associated with *freeze* denote different semantic concepts. Take, for example, the event-frame of *freeze-out* describing a situation in which somebody is eliminated from a competition (*Turn up the heat unless you're trying to freeze your friends out!)* The event-frame of *freeze-over*, on the other hand, denotes a situation in which a surface becomes covered with a layer of ice (*Last night's frost was enough to freeze over the lake*).

f. *They froze themselves over the fridge/ to exhaustion.
g. The ice froze solid.

Next, let us turn to the event-frames of the prototypical senses of *kill* and *bayonet* as well as to the types of arguments they license.

7.2.1.1.4 Kill

(7.10) Event-based frame semantic representation of the prototypical sense of *kill*

GOAL
Ag Pt (p3)

Ag: Entity causing an entity to be dead
Pt: Object or event which dies
p3: LEX: *dead*

(7.11) a. *Kenny killed.
b. Kenny killed us (dead).
c. *Kenny killed us into the house.
d. *Kenny killed us to death.
e. *Kenny killed us dark.
f. Kenny killed himself.
g. Kenny killed himself dead.
h. *Kenny killed himself to exhaustion.
i. *We killed dead.

The event-frame of prototypical *kill* differs from *shatter*, *melt*, and *freeze* in three ways. First, the LEX (for lexical specification) notation shows that *kill* prescribes a specific type of resultative phrase, namely *dead*, to denote the outcome of the patient participant (note that modifications of *dead* such as *stone dead* are permitted). This specification rules out sentences like (7.11c), (7.11d), and (7.11e). Second, the patient event participant may be co-referential with the agent, cf. (7.11f) and (7.11g). This is possible because the event-frame of prototypical *kill* does not allow its agent participant to be omitted (cf. the missing parentheses around 'Ag' in (7.10)). Note that in (7.11g) the patient participant is not construed as a divided person as is the case with fake objects (cf. Section 7.2.3 below) because the reflexive may occur by itself without the resultative phrase as in (7.11f).[5] This is tied to the third difference between *kill* and *shatter*, *melt*, and *freeze*. The agent event participant may not be omitted, cf. (7.11h). Again, the event-frame indicates this requirement by the fact that the agent 'Ag' is not surrounded by parentheses.[6]

Since the event-frame for *bayonet* exhibits the same architecture as that of *kill*, except for the specification of the resultative phrase as *to death* instead of *dead*, we do not need to discuss it in detail.[7] Note, again, that the resultative-phrase specifications of *kill* and *bayonet* (*dead* vs. *to death*) are idiosyncratic and conventionalized which means that they need to be listed at the level of the event-frame and cannot be predicted on general grounds.

7.2.1.1.5 Summary

In this section we discussed a number of verbs whose prototypical event-frames lexically subcategorize for a specific type of optional resultative phrase. I have shown that the event-frames of *shatter*, *melt*, and *freeze* also encode information that allows the backgrounding of the agent event-participant in order to profile the patient participant (intransitive use). The event-frames of prototypical *kill* and *bayonet,* however, do not allow for this option. Instead, they necessitate the construal of the agent participant in terms of a true patient participant and not in terms of a divided agent participant (fake object). This is not possible with the event-frames that allow omission of the agent participant.

In each of the attested cases, the resultative phrase serves to emphasize the viewpoint regarding the outcome of the event. Both the comparison with other verbs that are closely related in meaning but do not allow the same

---

[5]This shows that the reflexive is construed as a true patient in these cases and not in terms of a divided agent, i.e., a fake object (cf. *He ran his feet sore* vs. **He ran his feet*) (cf. our discussion of fake objects in Section 7.2.2). Another indication that the reflexive NPs licensed by the event frames in this section are not fake objects but rather conceptualized as true distinct prototypical patients is the fact that they allow passivization (cf. *Kenny killed himself/Kenny was killed (by himself)* vs. *Kenny ran himself to exhaustion/*Kenny was run to exhaustion (by himself)*).

[6]Other verbs that are closely related in meaning to *kill* do generally not allow the same type of resultative modification. This has probably to do with the fact that *kill* simply states a fact that an animate being has been deprived of life, whereas *murder* (**He murdered him dead/to death*), *slay* (**He slayed him dead/to death*) and *assassinate* (**He assassinated him dead/to death*) all include a more dramatic action, wantonness, motive, and intention which subsume the meaning expressed by the resultative phrase *dead* in combination with *kill*. This means that the event-frames of *murder*, *assassinate*, and *slay* each have event-frame semantic specifications that differ from that of *kill*.

[7]Of course, the event-frame also contains other types of off-stage and on-stage information that makes it different from *kill*.

type of resultative modification and the specific requirements of certain verbs with respect to the semantic and syntactic type of resultative phrase has shown that their distribution is not predictable on general grounds. This has led me to propose that each event-frame must contain lexical specifications (collocational restrictions) with respect to the possible distribution of its event participants in resultative constructions. We now turn to cases in which the resultative construction makes a vague interpretation of an end result state more precise.

7.2.1.2 Rendering a Vague Endpoint of an Event More Precise

Recall from Section 5.2.3.2 that the verbs in (7.12a)-(7.12f) convey information about the end result state of the patient argument and that without a resultative phrase this end result is vague in some regard. Based on this observation I proposed that the resultative phrase specifies the end result state of the prototypical patient participant.

(7.12)
a. Jack painted the house (red).
b. Anabel washed her sweater (clean).
c. Niko hammered the metal (flat).
d. Lilian cut the bread (to pieces).
e. Lane broke the vase (to pieces).
f. Jill strangled Kim (to death).

The corpus data discussed in Chapter 5 show that verbs are highly selective with respect to the types of resultative phrases with which they occur. This has led me to claim that each event-frame lexically selects for a specific type of resultative phrase. We now turn to a discussion of the licensing of different arguments by the respective event-frames. We begin with the event-frame of prototypical *paint*.[8]

[8] In this section we do not address the licensing of fake objects which are licensed by the same event-frames. The possibility for licensing fake objects is given by some of the event-frames, because they allow recruitment of off-stage information as is shown by the 'W' and 'p2' specifications. For a detailed discussion of how fake objects are licensed with these verbs, see Section 7.2.2.

7.2.1.2.1 Paint

(7.13) Event-based frame semantic representation of the prototypical sense of *paint*[9]

GOAL
Ag (W p2) Pt (p3)

Ag: Entity applying paint to a surface
Pt: Surface or object that is construed as exhibiting a surface
p3: SYN: AP or NP
SEM: denoting a color or a property associated with the prototypically intended end result of applying paint to a surface

(7.14) a. Jack painted the house {red/very bright/a pale shade of green/waterproof}.
b. *Jack painted the air red.
c. *Jack painted the house liquid.
d. *The house painted red.

(7.14a) is licensed by (7.13) since the patient argument *the house* has a surface and the resultative phrases all denote a color or a property associated with paint at the prototypical end result of applying it to a surface. Note that without the resultative phrase or the proper contextual background information, it is not clear what exact state the house is in as a result of Jack's painting activity.[10] In other words, the resultative phrase renders the interpretations of the end result state associated with *paint* more precise. (7.14c) is ruled out because *liquid* does not denote a prototypical intended end result state of applying paint to a surface. When a surface is painted, the prototypical end result includes the intended goal that the paint is dry at the end of the painting event. That is, although liquid is an inherent quality of paint,

---

[9]Other event-frames associated with *paint* denote different semantic concepts and thus contain different types of frame-semantic information. For a discussion of the Image-impression event-frame (*The visitors painted their symbolic image on galleries.* (BNC)), the Characterize event-frame (*If ministers spend this week in Blackpool trying to paint the Labour Party red...* (BNC)), and the 'Party'-sense *(Tonight we're going to paint the town red!* (BNC)), see Section 6.3.3.2.1.

[10]Note that it is not even necessary that the color of the surface changes. If a surface is painted with a liquid that makes it waterproof, for example, the color of the surface does not have to change.

it is not a prototypical intended end result of applying paint to a surface. (7.14b) is ruled out by (7.13) because *air* can typically not be construed as exhibiting a surface in this context.[11] Finally, the prototypical event-frame of *paint* does not allow realization of the patient argument in subject position under omission of the agent participant as the missing parentheses around 'Ag' in (7.13) and example (7.14d) show.

7.2.1.2.2 Wash

The prototypical sense of *wash* is equal to the removal-1 sense of *wipe* discussed in Section 6.3.3.2.2, i.e., the surface of the object from which an undesired substance is removed is profiled.

(7.15) Event-based frame semantic representation of the prototypical sense of *wash*[12]

GOAL
Ag (W p2) Pt (p3)

Ag: Entity exerting energy towards an object such that unwanted substances get removed from the object
Pt: Object or area that is host to unwanted substances
p3: SYN: AP
SEM: denoting a state of cleanliness[13]

---

[11]Verbs that are closely related in meaning such as *dye, stain*, and *color* typically occur with other types of patient arguments (as well as other off-stage information). For example, hair is typically dyed and not painted. This shows that although the respective event-frames show a great deal of overlap that might be abstracted away at a higher level, each event-frame exhibits its own idiosyncratic specifications.

[12]Other event-frames associated with *wash* denote different types of semantic concepts. These include, among others, the funnel-sense (*Kim washed the dirt into the sink*) and the removal-sense-2 (*I would wait as long as it took to wash the mess off the roof.* (BNC)). In this connection note that according to our event-frame analysis of resultatives *Stefan washed the soap out of his eyes* is not an instance of a fake object licensed by an event participant perspective shift based on the prototypical sense of *wash* as represented by the event-frame in (7.15). Instead, it is licensed by the removal-sense-2 that profiles the undesired substance instead of the surface or object from which it is to be removed (cf. also *Dawn washed the dirt off her car*). See Section 6.3.3.2.2 for a detailed discussion of these different event-frames associated with *wash*.

[13]This information may also be overruled by context, however, only within the semantic boundaries imposed by the 'state of cleanliness' specifications of 'p3'. In other words, other resultative phrases have to express either a modification of a state of cleanliness (e.g. *halfway clean*), or the opposite of *clean*, e.g., *dirty*.

(7.16) a. Anabel washed her {sweater/her car/her table/the bathtub} clean.
b. *Anabel washed her sweater {to cleanliness/to a bright shine/a great cleanliness}.
c. *Anabel washed the mud clean.
d. *The sweater washed (clean).

The patient participants in (7.16a) are all licensed by (7.15) since they may be construed as an area hosting an unwanted substance. (7.16b) is ruled out by the event-frame of prototypical *wash* because the resultative phrases are not APs. Finally, under normal contextual conditions, *the mud* in (7.16c) cannot be construed as being host to an unwanted substance which leads to (7.16c) being ruled out by (7.15).[14] Note that besides the obvious differences in on-stage and off-stage information, the event-frame in (7.15) differs from that of prototypical *paint* in (7.13) in that the former does not allow a freedom of choice when it comes to the syntactic choice of resultative phrases. It is only at the lexical level of event-frames that this relevant distinction can be made. Let us now turn to the event-frame of prototypical *hammer*.

7.2.1.2.3 Hammer

(7.17) Event-based frame semantic representation of the 'form-changing' sense of *hammer*[15]

GOAL
Ag Pt p3

[14]The event-frame of the prototypical sense of *wash* also licenses fake objects, as is indicated by the 'W' and the 'p2' in the middle line between the agent and patient specifications. See Section 7.2.2.

[15]Other event-frames associated with *hammer* denote different types of semantic concepts (i.e. senses). These are, e.g., frames which describe (1) a forceful impact on an object so that it becomes part of another object (*Continue to hammer more nails into the back* (BNC)), (2) removing a physical property of an entity by applying strong force (*The blacksmith hammered the dents out of the shield of the knight* (BNC)), and (3) forceful impact of an object onto a surface without changing the property of either participant (*He hammered his rifle butt against the wooden paneling in the hallway* (BNC)), among others. The resultative phrases of each of these distinct event-frames denote a different semantic type of end result state. For an exhaustive BNC-list of other verbs patterning with *flat* as their resultative phrase, see Appendix A.16.

Ag: Entity exerting great amount of energy
Pt: Physical object
p3: SYN: AP
SEM: denoting a state of flatness or other state that can be construed as being directly caused by the energy emitted by the agent

(7.18) a. Niko hammered the metal {flat/thin}.
b. Niko hammered {the dough/the keychain/the carpet flat}.
c. ??Niko hammered the car flat.
d. The metal press hammered the car flat.
e. *Niko hammered the metal {to flatness/ to thinness}.
f. Niko hammered the metal hot. (resultative reading)
g. *Niko hammered the metal cold. (resultative reading)
h. *Niko hammered the metal.
i. *The metal hammered flat.

(7.17) differs from other event-frames in this section in that it obligatorily requires the overt realization of its resultative phrase, cf. (7.18h), which is indicated by the missing parentheses around 'p3' in (7.17) (note that without the resultative phrase, (7.18h) must be realized as *Niko hammered on the metal*).[16] The difference between (7.18c) and (7.18d) illustrates that contextual background information and pragmatic reasoning plays a role in the licensing of resultatives.[17] That is, although *Niko* is a person who can be construed as a hammerer, this construal sounds odd in (7.18c) given normal contextual background information. A different agent participant, such as a metal press in (7.18d), however, does not pose this problem because it is part of world knowledge that metal presses are able to exert great physical force. This shows that although a sentence like (7.18c) may be licensed by the event-frame in (7.17), it sounds pragmatically odd.[18] Sentence (7.18e) is

---

[16]The lexical default of this event-frame may be overridden by contextual default information or by other types of perspectivizing functions, such as the progressive form (cf. *Niko was hammering for five hours*).

[17]Note that a different event-frame denoting a different sense of *hammer* licenses *She hammered the metal to pieces,* in which the resultative phase specifications prescribe a PP denoting the loss of structural integrity. It is important to note that this event-frame describes a *different* semantic concept associated with the activity of hammering (i.e., loss of structural integrity (*to pieces*) vs. reduction of the physical expansion of the material (*flat*)).

[18]This oddness, however, does not arise when a given context is set up such that *Niko* has enough power to achieve this goal within a reasonable time. (*Niko took the wonderpill that made him 15 feet tall and stronger than superman. His friend brought him the biggest sledgehammer in town. Then, Niko hammered the car flat.*)

ruled out by (7.17) because the result phrase is not an AP. (7.18f) is licensed by the event-frame in (7.17) since *hot* denotes a state that is a direct result caused by the energy emitted by the agent. (7.18g) is ruled out since *cold* does not typically denote a direct result state caused by the energy emitted by the agent of a hammering activity.

7.2.1.2.4 Cut

(7.19) Event-based frame semantic representation of the prototypical sense of *cut*[19]

GOAL
Ag Pt (p3)

Ag: Entity exerting energy
Pt: Object that is divided as a result of applying force with a sharp instrument to it
p3: SYN: PP, AP
SEM: denoting the end result state of physical disintegration

(7.20) a. Lilian cut the bread.
b. Lilian cut the bread {to pieces/into thick slices/too short}.
c. Lilian cut the bread onto the plate.
d. *Lilian cut the bread {broken/a great slice}.
e. *The bread cut (to pieces/onto the plate).

[19]Note that the prototypical sense of *cut* profiles the whole object that is being affected by the activity of cutting. This means that the resultative phrase is only a specification of this event-frame (cf. *Lilian cut the bread (to pieces)*). Other event-frames associated with *cut* denote different semantic concepts. The event-frame of *cut-off*, e.g., profiles the entity which is removed from a larger object. The event-frame of *cut-off*, in contrast to that of *prototypical cut*, thus requires the resultative phrase *off* to be overtly realized (*Lilian cut a slice* vs. *Lilian cut a slice off*). Without the resultative phrase, the semantic concept denoted by this event frame cannot be properly construed. Other event-frames associated with *cut* denote semantic concepts which refer to (1) reducing somebody's arrogance (*cut down to size*: *Christian was boasting as usual about how much he could drink, but Bernie soon cut him down to size by drinking him under the table*), (2) exclude (*cut out*: *It was really bad for Stefan yesterday, because they kept cutting him out of the conversation*). All of these event-frames exhibit on-stage and off-stage information that is distinct from that associated with the event-frame of the prototypical sense of *cut*. In addition, these event-frames require overt realization of their respective result phrases.

(7.20b) and (7.20c) are licensed by (7.19) because they can be construed as specifying the end result state of the physical disintegration denoted by the event frame in terms of a PP. These phrases inform about the exact outcome of the event and thus help to eliminate vague interpretations. (7.20d), however, is ruled out by (7.19) since the resultative phrases are not PPs.[20] (7.20e) is not licensed by (7.19) because the event-frame's requirements for the obligatory realization of the agent argument are not met. Let us now turn to the event frame of the prototypical sense of *break*, a verb of surface contact.

7.2.1.2.5 Break

(7.21) Event-based frame semantic representation of the prototypical sense of *break*

GOAL
(Ag) Pt (p3)

Ag: Entity exerting energy
Pt: Object that loses its structural integrity as a result of applying force
p3: SYN: PP
SEM: denoting the end result state of physical disintegration[21]

---

[20]Note that verbs which are closely related in meaning to *cut* such as *carve, slit, slash,* and *hew* do not share the same distribution of resultative phrases as the prototypical event-frame of *cut,* because they denote different types of semantic concepts with greater connotational force and are associated with different types of on-stage and off-stage information. For example, *carve* and *slit* denote greater care, skill, and restraint (*?Lilian carved the bread to pieces/*Lilian slit the bread onto the plate*), whereas *slash* and *hew* (*??Lilian slashed the bread onto the plate/ *Lilian hewed the bread to pieces*) are associated with an action that is more violent and forceful than that denoted by *cut.* The blocking of resultative phrase realizations similar to that of prototypical *cut* is probably due to the fact that the more precise manner specifications of these verbs eliminates the option of further modifying the action by adding a resultative phrase as is the case with prototypical *cut.*

[21]For an exhaustive BNC-list of other verbs occurring with the same semantic types of resultative phrases, see Appendix A.1 for verbs patterning with *apart,* Appendix A.19 for verbs patterning with *into pieces,* and Appendix A.47 for verbs patterning with *to pieces.*

(7.22) a. She broke the vase.
b. She broke the vase {to pieces/into a thousand pieces/apart/in two}.
c. *She broke the vase broken.[22]
d. *She broke the water to pieces.
e. The vase broke to pieces.

(7.21) licenses only resultative phrases such as in (7.22b) that are PPs denoting the end result state of physical disintegration.[23] Furthermore, (7.22d) is ruled out because water is typically not construed as an object that can lose structural integrity as a result of the application of force.[24] The event-frame in (7.22e) differs from other event-frames in this section in that it optionally allows profiling of the patient participant (cf. the missing parentheses around 'Ag'). In this case, the patient participant is linked to subject position. *Break* differs from other verbs of surface contact in that its prototypical event-frame allows resultative modification which is not the case with all verbs of surface contact as the distribution of *break*, *strike*, and *touch* illustrate.

(7.23) a. *Stefan broke.
b. Stefan broke the vase.
c. Stefan broke the vase to pieces.
d. Stefan broke the vase with a hammer.

(7.24) a. ?Christian struck.
b. Christian struck the vase.
c. *Christian struck the vase to pieces.
d. Christian struck the vase with his hand.

(7.25) a. ?Dawn touched.
b. Dawn touched the vase.

---

[22]There is a general constraint that prohibits *broken* from appearing in English resultative constructions. In German, on the other hand, *kaputt* ('broken') is highly productive in resultative constructions (Cf. *Fritz schlug die Vase kaputt.* ('Fritz broke the vase to pieces')).

[23]The event-frame representing the prototypical sense of *break* does not permit fake objects, as is indicated by the missing diacritics 'W' and 'p2' that allow recruitment of world knowledge (cf. **She broke herself exhausted*, **She broke the hammer to pieces* (on the resultative reading in which the hammer is employed as an instrument to break an object)).

[24]Technically, of course, water may be broken down into atoms. Other event-frames associated with *break* denote different types of semantic concepts, e.g., *break X up*, *break X off*, and *break X down*. For a detailed discussion of these separate event-frames see Section 6.3.1.

c. *Dawn touched the vase to pieces.
d. Dawn touched the vase with her hand.

The examples show that *strike* and *touch* show syntactic distributions outside of resultative constructions similar to *break*. However, they do not allow the same type of resultative modification as *break*. This difference in distribution is reflected by the architecture of the respective event-frames of *strike* and *touch* which indicate that no result specification is allowed (no 'p3' specification following 'Pt', as opposed to the event-frame of prototypical *break* in (7.21)) by the prototypical senses of *strike* and *touch*.

(7.26) Architecture of the event-frames of prototypical *strike* and *touch*.

GOAL
Ag
Pt

Finally, let us turn to the event-frame of prototypical *strangle*.

7.2.1.2.6 Strangle

(7.27) Event-based frame semantic representation of the prototypical sense of *strangle*

GOAL
Ag
Pt (p3)

Ag: Entity obstructing the flow of air in the patient
Pt: Animate being that breathes
p3: LEX: *to death*[25]

(7.28) a. Jill strangled Kim.
b. Jill strangled Kim to death.
c. *Jill strangled Kim dead.

[25]Note that *strangle*, unlike other verbs discussed in this section only allows *to death* as its resultative phrase. For an exhaustive list of verbs also occurring with *to death* in the BNC, see Appendix A.43.

d. *Jill strangled Kim off the bridge.
e. *Jill strangled the beer case to death.
f. *Kim strangled to death.

The event-frame specifications for the patient participant and the resultative phrase of (7.27) license both (7.28a) and (7.28b). (7.28c) and (7.28d) are ruled out because of a violation of the resultative phrase requirement. Since the postverbal NP in (7.28e) cannot be construed as fulfilling the semantic requirements for the patient argument imposed by (7.27), it is ruled out on semantic/pragmatic terms. Note that without the result phrase it is not clear what state *Kim* is in as a result of Jill's strangling activity (she could be dead or alive). The function of the resultative phrase is thus to render the interpretation of the end result state more precise.

7.2.1.2.7 Summary

We have seen that the function of the resultatives in this section differs from the types of resultatives discussed in Section 7.2.1.1. Whereas the latter only serve to highlight the outcome of an event, the former are used to specify the outcome of an event, thereby conveying a more precise viewpoint about the result state of an event participant. In this section I have shown that each event-frame licenses the resultative by lexically subcategorizing for the semantic and/or syntactic type of the resultative phrase. The comparison with verbs that are closely related in meaning but do not allow the same type of resultative modification has shown that the ability to occur with a resultative is a matter of conventionalization and cannot be predicted on general grounds. It therefore must be marked on an individual basis for each event-frame.[26]

Although the event-frames surveyed in this section are constructions and as such exhibit the same overall architecture (pairings of form with meaning), they differ with respect to the types of restrictions they impose on resultative phrases. Whereas some event-frames like that of prototypical *paint* state more general semantic requirements with respect to collocational restrictions on resultative phrases, *strangle* lexically subcategorizes for *to death* as its resultative phrase. Except for the event-frame associated with the prototypical sense of *hammer*, the overt syntactic realization of the resultative phrase is optional as is the case with the resultatives surveyed in Section 7.2.1.1. The crucial point here is that there is a link between the

[26]As pointed out in Chapter 6, this does not mean that larger generalizations are not possible. However, in order to arrive at a system that is able to deal with the entire distribution of attested resultative constructions it is necessary to follow a bottom-up approach.

degree of collocational restriction a verb exhibits in the resultative pattern and conventionally expected results. To be more precise, a speaker's world knowledge about different types of conventionally expected results determines the range of possible resultatives and as such reflects the degree of linguistic conventionality (the extent to which a given verb may or must occur with a particular resultative phrase or not). The influence of a speaker's world knowledge about conventionally expected results on the degree of collocational restrictions exhibited by verbs becomes even more apparent in cases in which verbs always require the overt realization of a specific type of resultative phrase as the following section illustrates.

7.2.1.3 Obligatory Resultatives

The event-frames in this section require the overt realization of the resultative phrase due to semantic spreading 'whereby instead of packing a fat bundle of semantic features into one word, matters can be made more flexible by packing thinner bundles into two or more words.' (Bolinger 1971: 45)[27] This means that whereas the resultative meaning of the verbs in the last two sections can be interpreted to a certain degree without the resultative phrase, the semantic concepts denoted by the verb's event-frames in this section cannot be interpreted appropriately without the resultative phrase. The event-frames in this section capture this property by imposing tighter collocational restrictions that require overt realizations of very specific resultative phrases with certain verbs.

[27]For further studies of how different types of phrasal verbs with resultative meaning spread their semantic information over the verb and the resultative particle, see Nickel (1978) (who labels this phenomenon 'division of labour' (1978: 77)), and Quirk et al. (1985: 1401).

7.2.1.3.1 Drive-Crazy

(7.29) Event-based frame semantic representation of *drive-crazy*

GOAL
Ag Pt p3

Ag: Entity causing a (typically negative) mental impression
Pt: Animate object that has mental capabilities
p3: SYN: AP (77%), PP (23%)
SEM: (typically) negative mental state[28]

(7.30)
a. *Erin drove Eric.
b. Erin drove Eric {crazy/mad/to desperation/to insanity/to a drinking and gambling problem/bonkers/nuts/crackers/up the wall}.
c. *Erin drove Eric {wooden/to old age/into pieces}.
d. {The final score/the sound of the alarm clock/alcohol/free beer}drove Eric mad.
e. Erin drove {her dog/the birds/her goldfish}crazy.
f. *Eric drove crazy.

Note that 'p3' is not surrounded by parenthesis in (7.29) indicating that it must be overtly realized. The 'p3' specifications differ from those of other types of event-frames discussed so far in that their syntactic specifications include percentage numbers for APs and PPs. These specifications capture our observations made in Chapter 5 that *drive-crazy* shows a clear preference for APs over PPs.[29] The event-frame in (7.29) licenses (7.30b),

---

[28] Recall our discussion of corpus data of *drive-crazy* in Chapters 5 and 6. There we have seen that it is not possible to draw sharp boundaries between syntactic categories of resultative phrases (fuzziness of categories). However, I have shown that there is a clear tendency in favor of adjectival phrases. At the same time, some select types of PPs occurring with the *drive-crazy* sense in the BNC only occur with the *drive-crazy* sense of *drive* and no other verb in its resultative usage in the whole corpus. These PPs include *to madness, to insanity, to distraction, to desperation,* and *up the wall.* For a complete list of BNC-attested examples of *drive-crazy*, see Appendix B.1.

[29] The percentage numbers are based on the total distribution of resultative phrases with this sense of *drive* in the BNC. Note that if this event-frame were used to simulate real human language production on a Natural Language Processing System, it would be necessary to encode the entire list of attested corpus resultative phrases including the percentage numbers for

(7.30d), and (7.30e), and rules out (7.30a), (7.30c), and (7.30f).[30] Although this event-frame has specific semantic limitations with respect to the semantic boundaries it imposes on resultative phrases, the range of resultative phrases (and its event participants) shows great productivity within these boundaries.[31] Other event-frames do not allow for such a broad variety of resultative phrases but limit the range of resultative phrases, as the event-frame of *wipe-out* illustrates.

7.2.1.3.2 Wipe-Out

(7.31) Event-based frame semantic representation of *wipe-out*[32]

GOAL
Ag Pt p3

Ag: Entity exerting force that can destroy objects
Pt: Object or event
p3: LEX: *out* (+modification)

(7.32)
a. Hurricane Fran wiped Wrightsville Beach out.
b. They virtually wiped out a Japanese division. (BNC)
c. It points out that Stalin wiped out the entire leadership of the Polish Communist Party in 1937. (BNC)
d. The comprehensive schools should wipe the other schools out of existence. (BNC)
e. *Hurricane Fran wiped Wrightsville Beach.
f. *They wiped a Japanese division in.

---

each resultative phrase. Based on these lexical specifications it would then be possible to predict how often a certain resultative phrase would be used in discourse.

[30]The event-frame specifications of *drive-crazy* also indicate that it is difficult to derive them from a basic sense of *drive*. Compare the resultative specifications of the two frames (**Erin drove crazy/ Erin drove home*).

[31]Note that other verbs that denote motion by using a vehicle like *fly*, *sail*, and *bicycle* are not associated with an event-frame similar to *drive-crazy* (cf. **She flew him to madness*, or **Sam sailed her up the wall*). This shows that the distribution of *drive* with resultatives in this event-frame is not predictable on general grounds outside of this specific event frame which in turn means that it is conventionalized and must be listed as such with its individual properties in the lexicon. However, some select verbs do occur in the *drive-crazy* sense, but only very marginally (cf. *He's inhaled too much resin – sends you crazy after a while* (BNC)).

[32]For a complete list of BNC-attested examples of *wipe-out*, see Appendix B.3.

g. *Stalin wiped the entire leadership off.
h. *A Japanese division wiped out.

Note that whereas (7.31) licenses (7.32a)-(7.32d), it rules out (7.32e)-(7.32h) because these sentences do not contain *out* which is crucial for interpreting the specific semantic concept denoted by *wipe-out*. Also, (7.32e)-(7.32h) cannot be readily based on any other event-frames that are associated with *wipe*, such as *wipe-in*, *wipe-off*, or prototypical *wipe*. As with other types of event-frames discussed in this chapter, the information contained in (7.31) must be stated at the level of event-frames because *wipe-out* denotes a very specific semantic concept that cannot be generated using general compositional mechanisms alone. Notice that other verbs which share the 'removal of an unwanted substance from a surface' event-frame with *wipe*, such as *wash*, *sweep*, *polish*, and *dust*, do not share the 'physical elimination' sense with *wipe*. (cf. **Hurricane Fran swept Wrightsville Beach out*, **They washed a Japanese division out*, **Stalin polished out the entire leadership*, and **The schools should dust the other schools out of existence*.) This shows that *wipe-out* is a conventionalized form-meaning pair that must be stated at the lexical level.

While it might be argued that *out* in *wipe-out* and *blow-out* is responsible for 'delivering' the elimination sense associated with the respective event-frames and that it should therefore be possible to generate new verb meanings based on the existing base meanings of *wipe* and *blow*, this is very difficult. The problem is not only due to different lexical-semantic polysemy networks of the respective verbs, but also to the polysemy of *out*, as well as the fact that when *out* combines with other types of verbs it does not come to mean eliminate, cf. *take-out*, *work-out*, *push-out*, and *look-out*, but it forms other semantic concepts that do not mean *eliminate*. This comparison shows that the *verb-out* combinations are conventionalized and hard to predict on general grounds, i.e., on the basis of their meanings outside of resultative constructions. In order to predict the semantic range of event participants as well as the ability to occur with resultative phrases, it is thus necessary to first lexically list the properties of all of the conventionalized combinations denoting specific semantic concepts. Only with such a bottom-up approach will it be possible to arrive at valid generalizations. We now turn to the discussion of *blow-out*.[33]

---

[33]For the present discussion I label verbs such as *blow out* or *switch off* that are traditionally known as a subclass of 'phrasal verbs' (Bolinger 1971) or 'verb-particle constructions' (Lipka 1972) as resultative verbs because they denote a resultative meaning by focusing on the place, position, or state resulting from the situation expressed by the verb. This does not mean that all phrasal verbs exhibit resultative meanings, as Brinton (1988: 176-184) points out.

7.2.1.3.3 Blow-Out

(7.33) Event-based frame semantic representation of the prototypical sense of *blow-out*

GOAL
(Ag) Pt p3

Ag: Entity that makes air move
Pt: Flame or object associated with a flame[34]
p3: LEX: *out*

(7.34)
a. Sticks meant to blow it out. (BNC)
b. He entered the attic and blew the lamp out. (BNC)
c. The wind blew the fire out.
d. *He blew it. (on resultative reading)
e. *He blew the lamp {off/in/under/on/out of the house}.
f. *He blew {the table/the car/the beer}out.
g. *{The bottle/the CD-player/the dictionary} blew the candle out.
h. The candle blew out.

The semantic specifications of (7.33) license (7.34a)-(7.34c), and (7.34h) and rule out (7.34d)-(7.34g). The distributions in (7.34a)-(7.34h) illustrate that *blow* always has to occur with *out* to denote the specific semantic concept of elimination of a flame or object associated with a flame. (7.33) differs from (7.31) in that it also licenses an intransitive variant in which the patient is mapped to subject position (cf. parentheses surrounding the agent in (7.33) indicating that it may be backgrounded). This event-frame denotes a semantic concept different from the general caused-motion event-frame associated with *blow* which can also appear with *out*. The crucial semantic difference between the two (*eliminate a flame* vs. *make s.th. move*) also manifests itself in the fact that under normal contextual conditions the caused-motion event frame associated with *blow* has to occur with a PP denoting a final endpoint of the patient participant and not only with a sin-

[34]Note that the *blow-out* event-frame does not allow for fake objects as the option for recruitment of world knowledge ('W' and 'p2') is missing in this event-frame (**She blew herself to exhaustion out*/ **She blew the hairdryer to pieces out*).

gle preposition as is the case with the *blow-out* event frame. This is illustrated by the following sentences.

(7.35) a. He sucked on his funny cigarette and blew the smoke into my face. (COBUILD)
b. *... and blew the smoke into.
c. ... with the wind trying to blow me out to sea again. (BNC)
d. ?...with the wind trying to blow me out.

Besides the obvious differences in underlying semantic concepts between the two event-frames, the architecture of the caused-motion event-frame associated with *blow* shows different specifications when it comes to the resultative phrase. Consider the following event-frame architecture.

(7.36) Event-based frame semantic representation of caused-motion sense of *blow*

GOAL
(Ag) Pt p3

Ag: Entity that makes air move
Pt: Object that can be moved by air stream
p3: SYN: PP
SEM: construed as denoting a definite endpoint

(7.37) a. *Claire blew the dust.
b. Claire blew the dust {away/out/off}.
c. *Claire blew the dust into.
d. Claire blew the dust into his face.
e. The dust blew into his face.

The comparison of (7.37b) and (7.37c) shows that prepositions vary with respect to how they are construed in the caused-motion event-frame of *blow*. Whereas *away*, *out*, and *off* function as particles that do not require an NP, *into* is a preposition which requires an NP to achieve the definite endpoint interpretation. Besides denoting a semantic concept different from (7.33) (*caused motion* vs. *elimination of a flame*), the event-frame in (7.36) differs from that in (7.33) because it allows a broader variety of resultative phrases denoting the end state of the patient participant.[35]

7.2.1.3.4 Switch-Off

(7.38) Event-based frame semantic representation of *switch-off*

GOAL
Ag Pt p3

Ag: Entity that operates a switch
Pt: Object that is connected to a switch which regulates supply of energy
p3: LEX: *off*

(7.39) a. Jen switched {the computer/the light/the oven}off.
b. *Julio switched the TV {under/into/away/purple/to exhaustion}.
c. *Jen switched the TV.
d. *Julio switched himself off.
e. *The blanket switched the TV off.
f. *The TV switched off.

(7.38) requires overt realization of *off* and does not allow any other event participants besides the ones specified by the semantic requirements of its event-frame. This information rules out (7.39b)-(7.39f).[36]

7.2.1.3.5 Summary

The data discussed in this section illustrate that resultative phrases denoting a common semantic concept in combination with specific verbs have to be obligatorily realized at the syntactic level. The comparison with verbs that are closely related in meaning has led me to the conclusion that the verb-resultative combinations are highly conventionalized and not predictable on general grounds. By encoding the verb-resultative phrase combinations in

[35]Note that sentences like *The wind blew* are licensed by a different event-frame, namely the prototypical event-frame of *blow*.
[36]For a complete BNC-list of other verbs occurring with *off*, see Appendix A.23.

terms of tight collocational restrictions at the lexical level, it is not only possible to account for the distribution of different types of resultative phrases (either in terms of broader syntactic and semantic specifications as with *drive-crazy*, or very specific phrases, such as *out* in *blow-out*). In addition, it is also possible to state collocational restrictions that the verb imposes on its respective event-participants. Since each event-frame exhibits its own distinct specifications, each event-frame is to be considered as a construction *per se*. On this view, no additional structure needs to be added to a verb's semantic or syntactic structure (see our survey of other analyses in Chapters 2-4) because only specific senses of a verb are conventionally associated with a resultative pattern of the form [NP V NP XP].[37]

The data clearly demonstrate that knowledge about conventionally expected results ('off-stage information') determines the range of possible resultative phrases. In this case, there is almost no flexibility when it comes to substituting resultative phrases because the combination of verb and resultative phrase encodes the semantics of the event's outcome. Any substitution of the resultative phrase would alter this meaning and would thus lead to a different interpretation. In other words, the tight collocational restrictions prohibiting any substitution of the resultative phrase reflect the fact that the verb-resultative phrase combination denotes a very specific conventionally expected result. It is this link between collocational restrictions and conventionally expected results that illustrates how knowledge about the world may license linguistic structures.

7.2.2 Perspectivizing Non-Prototypical Patient Participants: Fake Objects

7.2.2.1 Fake Reflexives with Motion Event-Frames

In this section we discuss cases in which the end result state profiled is not that of the prototypical patient event participant. In particular, we look at the types of contexts in which fake reflexives occur in resultative constructions incorporating motion verbs. We first consider some cases in which an intransitive motion verb occurs with a fake reflexive and a location resultative as in (7.40).

[37] To this end, Bolinger's (1961: 381) alternative question 'Is grammar something where speakers produce (i.e. originate) constructions, or where they reach for them from a pre-established inventory, when the occasion presents itself?' must be answered in the affirmative for the second part with respect to the resultatives discussed in this section.

7.2.2.1.1 Location Resultatives

(7.40)
a. ... while Blair held onto the wall and walked *himself* back to bed. (www.assgm.com/a-b/All-you-need-is-a-cape-ellison-[file-4-140k].txt)
b. The soldiers slow-walked *themselves* towards the machine guns of the enemy.(www.Siol-nan.gaidheal.com/hrogr.htm)
c. The boy walked *himself* thirty-seven blocks to an emergency room. (www.Freepics.com/members/stories/strange/boywatch.txt)
d. After school, I marched *myself* down to the public library.
e. He crawled *himself* out of bed and into his chair.
f. Why not walk *yourself* down the aisle? (Message-ID: 20000118191605.03674.00000145@ng-fol.aol.com)
g. James walks *himself* down toward the ring, in a rather hushed tone, not turning his attention to the cameras or the fans. (Message-ID: 85h66r$vf8$2@news.datasync.com)
h. Hannah raced *herself* to the landing pad that Luke was taking off from. (www.fanfix.com/stories/newrep/context.txt)

The agent event participants in (7.40a)-(7.40h) are portrayed as overcoming an obstacle against which they have to use their own will in order to move to the intended location. In (7.40a), e.g., *Blair* is so weak that he has to hold onto the wall when walking back to bed. The reflexive indicates that Blair is overcoming his own weakness and has to put extra effort into walking in order to make it back to bed. Next, consider (7.40b) in which the fake reflexive is used to express the soldiers' efforts to overcome their survival instinct urging them against moving towards the enemy's machine guns. Similar observations with respect to the use of the reflexive can be made for (7.40c)-(7.40h). Note that the use of the reflexive is not obligatory in (7.40a)-(7.40h), i.e., it can be omitted as the following examples illustrate.

(7.41)
a. ... while Blair held onto the wall and walked back to bed.
b. The soldiers slow-walked towards the machine guns of the enemy.
c. The boy walked thirty-seven blocks to an emergency room.
d. After school, I marched down to the public library, ...

e. He crawled out of bed and into his chair.
f. Why not walk down the aisle?
g. James walks down toward the ring, in a rather hushed tone, not turning his attention to the cameras or the fans.
h. Hannah raced to the landing pad that Luke was taking off from.

When the reflexives are omitted, a different pragmatic effect is achieved. Instead of emphasizing the fact that the movers have to overcome some obstacle (typically the proclivity of their mind or body to resist movement in order to reach their destination), the sentences describe the moving event from a much more neutral perspective and consequently remain silent about the movers' attitudes or emotions towards their movement. The data in (7.40) and (7.41) suggest that the fake reflexive is not primarily motivated by syntactic or semantic factors, but rather by pragmatic factors. It serves to portray an event from an unusual perspective,[38] namely from a perspective that describes the agents' attitudes and emotions towards their movement.[39] Since the *–self* forms are employed to point out something special in discourse, I label them *perspectivizing –self.*

Let us now turn to the question of what mechanisms serve to license fake reflexives. We will first discuss how agents of moving events can be construed in different ways and will then turn to the question of how this information can be associated with different types of event-frames. The realization of fake reflexives in resultative constructions such as in (7.40) is a consequence of the fact that under certain circumstances humans perceive

[38]This function of *-self* is not special to resultative usages. Compare the following sentences in which *–self* is employed to convey emphasis with respect to the agent participant (for discussion of this communicative function of *–self* and its licensing conditions, see Kemmer (1995)).

a. Though quite attractive *herself,* Hughes had neither Rogers' beauty, nor ... (members.iquest.net /~taldr/index.html)
b. If I was 20 years younger, I'd be running *myself.* (www.washingtonpost.com/wp-srv/politics/ campaigns/ wh2000/stories/ames081699.html)

[39]Another communicative function of fake reflexives is to point out that something unexpected (typically bad from the perspective of the agent) happened to an agent. That is, in the following sentences *–self* conveys information about the agents' attitudes and emotions towards the unexpected situation they end up in as a result of their moving. Note that here, too, the *–self* can be left out and the sentence has a more neutral connotation.

a. I was running from something bad and ran *myself* clean into something worse. (www. Blackcity.com/empire/chapter1.html)
b. Am I embarrassing you? No, but you walked *yourself* into a lesbian political meeting. (www. Gaydaze.com/jun97/fran/f70604.htm)
c. Harvey, who had the reputation of a coureur, would run *himself* into more trouble if he were not careful. (BNC)

their bodies as two separate entities, namely as agents and patients.[40] Since bodies can be construed as patient arguments that are undergoing some change of state instigated by the agent (the conscious Self), the patient has to be explicitly mentioned in order to convey this specific viewpoint.

The proposal that event participants are not always conceptually construed and linguistically realized as single entities is supported by Dowty's (1991) views on thematic relations. He points out that there are no strict semantic boundaries between different thematic roles such as agent, patient, and instrument, and that one cannot refer to a strict thematic role hierarchy in order to make general predictions about how semantic arguments will be realized syntactically. Specifically, event predicates exhibit a clustering of so-called proto-agent and proto-patient properties. On this view, an event participant which has the most proto-agent properties will be identified as the proto-agent of the event whereas the event participant with the most proto-patient properties will be identified as the proto-patient of the event. Dowty (1991: 572) presents a list of proto-agent and proto-patient properties.

Agent proto-role	Patient proto-role
volitional involvement in event	undergoes change of state
sentience/perception	incremental theme
causing event/change in another participant	causally affected by another participant
movement relative to another participant	stationary relative to movement
(exists independently of event)	(doesn't exist independently)

(cf. Dowty 1991: 572)

[40]To this end, compare Lakoff's (1996: 102) description of the 'Divided-Person Metaphor:' 'The Subject is supposed to be in control of the Self. The Subject can reason, but cannot function directly in the world, as the Self can. The Subject is always the locus of consciousness, subjective experience, perception, reason, and judgment. The Self consists of other aspects of a whole person – the body, emotions, a past history, social roles, and much more.' This type of metaphor is found in many different contexts, cf. the following sentences.

a. I lifted *my arm*.

b. I made *myself* get up early. (Lakoff 1996: 113)

(7.42) Linking including on-stage and off-stage frame semantic information

Ag: animate object moving legs quickly
p1: directional PP
W: world knowledge containing knowledge about
non-prototypical event-participants of running events
p2: change in state or location of event-participant from 'W'

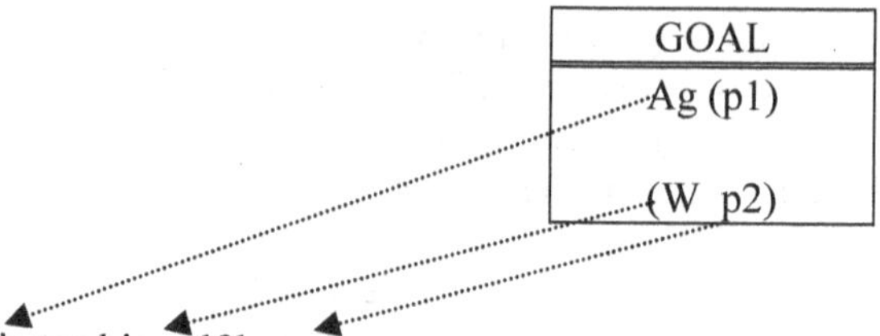

Chris ran himself home.
SU DO ResP
NP V NP XP

(7.43) <u>Fake Object Licensing Conditions</u>

(1) Agents are linked to subject position, patients are linked to direct object position.
(2) Resultative phrases conveying information about the prototypical end location of the agent are realized in immediate postverbal position.
(3) Resultative phrases conveying information about the end result state or location of the non-prototypical patient are realized in immediate post-patient position.

The linking between the semantic event-frame information and the syntactic level follows the principles in (7.43). The fake reflexive is licensed by world knowledge about running events that is contained in the 'W' off-stage information of the event-frame for *run*. In other words, when a running event is conceptualized from a non-prototypical perspective then – based on world knowledge – it is possible to recruit information about the fact that runners are patients as well as agents. Because of this knowledge, the *–self* indicating the patient qualities of the agent is automatically realized in immediate postverbal position according to Linking Principle 1. The result phrase *home* is subsequently realized in the position following the patient argument in direct object position.[41] Let us now examine whether there are any verbs denoting motion that disallow the perspective shift exhibited by *run*:

(7.44) a. *Chris entered himself into the room.
b. *Ed returned himself to the bar.
c. *Pat zigzagged herself across the street.
d. *Eric roamed himself downtown.

The above examples show that some verbs denoting motion do not allow realization of fake objects.[42] This behavior is captured by the architecture of their respective event frames. The event-frames for *enter, return, zigzag,* and *roam* do not allow such a change in perspective as is shown in the following diagram.

(7.45) Event-based frame semantic information representing the verbs in (7.44)

Ag: enterer, returner, zigzagger, roamer
p1: directional PP

GOAL
Ag (p1)

(7.45) differs from the event-frame for *run* in (7.42) above in that it only includes the information representing the Agent 'Ag' and its directional property 'p1.' Whenever the event-frame is employed to convey information about a change of location, the event-frame requires immediate realization of the directional PP in postverbal position without any intervening lexical material that might be recruited from world knowledge (cf. **Ed re-*

[41] The licensing principles also correctly predict that under 'normal' perspectivizing conditions (i.e., in those in which no perspective shift takes place that profiles the agent in terms of agent and patient) (7.43) licenses sentences such as *Chris ran home*. In this case, Licensing Principle 1 determines that *Chris* is linked to subject position, whereas Licensing Principle 2 correctly determines that the resultative phrase follows in immediate postverbal position. Also note that *Chris ran* is licensed.

[42] This does not mean that the agent may not be conceptualized as a patient, but this construal cannot be overtly expressed by the verb in combination with a fake reflexive, because the event-frame lexically blocks such a linguistic realization.

turned himself to the bar vs. *Ed returned to the bar*). In other words, it does not allow any resultative licensing based on off-stage information in order to convey the 'overcoming an obstacle sense' of a prototypical moving event. By lexically distinguishing at the level of event-frames what types of on-stage and off-stage information are included and how they may be syntactically realized, we are thus able to encode which motion verbs may occur with a fake reflexive to denote the 'overcoming an obstacle sense' and which ones may not. Note that while the event-frame architecture rules out the fake reflexive for the verbs in (7.44), it still licenses the standard motion linking pattern of those verbs as the following sentences show.

(7.46) a. Chris entered into the room.
b. Ed returned to the bar.
c. Pat zigzagged across the street.
d. Eric roamed downtown.

That is, based on the event-frame in (7.45), the agent is obligatorily linked to subject position, followed by the verb and the directional PP represented by 'p1' in (7.45). So far, we have seen that our event-frame architecture allows a motion verb's ability to occur with a fake reflexive on a result-location reading to be lexically encoded, thereby enabling us to make the correct characterizations about which verbs allow this pattern and which verbs do not. We now turn to property resultatives of motion verbs with fake reflexives.

7.2.2.1.2 Property Resultatives

Whereas perspectivizing *–self* is optional with motion resultatives that occur with a location phrase, cf. (7.47), it is required with motion resultatives that occur with property resultatives, cf. (7.48)-(7.50).

(7.47) a. Kim ran *herself to the store.*
b. Kim ran *to the store.*

(7.48) a. Kim ran *herself to exhaustion.*
b. *Kim ran *to exhaustion.*

(7.49) a. He had jogged *himself out of breath.*
b. *He had jogged *himself breathless.*

(7.50) There once was a turkey named Skinner
Who fasted and jogged *himself thinner*
His plan was so clever,
The farmer would never ...
Select him for Thanksgiving dinner. (Author unknown)

The property resultatives in (7.48)-(7.50) differ from location resultatives such as in (7.47) in that they take a radically different perspective of a running event. In this case, the primary perspective highlights the runner's exhaustion rather than his change of location; the latter is only implicitly understood or backgrounded. For this perspective shift to be realized, it is necessary not only to conceptualize the agent as two event participants and to express this conceptualization linguistically but to recruit other kinds of world knowledge, namely that one may become tired as a result of running. This specific world knowledge is so deeply entrenched that it is normally completely irrelevant. However, if a specific perspective of an event's outcome is to be emphasized, this world knowledge may be recruited and subsequently overtly expressed. Compare the following linking from the event-frame for prototypical *run* to the syntactic level.

(7.51) Linking from the event-frame for the prototypical sense of *run* (including on-stage and off-stage frame semantic information): Perspective shift.

Ag: animate object moving legs quickly
p1: directional PP
W: world knowledge containing knowledge about non-prototypical event-participants of running events
p2: change in state or location of event-participant from 'W'

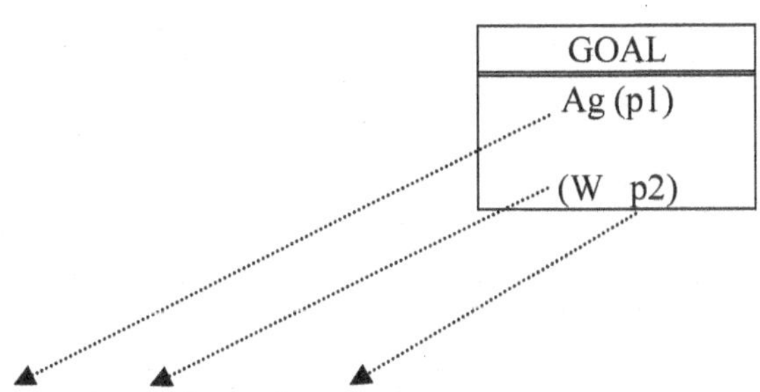

Kim ran herself to exhaustion.
SU DO ResP
NP V NP XP

The linking is similar to that of *Chris ran himself home* in (7.42) above in that the agent participant is linked to the subject position followed by the verb.[43] Furthermore, the conceptualized patient part (the Self) of the agent is recruited from world knowledge 'W' and subsequently linked to the direct object position. What is relevant to the viewpoint in (7.51) is that the agent, *Kim*, is exhausted as a result of the running activity. The arrow leading to the resultative phrase *to exhaustion* indicates that the relevant information about the property end result state is recruited from world knowledge. This includes, among many other things, knowledge about the fact that running, like other physical activities, can be potentially tiring. But note that not every verb allows recruitment of this type of world knowledge. Compare the following sentences.

(7.52) a. *Chris entered himself to exhaustion.
b. *Ed returned himself to exhaustion.
c. Pat zigzagged herself to exhaustion.
d. *Eric roamed himself to exhaustion.

The sentences illustrate that only *zigzag* (but not *enter*, *return*, and *roam*) allows a property end result construal and subsequently requires a perspectivizing *–self* to be acceptable. This difference in distribution is captured by the difference in event-frame architecture between (7.53) and (7.54).

(7.53) Event-based frame semantic architecture for the prototypical senses of *enter*, *return*, and *roam*

GOAL
Ag (p1)

Ag: Enterer, returner, roamer
p1: directional PP

Recall that according to our Licensing Condition 'Ag' and 'p1' in the event-frame architecture for *enter*, *return*, and *roam* need to be realized in immediate preverbal and postverbal position respectively, thereby ruling out un-

[43] Recall that the parentheses that encompass 'W' and 'p2' mean that whenever a non-prototypical event-participant is recruited from world knowledge and subsequently realized at the linguistic level, then a resultative phrase has to predicate over this non-prototypical event participant. This rules out sentences such as **Kim ran herself* (on a resultative interpretation).

attested instances with fake reflexives as in (7.52 a,b,d). This event-frame does not allow recruitment of world knowledge in order to overtly realize it at the linguistic level in the form of resultative constructions. This lexical specification precludes sentences such as (7.52 a,b,d). Let us now turn to the representation for *zigzag*.

(7.54) Event-based frame semantic architecture for the prototypical senses of *zigzag*

GOAL
Ag (p1) (W p2)

Ag: zigzagger
p1: directional PP
W: world knowledge containing knowledge about non-prototypical event-participants of zigzagging events
p2: change of state of event-participant from 'W'

The event-frame semantic representation shows that the prototypical sense of *zigzag* also requires immediate postverbal realization of the directional PP, meaning that fake reflexives in the locative interpretation as in (7.44c) above are ruled out. The event-frame differs, however, from the event-frame of prototypical *roam*, *enter*, and *return* in that it allows recruitment of general world knowledge 'W' in order to be realized at the linguistic level in combination with 'p2.'[44] This explains why (7.52c) is acceptable.

7.2.2.1.3 Summary

In the last sections I have argued that fake reflexives are motivated by the speaker's divided conceptualization of the agent participant in terms of two separate participants, an agent and a patient. Fake reflexives as well as resultative phrases are licensed by semantic off-stage information contained in the event-frames associated with verbs. On this view, it is possible to motivate mechanisms adding semantic roles because of information that is already associated with the respective event-frames in terms of general world knowledge. In cases where a specific viewpoint of an event is to be conveyed, it is then possible to recruit off-stage information associated with

[44] This rules out sentences such as **Chris zigzagged himself* (on a resultative interpretation). Note that this event-frame differs from that of *run* in that it does not allow a directional PP to predicate over the non-prototypical event-participant recruited from world knowledge, thereby ruling out sentences such as **He zigzagged himself up the stairs.*

the respective event-frames and make them linguistically relevant by overtly realizing them at the syntactic level. We have seen that the fake reflexive serves as a conceptual marker that points out a specific viewpoint of an event's outcome. I have discussed three types of event-frames that differ with respect to how much off-stage information they allow to be realized at the syntactic level. I have shown that once event-frame semantic information is recruited for overt linguistic realization, linking to the syntactic level follows the same procedure as the linking patterns in regular resultatives. Our discussion has shown, though, that it is ultimately the information associated with the event-frames that determine whether off-stage information may be recruited in order to be overtly realized.

7.2.2.2 Non-Reflexive Fake Objects with Motion Event-Frames

In this section we address the licensing conditions of other nonsubcategorized postverbal NPs, so-called regular fake objects as found in the following sentences.

(7.55) a. Carol ran her feet sore.
b. Jim jogged his Nikes to threads.
c. Dave ran the pavement thin.
d. Claudia walked her shoes threadbare.

(7.55a)-(7.55d) are structurally identical to the sentences discussed in the last section in that the postverbal NPs and the resultative phrases are not subcategorized for by the intransitive matrix verb. They differ from the sentences above in that the postverbal NP is not a perspectivizing *–self* that serves to point out the patient properties of the mover, but rather a referential noun phrase which is construed as the patient of the event.

Parallel to the arguments put forward in the previous sections, I suggest that the postverbal NP and the resultative phrase are motivated by the conceptualization of the motion event from a different viewpoint. However, in contrast to the section above, where the mover was conceptualized as a divided person, namely both an agent and a patient at the same time, the postverbal NPs are not part of the patient *per se*. Instead, they are either a physical extension of the mover that is affected by the energy emission during the motion activity (feet, shoes, legs), or an entity which is not a direct physical extension of the mover, but that is nevertheless directly affected by the energy emitted during the moving activity (e.g., the pavement).

(7.56) Perspective shift based on the prototypical sense of *run*

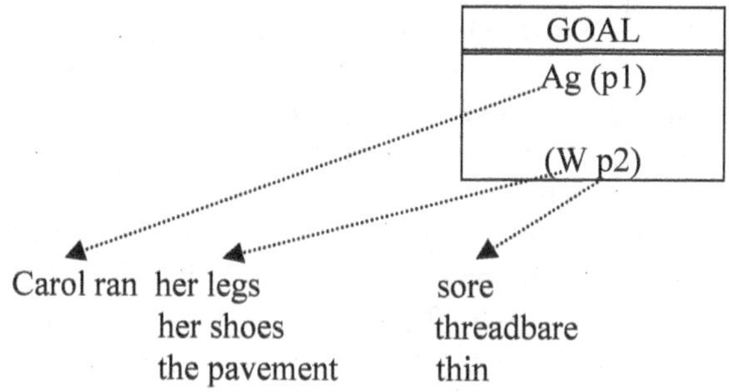

(7.56) captures how off-stage information associated with the event-frame of the prototypical sense of *run* is made linguistically relevant. The fake objects *her legs*, *her shoes*, and *the pavement* are recruited from general world knowledge 'W' about what it means to run (running involves feet, legs, shoes, and often takes place on pavement). Since the fake objects are directly affected by the energy emitted during the running activity, they may be overtly expressed (cf. licensing condition in (7.43) above).[45] While in languages like German fake objects are case-marked by accusative case reflecting their object status, Korean exhibits case concord between the agent and the fake object as is evident in:

(7.57) Franz lief seine Füße wund.
Franz:NOM ran his feet:ACC sore
'Franz ran his feet sore.'

(7.58) Chris-ka palpatak-i talh-key talli-ess-ta
Chris:NOM feet:NOM worn run-Pst-Ind
'Chris ran her feet sore.' (Kim and Maling 1997: 192)

The comparison between German and Korean shows that Korean overtly marks the identity of the fake object as a part of the agent, whereas German and English do not. Consider the following examples.

[45]Recall that 'p2' must automatically be realized due to the parentheses that enclose 'W' and 'p2'. This means that whenever a non-prototypical event-participant is recruited from world knowledge, then it has to be predicated over. This rules out sentences such as **Carol ran her legs* and **Carol ran sore*.

(7.59) a. *Kim ran the walls thin.
b. *Kim ran her hands sore.
c. *Kim ran her hat threadbare.

(7.59a) is ruled out because general world-knowledge dictates the impossibility of running on walls.[46] (7.59b) and (7.59c) are ruled out since neither hands nor hats are directly affected by the flow of energy during a running event such that they could become sore or threadbare, respectively.[47] The following constraints on the licensing of fake objects rule out the unacceptable sentences in (7.59a)-(7.59c).

(7.60) Constraints on the recruitment of off-stage information for the licensing of fake objects

(1) The fake object has to be directly affected by the energy emitted during the prototypical activity denoted by the event-frame.

(2) The resultative phrase has to denote a property that is construable as a change of state of the fake object resulting from the prototypical activity denoted by the event-frame.

Let us now turn to some verbs that never allow fake objects. Compare the following sentences.

(7.61) a. *Julia entered her shoes threadbare.
b. *Nick roamed the pavement thin.
c. *Chip returned his legs sore.

The unacceptability of (7.61a) – (7.61c) is explained by the event-frames of the verbs discussed in the previous section, which do not permit recruitment of off-stage information for overt linguistic expression, cf. event-frame (7.53) above. This does not mean that one has no knowledge whatsoever about the fact that the activities denoted by the respective event-frames in-

[46]Recall that all of this is lexical default information and may be overridden given the proper contextual background conditions (a good example are Science Fiction stories).

[47]Other fake objects that are not directly affected by the energy of a prototypical running activity are licensed by different semantic concepts. That is, *Dave ran Jim off the street* is licensed by a separate conventionalized event-frame denoting a different type of semantic concept associated with *run*.

volve feet, legs, shoes, and typically take place on a surface that may be affected by the activity. From a purely linguistic point of view, however, it means that the verbs do not allow overt realization of this type of off-stage information.[48] This shows that although off-stage information is associated with prototypical event frames of verbs such as *enter*, *return*, and *roam*, some verbs lexically block overt realization of this knowledge. Since this variable verb behavior is a matter of conventionalization, as pointed out at the beginning of Chapter 5, a detailed description of verbal semantics and its different syntactic realization patterns is the only adequate way to capture the distribution of fake objects in resultative constructions.

7.2.2.3 Fake Objects With One-Participant Non-Motion Event-Frames

This section is concerned with the licensing of postverbal NPs and resultative phrases in sentences such as the following.

(7.62)
a. A trader yells *himself hoarse* in the deafening pit where fortunes changed hands. (BNC)
b. The dogs were unhappy and would bark *themselves hoarse*. (BNC)
c. And she drunk *herself to sleep*. (BNC)
d. All he'd do was sit and drink *himself stupid*. (BNC)
e. In the small hours of the next morning, when they were back at La Gracieuse, after dancing *her feet raw* with Sam ... (BNC)
f. Imagine how key that would be to have in those overheated venues while everyone proceeds to dance *themselves to a heat stroke*. (Message-ID: Pine.GSO.3.96.1000113145531.7726B-100000@oats.farm.niu.edu)

The sentences in (7.62a)-(7.62f) describe exceptional outcomes of events that are beyond the conventional prototypical goal of the respective activities denoted by the verbs and must thus be expressed differently (i.e., by a resultative construction in this case) in order to highlight their exceptionality. Take, for example, yelling and barking the primary prototypical goals of

---

[48]Note that although the respective verbs may not be used to overtly express this type of off-stage information, there are other options of expressing it. Cf. *Bill entered and exited the room 800 times a day. This made his feet sore.*

which are to emit loud sounds but not to become hoarse. Similarly, the prototypical goal of drinking is not to become sleepy. In other words, in (7.62a)-(7.62f), the resultative construction has the pragmatic/communicative function of pointing out an unconventional result state of an event participant. To achieve this, off-stage information connected with the respective event-frames is recruited as the following diagram illustrates.

(7.63) Perspective shift based on the prototypical senses of *bark*, *yell*, and *drink*[49]

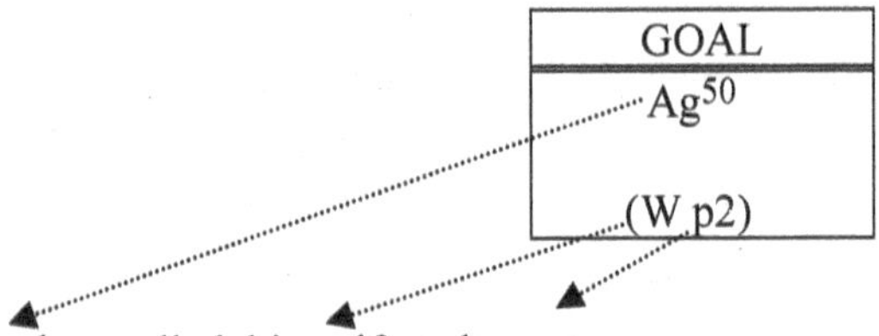

The trader yelled himself hoarse
The dogs barked themselves hoarse.
She drank herself to sleep.

Note that the linking from the underlying event-frame to syntax follows the same general principles as that of motion verbs in the last sections. That is, the agent participant is automatically linked to subject position followed by the verb. Due to the divided person conceptualization, the agent's Self is construed as the patient of the activity denoted by the event-frame.[51] This knowledge is part of the general world knowledge 'W' associated with the respective event-frames and thus serves to license its linguistic realization in terms of a patient which is subsequently linked to direct object position according to Linking Principle 1 in (7.43). The resultative phrases are li-

---

[49]Note that the event-frame for prototypical *drink* also includes a prototypical patient participant. This has been omitted here in order to make the comparison between the three verbs easier.

[50]The semantic specifications of the event-participants look as follows: *Yell*: Ag: Entity emitting loud sounds in order to communicate. W: world knowledge containing information about non-prototypical event-participants of yelling events. P2: change of state of event-participant from 'W.' *Bark*: Ag: Entity emitting short loud sounds. W: world knowledge containing information about non-prototypical event-participants of barking events. P2: change of state of event-participant from 'W.' *Drink*: Entity swallowing liquid after putting it into the mouth. W: world knowledge containing information about non-prototypical event-participants of running events. P2: change of state of event-participant from 'W.'

[51]To be more precise, it is only a part of the agent's self, i.e., the head, the voice, or the feet that are directly affected by the energy emission during the activity.

censed by off-stage information in combination with Linking Principle 3.[52] Constraint 1 in (7.60) rules out instances of fake objects that are not directly affected by the energy emitted by the activity, cf. (7.64a)-(7.64c), whereas Constraint 2 in (7.60) rules out instances in which the result phrase does not denote a patient's change of state resulting from the prototypical activity denoted by the event frame, cf. (7.65a)-(7.65c).[53]

(7.64) a. *The trader yelled his dog hoarse.
b. *The dog barked the postman hoarse.
c. *She drank her best friend to sleep.

(7.65) a. *The trader yelled purple.
b. *The dog barked itself broken.
c. *She drank herself into pieces.

The event-frame in (7.63) differs from the event-frames associated with motion verbs above in that it does not allow any locative specification of the agent participant, cf. the missing 'p1' specification in (7.63) following 'Ag.' In addition, the event-frame specifications for 'p2' in (7.63) are specified for change of state, not location. This rules out sentences as the following.

(7.66) a. *The trader yelled himself into the room.
b. *He drank himself into the bar.[54]

Finally, let us compare these verbs with closely related verbs that do not allow this type of licensing of fake objects.

(7.67) a. ??The trader whispered himself hoarse.
b. *The dog wheezed itself hoarse.
c. *He slurped himself to sleep.

---

[52]For an exhaustive list of other verbs occurring with *hoarse* as a resultative phrase in the BNC, see Appendix A.16.

[53]Note that the cases of fake reflexives discussed here are based on the prototypical sense of the respective verbs. Besides the event-frames representing the prototypical senses of these verbs, there are other conventionalized event-frames associated with these and related verbs. Take, for example, prototypical *talk* which would only allow a change of state as a 'p2' specification. Sentences like *The salesman talked himself into the Jones' living room*, however, are licensed by a different conventionalized event-frame associated with *talk* (the persuasion event-frame, with its own frame semantic specifications that sets it apart from the prototypical sense of *talk* (e.g., intention of the talker to achieve something, etc.)).

[54]Phrases such as *to drink somebody out of house and home* are considered as conventionalized idiomatic constructions (event-frames) with their own specific semantics and syntax.

The examples suggest that *whisper*, *wheeze*, and *slurp* do not allow the same type of perspective shift (including a fake reflexive) as *yell*, *bark*, and *drink*. This is reflected in the architecture of their event-frames which do not allow recruitment of off-stage information.

(7.68) Event-frame architecture of the prototypical senses of *whisper*, *wheeze*, and *slurp*[55]

GOAL
Ag

7.2.2.4 Fake Objects With Two-Participant Event-Frames

In this section I address the licensing of fake objects with verbs associated with two participant event-frames such as the following.

(7.69) a. Jackie painted the brush to pieces.
b. Pam swept the broom to pieces.
c. *Beryl opened the key to pieces.

In these sentences the outcome of the respective event participants is portrayed from a perspective that gives a non-prototypical viewpoint of the events' outcome. That is, world knowledge tells us that the prototypical goal of painting is to apply paint to a surface in order to change the appearance of a surface, not to ruin the instrument used in this activity. Similar observations can be made for sweeping and opening. This means that under 'normal' perspectivizing conditions, the prototypical outcome of the respective events are directly linked to syntax from the underlying event frames according to the Licensing Conditions in (7.43) above (cf. also our discussion of two-participant event frames in Chapter 6).

[55]Note that the event-frame denoting the prototypical sense of *slurp* also includes a prototypical patient argument. This has been omitted here in order to make a comparison between the three verbs easier.

(7.70) Perspective of the prototypical senses of *paint, sweep*, and *open* (first approximation)

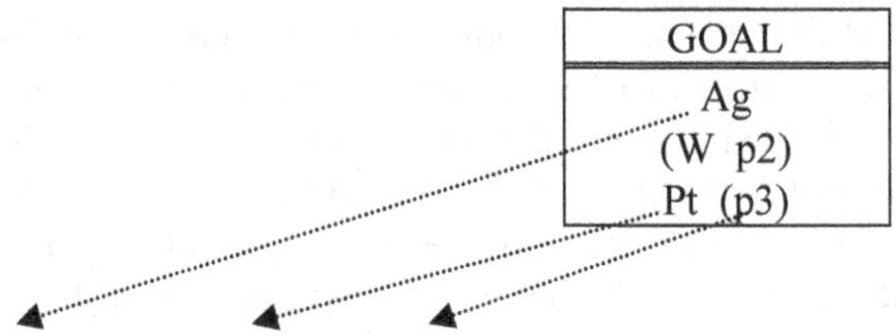

Jackie	painted	the barn	red.
Pam	swept	the floor	clean.
Beryl	opened	the door	wide open.

Note, however, that if the viewpoint of the outcome of the event is a different one, the fake objects are licensed by off-stage information associated with the event-frames of the respective verbs. Although the event-frames for *paint*, *sweep*, and *open* are all associated with off-stage information regarding the necessary use of an instrument to complete the activity as the sentences in (7.71) and the image in (7.72) show, the three verbs differ with respect to whether this type of information may be overtly realized in the form of resultatives, cf. (7.69) above.

(7.71) a. Jackie painted the house with a brush.
b. Pam swept the floor with a broom.
c. Beryl opened the door with a key.

(7.72) Conceptualization of events

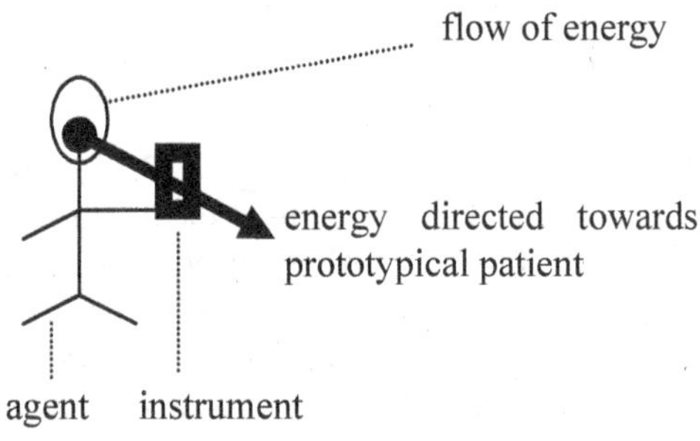

This diagram is meant to express the fact that even though each event-frame encodes a prototypical end goal of the activity denoted by the event-frame (surface changing color, floor being clean, door opened), not every event-frame allows a shift in perspective in order to perspectivize the instrument that is backgrounded. The conceptualization in (7.72) illustrates that the event-frames for *paint*, *sweep*, and *wipe* describe events in which energy is directed from the agent's body through the instrument and towards the prototypical patient (surface, door) in order to change one of its properties. Since *open* exhibits a different distribution of fake objects than *paint* and *sweep*, the architecture of the respective event-frames have to differ with respect to whether they allow recruitment of off-stage information in order to license a fake object that overtly expresses the shift in perspective to profile the instrument participant.

(7.73) Perspective shift based on the prototypical senses of *paint* and *sweep*

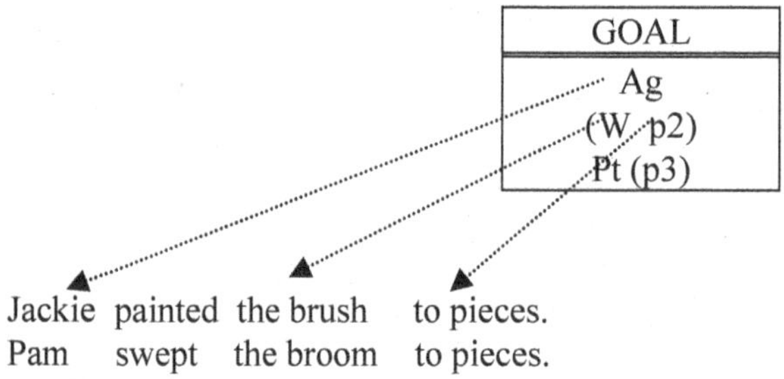

(7.74) Event-based frame semantic architecture for the prototypical sense of *open*.

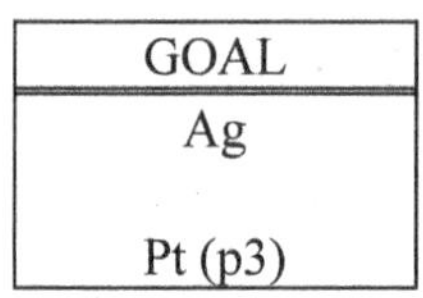

The event-frames in (7.73) and (7.74) differ from each other in that *paint* and *sweep* allow recruitment of off-stage information about the instrument participant to be overtly realized, whereas *open* does not. The two different types of event-frames in (7.73) and (7.74) describe not only the distribution of fake instrument objects as in (7.69a)-(7.69c) above but also the distribution of fake reflexive objects as in the following examples.

(7.75) a. Jackie painted herself to exhaustion.
b. Pam swept herself to exhaustion.
c. *Beryl opened herself to exhaustion.

Whereas the event-frames for *paint* and *sweep* allow recruitment of world knowledge to convey a different viewpoint of the outcome of an event (cf. the 'W' and 'p2' between agent and patient participants in (7.73)), the event-frame for *open* does not allow for this option.

7.2.3 Summary

In this section I have argued that fake objects are the result of taking a different viewpoint of the prototypical outcome of an event. Whereas each event-frame contains on-stage and off-stage information about the prototypical outcome of an event that it describes, it also contains off-stage information about event-participants that is typically left unexpressed outside of resultative constructions. However, if a speaker wishes to point out something special about an event, she can recruit this off-stage information from world knowledge and make it linguistically relevant. We have seen that although all event-frames follow general linking patterns, there are individual differences between motion, non-motion, one-event participant, and two-event participant event-frames. These differences as well as individual idiosyncratic properties of certain verbs license and regulate the distribution of fake objects. The data reveal another interesting difference between resultatives constructions. That is, resultatives with 'regular' objects tend to exhibit stronger collocational restrictions with respect to the range of the verbs' postverbal constituents.

In Section 7.2.1 I have shown that verbs such as *kill*, *wipe-out*, *paint*, and *wash* exhibit very specific collocational restrictions with respect to the types of resultative phrases that may pattern with them. I have argued that the tight collocational restrictions exhibited by these verbs reflect the knowledge a speaker has about conventionally expected results of activities denoted by these verbs. In other words, the fact that the prototypical sense of *kill* expresses an activity that has a strictly pre-determined expected result and therefore requires no off-stage information is reflected linguistically by the fact that it only allows a narrow set of resultative phrases. In this case, the only resultative phrase allowed with *kill* is *dead*. While verbs such as prototypical *paint* and *wash* exhibit considerably less collocational restrictions than *kill* or *wipe-out*, they share with these verbs the property of requiring extremely little off-stage information when they occur in resultatives with regular objects.

In contrast, verbs with fake objects require a great deal more off-stage information in order to license their postverbal constituents in resultatives. This is because the result state expressed by fake object resultatives involves non-prototypical event participants and as such does not denote conventionally expected results that are directly inferable on the basis of on-stage information. Take, for example, the verb *run* which may occur with a wide variety of non-prototypical event participants such as *the pavement, herself, the shoes, his feet*, etc. as fake objects in resultative constructions. In this case, off-stage information is recruited in order to license non-prototypical event participants besides the prototypical running event participant. In addition, off-stage information needs to be recruited about possible end result states of each of the fake objects since they do not typically denote conventionally expected results. The fact that more off-stage information is required to license non-prototypical event participants such as fake objects and their resultative phrases is reflected linguistically. That is, because more off-stage information is required, event-frames impose fewer collocational restrictions on postverbal constituents in resultatives with fake objects than in resultatives with regular objects.

On the view presented here, no syntactic transformations, independently existing constructions, or template augmentation mechanisms are needed to license the occurrence of fake objects. Instead, the necessary information that licenses the distribution of fake objects is already associated (in terms of world knowledge) with the event-frames that are part of a verb's lexical entry. Depending on what perspective of an event is to be conveyed, different parts of an event frame may be chosen for overt linguistic realization. What this means is that the distribution of syntactic arguments in a sentence can be directly projected from a verb's lexical semantic structure without elaborate linking mechanisms or additional levels of representation. We now turn to resultatives that are not directly licensed by conventionalized event-frames.

7.3 Nonconventionalized Resultatives Based on Analogy

The analysis presented so far is at variance with Goldberg (1995), who proposes a constructional approach in which meaningful constructions add arguments to a verb's argument structure. One of the main motivations for her constructional account of resultatives, is her wish to 'avoid the problem of positing implausible verb senses.' (1995: 224). Among other examples, she lists the following sentences as support for her constructional account of caused-motion and resultative constructions.

(7.76)
a. He sneezed the napkin off the table.
b. Dan talked himself blue in the face. (Goldberg 1995: 224)
c. In the last Star Trek episode, there was a woman who could think people into a different galaxy. (1995: 154)
d. She drank him under the table. (1995: 157)

Clearly, (7.76d) is a conventionalized idiomatic construction representing a conventionalized sense of *drink* which is not formed by a construction adding additional argument roles to a verb's participant roles to expand the basic meaning of *drink*. In contrast, (7.76b) is a special case of a conventionalized construction that roughly means 'to overdo an activity' (the agent does not really get blue in the face) rather than a true resultative construction.[56] Other constructions belonging to this family of 'overdoing an activity' are 'to verb X to death' (cf. *It frightened me to death if you want to know* (BNC)) and 'to verb X's body part off' (cf. *Which made everyone else laugh their heads off* (BNC)).[57] As (7.76b) and (7.76d) are not true resultatives, we will thus primarily focus on capturing how resultatives as in (7.76a) and (7.76c) are licensed.

7.3.1 Conventionalization and Analogy

When we take a closer look at Goldberg's reasoning, we need to ask what 'intuitively' and 'implausible' (Goldberg 1995: 224) really mean in the context of linguistic analysis. Does this mean 'implausible' and 'intuitively' are a matter of stylistics and therefore one style is preferred over the other? Or do 'intuitively' and 'implausible' really relate to the observation that the postverbal arguments and the respective verbs in (7.76a) and (7.76c) do not form a linguistically related unit with a distinct and established meaning? I suggest the latter, i.e., the use of these verbs in the resultative pattern sounds odd not because they fail to form a distinct sense of a verb such as *drive-crazy*, e.g., but because they are not conventionally associated with the resultative pattern. Thus, *sneeze* in (7.76a) sounds odd because it is associated with an unconventional syntactic pattern, in this case the resultative [NP V NP XP] pattern, producing a resultative meaning that sounds odd to a large percentage of the speech community.

This partially explains why many people unfamiliar with Goldberg's example sentences only accept this particular use of *sneeze* after being given the proper contextual background information, including some 'help' by suggesting that *sneeze* be interpreted as *to blow*. Thus, the resultative use

---

[56]The Oxford English Dictionary lists 1604 as the year of first occurrence of this *drink a person into some condition* sense of *drink*. In this connection, note that verbs that are related in meaning to *drink* do not exhibit this property. Cf. **She sipped him under the table*, or **She gulped him into bed.*

[57]In fact, the 'V-bodypart-*off* construction' subsumes both body parts as well as 'extended' body parts such as clothing, etc. (cf. ... *slickly eluded our lensman and left after about ten minutes to dance his studded boots off at some West End nightclub* (BNC), *I expect she would laugh her socks off if she found you here in royal regalia* (BNC)).

of *sneeze* sounds odd because this usage pattern is not yet conventionalized and is therefore unfamiliar to many members of the speech community.[58] Clark (1993: 67ff.) points out that 'what makes terms conventional is that everyone in a speech community agrees with everyone else on which words or expressions denote which kinds. (...) To count as conventional, such meanings must be consistent from one occasion to the next. (...) Conventionality in the lexicon, then, works in the same way as convention elsewhere.' *Sneeze* is not immediately recognized as a conventionalized linguistic form-meaning pair because it is not consistently associated with the resultative semantics in combination with a surface [NP V NP XP] pattern by all members of the speech community. *Blow*, on the other hand, sounds acceptable to speakers in contexts such as *The wind blew the leaves off the street*, or *Jack blew the napkin off the table* because it has been conventionally associated with the [NP V NP XP] caused-motion/resultative pattern since at least 1382, according to the Oxford English Dictionary.[59] This explains Goldberg's intuition that it is 'implausible' to posit a distinct sense for the unconventional usages of verbs such as *sneeze* with the [NP V NP XP] pattern.

In the first sections of this chapter we have seen that it is necessary to lexically list the conventionalized event-frames for each verb in order to capture the distribution of resultatives. Since we obviously cannot apply the same type of analysis to non-conventionalized resultatives, I propose that these resultative usages are motivated by analogy.

Since the Neogrammarians' late nineteenth-century investigations into the nature of language change, analogy and analogical change have been identified as a major force in language change based on vast amounts of attested historical data. Winters' (1997) characterization of analogy states that it

> is based on the mental process by which speakers perceive certain linguistic units as related because of some shared feature(s) of their structure or meaning. Over time, these units may then become even more similar be-

---

[58]Note that people differ widely with respect to acceptability judgements of resultative constructions, much to the frustration of the author. The most common answer given by informants when asked why a resultative does not sound acceptable is 'I just haven't heard it before' or 'I really wouldn't say it like that.'

[59]The fact that this specific sense of *blow* dates back so far is, in my opinion, a good indication for the fact that it is conventionalized, as opposed to *sneeze*, which does not have any such conventionalized association, according to the OED. I am aware of the fact that dictionaries only give a rough approximation of actual language use. However, I concur with Clark (1993) who observes that '[d]ictionaries list only words that are well established, but speakers can also construct new words, made just for the occasion.' (1993: 67)

> cause features of one or the other change, with the result that the units resemble each other to an even greater degree. These subsequent changes are motivated ultimately by some original judgment of resemblance.
>
> (Winters 1997: 360)

Some linguists have extended the notion of analogy to cover cases in which a new form that has previously not existed is formed in relation to already existing linguistic forms. Consider the following example. [60]

(7.77) work : workaholic :: news : 0
0 → newsaholic
(Winters 1997: 362)

In her discussion of (7.78), Winters explains the mechanisms behind this 'creation' analogy as follows.

> When a strong enough similarity between two forms is perceived, a new form may be devised, created expressly to fill a gap which was in turn identified by an examination (at some degree of linguistic consciousness) of the better established relationship.
>
> (Winters 1997: 362)

Note that such innovations are not isolated phenomena but occur quite frequently when the need arises to express a specific situation or concept. Clark (1993: 78) points out: 'Speakers of a language often need to convey meanings for which there is no ready-made, conventional expression. On such occasions, they turn to innovative lexical items – forms constructed to carry novel meanings interpretable in context, given the shared assumptions and mutual knowledge of speaker and addressee.' The difference between the analogy in (7.77) and the analogy of *sneeze* to be discussed in the following section is that the former is an analogy that has become conventionalized (lexical innovation), whereas *sneeze* has not yet been conventionalized with a [NP V NP XP] frame and is thus not yet part of a typical speaker's mental dictionary. We now turn to the question of how *sneeze* can

---

[60] Whereas the role of analogy in language change has been recognized as a linguistic phenomenon for a long time, it has also been shown to play a major role in psychology (Vosniadu and Ortony (1989) and Gentner (1989)). Janda (1996), in her study of how relic forms in Slavic languages serve as source material for analogical extension, points out that 'analogical thought is not unique to linguistic behavior' (1996: 1) and cites Rumelhart (1989: 300) who observes that the ability to find patterns is 'probably *the* essential component in most cognitive behavior.'

be associated with a new meaning and subsequently acquires a novel syntactic frame.

7.3.2 Analogy as a Licensing Factor for Nonconventionalized Resultatives

7.3.2.1 Motivation for Analogy

Suppose a speaker witnesses a scene in which a strong airflow emitted by a person causes a napkin to fly off the table. In order to describe this scenario, the speaker has the following two options (among others).

(7.78) a. Tom sneezed. As a result of Tom's sneezing, the napkin flew off the table.
b. Tom sneezed the napkin off the table.

Both versions serve the same communicative function, i.e., they impart information about what Talmy (1996) calls a 'causal sequence' from its beginning to its end. Yet note that (7.78b) eases the 'cognitive processing load' for both the speaker and hearer by reducing two separate utterances to a single utterance.[61] Rather than going through the three stages of language production (conceptualization, formulation, and articulation) twice to produce two utterances as in (7.78a), the speaker will most likely choose the more efficient variant in (7.78b).[62] Since *sneeze* is not yet conventionally associated with a resultative meaning that may be expressed as [NP V NP XP], the speaker will thus look for a way of creatively expanding the existing semantic concepts associated with *sneeze* in order to express the observed scenario more efficiently. The semantic expansion of a word's sense and combined syntactic frame in order to express a broader variety of situations in the world (such as causal chains) thus follows principles similar to those observed by Bolinger (1975) for the coinage of new words.

> Words are not coined in order to extract the meanings of their elements and compile a new meaning from them. The new meaning is there FIRST,

---

[61] Fauconnier and Turner (1996: 117) call this type of association with a new syntactic frame 'conceptual blending' and point out that the motivation behind it is the push to consolidate several events into a single unit. On this view, it is possible to merge two inputs when they are similar enough such that a single syntactic configuration may be used to articulate the integrated conceptual structure created by the blend.

[62] According to Levelt (1989), language production involves three distinct stages. First, the speaker has to conceptualize the message, then she has to formulate the grammatical characteristics of the message, and finally she has to articulate it.

and the coiner is looking for the best way to express it without going through too much trouble.

(Bolinger 1975: 109)

Thus, the speaker in (7.78b) is motivated to express himself as efficiently as possible. Yet how does a speaker come to associate the [NP V NP XP] syntactic frame with *sneeze*? The answer is best summarized by Anttila (1977) as follows.

(7.79) A intends to bring about p
A considers that he cannot bring about p unless he does a

Therefore A sets himself to do a (Anttila 1977: 126)

In the following section I address the individual steps 'a' necessary to bring about 'p,' i.e., the individual steps necessary for the licensing of the resultative [NP V NP XP] pattern with *sneeze*.

7.3.2.2 Factors Determining Analogical Creativity

Rather than positing an abstract meaningful construction for the licensing of resultatives with *sneeze* (cf. Goldberg 1995), I propose that the speaker utilizes a much more concrete conventionalized form-meaning correspondence that is already part of her existing inventory of linguistic signs and takes it as the basis for analogy. Thus, the speaker places *sneeze* (the target) in correspondence with another verb (the source) that is (1) closely related in meaning by virtue of having a similar role in common relational structures outside of resultative constructions and (2) conventionally associated with a resultative meaning that is overtly realized in terms of a syntactic [NP V NP XP] frame. If the situational conditions of *sneeze* (the target) overlap with the situational conditions associated with the resultative usage pattern of the source verb, the conventionalized resultative usage pattern of the source may be associated and thereby extended to *sneeze*.[63] In search of a potential source for creatively expanding the usage pattern of *sneeze*, the speaker adheres to the following two principles suggested by Israel (1996).

---

[63]This approach to pattern recognition is not particular to linguistics, but can be found in cognition in general, as Langacker (2000) points out: 'A particular target of categorization tends to activate a variety of established units, any one of which could in principle serve to categorize it.' (2000: 15)

(7.80) **The Production Principle (Analogical Usage):**
Utterances should sound like things the speaker has heard before.

(7.81) **The Comprehension Principle (Schema Abstraction)**
Representations should capture similarities across experienced usages.

(Israel 1996: 228)

Based on these principles, the appropriate source for the analogical association of *sneeze* with the resultative pattern must be a verb that is related in meaning, i.e. which is also an air-emission verb, and which is conventionally associated with the resultative [NP V NP XP] pattern to denote the change of an object's location by an air stream. The prototypical air emission verb conventionally associated with this sense is *blow* (first attested use with this meaning and syntactic frame is 1382, according to the OED). The event-frame for this sense of *blow* as well its linking of arguments is given in (7.82) and the event frame for the prototypical sense of *sneeze* and its linking of arguments is given in (7.83). Note that the event-frames not only differ with respect to the number of event participants but also with respect to their temporal and force-dynamic specifications.

(7.82) Event-based frame semantic representation of caused-motion/resultative *blow*

Ag: entity that makes air move
Pt: object that is moved by air stream emitted by Ag
p3: directional PP

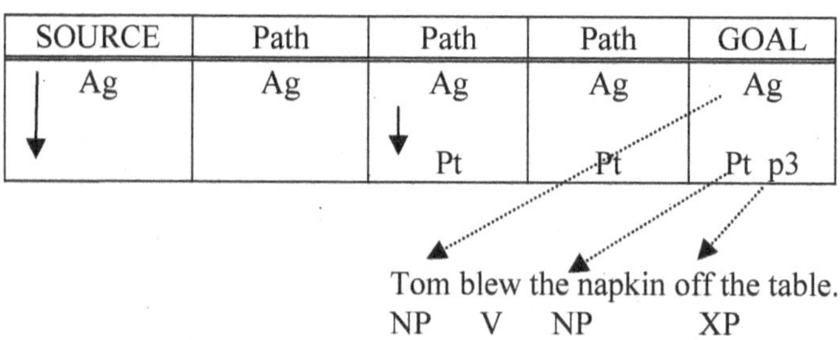

(7.83) Event-based frame semantic representation of the prototypical sense of *sneeze*

Ag: entity that makes air move as the result of an involuntary and convulsive or spasmodic action

SOURCE	Path	Path	Path	GOAL
Ag	Ag	Ag	Ag	Ag

Tom sneezed.
NP V

Since *sneeze* is not yet conventionally associated with a [NP V NP XP] syntactic frame indicating a resultative/caused-motion sense, the speaker follows Israel's (1996) Production and Comprehension Principles in finding a verb that is conventionally associated with this pattern. If the semantic overlap in their other conventionalized non-resultative usages is similar, and, given the proper contextual conditions and situational overlap, the speaker associates the resultative meaning stemming from the conventionalized [NP V NP XP] syntactic frame of *blow* (the source) with *sneeze* (the target), the following (abbreviated) diagram results.

(7.84) Analogical association of a verb's target event-frame with the event-frame of a source verb

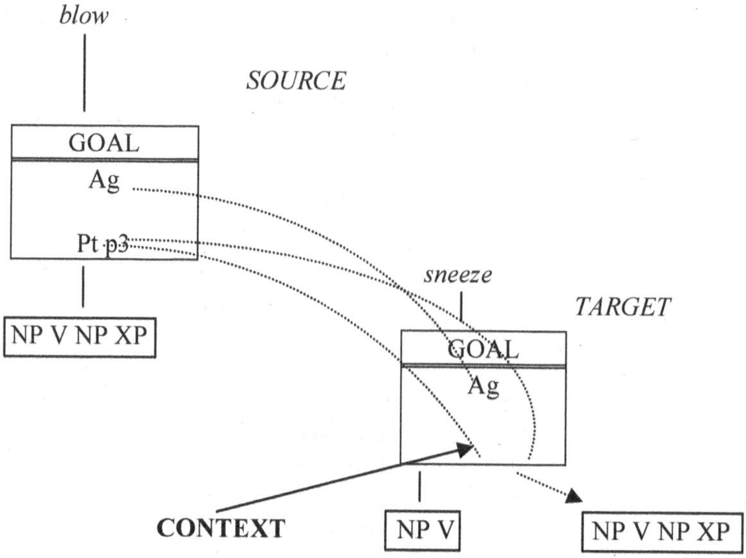

(7.84) includes a simplified representation of the event-frames of the caused-motion/resultative event-frame associated with *blow* that is conventionally associated with the [NP V NP XP] syntactic frame, as well as the event-frame representing the prototypical sense of *sneeze* that is conventionally associated with the [NP V] syntactic frame. The dotted lines between the two event-frames illustrate how the event-semantic information (event participant 'Ag') associated with *sneeze* is compared to the event-semantic information of *blow*. This is the crucial point at which the association process takes place, i.e., the frame-semantic information associated with *sneeze* (the target) is compared with the frame-semantic information of *blow* (the source) in combination with contextual background information that is indicated by the black arrow. Context provides the type of information for the target verb with which it is not conventionally associated (that is why the context-arrow points to the event-frame of *sneeze*). If there is a large enough overlap in on-stage and off-stage information between *blow* and *sneeze* in combination with contextual background information, the event-frame of *sneeze* may acquire the syntactic [NP V NP XP] frame associated with the event-frame of *blow*. The analogical process by which *sneeze* acquires the [NP V NP XP] frame from *blow* is constrained by a general restriction on the use of new words pointed out by Lehrer who cites Rudzka-Ostyn (personal communication): 'If there is a single general word that fits a new context, do not use a more specific word unless the use of the latter can be (fully) justified.' (Lehrer 1990: 229) In order to avoid overgeneration of structures yielding unrestrained analogical usages, it is necessary to investigate in more detail the conditions under which such analogical creativity may take place. We now turn to the individual licensing conditions under which *sneeze* may be used with the conventionalized [NP V NP XP] frame of *blow*.

7.3.2.2.1 Overlap of Conventionalized Frame-Semantic Information

The first set of licensing conditions in (7.80) requires that there be the greatest possible overlap of existing conventionalized frame-semantic information associated with the respective frames. This means that the conventionalized frame-semantic information associated with the prototypical event-frame of *sneeze* in (7.83) must show similar semantic properties to the respective counterpart information associated with *blow* in (7.82) in order for *sneeze* to be readily associated with the same sense and syntactic frame as *blow*.[64] Compare the following two sentences and the diagram in (7.86).

(7.85) a. Tom blew the napkin off the table.
b. Tom sneezed the napkin off the table.

(7.86) Simplified representation of (7.85a) and (7.85b)

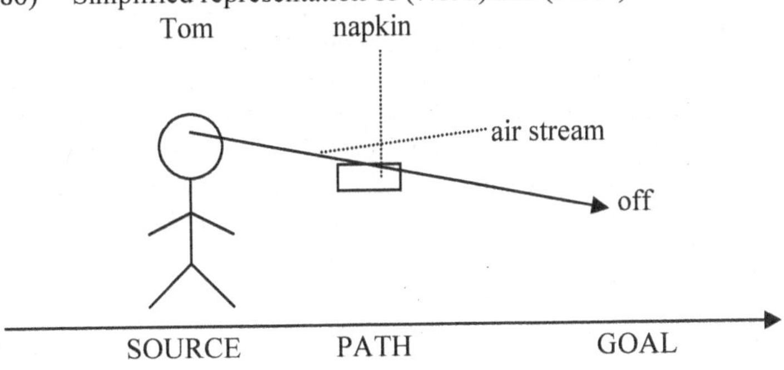

[64]The smaller the frame-semantic overlap, the smaller will be the chance that the target verb (*sneeze*) will be associated with the syntactic frame of the source verb (*blow*). However, as we will see below, it is possible for contextual background information to provide the required types of semantic/pragmatic knowledge in order to 'fill in' potential overlap gaps between the two event-frames. This means that contextual background information can contribute to a large degree to (and sometimes even trigger) the associative patterning matchings that lead to analogy.

The diagram illustrates that in both sentences, an agent emits an air stream. Comparing the event-frames of *blow* and *sneeze* in (7.82) and (7.83), we see that the semantic specifications for agent given by *sneeze* are completely subsumed by the semantic specifications for the agent participant of *blow*. This means that there is a frame-semantic compatibility of the two types of agent participants (represented by 'Ag' in (7.84)). The diagram also illustrates that in both a sneezing and a blowing event, there is a strong airflow originating from the agent and moving in a specified direction. Because of the semantic overlap there is also a frame-semantic compatibility between the two types of causing force dynamics (represented by the arrow in the SOURCE slot).[65] So far we have seen that the frame-semantic information contained in (7.82) and (7.83) overlap with respect to the causing event of blow's event frame (SOURCE-slot) in (7.84). Notice, however, that the rest of the conventionally associated frame-semantic information of *blow* in (7.82), namely information about the caused event (patient participant and result state), is not contained in the event-frame of *sneeze* in (7.83) but must be provided by context, an issue to which we now turn.

7.3.2.2.2 The Role of Discourse Context in Providing the Link to the Syntactic Frame of the Source Verb

Discourse information includes the force dynamic relations consisting of a patient participant that changes location as a result of air emission by the agent. Note that the force-dynamic 'base' is identical with *sneeze* and *blow* in (7.86), (7.82) and (7.83), i.e. in both cases a strong air stream is emitted that moves away from the agent.[66] The only way in which they differ is that the event-frame of *blow* in (7.82) comes lexically preassembled with a caused event including a patient participant and an end-result location of that participant, cf. the PATH and GOAL specifications in (7.82). That is, this specific sense of *blow* has a causal chain 'built in,' whereas *sneeze* does not.

---

[65]To this end, compare the following corpus examples illustrating how *sneeze* is used outside of resultatives to denote directed motion of an air stream (but without moving any objects) caused by sneezing: *Like not being able to sneeze on the cheese*. (BNC). *Sneezing in his fucking beer*. (BNC)

[66]This explains why outside of the resultative construction, *blow* and *sneeze* are not only used intransitively, but in other syntactic patterns as well. Note that whereas in sentences such as *Kim blew* or *Pat sneezed* it is only the agents that are profiled, whereas in sentences such as *Kim blew at Chris* and *Pat sneezed at Joe*, different event participants are profiled. This shows that different temporal instances of a blowing or sneezing event-frame may be profiled in order to express different end result states of event participants.

Thus, when a speaker observes a scene in which an object is being blown away by an air stream, she can express this cause-effect relation in a conventionalized preassembled way by employing the event-frame associated with *blow* in (7.82). In the case in which this movement is caused by sneezing, however, she does not have the same option readily available. Yet, by virtue of the *visual input* perceived, she is able to fill in the information about the cause and effect relation (the air stream is of the same type), thereby creating a causal link that makes it possible to associate *sneeze* with the semantic template and syntactic realization [NP V NP XP] of *blow*.[67] In other words, *sneeze* provides the necessary 'basic' semantics for an association with *blow*'s [NP V NP XP] frame in terms of yielding an agent participant, force dynamics, and associated world knowledge (e.g., that as a result of sneezing, a strong air stream goes away from the agent). The remaining information needed to associate *sneeze*'s basic semantics with *blow*'s causal chain is provided by contextual input that motivates the association with the closely related conventional form-meaning pairing of a particular sense of *blow* which includes the causal link.

Note, however, that the circumstances under which the cause-effect relation may be associated with *sneeze* are subject to the same pragmatic restrictions as imposed on the construal of *blow*. That is, the semantic range of patient arguments and directional PP phrases to be integrated into the semantics associated with *sneeze* are limited by contextual factors (within the limits imposed by the event-frame of *blow*) and thus restrict the range of contexts under which *sneeze* may be associated with *blow*'s [NP V NP XP] frame as the following sentences show.

(7.87) a. Lars blew the napkin off the table.
b. ?Lars blew the book off the table.
c. *Lars blew the beer case off the table.

(7.88) a. Rachel sneezed the napkin off the table.
b. ?Rachel sneezed the book off the table.
c. *Rachel sneezed the beer case off the table.

---

[67]*Blow* itself is the most prototypical instantiation of an air emission verb associated with the [NP V NP XP] pattern. *Blow* is a more concrete instantiation of prototypical *push* denoting a caused-motion sense. Although *push* may serve as source for the analogy as well, I have chosen *blow* because it is semantically closer to *sneeze* than *push*. Ultimately, it might be possible to construct a multiple inheritance hierarchy of constructional inheritance relations with different 'basic verbs' (*push, pull, take, move, make, put*) towards the top and other, more specific verbs further down in the hierarchy. On this basis it would be possible to see how specific the semantics of a verb have to be in order for it to serve as the source verb for an analogy with a target word.

The examples illustrate that the use of the target verb *sneeze* with the [NP V NP XP] pattern is subject to the same semantic/pragmatic restrictions as those of the source verb *blow* when it comes to the construal and subsequent overt linguistic realization of event participants and force-dynamic relations between them. Whereas (7.87)-(7.88) illustrate this with respect to patient event participants, this is also true in the case of agent participants and their force dynamic contribution to the construal of the event as the following examples show.

(7.89) a. Lars blew the napkin off the table.
b. ?The baby blew the napkin off the table.
c. *The mouse blew the napkin off the table.

(7.90) a. Mary sneezed the napkin off the table.
b. ?The baby sneezed the napkin off the table.
c. *The mouse sneezed the napkin off the table.

The above sentences demonstrate that the force-dynamic relationships between agents, patients, and end locations are parallel for the source verb *blow* and the target verb *sneeze*. That is, if in addition to the frame-semantic overlap sketched out in 7.3.2.2.1 the same force-dynamic relations can be construed for *sneeze* as for *blow*, then *sneeze* may be associated with the syntactic [NP V NP XP] frame of the source verb *blow*. This means that contextual background information is crucial to providing the missing link in order for *sneeze* to be associated with *blow*'s [NP V NP XP] pattern. Once this missing link is provided, however, analogy may take place. On this view, the combination of overlapping conventionalized frame-semantic information and pragmatically induced contextual background information helps *sneeze* to acquire a similar meaning and thus pattern with *blow* in its caused-motion/resultative sense.

7.3.2.2.3 Discourse Context and Event-Frames as Determining Factors

Let us turn to other air emission verbs that are related to *sneeze* and *blow* to see whether they can also be associated with *blow*'s [NP V NP XP] frame.

(7.91) a. Marc coughed the napkin off the table.
b. ?Kirsten breathed the napkin off the table.[68]

[68] Under different contextual circumstances, no additional context is required for *breathe* to take on a caused-motion/resultative interpretation, cf. *You like garlic? he asked, breathing it over me. (BNC)*

c. ?Jenn panted the napkin off the table.
d. ??Julio wheezed the napkin off the table.
e. *Katie exhaled the napkin off the table.
f. *Joshua inhaled the napkin off the table.

The examples demonstrate that not every air emission verb may be associated with the [NP V NP XP] frame of *blow*. I claim that there are different reasons for this phenomenon. The first reason has to do with the intensity of the force dynamics associated with an event-frame. Whereas *cough* in (7.91a) may be readily associated with *blow*'s [NP V NP XP] pattern, the verbs *sneeze*, *breathe*, *pant* and *wheeze* do not 'sound' as acceptable as *sneeze* and *cough* in the [NP V NP XP] frame. That is, although they are also air emission verbs and show a similar type of frame-semantic overlap of conventionalized information with *blow*, it is not possible to straightforwardly associate these verbs with *blow*'s [NP V NP XP] pattern. This problem is due to the fact that the force-dynamic relations between the event-participants that are to be integrated into the causal chain of the source verb *blow* do not exhibit the same semantic/pragmatic relationship as those of *blow*, *sneeze*, and *cough*. Since *breathe*, *pant*, and *wheeze* do not (in neutral context) denote a very strong emission of air, they are harder to associate with the caused-motion usage pattern of *blow*. But note that in cases in which the force-dynamic relations between the event-participants that are to be integrated into the causal chain are 'fixed' by contextual background information, the causal link between causing and caused event can be readily associated with these verbs as with *blow*, *sneeze*, and *cough*, thereby facilitating association of the target verbs with the [NP V NP XP] syntactic frame of the source verb *blow*.

(7.92) a. Kirsten came back from a 5k run and was out of breath. Breathing heavily, she sat down and breathed the napkin off the table.
b. Jen held her breath for 45 seconds. Then she panted the napkin off the table.
c. Julio wheezed the feather off the table.

The above sentences show that the force-dynamics conventionally associated with *breathe*, *pant*, and *wheeze* may be changed by context. Providing contextual background information to the event-frame's lexical force-dynamics makes it thus possible to associate a target verb with a given syntactic frame of the source verb, even if the basic conventionalized frame-semantic information does not readily allow for this association. Note that it is hard to exactly quantify the amount of force-dynamic information that needs to be provided by discourse in order for the association to be made, because the two types of information are on a sliding scale. The only broad-scale generalization that seems to hold is that the force-dynamic relations of the target verb (*breathe*, *wheeze*, *sneeze*, etc.) in combination with the force dynamic information provided by the context have to be equivalent to the type of force-dynamic relations exhibited by the source verb (*blow*). This is captured by the following diagram.

(7.93) Relation between force-dynamic information provided by a target verb's event-frame and by contextual background information in order to match the source verb's force dynamic specifications

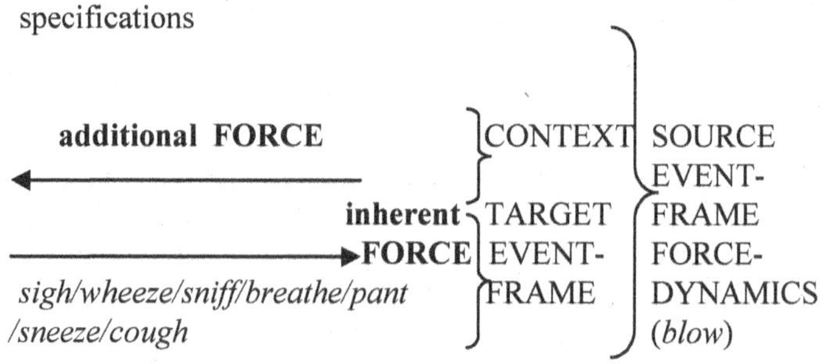

The diagram illustrates the difference in force-dynamic information associated with the event-frames of different air emission verbs that are target verbs to be associated with *blow*'s [NP V NP XP] frame. Since every verb has to somehow be construed as denoting the same force-dynamic relations in context as prototypical *blow*, there are different options available. If a verb's event-frame is already lexically associated with this type of force-dynamic information, then no extra context is needed, cf. *sneeze* and *cough*. However, if a verb's event frame does not lexically denote such strong force dynamics, cf. *breathe*, *wheeze*, and *sigh*, the force-dynamic information has to be provided by context. That is, *sigh* and *wheeze* will require more contextual force dynamic information in order to be associated with *blow*'s [NP V NP XP] frame than *breathe* and *pant*.[69] The amount of force-dynamic

[69]This observation is not only true for air emission verbs covered in this section. It holds for the principles of analogical association across the board. Compare, e.g., the conventionalized caused-motion frame of *run* as in *Jack ran Bob off the street*. Other verbs that are to acquire the same syntactic pattern must lexically denote strong force that can be construed as pushing another person away. If event-frames are not lexically associated with the proper force-dynamics, then context has to provide the necessary information. The following verbs thus need in descending order more contextual background information in order to be associated with *run*'s [NP V NP XP] frame: *jog, dance, walk, crawl, creep*.

information provided by the lexicon and by discourse is therefore not constant and varies with each verb. Ultimately, the construal of the event-frame information in combination with discourse information triggering the target verb's association with *blow*'s [NP V NP XP] pattern follows the same pragmatic principles of interpretability as those of *blow*. This is illustrated by the following sentences.

(7.94) a. Jack sneezed the napkin off the table.
b. ?Jack sneezed the book off the table.
c. *Jack sneezed the bookcase over.

(7.95) a. The elephant sneezed the napkin off the table.
b. The elephant sneezed the book off the table.
c. The elephant sneezed the bookcase over.

Let us now turn to the second type of verbs in (7.91) that is to say the ones that do not allow association with *blow*'s [NP V NP XP] pattern. *Exhale* and *inhale* differ from *sneeze*, *cough*, *wheeze*, *breathe*, and *pant* in that they lexically block any association with *blow*'s [NP V NP XP] pattern. That is, whereas the latter group of verbs shows a great deal of conventionalized frame-semantic overlap with the event-semantics of the caused-motion sense of *blow* and only needs contextual background information in order to be associated with *blow*'s resultative sense, the former group does not exhibit the same amount of frame-semantic overlap with *blow*.

(7.96) a. Katie blew.
b. *Katie blew the napkin.
c. Katie blew the napkin off the table.

(7.97) a. Katie exhaled.
b. Katie exhaled {the air/*the napkin}.
c. *Katie exhaled the napkin off the table.

(7.98) a. Joshua inhaled.
b. Joshua inhaled {the air/*the napkin}.
c. *Joshua inhaled the napkin off the table.

The sentences illustrate that *exhale* and *inhale* are conventionally associated with both an intransitive and a transitive usage whereas *blow* is not. There are also different types of event-semantic relations associated with these different usage patterns. When *exhale* and *inhale* are used in the transitive pattern they imply that the postverbal object either originates or ends within the lungs.[70] While this is very well possible with air, it is normally not possible with napkins. This means that when *exhale* and *inhale* are to be associated with *blow*'s [NP V NP XP] interpretation, their frame-semantic information blocks this association because readings such as in (7.97c) and (7.98c) would assume that the napkin either originates or ends up in the lungs. In other words, frame-semantic information about what it means to *inhale* and *exhale* as opposed to *blow* and *sneeze* blocks any possible association of these verbs with *blow*'s [NP V NP XP] pattern. This means that the event-frames of *exhale* and *inhale* do not allow any recruitment of world knowledge in order to perspectivize any other event participants than those already associated with their conventionalized event-frames (a similar case is *open*, cf. Section 7.2.3 above). In addition, note that *exhale* and *inhale* are already conventionally associated with an optional caused-motion/resultative interpretation.

(7.99) a. She exhaled the smoke into his face.
b. He inhaled her perfume into his lungs.

(7.100) Simplified event-frame architecture of *inhale* and *exhale*

GOAL
Ag (Pt) (p3)

Ag: Entity moving air or gas in or out of lungs
Pt: Objects and gases moved into (inhale) or out of (exhale) lungs
p3: Directional PP denoting the final location of patient

The event-frame expresses the fact that the optional conventionalized caused-motion senses of *inhale* and *exhale* do not allow any recruitment of world knowledge. Therefore, these verbs may not be associated with syntactic event-frames of verbs closely related in meaning that yield an interpretation different from their own specifications. Since the event-frames of *exhale* and *inhale* lexically block any analogical associations, it is also not

70 The difference between the frame-semantics of *exhale* and *blow* is in profiling. Normally, *exhale* profiles the lungs as the 'source' of the air leaving the body, whereas *blow* profiles the mouth as the 'source' of the air leaving the body.

possible to have the necessary information to trigger an association with *blow*'s [NP V NP XP] frame above.[71]

The examples discussed in this section show that there are in principle two cases in which an analogy with a verb closely related in meaning is blocked. The first type is exemplified by verbs such as *wheeze*, *pant*, and *breathe* and may be 'fixed' by contextual background information. The second type is exemplified by verbs such as *exhale* and *inhale* which lexically block any analogical association with syntactic frames of other event-frames and may therefore not be 'fixed' by contextual background information.[72]

The analysis presented in this section suggests that the production and interpretation of nonconventionalized resultatives is based upon analogical associations with existing conventionalized resultative patterns of verbs in combination with contextual background information. As such, nonconventionalized resultatives based on analogy are constrained by both lexical (on-stage and off-stage information) as well as contextual factors. The relationship between conventionalized and nonconventionalized resultatives discussed in this chapter is what Lehrer (1990: 240) characterizes in her discussion of conventionality as follows: 'In most cases, however, because productivity is partial, the lexicon must contain the existing conventional senses as well as the rule.'

---

[71]Ultimately, *exhale* and *inhale* may not be associated with *blow*'s semantics because of the principle of contrast, i.e., because these verbs are already associated with a specific meaning that is represented by the [NP V NP XP] pattern. To this end, Clark (1992: 178) points out that 'speakers systematically contrast their new terms with what is already available in the conventional lexicon.'

[72]In some cases, contextual background information may also be employed to override a lexical specification of a conventionalized event-frame. Take, e.g., *Ed hammered the metal safe.* Given contextual background information about the fact that somebody cut himself on a piece of metal sticking out of Ed's car door the day before, the sentence is interpretable as *Ed hammered the metal and as a result of Ed's hammering the metal became safe*. In this case, the speaker needs to convey a meaning for which there is no ready-made, conventional expression that can be employed to readily express the immediate causation relationship between the causing event (Ed hammering) and the caused event (The metal becoming safe). In this case, the resultative phrase specifications imposed on *hammer* by the *hammer-flat* event-frame are loosened and replaced by contextual factors in combination with analogy. In this case, *make-safe* serves as the target for the analogical association of the *hammer-flat* event-frame with a different type of semantic resultative phrase ('*flat*' being replaced by *safe* due to analogy with *make*). The *make-safe* event-frame serves as the source because there is no other verb belonging to the verb class of *hammer* that has a similar conventionalized usage pattern as *make*. In this connection, note that *make* serves as the prototype for this sort of analogy. In combination with *safe*, *make* occurs a total of 67 times in the BNC, making up for 100% of all resultative uses of *safe* in the BNC. Compare Appendix A.29 for the exhaustive list of *make-safe* occurrences in the BNC.

7.4 Conclusions

In this chapter I have laid out the details of an alternative account of resultative constructions that regards the role of the verb and its individual senses as central in determining the occurrence and distribution of resultatives. On the view advocated here, a verb is a collection of different types of event-frames that contains information about the respective senses associated with it. Each event-frame is its own construction that includes different frame semantic (and sometimes syntactic) information bundles. This means that each verb also exhibits distinct properties when it comes to the selection and realization of resultatives with a specific event-frame (i.e., sense of a verb).[73]

While on-stage information such as information about event participants is typically of immediate relevance and must thus be realized at the linguistic level, off-stage information such as information about force-dynamics or general world knowledge is usually irrelevant and does not have to be overtly expressed when a verb occurs in a sentence. However, when a speaker wishes to give a specific viewpoint of the outcome of an event, she may recruit this knowledge and make it linguistically relevant. I have argued that resultatives are motivated by the speaker's intention to point out a specific perspective of an event participant's end result state. The resultative is licensed by event-frame semantic information that determines (a) whether a given verb may occur with resultatives, and (b) what type of resultative a given verb may occur with.

The corpus evidence suggests that there are conventionalized resultatives based on lexicalized event-frames and nonconventionalized resultatives based on analogy with conventionalized event-frames. Conventionalized resultatives lexically specify the prototypical patient participant and the type of resultative phrase that may occur with a given sense of a verb (event-frame).[74] There are three different subclasses that each fulfill a different communicative function. The first class of conventionalized resultatives is employed to highlight the outcome of an event (cf. *kill*). The second type serves to specify a possible end result state that could hold of an event

[73]Although we have not been able to give in-depth semantic descriptions of the relevant event-participants and how they differ exactly from event-participants of other types of event-frames, we have attempted to define the relevant event participants in relation to each other and in relation to their individual usage in the given sense. This type of characterization of semantic relations that hold for different meanings of a verb is still unsatisfactory. However, we have taken a first step towards accounting for the distribution of resultatives in terms of individual verb senses defined over different semantic types of event participants instead of generatively deriving verb senses based on a basic verb sense.

[74]Besides other on-stage and off-stage information.

participant (cf. *paint*, *strangle*), thereby rendering it more precise. The third class of conventionalized resultatives, fake objects, is based on recruitment of off-stage information associated with event-frames. By recruiting this off-stage information, the outcome of an event is perspectivized from the viewpoint of a non-prototypical patient participant (cf. *Flora painted the brush to pieces*).

Nonconventionalized resultatives are based on analogy with conventionalized event-frames. In discussing verbs of air emission, we have seen that verbs may be associated with the semantics and the syntactic frame [NP V NP XP] of *blow*'s caused-motion/resultative event-frame. In order to be associated with the event-frame of a source verb (*blow*), event-frames of target verbs have to overlap in frame semantic information with the frame-semantic information contained in the event-frame of the source verb. The parts of frame-semantic information that are missing have to be provided by context. In the case of *sneeze*, e.g., the information provided by context has to contain information about a patient participant and the force-dynamics of the respective sneezing event. Once the frame-semantic overlap of the conventionalized event-frames in combination with contextual background information is given, the target verb may be associated with the [NP V NP XP] pattern of the source verb (*blow*). In cases in which a target is not lexically specified for the necessary force-dynamic information that can be construed as being able to move an object as a result of air emission, the context has to provide the extra information about the force dynamics.[75] In this connection, I have argued that event-frame semantic information and force dynamics vary regarding how much information about the force dynamics involved needs to be provided by context. Finally, I have pointed out that air emission verbs like *exhale* and *inhale* lexically block any association

[75]The proposals regarding analogical creativity made in this section are supported by recent findings in child language acquisition. Based on a number of studies, Tomasello (2000) elaborates on his (1992) Verb Island hypothesis which claims that 'children have an early period in which each of their verbs forms its own island of organization in an otherwise unorganized language system.' He observes 'in the vast majority of cases, this child's creative utterances were based directly on things she had said before many times previously. Moreover, in the vast majority of cases, one of the pieces of language on which the child's creative utterance was based was what we called an utterance schema.' The proposals made in this section provide evidence that the application of utterance schemas – in our case the combination of a verb typically closely related in meaning that is already conventionally associated with the [NP V NP XP] pattern in combination with contextual background information - is not only limited to child language acquisition, but also holds for innovative analogical associations in adult speech by which verbs may acquire new syntactic frames if needed.

with *blow* because their event-frames denote different profiling patterns of temporal and force-dynamic relations.[76]

The corpus data show that event-frames lexically subcategorize for specific types of resultative phrases. While in some cases the collocational restrictions are very broad and only require a resultative that expresses a certain state of affairs (e.g., a state of cleanliness), in other cases the lexical requirements are very specific and only allow one particular type of resultative phrase (e.g., *dead*). Furthermore, we have seen that event-frames differ with respect to whether they require the resultative phrase to be overtly expressed as is the case with phrasal verbs (e.g., *wipe-out*) and some other select event-frames, or whether this is only an optional feature (e.g., *break*).

The different categories of resultatives discussed in this chapter reveal an interesting connection between world knowledge and linguistic structure. That is, there is a link between knowledge about conventionally expected results and collocational restrictions imposed by an event-frame on constituents in resultative constructions. In Section 7.2.1 I have shown that verbs such as *kill*, *wipe-out*, *paint*, and *wash* exhibit very specific collocational restrictions with respect to the types of resultative phrases that may pattern with them. I have argued that the tight collocational restrictions exhibited by these verbs reflect a speaker's knowledge about conventionally expected results of activities denoted by these verbs. In other words, the fact that the prototypical sense of *kill* expresses an activity that has an extremely predetermined conventionally expected result and therefore requires no off-stage information is reflected linguistically by the fact that it only allows a narrow set of resultative phrases expressing the outcome of the activity of killing. In this case, the only resultative phrase allowed with *kill* is *dead*. While verbs such as prototypical *paint* and *wash* exhibit considerably less collocational restrictions than *kill* or *wipe-out*, they share with these verbs the property of requiring extremely little off-stage information when they occur in resultatives with regular objects.

In contrast, I have argued in Section 7.2.2 that verbs with fake objects require a great deal more off-stage information in order to license their

[76]Based on the observations made in this section I suggest that other types of non-conventionalized resultatives are formed in a similar way by means of analogy. This means that on a case-to-case basis a given target verb will have to be associated with a source verb in order to acquire the non-conventionalized syntactic pattern. In cases in which the semantic class to which the target verb belongs does not contain a source verb that is already conventionally associated with the [NP V NP XP] pattern, other, more general verbs that express the respective force-dynamic relationships will have to function as source verbs in combination with the proper contextual background information. Such verbs include *make, push, pull, take, move*, etc.

postverbal constituents in resultatives. This is because the result state expressed by fake object resultatives involves non-prototypical event participants and as such does not denote conventionally expected results that are directly inferable on the basis of on-stage information. Take, e.g., the verb *run* which may occur with a wide variety of non-prototypical event participants such as *the pavement*, *herself*, *the shoes*, *his feet*, etc. as fake objects in resultative constructions. In this case, off-stage information is recruited in order to license non-prototypical event participants besides the prototypical runner event participant. In addition, off-stage information needs to be recruited about possible end result states of each of the fake objects since they do not typically denote conventionally expected results. The fact that more off-stage information is required to license non-prototypical event participants such as fake objects and their resultative phrases is reflected linguistically. That is, because more off-stage information is required, event-frames impose fewer collocational restrictions on postverbal constituents in resultatives with fake objects than in resultatives with regular objects.

In contrast to conventionalized resultatives requiring different amounts of off-stage information, nonconventionalized resultatives form yet another category. That is, since they are formed by analogy on the basis of conventionalized resultatives in combination with contextual background information, they need to provide as much off-stage information as possible in order to be available for a potential analogical association. In the case of *sneeze* we have seen that in order for the analogical process to take place, the speaker needs to know as much as possible about what it means to sneeze in order to associate *sneeze* with the resultative semantics of *blow,* and, subsequently, with the syntactic frame [NP V NP XP] expressing the resultative semantics. This is because the resultative semantics does not describe a conventionally expected result of sneezing.[77] The recruitment of off-stage information about what it means to *sneeze* therefore requires information not only about the prototypical event participants but also about non-prototypical event participants that lie outside of the scene described by the prototypical sense of *sneeze*. While the range of postverbal arguments occurring with the nonconventionalized resultative sense of *sneeze* is constrained by the resultative event-frame of *blow* and contextual background information, it is nevertheless greater than that of intransitive *sneeze* which does not allow postverbal NPs or resultative phrases. In other words, the fact that more off-stage information is recruited in order to license non-prototypical event-participants with *sneeze* is reflected linguistically by the fact that the collocational restrictions of intransitive *sneeze* become less

[77]As discussed Chapter 4, I regard what Goldberg (1995) classifies as resultative and caused-motion constructions as a unified phenomenon, namely as resultatives.

strict as to allow for postverbal constituents. This means that the large amount of off-stage information directly influences the range of possible postverbal constituents, or, put differently, that the fewer collocational restrictions directly reflect the large amount of off-stage information needed in order to license a resultative with *sneeze*.

To sum up, the distribution of resultatives reveals an interesting fact about the influence of knowledge about conventionally expected results on collocational restrictions. That is, the more off-stage information is needed to license a resultative with a given verb, the fewer are the collocational restrictions that an event-frame imposes on the verb's postverbal constituents. What is important here is that event-frames licensing different types of resultatives are found at different points between two ends of a continuum.

On one end of the continuum are totally fixed resultatives such as *break-(in)to-pieces*, *kill-dead* and *wipe-out.* These resultatives require very little, if any, off-stage information in order to be licensed because speakers typically have a clear understanding about the types of conventionally expected results associated with activities described by the event-frames.[78] The fact that speakers have this knowledge about conventionally expected results readily available is reflected linguistically in that the event-frames impose very tight collocational restrictions on the postverbal constituents. On the other end of the continuum are extremely free combinations such as *sneeze-off-the-table*. The licensing of these resultatives requires a great deal of off-stage information because speakers typically do not have knowledge about the conventionally expected results of sneezing in terms of objects being moved by the emitted air flow. The fact that speakers are capable of making analogical associations on the basis of already conventionalized event-frames (such as *blow*) in combination with context requires large amounts of off-stage information about what it means to sneeze. Since speakers are capable of recruiting all sorts of off-stage information about what it means to sneeze, the influence of this knowledge is reflected linguistically in that the event-frames of verbs such as *sneeze* impose very little collocational restrictions on the postverbal constituents. In fact, as we have seen in Section 7.3.2.2, the collocational restrictions are imposed by the target event-frame of *blow* in combination with contextual background information. This means that in theory all sorts of nonconventionalized resul-

---

[78]Note that this statement only refers to the semantic and syntactic range of resultative predicates and postverbal NPs, but not to the obligatoriness of the resultative phrase. While there is some overlap between an event-frame's requirement for a resultative phrase to be licensed (see Section 7.2) and the amount of off-stage information correlating to the collocational restrictions on the postverbal constituents, the two are rarely identical.

tatives could be formed with *sneeze* as long as there is a source event-frame and contextual background information capable of licensing the analogical process underlying such resultatives as *Miriam sneezed the cockroach out of the cup*, *Lila sneezed her neighbors sick*, *Chuck sneezed his dog to madness*, and *Joe sneezed his keyboard wet* (always keeping in mind the restrictions in 7.3.2.2.3 that constrain productivity).

Other types of resultatives are to be found in the fuzzy area between the two ends of the continuum. For example, resultatives involving regular objects such as *Carlos painted the house blue* will require considerably less off-stage information about non-prototypical event participants because they typically involve a prototypical patient (e.g., *the house*). In this case, speakers have knowledge about what types of results to expect of a painting activity (houses being painted typically end up with new color). This means that there is no need to recruit off-stage information about non-prototypical event participants and the different types of result states they could end up with because of the activity denoted by the verb. More knowledge about conventionally expected results (with respect to prototypical event participants) thus means tighter collocational restrictions with respect to resultative phrases. In contrast, resultatives involving fake objects such as *Collin swept the broom to pieces* require a great deal more off-stage information about non-prototypical event participants because speakers typically do not associate conventionally expected results of prototypical event participants with non-prototypical event participants (e.g., **Collin swept the floor to pieces*). Since non-prototypical event participants of fake object resultatives could theoretically end up in all sorts of different result states, speakers will typically not associate conventionally expected result states with them as they do with regular object resultatives. Less knowledge about conventionally expected result states thus not only requires more off-stage information but also imposes fewer collocational restrictions on a verb's postverbal constituents.

The alternative proposal presented in this chapter has a number of important implications for other analyses of resultatives. First, the ability to occur with resultatives is determined by lexical features of verbs in combination with contextual factors. Second, the frame-semantic information contained in an event-frame determines not only the semantic and syntactic properties of resultative phrases, but also those of agent and patient participants. Third, since all of this information is lexically specified for each of a verb's multiple event-frames (i.e., each of its senses), no intervening levels of representation or generative mechanisms adding or subtracting information or structure to or from a verb's lexical-semantic information are needed for the linking of frame-semantic information to the syntactic level. The advantage of this approach for a theory of resultatives is that it does not have to determine the domains of application for generative mechanisms to cover the full range of empirical data. Instead, each verb forms its own domain of application for resultatives by lexically listing the information necessary for the licensing of resultatives in terms of multiple event-frames associated with a verb.

8

A Contrastive Look at Resultatives in English and German

> If we accept the reality that in everyday language total equivalence does not exist for words in isolation, we can still find satisfactory *working equivalents* for a large number of words (or translation units) in context. (...) The more transparent the context and the more semantic redundancy there is, the easier the translation will be. It is perhaps the stumbling-block of the conventional bilingual dictionary that it operates with words in isolation, yet functions according to the principle of working equivalence, whereby a context would be required. Sometimes however the foreign language cannot provide a working equivalent.
>
> (Snell-Hornby 1983: 215)

8.1 Introduction

In order to see how the constructional approach proposed in the last three chapters can be applied to languages other than English, this chapter looks at the differences in resultative formation between English and German. First, I discuss a set of contrastive data in order to assess the similarities and differences with respect to resultatives. Then I offer an explanation for the differences between English and German resultatives along the lines given in the previous chapter. We will see that the differences in resultative formation can be partially accounted for by more general properties of the two languages and are thus not a phenomenon particular to resultatives. Finally, I compare the constructional approach with other analyses proposed for German resultative constructions.[1]

---

[1]Parts of this chapter are based on Boas (2001), Boas (2002a), Boas (2002b), and Boas (2002c).

8.2 Differences and Similarities between English and German Resultatives

There is a large class of German verbs whose distribution in resultative usage patterns is similar to that of their English counterparts. As the English examples in (8.1) and their German counterparts in (8.2) demonstrate, the two languages allow the use of the same types of verbs (denoting identical situations) in both non-resultative and resultative patterns.

(8.1) a. Claire wiped the table (clean).
b. Natasha painted the house (red).
c. David ran himself tired.
d. Renate washed the soap out of her eyes.

(8.2) a. Ursula wischte den Tisch (sauber).
Ursula wiped the table clean
'Ursula wiped the table (clean).'
b. Ulrich strich das Haus (rot).
Ulrich painted the house red
'Ulrich painted the house (red).'
c. Fritz lief sich müde.
Fritz ran himself tired
'Fritz ran himself tired.'
d. Ruth wusch sich die Seife aus den Augen
Ruth washed herself the soap out of the eyes
'Ruth washed the soap out of her eyes.'
e. Magdalena hustete die Serviette vom Tisch.
Magdalena coughed the napkin from the table
'Magdalena coughed the napkin off the table.'

However, there are also numerous instances in which an English verb may occur both with and without a resultative, but its German counterpart may not occur with a resultative. The differences in distribution between English and German verbs in resultative constructions are shown in (8.3) – (8.18). In each case, notice how the two languages require different verbs to express the resultative meaning.

(8.3) a. Jim rolled the window up.
b. Altin rolled his sleeve up.
c. Dave rolled the ball down the street.

(8.4) a. Karsten kurbelte das Fenster hoch.
Karsten wound the window up
'Karsten rolled the window up.'
b. Jens krempelte seinen Ärmel hoch.
Jens moved his sleeve up
'Jens rolled his sleeve up.'
c. Sascha rollte den Ball die Strasse runter.
Sascha rolled the ball the street down
'Sascha rolled the ball down the street.'

(8.5) a. Martin ran Ed off the road.
b. *Martin rannte Ed von der Strasse ab.
Martin ran Ed from the street off
c. Martin drängte Ed (beim Rennen) von der Strasse ab.
Martin pushed Ed by running from the street off
'Martin ran Ed off the street.'

(8.6) a. Der Mann betete seine Tochter gesund.
the man prayed his daughter healthy
'The man prayed. As a result of his praying, his daughter became healthy.'
b. ?The man prayed his daughter healthy.
c. The man prayed. As a result of his praying, his daughter became healthy.

(8.7) a. Terry wiped the crumbs into a pile.
b. *Terry wischte die Krümel zu einem Haufen.
Terry wiped the crumbs to a pile
c. Terry wischte die Krümel zusammen.
Terry wiped the crumbs together
'Terry wiped the crumbs into a pile.'

(8.8) a. The doctors starved the patients to death. (BNC)
b. *Die Ärzte hungerten die Patienten zu Tode.
the doctors starved the patients to death
c. Die Ärzte liessen die Patienten verhungern.
the doctors let the patients starve
'The doctors starved the patients to death.'

(8.9) a. The coach ran the athletes around the track.
b. *Der Trainer rannte die Athleten um das Sportfeld
the coach ran the athletes around the track field
herum.
around
c. Der Trainer liess die Athleten um das Sportfeld
the coach let the athletes around the trackfield
herumrennen.
around-run
'The coach ran the athletes around the track.'

(8.10) a. I'll see you to the door.
b. *Ich sehe Dich zur Tür.
I see you to the door
c. Ich begleite Dich zur Tür.
I accompany you to the door
'I see you to the door.'

(8.11) a. The media have painted a picture of us as rivals.
b. *Die Medien haben ein Bild von uns als Rivalen gemalt
the media have a picture of us as rivals painted
c. Die Medien haben uns als Rivalen dargestellt.
the media have us as rivals depicted
'The media have painted a picture of us as rivals.'

(8.12) a. He laughed his butt off.
b. *Er lachte seinen Hintern ab.
he laughed his butt off
c. Er lachte sich schief.
he laughed self crooked
'He laughed his butt off.'

(8.13) a. I'm surprised the guy didn't beat the shit out of me. (BNC)
b. *dass der Typ die Scheisse aus mir herausgeschlagen hat.
that the guy the shit out me out-beat has
c. dass der Typ mich nicht zusammengeschlagen hat.
that the guy me not together-beat has
'... the guy didn't beat the shit out of me.'

(8.14) a. It broke me up when I learned about Bernadette's baby. (BNC)
b. *Es hat mich aufgebrochen als ich von Bernadettes
it has me open-broke as I from Bernadette's
Baby gehört habe.
baby heard have
c. Es hat mich total gewundert als …
it has me totally surprised as …
'It broke me up when …'

(8.15) a. This thing breaks it down by age, as I say, we're looking at seventy-fives and over. (BNC)
b. *Dieses Ding bricht es runter nach Alter, ...
this thing breaks it down after age
c. Dieses Ding teilt es nach Alter auf ...
this thing divides it after age up
'This thing breaks it down by age…'

(8.16) a. They broke them in like a horse, … (BNC)
b. *Sie brachen sie ein wie ein Pferd, ...
they broke them in like a horse
c. Sie ritten sie zu wie ein Pferd, ...
they rode them in like a horse
'They broke them in like a horse …'

(8.17) a. Unable to break them free, waves thrashed the jagged tubes of aluminum over the foredeck. (BNC)
b. *Unfähig sie freizubrechen, ...
unable them to free-break
c. Unfähig sie loszulösen, ...
unable them free-loosen
'Unable to break them free …'

(8.18) a. Beryl was poorly this morning and I had to run her to the doctors. (BNC)
b. *... ich musste sie zum Arzt rennen.
I had-to her to-the doctor run
c. ... ich musste sie zum Arzt bringen.
I had-to her to-the doctor accompany
'… I had to run her to the doctors.'

The sentence pairs illustrate that in many cases there are no direct German translation equivalents of English resultatives that include the verb which has a similar meaning outside of the resultative construction to the respective historically related English verb.[2] This difference is due to the conventionalized meanings associated with the resultative usages of verbs in particular contexts in each language which in turn means that they can only refer to events and causal chains that can be conventionally described by a verb of that language.[3] The fact that German verbs do not show the same type of flexibility with respect to their conventionalized usage patterns is not a phenomenon specific to resultative constructions. Hawkins' (1986) contrastive study of English and German observes that verb meanings in the two languages are distributed in different and often unpredictable ways:

> English regularly disposes of semantically very general lexemes (...) which have no exact and correspondingly broad translation equivalents in German. Hence, German speakers must make a choice between the type of knowing, leaving, putting, etc., whereas this can be left unspecified in English. Once again, it is not being claimed that English necessarily lacks lexemes of corresponding specificity to those of German (though this will often be the case). But rather English regularly contains additional lexemes which are neutral to the semantic distinctions that must be drawn in German, and in actual language use these more general terms will commonly be preferred, so that the substitution of a more specific for a more general term will be a regular feature of translation from English to German. (...) As a result (as Leisi 1975: 71 points out) the class of real-world

---

[2]Some people claim that there is a strict difference between a 'sense of a verb,' and an idiomatic phrase. The examples in (8.3) – (8.18), however, illustrate that such a distinction cannot be clearly drawn in many cases, i.e., the boundary between individual word senses and idiomatic phrases is fuzzy. Based on our observations made in the last chapter this should come as no surprise, since as we have seen there, each event-frame exhibits its own particular frame-semantic bundle of information. In other words, different senses of a verb and idiomatic phrases are treated equally with respect to the architecture of their event-frames and with respect to the specifications of semantic information and how that information gets mapped to syntax. What this means is that there is no strict division between senses of a word and idiomatic phrases that are based on a word. On the view advocated here, there are only different levels of semantic specificity requirements that each event-frame representing a particular 'sense' or idiomatic phrase imposes on its arguments. In principle, then, each event-frame is regarded as its own mini-construction with its own conventionalized semantic and syntactic requirements.

[3]With respect to German translation equivalents of English verbs, Snell-Hornby (1983: 214) points out that 'verb-descriptivity demonstrates more frequently the absence of an equivalent in the foreign language than the existence of one. Indeed, rather than functioning in terms of equivalence, the analysis showed lexemes to cover each other to a greater or lesser extent, and we will here place beside the absolute concept of equivalence the relative concept of extent of coverage.'

> situations that English sentences containing these general predicates can describe is very broad, whereas the German translations describe a much narrower class of situations. And there is that much more vagueness in these English lexemes that impose minimal selectional restriction requirements.
>
> (Hawkins 1986: 29-30)[4]

Hawkins' observations indicate that the selected semantic distribution of verbs in the two languages is not particular to resultatives but holds for English and German in general.[5] That is, due to historical developments that took different paths in each language, verbs that have descended from a common Germanic source have developed differently in English and German and therefore exhibit different usage conventions as illustrated by the data in (8.3)-(8.18). Leisi and Mair (1999) explain the historical background underlying the different verbal distributional patterns of the two languages as follows.

> ... da das Englische für viele neue Bezeichnungen nicht wie das Deutsche zur Lehnübersetzung, sondern zum direkten Latinismus gegriffen und seine alten einheimischen Wortbildungsmöglichkeiten (Vor- und Nachsilben, Komposition) weitgehend verloren hat. (...) Dadurch, dass diese einheimischen Wörter für alle möglichen Funktionen, gleichsam als universale Hilfsmittel, einspringen mussten, ergibt sich die gewaltige Bedeutungserweiterung oder gar Überhäufung, die sie im Lauf der mittel- und neuenglischen Zeit erfahren haben. Aus ihren ursprünglichen konkreten und speziellen Bedeutungen, z.B. *give, take* = mit der Hand geben und nehmen, *get* = erlangen, *run* = rennen, *put* = stossen, *set* = hinsetzen, *job* = bestimmtes Stück Arbeit, *glass* = das Material, haben sie sich zu ganz allgemein und universal verwendbaren Funktionselementen entwickelt. Dies gilt besonders für die Verben; die meistgebrauchten von ihnen, etwa *go, come, run, fall, turn, stand, get, take, look, put, set, lay*, haben ihre Bindung an ein bestimmtes Subjekt oder Objekt und damit die Assoziation an eine Tätigkeit bestimmter Form ganz verloren; sie sind heute nur noch elementare dynamische *operators*, die sich mit fast allem

---

[4] With respect to the difference in semantic flexibility, Hawkins (1985: 67) proposes that 'the loss of the case system is ultimately responsible for the greater semantic diversity of basic grammatical relations in English.'

[5] For a critical investigation of Hawkins' (1986) claims, see Fischer (1997) who supports Hawkins' thesis only in a weaker and thus modified version. In this connection note that in the area of resultative constructions Hawkins' claim cannot be upheld in its present form. As the tables in (8.19) and Appendix (C.1) – (C.4) show, there are also German verbs that are much more flexible when it comes to denoting semantic concepts different from their English counterparts.

> verbinden lassen und mit denen alle Arten von menschlichen und anderen Bewegungen wiedergegeben werden können.
>
> (Leisi and Mair 1999: 67, 72)[6]

For the sake of the present discussion, let us briefly consider how the information about a resultative outcome of an event is expressed differently in English as opposed to German: First, the resultative can be split into two separate sentences with two different verbs relating to separate parts of the causal chain (cf. (8.6) and (8.7)). Second, a verb with a completely different meaning can be used to describe the two subevents of the causal chain (cf. (8.10)). Third, a different kind of resultative phrase can be employed to denote the caused event (cf. (8.12)). The data in (8.3)-(8.18) suggest that the kinds of events and the types of causal chains that a verb can refer to in a resultative construction are conventionalized.

These claims are also supported by the observation that historically related English and German verbs, such as *run/rennen* (OE *rinnan*, OHG *rinnan*), *blow/blasen* (OE *blāwan*), *suck/saugen* (OE *sūcan*), *break/brechen* (OE *brecan*), and *wipe/wischen* (OE *wīpian*) (and which additionally show a great overlap in meaning outside of the resultative construction) cannot describe the same kinds of causal chains in the two languages. Thus, even when a speaker intends to refer to a causal chain using a resultative construction, she is limited by the amount of semantic information that a verb can conventionally refer to. If a single verb is not suited for relating information about the entire causal chain, then one has to either pick a different verb (cf. *run* vs. *abdrängen* in (8.5)), or use two verbs to describe each part of the causal chain individually (cf. *wipe* vs. *zusammenwischen* in (8.7)). The contrastive data thus illustrates that the semantic information that can

---

[6]Translation: ... because English did not make use of loan translations like German, it made more use of true Latinisms and has thus lost its own native word formation possibilities (pre- and suffixation, composition). Since native words had to take over all sorts of functions (like a universal aid), this explains the enormous expansion or overload of meanings during the middle and modern English period. From their very specific meanings, *give*, *take* = to give and take with hands, *get* = receive, *run* = run [i.e., fast energetic movement involving the legs, HCB], *put* = thrust, *set* = set down, *job* = certain piece of work, *glass* = the material, they have developed to universal applicable functional elements. This is especially true for verbs. The ones that are most frequently used, like *go, come, run, fall, turn, stand, get, take, look, put, set, lay*, have lost their ties to a specific subject or object and have thus completely lost the association with a specific activity; today they are only elementary dynamic operators that are combinable with almost anything and all sorts of human and other motion may be described with them.

be conveyed by each verb is constrained by the kinds of scenes it can describe, i.e., by its usage conventions.

In this connection, consider the tables in (8.19) as well as the additional tables in Appendix (C.1) – (C.4). The German equivalents of many English resultative constructions that are usually characterized as 'constructions' (i.e., being formed by a generative mechanism adding additional arguments to a verb's semantic frame) are conventionalized and idiosyncratic preverb-verb combinations that are lexicalized. The tables are organized as follows. The first column contains lexicalized German preverb-verb combinations which denote specific semantic event frames. Column 2 lists a German example sentence for the respective semantic event-frame followed by an English translation in column 3 and the English translation of the German sentence in column 4.

(8.19) Preverb-verb combinations with *brechen* ('break') and their English equivalents

	German verb	Sentence	English equivalent	English sentence
1	Ab-brechen-1	Stefan brach die Spitze des Bleistifts ab.	break off	Stefan broke off the point of the pencil.
2	Ab-brechen-2	Karsten brach die Schule ab.	demolish, tear down	Karsten tore the school down.
3	An-brechen-1	Jens brach die Packung Chips an.	break into, start (on)	Jens started on the package of chips.
4	An-brechen-2	Sascha brach den Ast an.	crack, break (s.th.) partially	Sascha partially broke the twig.
5	Durch-brechen	Christian brach den Ast durch.	break s.th. in two/ through	Christian broke the twig in two.

Continued on next page.

Table 8.19 - Continued

	German verb	Sentence	English equivalent	English sentence
6	Erbrechen	Gustl erbrach die Schokolade.	to vomit, to throw	Gustl threw up the chocolate.
7	Um-brechen-1	Mathias brach den Baum um.	break s.th. down	Mathias broke the tree down.
8	Um-brechen-2	Hennig brach den Acker um.	turn (over), plow	Henning ploughed the acre.
9	Um-brechen-3	Der Computer brach die Zeile um.	overrun	The com-puter over-ran the line.
10	Zerbrechen	Chris zerbrach die Vase.	break s.th. to pieces	Chris broke the vase to pieces.

The tables in (8.19) and in Appendix (C.1) – (C.4) do not cover the entire spectrum of preverb-verb combinations of the respective verbs. In some cases the tables also include non-resultative senses to illustrate the polysemy of the respective preverb-verb combinations. Although some of the preverb-verb combinations seem to denote very similar concepts, I have chosen to split senses rather than to lump them together in order to achieve a more fine-grained description. The (rough) English translations indicate that there are sufficient differences in meaning that justify this splitting.

The preverb-verb combinations are lexicalized instances and refer both to related event-frames as well as to semantically unrelated event frames. Compare, for example, the different meanings of *brechen* in (8.19). The English translations show that the event frames denoted by the respective 'versions' of *brechen* are quite different and vary with respect to their event-semantic information (cf. *break off, open, vomit, overrun*, etc.). We need to posit separate event frames not only for the distinct senses of *bre-chen* but also for cases in which a given preverb-verb combination (i.e., the phonological string) refers to two different types of events. This is the case with *abbrechen-1* and *abbrechen-2*. The former means to remove an object that is attached to a larger object whereas the latter means to demolish an object, typically a building. The same observations can be made for the verbs listed in Appendix C: *abschiessen* in (C.1) (*shoot down* vs. *shoot off*), *anschiessen* (C.1) (*wound by shooting* vs. *test-fire*), *verschiessen* (C.1) (*fire off* vs. *miss*), *abschlagen* (C.2) (*refuse* vs. *kick off* vs. *urinate*), and *abfahren* (C.3) (*wear down* vs. *use up* vs. *cart away* vs. *cut off*). The comparison between German and English in (8.19) and in (C.1)- (C.4) also shows that for most of the conventionalized German resultatives that contain the same 'base verb,' English employs different verbs in order to express the resultative sense.

Having compared German resultatives with English resultatives, let us now change perspectives and see how resultatives based on polysemous English verbs are realized differently in German. The tables in (8.20) as well as those in Appendix (C.5) – (C.8) follow a similar format as that in (8.19) above. As with the table above, the senses listed for each verb are not exhaustive; their purpose is simply to illustrate that verbs have different types of event-frames (senses) that give rise to different types of resultative interpretations.

(8.20) Resultatives based on *drive* and their German equivalents

	Description of sense	Resultative	German equivalent	Resultative
1	To guide, control, or direct (a vehicle)	He drove the car into the ditch/ to pieces.	fahren	Er fuhr das Auto in den Graben/ kaputt.
2	To convey transport in a vehicle.	She drove the kids to school.	befördern/ fahren	Sie beförderte/fuhr die Kinder zur Schule.
3	To penetrate	Kim drove the stake into the ground.	(ein)-schlagen	Karla schlug den Stock in den Boden (ein).
4	To repulse forcefully; put to flight	We drove the attackers away.	wegjagen/ vertreiben	Wir jagten die Angreifer weg./ Wir vertrieben die Angreifer.
5	To throw, strike, or cast	He drove the ball into the goal.	treten	Er trat den Ball in das Tor.
6	To change the mental state of somebody	She drove me crazy.	treiben	Sie trieb mich in den Wahnsinn.

The comparison of the contrastive data with the proposals made in the last chapter support our observation that each verb in English and German is associated with a variety of different semantic event-frames (senses) which each contains idiosyncratic event-based frame semantic information (and in some cases information about how the event participants and their possible end result states are realized syntactically). This means that although the two languages exhibit almost the same types of combinatorial possibilities when it comes to a verb's various usages to denote different types of events, the determining force whether a given resultative is licensed or not lies with the conventionalized senses (described by event-frames) associated with a verb. That is, each event-frame associated with a verb lexically prescribes the semantic (and often syntactic) type of resultative phrase for each event participant. Event-frames differ with respect to whether they allow resultative phrases at all, whether they require the overt realization of a specific syntactic realization of the result (cf. *off*, *away*, etc.), or whether the resultative phrase is optional.

The distinct meanings of the individual event-frames demonstrate how problematic it is to build verb meanings by using Rappaport Hovav and Levin's (1998, 2001) template augmentation mechanisms. This system makes it difficult to account for the range of resultative phrases (or preverbs) that may combine with a given verb to yield a distinct meaning. Whereas on the present account an event-frame is regarded as a distinct collection of conventionalized lexical semantic information (a 'sense') capturing the relevant knowledge associated with a specific sense of a verb (or idiomatic phrase that contains the verb), Rappaport Hovav and Levin (1998, 2001) aim to reduce the information needed to capture the distribution of resultatives to mere aspectual templates. However, as we have seen in Chapter 3, this reductionist approach to verb meaning seems misguided when it comes to capturing the full range of possible resultatives based on a 'base' verb. Instead, we need to list for each verb the types of event-frames (senses) it is associated with. We now sketch out a series of simple event-frames for the English and German verbs discussed in (8.20) (for those verbs in Appendix (C.1) – (C.4), see Appendix (C.5) – (C.8)).

8.3 Contrastive Lexical Entries of English and German Verbs

In this section we lay out the architecture of the lexical entries for English *drive* and its German counterparts that occur with resultatives. We follow the notation and linking conventions employed in Chapters 6 and 7. The lexical entries do not claim to be complete with respect to full coverage of either all the event-frames (senses) associated with a verb, or with all the senses that can give rise to resultative interpretations. Instead, they contain a few distinct event-frames that are necessary in order to distinguish the distribution of English and German verbs illustrated in (8.20) (and Appendix (C.5) – (C.8)).

These sample lexical entries are structured as follows. They consist of two separate parts, one for each language. The top part lists the individual event-frames of the English verb that gives rise to the different types of resultatives illustrated in (8.20). Beneath each English event frame we find linked by two-way arrows the corresponding German event frame which in turn is linked to the respective German verb it belongs to. Note that in this case we only list the single German counterparts to the respective English event-frames, i.e., other event-frames linked to that German verb are not given here.

Identity between event-frames is indicated by co-indexing. English event-frames are marked with (a), German event-frames are marked with (b). In case a given event-frame associated with one of the verbs in a language does not have a direct equivalent in the other language, we will indicate this by a series of three question marks following the translation equivalent. Consider a comparison of resultatives based on the different senses of English *drive* and its German counterparts as illustrated in Table (8.20) above. The numbers in diagram (8.21) indicate identity with the respective senses in Table (8.20).

(8.21) Partial lexical entry of *drive* (containing event-frames that give rise to resultatives) and their German counterparts[7]

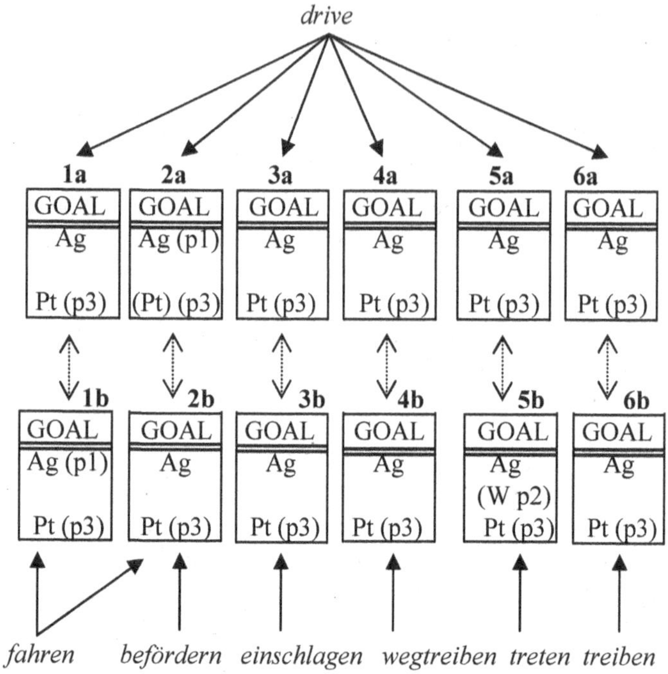

Table (8.22) lists the frame-semantic specifications of the individual event-frames in (8.21) in very general terms.[8] Since the semantic concepts denoted by the event-frames of English and German verbs are identical, we do not need to list the same information twice, i.e., the information stated for the English event-participants and resultative phrases also holds for their German counterparts. For that reason the column for German event-frames on the right hand side lists only event-frame specifications that differ from those of English.

[7]For individual sense descriptions, see table (8.20) above.

[8]The broad semantic characterization is, as it stands, not precise enough and needs to be further specified. For this purpose, it is necessary to do a large-scale corpus study of how the respective event participants and resultative phrases are realized and then derive the proper generalization. The present format of semantic specifications of event-frame information primarily illustrate that there are distinct semantic specifications for each event-frame.

(8.22) Individual frame-semantic specifications of event-frames of *drive* and its German counterparts in (8.21)

	English (a)	German (b)
1	Ag: animate being operating a vehicle Pt: vehicle p1: directional PP p3: directional PP or PP denoting state of physical disintegration	p3: additionally *kaputt* ('broken')
2	Ag: animate being operating a vehicle Pt: objects that fit in or onto the vehicle p3: directional PP	
3	Ag: entity exerting energy Pt: object that may penetrate the surface of an object as a result of the agent's activity p3: directional PP denoting a location that lies below the surface from the point of entry of the patient through the surface	p3: optionally *ein* ('into') following the PP
4	Ag: entity capable of causing a mental impression of them as being in control of the situation Pt: animate object with mental capabilities p3: directional PP	p3: *weg* ('away')
5	Ag: animate being handling a ball Pt: ball p3: directional PP	

Continued on next page.

Table 8.22 - Continued.

	English (a)	German (b)
6	Ag: entity causing a (typically negative) mental impression Pt: animate being that has mental capabilities p3: (typically) negative mental state, preferably expressed by APs and some select PPs (cf. Chapter 7.2.1.3.1)	p3: *in den Wahnsinn* ('to madness')

The contrastive lexical entries in (8.21) in combination with their frame-semantic event information in (8.22) license the following types of resultative constructions while ruling out other unattested cases. The linking of the event participants from the event-frames follows the general linking rules in Chapters 6 and 7.

(8.23) Licensing by (8.21.1a)

a. Dave drove the car into the ditch.
b. Dave drove the car to pieces.
c. *Dave drove the children to pieces.
d. *Dave drove the car crazy.

(8.24) Licensing by (8.21.1b)

a. Fritz fuhr das Auto in den Graben.
Fritz drove the car into the ditch
'Fritz drove the car into the ditch.'
b. Fritz fuhr das Auto kaputt.
Fritz drove the car broken
'Fritz drove the car to pieces.'
c. *Fritz fuhr die Kinder kaputt.
Fritz drove the children broken
d. *Fritz fuhr das Auto wahnsinnig.
Fritz drove the car crazy

(8.25) Licensing by (8.21.2a)

a. Dave drove the kids to school.
b. *Dave drove the children to pieces.
c. Dave drove himself to school.

(8.26) Licensing by (8.21.2b)

a. Fritz fuhr die Kinder zur Schule.
   Fritz drove the children to the school
   'Fritz drove the children to school.'
b. *Fritz fuhr die Kinder kaputt.
   Fritz drove the children broken
c. *Fritz fuhr die Kinder wahnsinnig.
   Fritz drove the children crazy

(8.27) Licensing by (8.21.3a)

a. Kim drove the stake into the ground.
b. *Kim drove the stake to pieces/crazy.
c. *Kim drove the children into the ground.
d. *Kim drove herself into the ground.

(8.28) Licensing by (8.21.3b)

a. Wir schlugen den Stock in den Boden (ein).
   we hit the stake in the ground in
   'We drove the stake into the ground.'
b. Wir schlugen den Stock kaputt.
   we hit the stake broken
   'We hit the stake to pieces.'
c. *Wir schlugen die Kinder in den Boden (ein).
   we hit the children into the ground into
d. *Wir schlugen uns selbst in den Boden (ein).
   we hit our self into the ground in

(8.29) Licensing by (8.21.4a)

a. They drove the attackers away.
b. *They drove the stake away.
c. *They drove the attackers to pieces.
d. *They drove the ball away.

(8.30) Licensing by (8.21.4b)

a. Sie trieben die Angreifer weg.
they drove the attackers away
'They drove the attackers away.'
b. *Sie trieben {das Auto/den Stock/den Ball}weg.
they drove the car/ the stake/ the ball away
c. *Sie trieben die Angreifer kaputt.
they drove the attackers broken
d. *Sie trieben die Angreifer in den Boden.
they drove the attackers into the ground

(8.31) Licensing by (8.21.5a)

a. He drove the ball into the goal.
b. *He drove the ball crazy.
c. *He drove the ball to pieces.
d. *He drove the stake into the goal.

(8.32) Licensing by (8.21.5b)

a. Er trat den Ball in das Tor.
he kicked the ball into the goal
'He drove the ball into the goal.'
b. *Er trat {die Angreifer/das Auto}in das Tor.
he kicked the attackers/the car into the goal
c. Er trat den Ball kaputt.
he kicked the ball broken
d. *Er trat den Ball wahnsinnig.
he kicked the ball crazy
e. Er trat sich müde.
he kicked self tired
'He kicked himself tired.'

(8.33) Licensing by (8.21.6a)

a. She drove me crazy.
b. *She drove {the ball/the car/the stake} crazy.
c. *She drove me into the ground.

(8.34) Licensing by (8.21.6b)

a. Sie trieb mich in den Wahnsinn.
she drove me into the madness
'She drove me mad/to madness.'

b. *Sie trieb mich {Nüsse/wild}.
she drove me nuts/ wild

c. *Sie trieb {das Auto/den Ball/den Stock}wahnsinnig.
she drove the car/ the ball/ the stake crazy

The examples in (8.23) – (8.34) illustrate the range of acceptable sentences licensed by the individual event-frames in (8.21) in combination with their frame-semantic specifications in (8.22). Whereas English *drive* is highly polysemous with its various senses giving rise to multiple resultative senses that have to be captured in terms of individual event-frames with their own distinct frame-semantic specifications, their German equivalents exhibit identical semantic specifications (except for some idiosyncratic differences that have to do with conventionalization of certain resultative phrases) but are linked to different types of verbs. In other words, German does not allow the phonological string *fahren* ('drive, i.e., operate a vehicle') to identify the multitude of distinct event-frames. Rather, German links each event-frame to a separate phonological string that identifies the respective event-frame straightforwardly. A similar state of affairs holds for the other verbs in Appendix C (see (C.5) – (C.8)) whose lexical entries are also listed in Appendix C (see (C.9) – (C.16)).

The analyses in this section of how distinct senses of polysemous English verbs give rise to different types of English resultatives and the comparison of German counterparts of these English resultatives show that although the underlying semantic concepts (represented in this work in terms of event-frames) are identical, their realization varies in the two languages. In other words, in the English examples in (8.20) and (C.1) – (C.5) it is possible to combine many different types of resultative phrases with the same verb, whereas in German each sense is expressed by a different verb in combination with a resultative phrase (for the opposite case, in which the semantic concepts represented by a single German verb in combination with different preverbs is mirrored by separate English verbs in combination with resultative phrases, see the tables in Section 8.2, cf. (8.19) and (C.1) – (C.4)). These contrastive observations support our proposals made in the last chapter with respect to the licensing of resultatives based on individual event-frames representing different senses of a verb. That is, the ability to occur with a resultative is not a property of a specific verb *per se*, but it is determined by a given sense of a verb (represented by an event-frame) that is conventionalized in such a way that it is open for resultative modification. As such, our account of different polysemy networks associated with English and German verbs yields similar results as other research on contrastive lexical semantics (see, e.g., Esser 1998, Weigand 1998, Altenberg and Granger 2002, and Viberg 2002). For example, Fillmore and Atkins (2000) show that although there are similar types of meaning extension mechanisms associated with *crawl* and its French counterpart *ramper*, it is generally not possible to predict which mechanism will apply in a language and why. If one of the main goals of linguistics is to arrive at an adequate theory of language, this leaves linguists with the sole option of pursuing a detailed bottom-up approach to the description of verbs and their distribution as outlined in this work (see also Gross 1994).

The comparison between English and German clearly shows that although there is an overlap between English and German verbs denoting the same semantic concept (i.e., those verbs which have the same historical origin and show a large meaning overlap outside of resultative constructions, e.g. *drive* vs. *treiben*, *break* vs. *brechen*) and their ability to license resultatives, there is also an unpredictable discrepancy between historically related verbs that exhibit the same meaning outside of resultative constructions. Due to different historical developments, the respective verbs have become conventionalized with distinct senses and idiomatic phrases which need to be accounted for in the lexicon in terms of event-frames specifying the frame-semantic information denoted by the respective senses of a verb.

8.4 Other Accounts

In Chapters 2-5, proposals by various authors to compositionally derive the meaning and distribution of English resultative constructions from their component parts were critically reviewed. In this section, we compare and contrast several analyses that are in some way related to the account of German resultatives put forward in this chapter.

8.4.1 Small Clauses (Staudinger 1997)

Adopting ideas from Hoekstra's (1988) and Aarts' (1992) Small Clause analyses of English resultative constructions (cf. our discussion in Chapter 2), Staudinger (1997) proposes that in sentences such as *Claire strich das Haus rot* ('Claire painted the house red') and *Christian trank Bernd unter den Tisch* ('Christian drank Bernd under the table') there exists a semantic predication relation between the resultative phrases and the postverbal patient NPs.[9] According to Staudinger, this semantic predication relation parallels that of a subject and a predicate in full clauses and should thus be encoded syntactically in terms of a pair of sister constituents that form a Small Clause. On this view, the resultative Small Clause is thematically independent of the matrix verb (1997: 206). This assumption in turn forces the author to assume a number of detransitivization and argument reduction processes.

The assumption that the Small Clause is thematically independent of the matrix verb poses a serious problem for Staudinger's approach. That is, he has no principled way to constrain the range of postverbal constituents in German resultatives, thereby leading to overgeneration of unacceptable sentences. More specifically, by denying that matrix verbs do not semantically select for their postverbal constituents, Staudinger's analysis cannot account for the different types of collocational restrictions in resultative constructions (for a more detailed critique, see Boas (2002a) and our discussion of Small Clause analyses in Chapter 2.2). Another problem with Staudinger's account is that he does not consider the influence of contextual background information on the formation of resultatives. Since non-conventionalized resultatives such as *Seppi niesste die Serviette vom Tisch* ('Seppi sneezed the napkin off the table.') are also possible in German, Staudinger's analysis begs the question of accounting for the distribution of postverbal elements in the full range of German resultative constructions.

8.4.2 Event Structure Composition (Rapp 1997)

Rapp's (1997) analysis aims for a treatment of German resultative constructions in terms of event structure composition. She proposes that the semantic structure of resultative constructions should be mirrored at the syntactic level in terms of a complex predicate and proposes that the occurrence of resultative predicates is licensed by a process of event composition which combines the matrix verb with the resultative phrase (much like Rappaport Hovav and Levin's (1998, 2001) approach discussed in Chapter 3). Rapp distinguishes between different classes of resultative constructions, namely resultatives based on (1) intransitive non-motion verbs, (2) transitive non-motion verbs, and (3) motion verbs. Based on different types of event structure compositions, Rapp claims to be able to account for the fact that each class of verbs shows distinct behaviors in resultative constructions (for a detailed discussion, see Boas (2000b: 160-178)).

The problem with this account is that although members of the three classes exhibit different behavior based on their transitivity (see similar arguments made by Hoekstra (1988) and Carrier and Randall (1992)), mem-

[9]This section is based on Boas (2002a).

membership in such a class does not allow us to make exact predictions about what types of resultative phrases may occur with a given verb. Compare, for example, change of state verbs as in (8.35) which – according to Rapp (1997: 107) – do not participate in event composition. For sentences such as (8.35a) and (8.35b) Rapp proposes treating resultative phrases as simple modifications of the inherent semantics expressed by the matrix verb.

(8.35) a. Er heilte den Kranken ganz gesund.
he healed the sick completely healthy
'He healed the sick person so he became completely healthy.'
b. Er fütterte die Katze satt.
he fed the cat stuffed
'He fed the cat so she became stuffed.'(Rapp 1997: 108)

(8.36) a. Er heilte den Kranken tot.
he healed the sick dead
'He healed the sick and the sick became dead as a result of it.'
b. Er fütterte die Katze müde.
he fed the cat tired
'He fed the cat tired.'

The sentences in (8.36) raise the question of what it exactly means for Rapp that resultative phrases always modify an inherent resultant state of change-of-state verbs ('dem Verb inhärierenden Resultatszustand' (1997: 107)). If one were to follow this line of argumentation, it would entail that *heilen* ('to heal') in (8.36a) has an inherent resultant state that includes *tot* ('dead'). However, Rapp does not address the issue of how to account for the various meanings of words in order to determine which parts of their meanings can be subject to a resultant state interpretation in a given context. What is needed, then, is a lexical-semantic representation of verbs that lists all the properties that can (potentially) undergo a change of state and therefore lead to a resultant state. However, Rapp's treatment of change-of-state verbs in resultative constructions remains silent on what constitutes an inherent resultant meaning of a verb, and therefore cannot account for the full range of resultative constructions.

Adopting our analysis of English resultatives for the data in (8.35) and (8.36) allows us to encode specific types of on-stage and off-stage information in the respective event-frames of *heilen* ('to heal') and *füttern* ('to feed'). As demonstrated by our treatment of English resultatives in Chapters

5-7, this approach successfully accounts for the influence of idiosyncratic lexical semantic information associated with a verb's various event-frames as well as the influence of contextual information on the licensing of non-conventionalized resultative constructions.

8.4.3 Strong and Weak Reflexives (Oya 2002)

Oya (2002) argues that English and German resultative constructions based on unergative verbs differ when it comes to the distribution of reflexive pronouns. Whereas German requires the presence of a reflexive pronoun with verbs describing movement, English does not as the following sentences illustrate.

(8.37) a. (Levin and Rappaport Hovav 1999: 27)
A bantam chick kicks free from its shell.
b. Ein Küken kickt *(sich) von seiner Schale frei.
a chick kicks itself from its shell free
(Oya 2002: 962)

Another difference pointed out by Oya is that German resultatives allow a greater range of unergative verbs than their English counterparts. That is, German resultatives allow 'verbs of activities that express the subject's maintenance of a spatial configuration.' (2002: 961), whereas English resultatives do not allow for this option as the following examples demonstrate.

(8.38) a. Der Kranke lag sich wund.
the patient lay himself sore
b. Er stand sich müde.
he stood himself tired
c. Er hungerte sich schlank.
he hungered himself thin (Oya 2002: 975)

(8.39) a. *The patient lay himself sore.
b. *He stood himself tired.
c. *He hungered himself slim. (Oya 2002: 975)

Oya argues that the difference between English and German resultatives is ultimately due

> to the availability of the reflexive pronoun in constructions expressing body activities. Since German possesses a weak reflexive pronoun that is compatible with predicates expressing body activities, resultative con-

> structions of the language can describe body activities that take place within the sphere of the subject. In contrast, the reflexive pronoun in English is basically a strong form and it occurs in resultative constructions when it bears the patient role in the sense of Jackendoff (1990).
>
> (Oya 2002: 961)

The problem with this approach is that although Oya cites numerous examples from English and German, the comparisons do not always include 'equal' resultative constructions *per se*. Compare, e.g., the following sentences.

(8.40) a. She danced free of her captors.
b. Sie tanzte sich von ihren Verfolgern frei.
she danced herself of her pursuers free
(Oya 2002: 972)

Note that example (8.40a) does not include a patient argument that has to be present in resultative constructions. That is, *free of her captors* is interpreted as a locational phrase modifying the endpoint of the activity denoted by the intransitive use of *dance* as in *She danced out of the room*. Comparing (8.40a) with (8.40b) is misleading because the latter contains a patient argument whereas the former does not. Note that in cases in which a special perspective of an event is described, English does allow inclusion of a fake object as in *She danced herself free of her captors*. This means that the difference between the two languages lies in the fact that German provides a pre-assembled event-frame that requires *tanzen* ('to dance') to occur with a fake object whenever it occurs with an adjectival resultative phrase (see Kunze (1997: 83-180) for a detailed description and classification of reflexive Verbs in German).[10] The event-frame for *dance* does not encode this requirement, but allows both options (fake object as well as no object).

In contrast to (8.40a), *wash* in (8.41) is a true resultative construction that includes a postverbal argument (see Section 7.2 for licensing of fake objects) and which is based on the transitive use of the verb.

[10]Note that this requirement holds only for adjectival resultative phrases, but not for prepositional resultative phrases as in *Sie tanzte aus dem Zimmer* ('She danced out of the room.'). This means that the event-frame for *tanzen* ('to dance') includes specific information about the different types of requirements imposed on postverbal arguments depending on the choice of resultative phrases.

(8.41) a. *He washed clean.
b. He washed (himself).
c. He washed himself clean. (Oya 2002: 973)

As we have seen in Chapters 5-7, the event-frame of *wash* requires the presence of a (fake) object whenever the outcome of the activity denoted by the verb is specified by a resultative phrase. The fact that the event-frame of the removal sense of *wash* selects for a semantically coherent class of resultative phrases (expressing the final state resulting from the activity denoted by the verb, see Section 6.3.3.2.2) does not correspond to Oya's observation that in sentences such as (8.41c) 'no semantic coherence is found between the verb and resultative phrase.' (2002: 974) To the contrary, our discussion in Chapters 6 and 7 has shown that the event-frame representing the removal sense of wash imposes very specific collocational restrictions on its postverbal arguments.

There is a more serious problem with Oya's account. It is claimed that the difference between German and English resultatives observed in (8.38) and (8.39) above is due to the fact that 'these sentences describe activities carried out on one's body; that is, the events expressed are not directed at others and take place only within the sphere of the subject.' (2002: 975) Oya goes on to explain: 'the reason why the sentences (…) are not possible consists of the nature of the reflexive pronoun in English, that is, it does not occur in body-activity contexts.' (2002: 975-76) However, Oya's proposal does not make the right predictions as the following sentences demonstrate.

(8.42) a. That may have been the question in Hagar's mind as she cried herself sore. (http://www.focusctr.or.ke/Newslet/2002Apr/2002Aprpage1.htm).
b. Why, she laughed herself lame - she did, indeed; (http://www.eastoftheweb.com/short-stories/UBooks/MilPou.shtml.)
c. Worked myself tired over the weekend and loved it. (http://www.livejournal.com/users/nutties/)
d. When I was done, I had not only laughed myself sore, I had been … (http://www.wordboost.com/a/A_Working_Stiffs_Manifesto_1569472807.html.)
e. It must be because of her weight loss, so she continues to starve herself thin. (http://www.ihigh.com/cheerleading/stories/eatingdisorders.html)

The examples include verbs such as *laugh*, *cry*, *work*, and *starve*, each of which denotes an activity that typically takes place only within the sphere of the subject. Therefore the claim that it is not possible to have English resultative constructions in which a reflexive pronoun occurs in body-activity contexts is unwarranted. This means that in attributing the differences in distribution of English and German resultatives to strong and weak reflexives, Oya's proposal is too restrictive.

Another problem with this analysis is that Oya claims to be able to account for the distribution of reflexives in resultatives in terms of verb classes, such as 'body-activity contexts', 'perceptual events' (2002: 976), and 'body movement' (2002: 977). However, as I have argued in Sections 5.3.2 and 6.3.3.2, applying notions such as verb class is problematic as soon as exceptions to a general class are found. The examples in (8.56) strongly suggest that Oya's verb classification is too restrictive and is incapable of accounting for the full range of attested resultatives. This demonstrates that a bottom-up approach employing event-frames to account for the distribution of resultatives as outlined in Chapters 5-7 yields a descriptively and explanatorily more adequate account of the distribution of reflexives than that by Oya (2002).

8.4.4 Complex Predicates (Müller 2002)

Müller (2002) offers an analysis of German resultative constructions in terms of complex predicates. Working within Head-Driven Phrase Structure Grammar (Pollard and Sag 1994), Müller argues that the resultative predicate is a complement of the resultative construction which is itself modeled in terms of a complex predicate that is licensed in the lexicon by a lexical rule. Since the lexical rule 'accounts both for the resultative semantics of the resulting complex predicate and for the valence change,' it also licenses 'for every input entry another lexical item that has the potential to combine with another predicate.' (Müller 2002: 250) More specifically, Müller assumes that there is 'a lexical rule that has an intransitive verb as input and licenses a lexical item for a verb that contains the subject of the embedded predicate on its SUBCAT list.' (2002: 240) For sentences like *Sie fischten den Teich leer* ('They fished the pond empty'), Müller proposes that the theme role in the lexical entry of the intransitive verb *fischen* is 'not linked to any element in the valence representation' (2002: 242). Taking this lexical entry as an input, the lexical rule generates an output consisting of a complex predicate that subcategorizes for both the resultative predicate and the postverbal NP. The crucial point in Müller's analysis is his assumption that the 'resultative meaning of the whole construction is represented under

CONT in the output of the rule. Following Dowty (1979: 99), I assume that *cause* is an abstract logical operator that relates two events.' (2002: 241)

Müller's lexical rule approach is not restrictive enough. That is, his assumption of an 'abstract logical operator that relates two events' is incapable of ruling out impossible situations such as *Sie fischten den Teich voll* ('They fished the pond full') or *Sie fischten das Telefon leer* ('They fished the telephone empty.'). In order to deal with this issue, one could introduce constraints on postverbal constituents. Although Müller does mention the possibility of stating restrictions on the postverbal NP in terms of constraints on the value of the BACKGROUND feature (which is 'a set that contains appropriateness conditions associated with a given type of phrase' (Müller 2002: 245)), he does not go into any detail about how such restrictions could be implemented under his analysis. In other words, positing an abstract operator *cause* does not go far enough when it comes to restricting the range of possible postverbal constituents that may occur with a matrix verb.

Müller's analysis also begs the question of accounting for the collocational restrictions imposed by matrix verbs on their resultative phrases (see our discussions in Chapters 5-7). Although he acknowledges this point by noting that '[s]ince all information about the involved elements is available in the lexical rules, restrictions on possible resultative predicates can also be formulated' (2002: 245), Müller does not elaborate on how lexical rules would be able to decide on the range of resultative phrases based solely on information provided by the input to the rule. This problem becomes obvious in his syntactic classification of the resultative predicate as 'adj-or-prep' meaning adjective or preposition (cf. in (576) on p. 241, his Lexical Rule for Resultatives with Unergative Verbs). Our discussions throughout this monograph have demonstrated numerous times that it is often necessary to state the resultative phrase's syntactic category as part of a verb's event-frame in order to adequately capture the distribution of resultative constructions. Without such a detailed bottom-up approach, Müller's (2002) complex predicate analysis of resultatives based on lexical rules makes the wrong predictions and is thus not tenable.

8.5 Conclusions

This chapter has shown that English and German exhibit similar types of resultative constructions. Moreover, we have seen that verbs which show an almost identical overlap in meaning outside of resultative constructions often allow the same resultative pattern in the two languages. However, whereas some English verbs show a greater flexibility when it comes to their distribution in a broad variety of different resultative constructions denoting distinct types of semantic concepts, German verbs do not always exhibit such flexibility. I have demonstrated that in this case, a different verb has to be employed in order to express the same semantic concept in German. In this connection, I have shown that in some cases German verbs exhibit a greater flexibility than English verbs when it comes to denoting different semantic concepts. This means that a different English verb has to be employed in order to express the same type of resultative construction (in (8.19) and Appendix C (see (C.1) – (C.4))).

Based on contrastive distribution lists of English and German verbs, I have captured the respective verbs' distributional patterns in resultative constructions in terms of event-frames. More specifically, I have shown that it is possible to account for the different distribution patterns of English and German verbs in resultative constructions in terms of differently structured event-frames. These observations have led me to the conclusion that the difference in distribution in resultative constructions between English and German verbs is due to the different polysemy networks these verbs exhibit in the lexicons of the respective languages.

9

Conclusions

9.1 Summary

In this book, I have presented a constructional analysis of English resultatives. In Chapter 1, I set out to determine the licensing factors underlying the distribution of resultatives and to find an answer to the question of whether it is possible to capture the distribution of resultatives based on such licensing factors.

In Chapter 2, I first discussed several Small Clause analyses, which suggest that the two postverbal constituents – the resultative NP and the resultative phrase – form a syntactic clause for which the matrix verb subcategorizes. I showed that SC analyses are problematic when it comes to determining the full range of verbs that can occur in resultative constructions because they analyze resultatives primarily in terms of syntactic licensing mechanisms without taking into detailed consideration the semantics of the constructions' individual constituents. Such an approach to resultatives seems questionable because by postulating syntactic rules to generate resultative constructions, it is also necessary to determine the complete domain of application for these rules in order to arrive at full coverage of the empirical data. The SC analyses fail to provide a complete description of the domain of application for the types of syntactic rules necessary to capture and characterize the full range of resultative constructions and are therefore ultimately inadequate.

In the second part of Chapter 2, I reviewed different accounts of resultatives nested in Predication Theory. These analyses posit a ternary branching structure for resultative constructions in order to be able to state selection restrictions between the matrix verb and the postverbal constituents. Although the predication-type analyses offer conceptual and empirical advantages over the Small Clause analyses, I demonstrated that they too are problematic when it comes to capturing the distribution of resultative constructions because they do not offer a detailed enough analysis of the semantic and pragmatic restrictions that hold between the matrix verb and its postverbal arguments.

In Chapter 3 I looked at the role of event structure for the licensing of resultative constructions. It turned out that resultative constructions exhibit a complex event structure consisting of a causing event and a caused event that sets them apart from other types of events such as activities. Accounts of resultatives based on event structure have in common that they aim to explain the licensing of postverbal arguments primarily in terms of mechanisms that are sensitive to event structure. On this view, resultative constructions are licensed in cases in which the aspectual properties of the matrix verb are compatible with the aspectual properties of both the resultative phrase and the postverbal NP such that they fit into a complex aspectual event structure template. Although event structure plays an important role in determining whether a given verb may occur with a number of postverbal arguments, I have shown that event structure alone is not sufficient for capturing the full range of resultative constructions. By comparing and contrasting verbs that are closely related in meaning and exhibit the same type of event structure, I demonstrated that verbs with identical event structures do not all exhibit the same distribution in resultative constructions. In particular, I argued that a verb's multiple idiosyncratic senses play a much more important role in determining its syntactic behavior than event structure and that it is difficult to derive extended meanings of verbs on the basis of aspectual structures.

In Chapter 4, I investigated a Construction Grammar account of resultatives that takes the notion of independently existing meaningful constructions as central to the licensing of a verb's arguments. On this view, resultative (and caused-motion) constructions are capable of supplying a verb's semantics with additional arguments such as resultative phrases and postverbal NPs. While this approach arrives at a much more detailed analysis of resultative constructions than other analyses, it also faces certain problems regarding how the range of application of constructions may be restricted. Our discussion of the role of constructional polysemy and the constraints imposed on the fusion of constructional and verbal semantics has shown that this approach is unconvincing when it comes to capturing the semantic and syntactic range of resultative phrases. I pointed out that this problem is partly due to the fact that the lexical entries of the respective verbs do often not distinguish between the individual conventionalized senses of verbs.

Thus, when a construction supplies additional roles to a verb's semantics, it faces problems in deciding whether a given verb may occur with a specific semantic and/or syntactic resultative phrase or not. This observation led me to suggest shifting the explanatory burden from the level of abstract constructional semantics to the level of concrete verbal semantics in order to be able to account for the distribution of resultative constructions that may occur with a given verb.

In Chapters 5 through 7 I presented an alternative constructional approach towards resultatives that regards the multiple conventionalized senses associated with verbs as central to a framework that aims at capturing the full range of resultative constructions. Based on corpus data from the British National Corpus which demonstrate that particular senses of verbs subcategorize for distinct semantic and/or syntactic classes of resultative phrases and distinct semantic classes of postverbal NPs, I argued that it is extremely difficult to predict the distribution of resultatives on the basis of compositional mechanisms and abstract semantic constraints alone. Instead, resultative constructions should be grouped into two main classes, namely conventionalized resultative constructions and nonconventionalized resultative constructions. Each particular sense of a verb constitutes a mini-construction represented by an event-frame with its own semantic/pragmatic and syntactic specifications. In what follows, I summarize the main properties of conventionalized and nonconventionalized resultative constructions discussed in Chapters 5 through 7.

The members of the class of conventionalized resultatives are accounted for in terms of event-frames that represent the conventionalized semantic/pragmatic as well as syntactic information about a particular sense of a verb. Adopting the main ideas of Frame Semantics, I proposed that event-frames contain two types of interrelated information, namely linguistically immediately relevant on-stage information that needs to be overtly realized because it is conceptually the most salient type of information, and conceptual off-stage information that may be realized linguistically given the proper contextual conditions. While the former captures the relevant semantic specifications of the prototypical event participants (agents and patients), the latter contains different types of information that is conceptually less salient and does not have to be realized linguistically but may be recruited in order to point out a specific perspective of an event. Off-stage information includes information about temporal sequences of an event denoted by an event-frame, force-dynamic relations between the event participants, general world knowledge, and specific world knowledge about possible end result states of the individual event participants.

I identified four different communicative functions of resultatives that motivate different types of licensing mechanisms for resultative constructions. In two cases, the resultative phrase either serves to emphasize the change of state of the prototypical patient participant denoted by an event-frame (the sense of a verb) (e.g., *Flora shattered the vase to pieces*) or to reduce the vagueness associated with the change of state of the prototypical patient participant (e.g., *Jack painted the house white*). Using corpus data from the British National Corpus, I demonstrated that it is possible to include precise semantic and syntactic specifications about the event participants as well as the resultative phrase. This makes it possible to state the relevant collocational restrictions on the range of resultative phrases at the level of event-frames, thereby allowing predictions about the types of resultative phrases that may occur with a given sense (event-frame) of a verb. I showed that these lexical specifications are default specifications and may thus be overridden by proper contextual background information. In addition, I argued that event-frames differ with respect to whether they require overt realization of resultative phrases or whether they optionally allow them.

The third class of conventionalized resultative constructions includes cases in which the resultative is used to point out an unconventional perspective of an event in which a non-prototypical event participant undergoes a change of state (e.g., *Dave ran his feet sore*). In this case, conceptually relevant off-stage information is recruited from world knowledge and made linguistically relevant in order to point out the specific perspective taken of the result state of a non-prototypical event participant (fake object). I have shown that although all event-frames are associated with off-stage frame semantic information about the respective events, they differ with regard to whether they allow recruitment of off-stage information in order to be realized linguistically with a given verb. In a sense, then, event-frames serve as a filter through which conceptual structures are sorted out with respect to whether they may be realized linguistically by an event-frame of a given verb or not. In cases in which event-frames allow recruitment of the relevant off-stage conceptual information, fake objects and their resultative phrases may be realized linguistically. Finally, we have seen that a small set of linking rules serves to spell out the event-based frame-semantic information contained in the event-frames.

The fourth type of communicative function of resultative constructions is concerned with perspectivizing a non-prototypical event participant that lies outside of the prototypical event-scene described by the respective target event-frame (e.g., *John sneezed the napkin off the table*). I argued that in these cases a target event-frame (e.g., *sneeze*) is associated with a new syntactic frame that is capable of overtly realizing the non-prototypical event participant as well as its result state. This analogical process, however, is only possible if the target event-frame (e.g., *sneeze*) shows a certain semantic overlap in conventionalized frame semantic information with a source event-frame that is conventionally associated with the given syntactic frame (e.g., *blow*).

In order to trigger an association of the target event-frame with the form-meaning pairing of the source event-frame, it is also necessary to have context provide additional information that makes it possible to interpret the event-based frame semantic information of the target event-frame in terms of the event-based frame semantic information of the source event-frame. In particular, this means that the force-dynamic and temporal relations holding between the event participants of the source event-frame have to be similar between the event participants of the target event-frame if the association is to take place. Furthermore, I showed that although contextual background information may in principle provide the necessary information in order for such an association to take place, this is not always possible because certain event-frames lexically block any type of extension that would result in their acquiring a new syntactic frame (reflecting a new meaning) (e.g., *exhale*).

The comparison between the different levels of collocational restrictions holding between verbs and their postverbal constituents in the four classes of resultative constructions reveals another interesting property of resultatives. That is, there is a link between conventionally expected result states and collocational restrictions. The degree to which an event-frame allows off-stage information to be recruited for the resultative influences the degree of collocational restrictions the verb imposes on its postverbal elements. For example, in restricted cases such as *wipe X out,* the conventionally expected result state is already known since it is encoded by *out* in combination with *wipe*. In this case, the resultative pattern is extremely restricted and allows very little off-stage information to be recruited because there is no need for it. Towards the other end of the spectrum are event-frames encoding the prototypical usages of verbs such as *wipe* or *paint*. In order to determine the resultative phrase, the event-frame has to allow access to off-stage information. In cases in which non-prototypical event participants (fake objects) occur with this event frame, even more off-stage information is needed about what types of participants and their possible result states are involved in the prototypical event denoted by the verb. In other words, in cases in which resultative constructions are employed to express results that are not conventionally expected, more off-stage information than usual is required. In the case of nonconventionalized resultatives, the licensing of postverbal constituents relies not only on off-stage information contained in the event-frames of the source and target verbs, but also requires additional contextual background information. The important point here is that there is a direct correlation between the degree to which off-stage information is involved in determining the range of postverbal constituents in resultatives and the degree of collocational restrictions that the verb imposes on these constituents.

In Chapter 8, I argued that the similarities and differences in distribution between resultatives in English and German are due to the distinct lexical polysemy networks of English and German verbs. In particular, I showed that historically related verbs show different distributions of resultative constructions because of the variances in conventionalized usage patterns. My observations suggest that general syntactic rules and semantic principles used for deriving resultative constructions are insufficient.

Counter to other current trends, I have demonstrated that there is no need for generative syntactic rules, event structure augmentation mechanisms, or independently existing constructions adding additional roles to a verb's argument structure to account for the licensing of resultative phrases and non-subcategorized NPs. On the alternative view proposed here, the relevant information that is contributed to a verb's lexical entry by some mechanism in other frameworks is already contained in one of the various conventionalized event-frames associated with a verb. In other words, each sense of a verb constitutes its own construction. This means that the only mechanisms being applied to an event-frame are perspectivizing mechanisms that highlight certain information of an event-frame in order for it to be linguistically realized. This is possible because event-frames are associated with both on-stage and off-stage event-based frame semantic information that contains all of the conceptual knowledge necessary in order to communicate about an event denoted by the respective verb.

9.2 Outlook

The choice of Construction Grammar as a linguistic framework for analyzing resultatives has been driven primarily by the need for integrating syntactic, semantic, pragmatic, and more general conceptual aspects of language in a non-modular way. Though the analysis I have proposed in this book is developed within Construction Grammar, it should transfer fairly straightforwardly to other constraint-based theories of grammar such as Head-Driven Phrase Structure Grammar (Pollard & Sag 1994) and Lexical-Functional Grammar (Bresnan 2001). However, theories within the Chomskyan framework (Chomsky 1981, 1995) and approaches that emphasize the role of event structures (Rappaport Hovav & Levin 1998, 2001), qualia structures (Pustejovsky 1995), or Representational Modularity (Jackendoff 1997) may have to be modified in order to account for the phenomena investigated in this book. That is, by adopting a different view of what has traditionally been called 'the lexicon,' the integration of event-frame information in terms of (mini-) constructions will allow for a more specific 'input' for generative mechanisms used to derive syntactic structures in other frameworks. Such a step holds the promise for other theories to arrive at more adequate predictions about the collocational restrictions holding between a verb and its postverbal arguments.

There are four main directions for future research that might shed light on aspects of resultative constructions that I have not been able to cover in this book. The first direction should be concerned with identifying the exact conditions under which resultative patterns that are not directly licensed by event-frames interact with event-frame semantic information. These types of resultative patterns are licensed by event-frames in combination with more general abstract constructions such as the 'overdoing of an activity' construction family containing the 'V X's body part off' (e.g., *Collin laughed his butt off*), 'V X-self blue in the face' (e.g., *Joe laughed himself blue in the face*), and 'V X to death' (e.g., *Miriam laughed herself to death*) constructions, for example. These constructions clearly have a distinct idiomatic meaning and must be described and subsequently accounted for on the basis of corpus data.

The second direction for further research should be concerned with the historical development of resultative constructions. In order to arrive at a more complete understanding of the overall distribution and development of resultative constructions, it is necessary to look at diachronic data. To this end, large amounts of English and German diachronic data from historical corpora might shed some light on the question of what the pragmatic contexts were under which a given usage pattern of a verb was extended and subsequently associated with a resultative usage pattern. In this connection, one could investigate whether the contexts that gave rise to new resultative usage patterns were the same in the two languages or not. Equipped with this sort of knowledge it might then be possible to investigate the factors that lead to a usage pattern becoming conventionalized over time.

The third direction in which this work should be extended concerns the question of verb descriptivity. It is absolutely crucial to gather more empirical data on the distributional patterns of verbs in English and compare these usage patterns with those of verbs denoting similar semantic concepts in other languages. By analyzing more corpus data it will also become possible to make the semantic restrictions encoded in the event-frames in this work more precise, thereby achieving a greater degree of explanatory power. Based on a large enough database in combination with a model that is able to adequately account for the influence of contextual background information on the interpretation of verb senses, it might then be possible to arrive at a linguistic framework that is able to capture the syntactic distribution of verbs based on their idiosyncratic semantic properties. However, before such a model may be constructed we must first have a solid understanding of all of a verb's usage patterns. Without such an understanding it will be difficult, if not impossible, to construct an adequate linguistic model.

The fourth direction for future research should be concerned with psycho- and neurolinguistic evidence that may shed light on the proposals put forward in this book. The model of resultative constructions proposed here heavily relies on the idea that different senses of a verb form their own specific constructions with idiosyncratic information associated with them. While research concerned with the question of how different senses of a word are stored in memory and accessed in discourse is just beginning to emerge, its findings will be crucial in determining whether the proposals presented in this book find empirical support outside of usage-based linguistic theorizing.

Appendix A

Resultative Phrases

Exhaustive corpus search in the British National Corpus (BNC). 'Size' lists the total number of occurrences of the target phrase found in the BNC. 'No. of occur.' lists the number of resultative usages of the target phrase found in [NP V NP XP] patterns in the BNC. For the complete list of examples, please go to http://cslipublications.stanford.edu/resultatives.html.

A.1 APART

Size: 3444 intervals/matches

Verb	No. of occur.
Tear	166
Take	48
Pull	41
Prise	26
Blow	24
Rip	21
Force	16
Drive	8
Split	7
Break, push	6
Draw	4
Brace, knock, place, tease, wrench	3

Continued on next page

Table A.1 – continued.

Verb	No. of occur.
Ease, pick, spread, sweep, wedge	2
Burst, rip, bust, tear, cut, drag, glimpse, nudge, plant, press, rub, shift, slide	1

A.2 AWAKE

Size: 1379 intervals/matches

Verb	No. of occur.
Shake	24
Jerk	4
Kiss	2
Frighten, grunt, kick, nudge, rock, shock, scream, clap, spear, tease, stretch	1

A.3 BLACK

Size: 19222 intervals/matches

Verb	No. of occur.
Paint	6
Beat (black and blue)	6
Dye	5
Turn	4
Make	2
Burn, get, render, spray, stain	1

A.4 CALM

Size: 2794 intervals/matches

Verb	No. of occur.
Make	2

A.5 CLEAN

Size: 6092 intervals/matches

Verb	No. of occur.
Wipe	41
Wash	11
Sweep	10
Scrub	9
Rub, make, lick	6
Scrape	5
Rinse, suck	3
Scour, pare	2
Whip, wag, swab, polish, pick	1

A.6 CROOKED

Size: 314 intervals/matches

Verb	No. of occur.
Knock	2
Make	1

A.7 DEAD

Size: 11644 intervals/matches

Verb	No. of occur.
Shoot	408
Cut	11
Kill	9
Strike	8
Stop	6
Make, knock	3
Make the ball	2
Flatten, kick, smite	1

A.8 DEAF

Size: 2120 intervals/matches

Verb	No. of occur.
Make	3
Strike	2

A.9 DIRTY

Size: 2591 intervals/matches

Verb	No. of occur.
Get	33
Make	8

A.10 DRY

Size: 6236 intervals/matches

Verb	No. of occur.
Suck	16
Make	8
Bleed	7
Towel, wipe, rub	6
Boil, pat, drink	5
Milk, squeeze	3
Hug, run, drain	2
Blow, brush, caress, cry, dab, drip, eat, scrub, weep	1

A.11 EMPTY

Size: 5409 intervals/matches

Verb	No. of occur.
Bang, ferry, rain, ring	1

A.12 FAMOUS

Size: 6344 intervals/matches

Verb	No. of occur.
Make	37

A.13 FAT

Size: 4137 intervals/matches

Verb	No. of occur.
Make	5

A.14 FLAT

Size: 5899 intervals/matches

Verb	No. of occur.
Press	8
Knock	5
Fling, lay, stretch	2
Beat, crush, dry, grind, hammer, make, pound, plough, throw, render, roll, slam, smooth, squash, stack, suck	1

A.15 FULL

Size: 26545 intervals/matches

Verb	No. of occur.
Enjoy to the	25
Exploit to the	17
Fill	14
Pump	10
Stuff	8
Load, make, spoon, suck	1

A.16 HOARSE

Size: 236 intervals/matches

Verb	No. of occur.
Shout	6
Yell, talk, scream, make	1

A.17 ILL

Size: 4808 intervals/matches

Verb	No. of occur.
Make	65

A.18 INSANE

Size: 384 intervals/matches

Verb	No. of occur.
Drive	23
Make	1
Send	1

A.19 INTO PIECES

Size: 74 intervals/matches

Verb	No. of occur.
Cut	20
Tear	7
Break	6
Chop	6
Hack, rip, shatter, split	2
Crumble, divide, mould, slice	1

A.20 INTO SHAPE

Size: 120 intervals/matches

Verb	No. of occur.
Get	27
Knock	16
Lick	9
Hammer, mould, pull	3
Kick, work, whip	2
Bang, bash, break down, baste, press, call, rub, clip, cut, ease, edit, hack, freeze dry, back, comb, tousle, lipgloss, knock, bend, form, tweak, pat, paw, pound, press, pummel, put, roll, pitch, rush, sand, scrunch, squash, heat, twist, batter, weave, whittle, work, wrestle	1

A.21 INTO THE GROUND

Size: 262 intervals/matches

Verb	No. of occur.
Run	6
Work	5
Put	4
Beat, Push	3
Drive, grind, hammer, ram, stick	2
Batter, screw, bulldoze, dig, catapult, dig, force, gallop, hand, knock, lower, peg, play, plough, pound, press, stake, stomp, trample, walk, wedge	1

A.22 MAD

Size: 2847 intervals/matches

Verb	No. of occur.
Drive	108
Make	35
Send	5

A.23 OFF

Size: 69250 intervals/matches

Verb	No. of occur.
Beat	108
Bite	87
Blow	75
Rip	56
Brush	52
Run	36
Drive	33
Break	32
Auction, cut	31
Wipe	29
Chop, shake	27
Bounce	26
Pull, scrape	25
Push, rub	19
Wash, slip, clean	17
Burn, take	16
Drag	15
Tear, snap, scare, shave, shrug,	14
See	13

Continued on next page.

Table A.23 - continued.

Verb	No. of occur.
Steam, syphon, scrap, lift, lick, bump, drop, sweep, whip	12
Strip, prise, force, ease	10
Chuck, pick, work, scream, scoop	8
Blast, charm, dry, march, polish	7
Draw, eat, freeze, smash, snip, wrench, skim, slice, dust	6
Allow, bear, chase, chew, jerk, marry, pack, pinch, rinse, sell, shut, talk, bore, cart, delete, bang, bear, boo	5
Shoot, shove, sleep, tub, switch, swing, throw, scrub, peel, raise	4
Squeeze, steal, suck, wave, shout, shovel, sing, smooth, smoke, rush, score, scratch, send, run, divide, haul, boot, bark, bawl, dance, hurl	3
Cool, blank, act, air, eat, drain, frighten, lever, fight, move, piss, pour, pray, saw, scalp, shift, walk, wheel, yell, wear, spirit, tow	2
Shake, brush, chop, bitch, blaze, bluff, boil, carry, chat, chip, clip, collect, crack, dash, drink, drill, dump, fling, flip, frig, lead, massage, nip, nudge, place, plane, pop, propel, prune, puff, rake, roll, scald, scramble, shag, shepherd, reel, shriek, shin, slag, slide, slit, sneak, sneeze, snort, towel, tweak, twist, wheech, wrestle, yawn, soak, soap, sob, sponge, sue, swear, sweat, swing	1

A.23 Open

Size: 20457 intervals/matches

Verb	No. of occur.
Push	119
Throw	103
Tear	29
Rip	23
Prise	20
Wrench	11
Crack, thrust, fling	8
Kick, pull	7
Cut, swing	6
Flip, smash, snatch, yank	4
Bust, snap	3
Blow, jerk, slice, slide, steam	2
Burst, crash, fix, force, hold, make, punch, shake, slash, whisk	1

A.25 OVER THE BRINK

Size: 5 intervals/matches

Verb	No. of occur.
Tip	2
Push	1

A.26 OVER THE EDGE

Size: 218 intervals/matches

Verb	No. of occur.
Push	4
Drive, send, tip	3
Ease, throw, topple	2
Drop, knock, launch, put, slide, trip	1

A.27 OVER THE TOP

Size: 727 intervals/matches

Verb	No. of occur.
Put	17
Place	4
Sprinkle, blaze	3
Pour, smooth, throw	2
Bend, blast, brush, draw, drive, fire, flick, lay, lead, play, push, slide, smear, spread, stretch	1

A.28 RED

Size: 11609 intervals/matches

Verb	No. of occur.
Color	4
Dye	4
Make	4
Paint	2
Stain	1

A.29 SAFE

Size: 8069 intervals/matches

Verb	No. of occur.
make	67

A.30 SHUT

Size: 5333 intervals/matches

Verb	No. of occur.
Slam	71
Snap	23
Squeeze	22
Pull	20
Bang	15
Screw	9
Clamp, push	6
Nail	4
Swing, drag	3
Slide, zip, clench, click, close, jam	2
Bolt, slam, cram, crash, slam, haul, seal, sow, shoulder, slap, squelch, tap, wedge	1

A.31 SICK

Size: 4243 intervals/matches

Verb	No. of occur.
Make	136
Worry	8
Laugh	5

A.32 SILLY

Size: 2625 intervals/matches

Verb	No. of occur.
Scare	4
Drink	4
Fuck, laugh	2
Eat, beat, bore, drug, knock, make, shit, smoke, stuff	1

A.33 SLEEPY

Size: 401 intervals/matches

Verb	No. of occur.
Make	19

A.34 SMOOTH

Size: 3045 intervals/matches

Verb	No. of occur.
Make	12
Rub	4
Polish	1

A.35 SOBER

Size: 605 intervals/matches

Verb	No. of occur.
Make	2
Will	1

A.36 SOFT

Size: 1107 intervals/matches

Verb	No. of occur.
Knock	1

A.37 SOLID

Size: 3990 intervals/matches

Verb	No. of occur.
Make	2

A.38 SORE

Size: 852 intervals/matches

Verb	No. of occur.
Make	11
Scratch	1

A.39 STUPID

Size: 3083 intervals/matches

Verb	No. of occur.
Make	5
Drink	3
Blow, drive, fuck, laugh, scare, smack, worry	1

A.40 TENDER

Size: 1632 intervals/matches

Verb	No. of occur.
Make	3

A.41 THIN

Size: 5081 intervals/matches

Verb	No. of occur.
Make	10
Cut	6
Wear	5
Spread	4

A.42 TIRED

Size: 3989 intervals/matches

Verb	No. of occur.
Make	18

A.43 TO DEATH

Size: 1766 intervals/matches

Verb	No. of occur.
Stab	114
Beat	74
Put	44

Continued on next page.

Table A.43 - continued.

Verb	No. of occur.
Batter	39
Frighten	34
Crush	25
Scare	24
Burn	18
Torture	16
Drink, starve	15
Bludgeon, hack	12
Shoot, kick	11
Club	9
Bore, knife, choke	8
Blast, trample, work, worry	7
Love	6
Strangle	4
Dash, poison, kiss	3
Ax, bayonet, boil, bring, clap, suffocate, kick, freeze, spear, spray, stone, suck, gun, hammer, hug, knock, nag, peck, play, rape, shag, sting	2
Annoy, eat, bleed, blend, bug, bully, stab, flog, frit, cudgel, curse, dance, feed, gas, flog, jog, stab, laugh, pitchfork, pound, run, schmaltz, scortch, scratch, seduce, shock, sing, smother, squash, squeeze, stamp, strike, suffocate, sweat, whip	1

A.44 TO FAME

Size: 158 intervals/matches

Verb	No. of occur.
Shoot	1

A.45 TO INSANITY

Size: 10 intervals/matches

Verb	No. of occur.
Drive	1

A.46 TO MADNESS

Size: 15 intervals/matches

Verb	No. of occur.
Drive	5

A.47 TO PIECES

Size: 461 intervals/matches

Verb	No. of occur.
Tear	73
Take	19
Smash	15
Blow, cut, rip	13
Pull	12
Hack	10
Shake	8
Shoot	6
Blast	4
Chop, rend	2
Beat, dash, grind, knock, pick, punch, scratch, splash, spoil, wear, wrench	1

A.48 TO SLEEP

Size: 2264 intervals/matches

Verb	No. of occur.
Put	63
Cry	24
Sing	5
Rock, soothe	3
Drink, send	2
Chant, drive, eat, murmur, mutter, nurse, sob, talk, teach	1

A.49 TO SUICIDE

Size: 35 intervals/matches

Verb	No. of occur.
Drive	8

A.50 UNCONSCIOUS

Size: 1386 intervals/matches

Verb	No. of occur.
Knock	18
Beat	11
Batter, shriek	1

A.51 WET

Size: 3787 intervals/matches

Verb	No. of occur.
Make	12

Appendix B

Verbs

Exhaustive corpus search in the British National Corpus (BNC). 'Resultative Phrase' lists the total number of occurrences of the target phrase found in the BNC (length of target phrase limited to three words). 'No. of occur.' lists the number of resultative usages of the target phrase found in the BNC. For the complete list of examples, please go to http://cslipublications.stanford.edu/resultatives.html.

B.1 'Drive-Mental State'

Total Number: 329

APs: 253 (77%)
PPs: 76 (23%)

Resultative Phrase	No. of occur.
Mad / to madness	108 / 5
Crazy	70
To distraction	27
Insane	23
Wild	22
Nuts	18
Up the wall	13
To suicide	9

Continued on next page.

Table B.1 – continued.

Resultative Phrase	No. of occur.
To despair	8
To desperation	7
Batty	4
Dotty	4
Crackers	4
Into a frenzy	3
Over the edge	3
To insanity	1

B.2 SWEEP

Total uses found in resultative pattern in the BNC: 97

Verb-Part-Comb.	No. of occur.
Sweep-away	37
Sweep-up	11
Sweep-into	8
Sweep-off	9
Sweep-ADJ	15
Sweep-aside	6
Sweep-from	2
Sweep-through	2
Sweep-up	2
Sweep-out	2
Sweep-down	1
Sweep-towards	1
Sweep-over	1

B.3 WIPE

Total uses found in resultative pattern in the BNC: 318[1]

Combinations with verb	No. of occur.
Wipe-out	164
Wipe-ADJ	53
Wipe-away	44
Wipe-from	27
Wipe-off	20
Wipe-up	5
Wipe-down	2
Wipe-through	1
Wipe-creation	1
Wipe-on	1

[1]The discrepancy between the number of sentences and the total number given above is caused by the fact that in some sentences there are two resultative predicates.

Appendix C

English and German Resultatives

C.1 Preverb-verb combinations with *schiessen* ('shoot') and their English equivalents

	German verb	Sentence	English equivalent	English sentence
1	Ab-schiessen-1	Sie schossen die Kugel ab.	shoot (off), to shoot a bullet (at s.o.)	They shot the bullet off.
2	Ab-schiessen-2	Sie schossen ein Flugzeug ab.	shoot down	They shot an airplane down.
3	An-schiessen-1	Sie schoss einen Vogel an.	wound (by a shot), shoot at and wound	She shot at and wounded a bird.
4	An-schiessen-2	Er schoss seine Winchester an.	test-fire	He test-fired his Winchester.

Continued on next page.

Table C.1 – continued.

	German verb	Sentence	English equivalent	English sentence
5	Erschiessen	Sie erschossen den Dieb.	shoot (dead)	They shot the thief dead.
6	Um-schiessen	Sie schossen den Dieb um.	to shoot s.o. or s.th. down	They shot the thief down.
7	Ver-schiessen-1	Er verschoss seine letzte Kugel.	dis-charge, fire (off)	He fired his last bullet off.
8	Ver-schiessen-2	Klinsmann ver-schoss den Elf-meter.	miss	Klinsmann missed the penalty kick.
9	Zerschiessen	Die Armee zer-schoss das Dorf.	to shoot to pieces	The army shot the village to pieces.

C.2 Preverb-verb combinations with *schlagen* ('strike', 'hit') and their English equivalents

	German verb	Sentence	English equivalent	English sentence
1	Ab-schlagen-1	Sie schlug den Henkel von der Tasse ab.	knock off	She knocked the handles off the cup.
2	Ab-schlagen-2	Er schlug die Bitte ab.	refuse, reject, turn down	He turned down the request.

Continued on next page.

Table C.2 – continued.

	German verb	Sentence	English equivalent	English sentence
3	Ab-schlagen-3	Sie schlug den Ball ab.	kick off	She kicked the ball off.
4	Ab-schlagen-4	Er schlug sein Wasser ab.	to urinate	He urinated.
5	An-schlagen-1	Er schlug die Leiste an die Wand.	fasten, fix, nail s.th. to s.th.	He nailed the board to the wall.
6	An-schlagen-2	Sie schlug die Glocke an.	strike, hit	She hit the bell.
7	Durch-schlagen-1	Er schlug das Brett durch.	cut (or hew) (s.th.) in two	He cut the board in two.
8	Durch-schlagen-2	Das Projektil durchschlug die Mauer.	knock a hole in s.th., pierce, penetrate	The projectile pierced the wall.
9	Erschlagen	Sie erschlug den Dieb.	strike (s.o.) dead, kill, slay	She stroke the thief dead.
10	Verschlagen	Sie verschlugen das Haus mit Brettern.	to board up/nail up s.th.	They boarded the house up.
11	Um-schlagen-1	Er schlug die Seite um.	turn over	He turned the page over.
12	Um-schlagen-2	Sie schlug den Baum um.	fell, cut down	She cut down the tree.

Continued on next page.

Table C.2 – continued.

	German verb	Sentence	English equivalent	English sentence
13	Um-schlagen-3	Er schlug den Schal um seinen Hals.	wrap s.th. around	He wrapped the scarf around his neck.
14	Zerschlagen	Sie zerschlug die Vase in Stücke.	break, smash s.th. to pieces	She smashed the vase to pieces.

C.3 Preverb-verb combinations with *fahren* ('drive') and their English equivalents

	German verb	Sentence	English equivalent	English sentence
1	Ab-fahren-1	Er fuhr seine Reifen ab.	to wear down	He wore his tires down.
2	Ab-fahren-2	Sie fuhr ihre Fahrkarte ab.	use up	She used her ticket up.
3	Ab-fahren-3	Der LKW fuhr den Schrott ab.	cart away	The truck carted the junk away.
4	Ab-fahren-4	Der Panzer fuhr ihm den Fuss ab.	to cut off, severe	The tank cut his foot off.
5	An-fahren-1	Sie fuhren Erde an.	carry, convey	They carried earth.
6	An-fahren-2	Er fuhr den BMW an.	run into, collide	He ran into the BMW.

Continued on next page.

Table C.3 – continued.

	German verb	Sentence	English equivalent	English sentence
7	An-fahren-3	Das Auto fuhr mit einem Ruck an.	start off, drive off	The car started off with a jerk.
8	Um-'fahren-1	Auf dieser Strasse kann man den See umfahren.	drive around, circumvent	On this road you can drive around the lake.
9	'Um-fahren-2	Kim fuhr Pat um.	run over s.th./s.b.	Kim ran over Pat.
10	Zer-fahren	Er zerfuhr den Apfel.	cruse (or break, smash) (s.th.) by driving over it	He smashed the apple by driving over it.

C.4 Preverb-verb combinations with *streichen* ('paint') and their English equivalents

	German verb	Sentence	English equivalent	English sentence
1	An-streichen	Sie strich das Haus blau (an).	paint, coat	She painted the house blue.
2	Ab-streichen	Er strich den Pinsel ab.	clean out the brush	He cleaned out the brush.

Continued on next page.

Table C.4 – continued.

	German verb	Sentence	English equivalent	English sentence
3	Be-streichen	Er bestrich das Brot mit Butter.	to spread (coat, cover) s.th. with s.th., to spread s.th. on s.th.	He spread butter onto the bread. (Holistic interpretation)
4	Durch-streichen	Sie strich das Wort durch.	cross out	She crossed the word out.
5	Um-streichen	Er strich den Wagen um.	repaint in a new color	He repainted the car.
6	Zer-streichen	Sie zerstrich die Farbe.	spread until evenly distributed	Mary spread the paint until it was evenly distributed.

C.5 Resultatives based on *run* and their German equivalents

	Description of sense	Resultative	German equivalent	Resultative
1	To go by moving the legs quickly	Chris ran himself to exhaustion/his shoes threadbare/home.	1. rennen 2. sich schleppen/ quälen	1. Chris rannte {sich müde/seine Schuhe kaputt}. 2. Chris schleppte/quälte sich (rennend) nach Hause.

Continued on next page.

Table C.5 – continued.

	Description of sense	Resultative	German equivalent	Resultative
2	To cause or allow to go in a specified manner or direction	1. She ran Jack off the road. 2. The coach ran the athletes around the track.	1. abdrängen 2. rennen lassen	1. Sie drängte Franz von der Strasse ab. 2. Der Trainer liess die Athleten um den Sportplatz rennen.

C.6 Resultatives based on *wipe* and their German equivalents

	Description of sense	Resultative	German equivalent	Resultative
1	To remove by or as if by rubbing	Greg wiped the crumbs off the table.	abwischen	Henning wischte die Krümel vom Tisch (ab).
2	To completely expunge	Greg wiped the table clean.	sauberwischen	Henning wischte den Tisch sauber.
3	To create a collection of objects by wiping	Greg wiped the crumbs into a pile.	zusammenwischen	Henning wischte die Krümel zusammen, so dass sie einen Haufen bildeten.

C.7 Resultatives based on *walk* and their German equivalents

	Description of Sense	Resultative	German Equivalent	Resultative
1	To move over a surface by taking steps with the feet at a pace slower than a run	They walked their shoes threadbare. They walked themselves to exhaustion.	laufen	Sie liefen ihre Schuhe durch. Sie liefen sich kaputt.
2	To move illegally while holding the ball (basketball)	He walked himself out of the game.	im Ballbesitz mehr als zwei Schritte machen	Er machte mehr als zwei Schritte als er im Ballbesitz war. Deshalb wurde er aus dem Spiel ausgeschlossen.
3	To cause or proceed at a walk	She walked the horse out of the barn.	führen	Sie führte das Pferd aus der Scheune.
4	To escort on foot	He walked her home.	begleiten	Er begleitete sie nach Hause.
5	To move (a cumbersome or heavy object) in a manner suggestive of walking	We walked the bureau into the hall.	schleppen	Wir schleppten den Schreibtisch in den Flur.

C.8 Resultatives based on *beat* and their German equivalents

	Description of sense	Resultative	German equivalent	Resultative
1	To hit repeatedly in order to knock something off or out	They beat the olives out of the tree.	schlagen von	Sie schlugen die Oliven vom Baum.
2	To bring about frothing by mixing with air by means of repeated strong turning, whirling, or agitating	They beat the eggs creamy.	schlagen	Sie schlugen die Eier schaumig.
3	To pound into a powder, paste, or pulp	They beat the pebbles to a fine dust.	zermahlen	Sie zermahlten die Steine zu Staub.
4	To force or drive home by repeated strong admonition or injunction	They beat some sense into these people.	überzeugen	Sie überzeugten diese Leute.
5	Bring or make by hard or crushing blows	The mob beat them to death.	schlagen	Der Mob schlug sie tot.

C.9 Partial lexical entry of *run* (containing event-frames that give rise to resultatives) and its German counterparts[1]

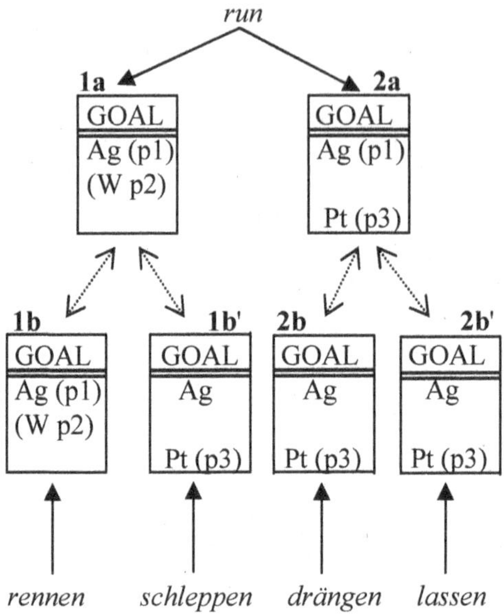

C.10 Individual frame-semantic specifications of event-frames of *run* and its German equivalents in (C.9)

	English (a)	German (b)
1	Ag: animate object moving fast and energetically p1: directional PP	p1': ( ) Pt': *sich* ('self') p3': directional PP
2	Ag: object or event capable of exerting great amounts of energy Pt: object that can be moved p3: directional PP denoting a location	p3: *ab* ('off') p3': + *rennen* ('run')[2]

[1]Compare with table (C.5) above. The single quotation mark notation on the numbers of the German event-frames indicates that German has two different types of event-frames for the respective single event-frame of English. For a more detailed discussion of polysemy networks of English and German motion verbs, see Boas (2001), for communication verbs, see Boas (2002c).

[2]The plus means in addition to the specifications of the English event-frame.

C.11 Partial lexical entry of *wipe* (containing event-frames that give rise to resultatives) and its German counterparts[3]

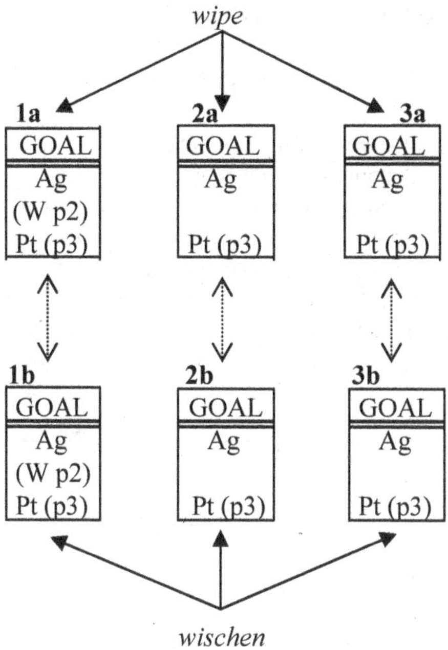

C.12 Individual frame-semantic specifications of event-frames of *wipe* in (C.11)

	English (a)	German (b)
1	Ag: entity removing unwanted substances from a surface Pt: unwanted substance p3: directional PP denoting a final endpoint that can be construed as not being on the surface	p3: *ab* ('off')

Continued on next page.

[3]Compare with table (C.6) above.

Table C.12 – continued.

	English (a)	German (b)
2	Ag: entity removing unwanted substances from a surface Pt: surface p3: AP denoting state of cleanliness	
3	Ag: entity removing unwanted substances from a surface Pt: unwanted substance p3: *into* followed by the entity that comes into existence as the result of the activity performed by the actor upon the patient.	p3: *zusammen* ('together') followed by a complementizer sentence describing the entity that comes into existence

C.13 Partial lexical entry of *walk* (containing event-frames that give rise to resultatives) and its German counterparts[4]

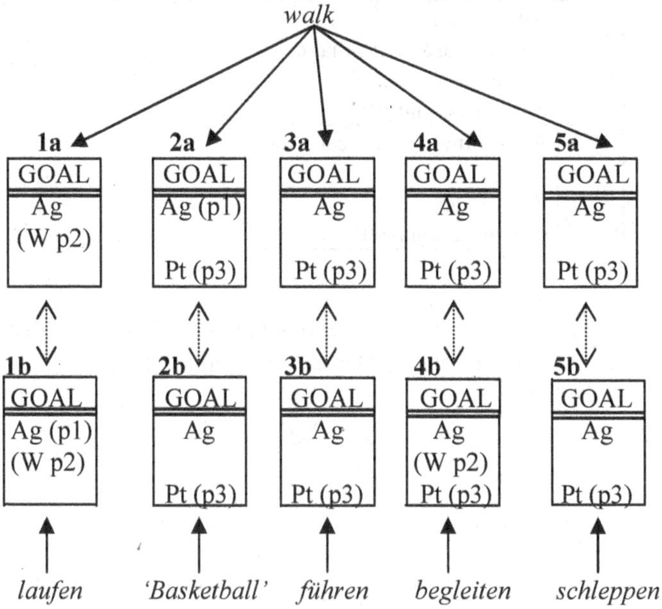

C.14 Individual frame-semantic specifications of event-frames of *walk* in (C.13)

	English (a)	German (b)
1	Ag: animate being moving p1: directional PP	
2	Ag: basketball player Pt: *-self* p3: *out* (of the game)	No direct equivalent
3	Ag: animate being, typically human Pt: animal p3: directional PP	

Continued on next page.

[4]Compare with table (C.7) above. For a detailed discussion of different polysemy networks of English and German motion verbs, see Boas (2001).

Table C.14 – continued.

	English (a)	German (b)
4	Ag: human Pt: animate being that can move p3: directional PP	
5	Ag: animate being carrying objects Pt: object p3: directional PP	

C.15 Partial lexical entry of *beat* (containing event-frames that give rise to resultatives) and its German counterparts[5]

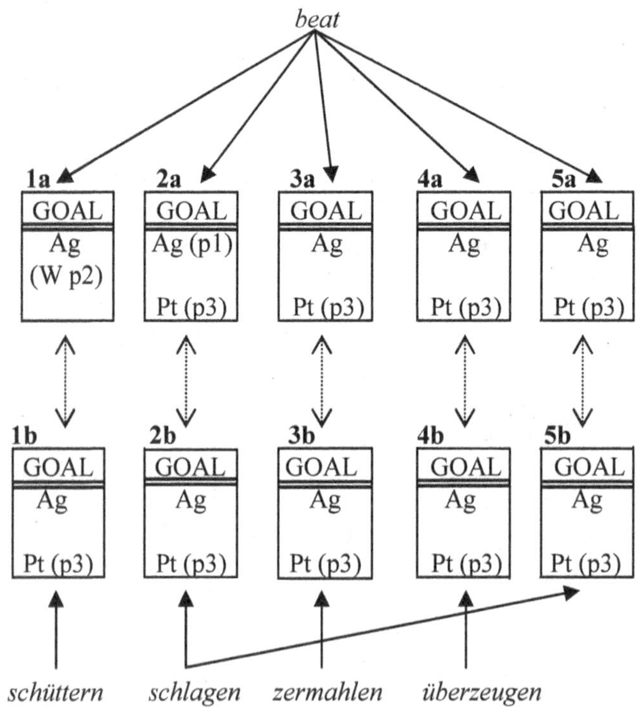

[5]Compare with table (C.8) above.

C.16 Individual frame-semantic specifications of event-frames of *beat* and their German counterparts in (C.15)

	English (a)	German (b)
1	Ag: object exerting force Pt: object that is part of a larger object p3: directional PP denoting the end point of a path that has as its starting point within the larger object	
2	Ag: object exerting stirring motions Pt: liquid mixture that can be made creamy or frothed (e.g., cream, eggs, milk) p3: AP or PP denoting the state of the Patient as a result of the stirring activity	
3	Ag: object exerting great amounts of energy Pt: object p3: PP denoting the state of the patient as a result of the agent's force exertion onto the patient	
4	Ag: human Pt: NP denoting an abstract idea (e.g., some sense, religion, etc.) p3: PP headed by *into* with an animate object with mental capabilities as its complement	Pt: animate being with mental capabilities p3: PP headed by *von* (from) with an abstract idea as its complement
5	Ag: human Pt: animate object p3: phrase denoting a state of the body after being violently hit (in case of death: *to death*)	p3: (in case of death: *zu Tode* ('to death'))

References

Aarts, B. 1989. Verb-preposition Constructions and Small Clauses in English. *Journal of Linguistics* 25: 277–90.

Aarts, B. 1992. *Small Clauses in English: The Nonverbal Types*. Berlin: Mouton de Gruyter.

Aarts, B. 1995. Secondary Predicates in English. *The Verb in Contemporary English*, eds. B. Aarts and C. F. Meyer, 75–101. Cambridge: Cambridge University Press.

Abney, S. 1987. The English Noun Phrase in its Sentential Aspect. Doctoral dissertation, MIT.

Abraham, W. 1995. *Deutsche Syntax im Sprachenvergleich*. Tübingen: Gunter Narr.

Ackerman, F., and G. Webelhuth. 1998. *A Theory of Predicates*. Stanford: CSLI Publications.

Adachi, K. 1985. Small Clauses are S's. *Metropolitan Linguistics* 5: 17–54.

Åfarli, T. A. 1991. On Sentence Structure. *Lingua* 84: 215–38.

Akmajan, A., R. Demers, A. Farmer, and R. Harnish. 1995. *Linguistics: An Introduction to Language and Communication*. Cambridge: MIT Press.

Allan, K. 1995. What Names tell about the Lexicon and the Encyclopedia. *Lexicology* 1: 280–325.

Allerton, D. J. 1982. *Valency and the English Verb*. London: Academic Press.

Altenberg, B., and S. Granger. 2002. Recent Trends in Cross-linguistic Lexical Studies. *Lexis in Contrast*, eds. B. Altenberg and S. Granger, 3–50. Amsterdam/Philadelphia: Benjamins.

Andersen, H. 1973. Abductive and Deductive Change. *Language* 49: 765–93.

Anttila, R. 1977. *Analogy*. The Hague: Mouton.

Arad, M. 1998. VP-Structure and the Syntax-Lexicon Interface. Doctoral dissertation, University College, London.

Arnold, J., T. Wasow, A. Losongco, and R. Ginstrom. 2000. Heaviness vs. Newness: The effects of structural complexity and discourse status on constituent ordering. *Language* 76: 28–55.

Apresjan, J. D. 1974. Regular polysemy. *Linguistics* 142: 5–32.

Aske, J. 1989. Motion Predicates in English and Spanish: A Closer Look. *BLS* 15: 1–14.

Atkins, B. T., J. Kegl, and B. Levin. 1988. Anatomy of a Verb Entry: From Linguistic Theory to Lexicographic Practice. *International Journal of Lexicography* 1: 84–126.

Atkins, B. T. S., J. Clear and N. Ostler. 1992. Corpus Design Criteria. *Literary and Linguistic Computing* 7: 1–16.

Bach, E. 1979. Control in Montague Grammar. *Linguistic Inquiry* 4: 515–31.

Bach, E. 1983. Semi-Compositionality. *GLOT* 6: 113–30.

Bach, E. 1986. The Algebra of Events. *Linguistics and Philosophy* 9: 5–16.

Baker, C. F. 1999. Seeing Clearly: Frame Semantic, Psycholinguistic, and Cross-Linguistic Approaches to the Semantics of the English verb See. Doctoral dissertation, University of California at Berkeley.

Baker, C. F., C. J. Fillmore and J. B. Lowe. 1998. The Berkeley FrameNet Project. *COLING-ACL '98: Proceedings of the Conference*: 86–90.

Baker, C. F., and J. Ruppenhofer. 2003. FrameNet's Frames vs. Levin's Verb Classes. *Proceedings of the 28th Annual Meeting of the BerkeleyLinguistics Society*, eds. J. Larson and M. Paster, 27-38. Berkeley: UC Linguistics Department.

Baker, M. 1997. Complex Predicates and Argument in Polysynthetic Languages. *Complex Predicates*, eds. A. Alsina, J. Bresnan and P. Sells, 247–88. Stanford: CSLI Publications.

Barlow, M., and S. Kemmer. 1994. A Schema-based Approach to Grammatical Description. *The Reality of Linguistic Rules*, eds. R. Corrigan, G. Iverson and S. Lima, 19–42. Amsterdam/Philadelphia: John Benjamins.

Baumgärtner, K. 1967. Die Struktur des Bedeutungsfeldes. *Satz und Wort im heutigen Deutsch*, ed. H. Moser, 165–97. Düsseldorf: Schwann.

Bausewein, K. 1990. *Akkusativobjekte, Akkusativsätze und Objektsprädikate im Deutschen*. Tübingen: Niemeyer.

Bennis, H. 1986. *Gaps and Dummies*. Dordrecht: Foris.

Benveniste, E. 1971. *Problems in General Linguistics*. (Translated by E. Meek). Coral Gables: University of Miami Press.

Bergenholtz, H., and U. Kaufmann. 1996. Enzyklopädische Informationen in Wörterbüchern. *Semantik, Lexikographie, und Computeranwendungen*, ed. N. Weber, 167–82. Tübingen: Niemeyer.

Berlin, B., and P. Kay. 1969. *Basic Color Terms: Their Universality and Evolution.* Berkeley: University of California Press. Re-published in 1999. Stanford: CSLI Publications.

Beukema, F., and T. Hoekstra 1984. Extractions from *With*-Constructions. *Linguistic Inquiry* 15:689–98.

Biber, D. 1993. Using Register-diversified Corpora for General Language Studies. *Computation Linguistics* 19: 219–41.

Biber, D., S. Conrad, and R. Reppen. 1998. *Corpus linguistics: Investigating Language Structure and Use.* Cambridge: Cambridge University Press.

Biber, D., S. Johansson, G. Leech, S. Conrad, and E. Finnegan. 1999. *Longman Grammar of Spoken and Written English.* London: Longman.

Binnick, R. I. 1991. *Time and the Verb. A Guide to Tense and Aspect.* Oxford: Oxford University Press.

Bierwisch, M. 1983. Semantische und konzeptuelle Repräsentation lexikalischer Einheiten. *Untersuchungen zur Semantik*, eds. R. Ruzicka and W. Motsch, 61–99. Berlin: Akademie Verlag.

Bloomfield, L. 1933. *Language.* NewYork: Holt.

Boas, H. C. 1998. *An Investigation into the Semantics of Resultative Constructions.* Manuscript, University of North Carolina, Chapel Hill.

Boas, H. C. 2000a. Resultatives at the Crossroads between the Lexicon and Syntax: Where are they formed? *Proceedings of the 1999 Western Conference on Linguistics*, eds., N. M. Antrim, G. Goddall, M. Schulte-Nafeh, and V. Samiian, vol. 11, 38-52.

Boas, H. C. 2000b. *Resultative Constructions in English and German.* Doctoral dissertation, University of North Carolina, Chapel Hill.

Boas, H. C. 2001. Frame Semantics as a Framework for describing Polysemy and Syntactic Structures of English and German Motion Verbs in Contrastive Computational Lexicography. *Proceedings of Corpus Linguistics 2001*, eds. P. Rayson, A. Wilson, T. McEnery, A. Hardie and S. Khoja, 64–73.

Boas, H. C. 2002a. Lexical or Syntactic Selection of Nonsubcategorized Nominal Arguments? The Case of German 'Sätzchen.' *New Insights in Germanic Linguistics III*, eds. I. Rauch and G. F. Carr, 9–26. New York: Peter Lang.

Boas, H. C. 2002b. On Constructional Polysemy and Verbal Polysemy in Construction Grammar. *Proceedings of the 2000 Western Conference on Linguistics*, ed. V. Samiian, vol. 12, 126-39.

Boas, H. C. 2002c. Bilingual FrameNet Dictionaries for Machine Translation. *Proceedings of the Third International Conference on Language Resources and Evaluation*, eds. M. González Rodríguez and C. Paz Suárez Araujo, vol. IV, 1364–71. Las Palmas, Spain.

Boas, H. C. 2002d. On the Role of Semantic Constraints in Resultative Constructions. *Linguistics on the Way Into the New Millennium*, ed. R. Rapp, vol. 1, 35–44. Frankfurt/M.: Peter Lang.

Boas, H. C. 2002e. When you Wanna look for Alternatives to Generative Accounts you Wanna Consider a Constructional Approach to Wanna-contraction. Talk given at: *Sixth Conference on Conceptual Structure and Discourse in Language. Rice University, Houston, TX, October 2002.*

Boas, H. C. 2002f. On the Structure of Lexical Entries and Grammatical Constructions. Invited Plenary Talk at the *Second International Conference on Construction Grammar*, University of Helsinki, Finland, September 2002.

Boberg, C. 2002. Fact or Opinion: A Sociolinguistic View of Native-Speaker Intuitions as Evidence in Linguistics. *LACUS FORUM XXVIII*: 3–13.

Bolinger, D. 1961. Syntactic Blends and Other Matters. *Language* 37: 366–81.

Bolinger, D. 1965. The Atomization of Meaning. *Language* 41: 555–73.

Bolinger, D. 1971. *The Phrasal Verb in English.* Cambridge: Harvard University Press.

Bolinger, D. 1975. Concept and Percept: Two Infinitive Constructions and their Vicissitudes. *Working Papers in Phonetics: Festschrift for Dr. Onishi's Kiju*, 65–91. Tokyo: Phonetic Society of Japan.

Booij, G. 1988. The Relation between Inheritance and Argument Linking: Deverbal Nouns in Dutch. *Morphology and Modularity: In Honour of Henk Schultink*, eds. M. Everaert, A. Evers, R. Huybregts and M. Trommelsen, 57–73. Dordrecht: Foris.

Borer, H. 1998. Passive without Theta Grids. *Morphological Interfaces*, eds. S. G. Lapointe, D. K. Brentari and P. M. Farrell, 60–99. Stanford: CSLI Publications.

Bouchard, D. 1995. *The Semantics of Syntax*. Chicago: University of Chicago Press.

Bouldin, J. M. 1990. The Syntax and Semantics of Postnominal Adjectives in English. Doctoral dissertation, University of Minnesota.

Bowerman, M. 1989. Learning a Semantic System: What Role do Cognitive Predispositions play? *The Teachability of Language*, eds. M. L. Rice and R. L. Schiefelbusch, 133–69. Baltimore: P. H. Brookes.

Bowers, J. 1983. Conditions on Logical Form. *Linguistic Analysis* 11: 27–101.

Bowers, J. 1993. The Syntax of Predication. *Linguistic Inquiry* 24: 591–656.

Bowers, J. 1997. A Binary Branching Analysis of Resultatives. *Proceedings of the 1997 Texas Linguistics Society Conference, The Syntax and Semantics of Predication. Austin: University of Texas at Austin (Linguistics Department)*, eds. R. C. Blight and M. J. Moosally, 43–58.

Bresnan, J. 1995. Linear Order, Syntactic Rank, and Empty Categories: On Weak Crossover. *Formal Issues in Lexical-functional Grammar*, eds. M. Dalrymple, R. M. Kaplan, J. T. Maxwell III and A. Zaenen, 241–74. Stanford: CSLI Publications.

Bresnan, J. 2001. *Lexical Functional Syntax*. Oxford: Blackwell Publishers.

Bresnan, J., and A. Zaenen. 1990. Deep Unaccusativity in LFG. *Grammatical Relations: A Cross-Theoretical Perspective*, eds. K. Dzwirek, et al., 45–57. Stanford: CSLI Publications.

Brinton, L. J. 1988. *The Development of English Aspectual Systems*. Cambridge: Cambridge University Press.

Brisson, C. 1994. The Licensing of Unexpressed Objects in English Verbs. *Papers from the 30th Regional Meeting of the Chicago Linguistic Society 1: The Main Session*, 90–102. University of Chicago: Chicago Linguistic Society.

Brugmann, C. 1988. *The Story of Over: Polysemy, Semantics and the Structure of the Lexicon*. New York: Garland.

Brugmann, K. 1906. *Grundriss der vergleichenden Grammatik der indogermanischen Sprachen.* 2nd ed., vol. 2, part 1. Strassburg: Trubner.

Burgschmidt, E., and D. Götz 1974. *Kontrastive Linguistik Deutsch/Englisch, Theorie und Anwendung*. München: Hueber.

Burzio, L. 1986. *Italian Syntax*. Dordrecht: Reidel.

Bybee, J. 1985. *Morphology: A Study of the Relation between Meaning and Form*. Amsterdam: Benjamins.

Bybee, J. 1998. The Emergent Lexicon. *Papers from the 34th Regional Meeting of the Chicago Linguistic Society: The Panels*, 421–435. University of Chicago: Chicago Linguistic Society.

Bybee, J., and D. Slobin 1982. Rules and Schemas in the Development and Use of the English Past Tense. *Language* 58: 265–89.

Cardinaletti, A., and M. T. Guasti. 1991. Epistemic Small Clauses and Null Subject. *ESCOL* 8: 23–33.

Cardinaletti, A., and M. T. Guasti. 1993. Negation in Small Clauses. *Probus* 5: 39–61.

Cardinaletti, A., and M. T. Guasti 1995. Small Clauses: Some Controversies and Issues of Acquisition. *Syntax and Semantics*, vol. 28: *Small Clauses*, eds. A. Cardinaletti and M. T. Guasti, 1–26. San Diego: Academic Press.

Carlson, G. 1977. A Unified Analysis of the English Bare Plural. *Linguistics and Philosophy* 1: 413–57.

Carrier, J., and J. Randall. 1988. From Conceptual Structure to Syntax: Projecting from Resultatives. Unpublished Manuscript, Harvard University and Northeastern University, Cambridge and Boston.

Carrier, J., and J. Randall. 1992. The Argument Structure and Syntactic Structure of Resultatives. *Linguistic Inquiry* 23: 173–234.

Carrier, J., and J. Randall. 1993. Lexical Mapping. *Knowledge and Language*, vol. 2, *Lexical and Conceptual Structure*, eds. E. J. Reuland and W. Abraham, 119–42. Dordrecht: Kluwer Academic Publishers.

Carrier-Duncan, J. 1985. Linking of Thematic Roles in Derivational Word Formation. *Linguistic Inquiry* 16: 1–34.

Carter, R. 1988. Compositionality and Polysemy. *On Linking: Papers by Richard Carter*, eds. B. Levin and C. Tenny, 167–204. *MIT Lexicon Project Working Paper no. 25*. Cambridge: Department of Linguistics and Philosophy, MIT.

Chafe, W. 1965. Review of Grammar Discovery Procedures, by R. E. Longacre. *Language* 41: 640–7.

Chafe, W. 1970. *Meaning and the Structure of Language*. Chicago: University of Chicago Press.

Chomsky, N. 1955. The Logical Structure of Linguistic Theory. Manuscript, Harvard University. Published, with an introduction by the author, Plenum Press, NewYork and London, 1973.

Chomsky, N. 1957. *Syntactic Structures*. The Hague: Mouton.

Chomsky, N. 1959. Review of Skinner, B.F. 'Verbal Behavior'. *Language* 35: 26–58.

Chomsky, N. 1965. *Aspects of the Theory of Syntax*. Cambridge: MIT Press.

Chomsky, N. 1977. *Essays on Form and Interpretation*. Amsterdam: Elsevier.

Chomsky, N. 1980. *Rules and Representations*. New York: Columbia University Press.

Chomsky, N. 1981. *Lectures on Government and Binding*. Dordrecht: Foris.

Chomsky, N. 1986. *Barriers*. Cambridge: MIT Press.

Chomsky, N. 1993. A Minimalist Program for Linguistic Theory. *The View from Building 20*, eds. K. Hale and S. J. Keyser, 1–52. Cambridge: MIT Press.

Chomsky, N. 1995. *The Minimalist Program*. Cambridge: MIT Press.

Chomsky, N., and H. Lasnik. 1991. Principles and Parameters Theory. *Syntax: Ein internationales Handbuch zeitgenössischer Forschung*, eds. J. Jacobs, A. v. Stechow, W. Sternefeld and T. Vennemann, 506–69. Berlin: Mouton de Gruyter.

Christ, O. 1994. A Modular and Flexible Architecture for an Integrated Corpus Query System. *Proceedings of COMPLEX 94*: 23–32.

Christ, O., and B. M. Schulze. 1995. Ein flexibles und modulares Anfragesystem für Textcorpora. *Tagungsbericht des Arbeitstreffens Lexikon und Text Tübingen*.

Chung, S., and J. McCloskey. 1987. Government, Barriers, and Small Clauses in Modern Irish. *Linguistic Inquiry* 18: 172–237.

Clark, E. 1978. Discovering what Words can do. *Papers from the Parasession on the Lexicon*, eds. D. Frakas, W. M. Jacobsen and Karol W. Todrys, 34–57. Chicago: Chicago Linguistic Society.

Clark, E. 1988. On the Logic of Contrast. *Journal of Child Language* 15: 317–35.

Clark, E. 1992. Conventionality and Contrast: Pragmatic Principles with Lexical Consequences. *Frames, Fields and Contrasts: New Essays in Semantic and Lexical Organization*, eds. A. Lehrer and E. Kittay, 171–88. Hillsdale: Erlbaum.

Clark, E. 1993. *The Lexicon in Acquisition*. Cambridge: Cambridge University Press.

Clark, E., and H. Clark. 1979. When Nouns Surface as Verbs. *Language* 55: 767–811.

Clark, H. 1996. *Using Language*. Cambridge: Cambridge University Press.

Close, R. 1975. *A Reference Grammar for Students of English*. London: Longman.

Collins, C., and H. Thràinsson. 1993. Object Shift in Double Object Constructions and the Theory of Case. *Papers on Case & Agreement II*, ed. C. Phillips. *MIT Working Papers in Linguistics* 19: 131–174.

Comrie, B. 1976. *Aspect.* Cambridge: Cambridge University Press.

Contreras, H. 1987. Small Clauses in Spanish and English. *Natural Language and Linguistic Theory* 5: 125–43.

Contreras, H. 1995. Small Clauses and Complex Predicates. *Syntax and Semantics*, vol. 28: *Small Clauses*, eds. A. Cardinaletti and M. T. Guasti, 135–52. San Diego: Academic Press.

Cowart, W. 1997. *Experimental Syntax: Applying Objective Methods to Sentence Judgments*. Thousand Oaks: Sage Publications.

Cowie, A. 1988. Stable and Creative Aspects of Vocabulary Use. *Vocabulary and Language Teaching*, eds. R. Carter and M. J. McCarthy, 126–37. London: Longman.

Cowie, A. 1994. Phraseology. *The Encyclopedia of Language and Linguistics*, eds. R. E. Asher and J. Simpson, 3168–71. Oxford: Pergamon Press.

Cowie, A. 1998. *Phraseology*. Oxford: Oxford University Press.

Cowie, A., and R. Mackin. 1993. *Oxford Dictionary of Phrasal Verbs. Oxford Dictionary Of Current Idiomatic English*, vol. 1. London: Oxford University Press.

Croft, W. 1991. *Syntactic Categories and Grammatical Relations: The Cognitive Organization of Information*. Chicago: University of Chicago Press.

Croft, W. 1998. Event Structure in Argument Linking. *The Projection of Arguments*, eds. M. Butt and W. Geuder, 21–64. Stanford: CSLI Publications.

Croft, W. 2000. *Explaining Language Change. An Evolutionary Approach*. Harlow: Pearson.

Croft, W. 2001. *Radical Construction Grammar*. Oxford: Oxford University Press.

Cruse, A. 1986. *Lexical Semantics*. Cambridge: Cambridge University Press.

Cruse, A. 2000. Aspects of the Micro-structure of Word Meanings. *Polysemy*, eds. C. Laecock and Y. Ravin, 30–51. Oxford: Oxford University Press.

Culicover, P. W., and M. S. Rochement. 1990. Extraposition and the Complement Principle. *Linguistic Inquiry* 21: 23–47.

Culicover, P. W., and W. Wilkins. 1984. *Locality in Linguistic Theory*. New York: Academic Press.

Curme, G. 1931. *Syntax*. Boston: Heath.

Czepluch, H. 1982. Case Theory and the Dative Construction. *The Linguistic Review* 2: 1–38.

Davidson, D. 1967. The Logical Form of Action Sentences. *The Logic of Decision and Action*, ed. N. Rescher, 81–120. Pittsburgh: University of Pittsburgh Press.

Davis, A. 2001. *Linking by Types in the Hierarchical Lexicon*. Stanford: CSLI Publications.

Deane, P. 1988. Polysemy and Cognition. *Lingua* 75: 325–361.

Deane, P. 1992. *Grammar in Mind and Brain: Explorations in Cognitive Syntax.* Berlin: Mouton de Gruyter.

Declerck, R. 1979. Aspect and the Bounded/Unbounded (Telic/Atelic) Distinction. *Linguistics* 17: 761–94.

Demonte, V. 1987. C-command, Preposition, and Predication. *Linguistic Inquiry* 18: 147–57.

Demonte, V. 1989. Remarks on Secondary Predicates: C-command, Extraction, and Reanalysis. *The Linguistic Review* 6: –39.

Deutschbein, M. 1939. *Grammatik der englischen Sprache auf wissenschaftlicher Grundlage*. Heidelberg: Quelle & Meyer.

Diersch, H. 1972. *Verben der Fortbewegung in der deutschen Sprache der Gegenwart. Eine Untersuchung zu syntagmatischen und paradigmatischen Beziehungen des Wortinhalts*. Berlin: Akademie Verlag.

Dikken, M. den. 1995. *Particles: On the Syntax of Verb-Particle, Triadic, and Causative Constructions*. Oxford: Oxford University Press.

Dikken, M. den, and E. Hoekstra. 1994. No Cause for a Small Clause? (Non-) arguments for the Structure of Resultatives. *Groninger Arbeiten zur Germanistischen Linguistik (GAGL)* 37: 89–105.

DiSciullo, A. M., and E. Williams. 1987. *On the Definition of Word.* Cambridge: MIT Press.

Dixon, R. 1982. *Where have all the Adjectives Gone? And other Essays in Semantics and Syntax*. Berlin: Mouton.

Dobrovol'skij, D. 1997. *Kognitive Aspekte der Idiom-Semantik.* Tübingen: Gunter Narr.

Dowty, D. 1976. Montague Grammar and the Lexical Decomposition of Causative Verbs. *Montague Grammar*, ed. B. Partee, 201–45. New York: Academic Press.

Dowty, D. 1978. Governed Transformations as Lexical Rules in a Montague Grammar. *Linguistic Inquiry* 9: 393–426.

Dowty, D. 1979. *Word Meaning and Montague Grammar*. Dordrecht: Reidel.

Dowty, D. 1991. Thematic Proto-roles and Argument Selection. *Language* 67: 547–619.

Eco, U. 1984. *Semiotics and Philosophy of Language*. Bloomington: Indiana University Press.

Eisenberg, P. 1989. *Grundriss der deutschen Grammatik.* Stuttgart: Metzler.

Emonds, J. 1976. *A Transformational Approach to English Syntax*. New York: Academic Press.

Emonds, J. 1985. *A Unified Theory of Syntactic Categories.* Dordrecht: Foris.

Endo, Y. 1990. On Small Clauses and Canonical Structure Realization. *English Linguistics* 7: 32–38.

Endo, Y. 1991. The Syntax and Semantics of Small Clauses. *Topics in Small Clauses (Proceedings of Tokyo Small Clause Festival),* eds. H. Nakajima and S. Tonoike, 59–74. Tokyo: Kurosio Publishers.

Engelberg, S. 1998. 'e' – Verben, Ereignisse und das Lexikon. Doctoral dissertation, University of Düsseldorf.

Erman, B., and B. Warren. 2000. The Idiom Principle and the Open-Choice Principle. *Text* 20: 29–62.

Erteschik-Shir, N., and T. R. Rapoport 1997. A Theory of Verbal Projection. *Interfaces in Linguistic Theory*, eds. G. Matos, et al., 129–48. Lisbon: APL.

Esser, J. 1998. Lexical Items and Medium-Transferability in English and German. *Contrastive Lexical Semantics*, ed. E. Weigand, 173–86. Amsterdam/Philadelphia: Benjamins.

Evens, M. 1988. *Relational Models of the Lexicon: Representing Models in Semantic Networks*. Cambridge: Cambridge University Press.

Fabb, N. 1984. Syntactic Affixation. Doctoral dissertation, MIT.

Faber, B., and R. Usón. 1999. *Constructing a Lexicon of English Verbs*. Berlin: Mouton de Gruyter.

Farmer, A. 1984. *Modularity in Syntax*. Cambridge: MIT Press.

Fauconnier, G. 1985. *Mental Spaces: Aspects of Meaning Constructions in Natural Language*. Cambridge: MIT Press/Bradford.

Fauconnier, G. 1994. *Mental Spaces*. Cambridge: Cambridge University Press.

Fauconnier, G., and M. Turner. 1996. Blending as a Central Process of Grammar. *Conceptual Structure, Discourse, and Language*, ed. A. Goldberg, 113–30. Stanford: CSLI Publications.

Filip, H. 1996. Psychological Predicates and the Syntax-Semantics Interface. *Conceptual Structure, Discourse, and Language*, ed. A. Goldberg, 131–48. Stanford: CSLI Publications.

Fillmore, C. J. 1968. The Case for Case. *Universals in Linguistic Theory*, eds. E. Bach and R. Harms, 1–88. New York: Holt, Rinehart, and Winston.

Fillmore, C. J. 1975. An Alternative to Checklist Theories of Meaning. *Proceeedings of the First Annual Meeting, Berkeley Linguistics Society*: 123–31.

Fillmore, C. J. 1976. Frame Semantics and the Nature of Language. *Origins and Evolution of Language and Speech*, eds. S. R. Harnad, et al., 20-32. New York: New York Academy of Sciences.

Fillmore, C. J. 1978. On the Organization of Semantic Information in the Lexicon. *Papers from the Parasession on the Lexicon*, eds. D. Frakas, et al., 148-73. Chicago: Chicago Linguistic Society.

Fillmore, C. J. 1982. Frame Semantics. *Linguistics in the Morning Calm*, ed. Linguistic Society of Korea, 111–38. Seoul: Hanshin.

Fillmore, C. J. 1985. Frames and the Semantics of Understanding. *Quadernie di Semantica* 6: 222–254.

Fillmore, C. J. 1988. The Mechanisms of Construction Grammar. *Proceedings of the Fourteenth Annual Meeting of the Berkeley Linguistic Society*, eds. S. Axmaker, A. Jassier, and H. Singmaster, 35–55.

Fillmore, C. J. 1989. Grammatical Construction Theory and the Familiar Dichotomies. *Language Processing in Social Context*, eds. R. Dietrich and C. F. Graumann, 17–38. Amsterdam: Elsevier.

Fillmore, C. J., and B. T. Atkins. 1992. Toward a Frame-based Lexicon: The Semantics of RISK and its Neighbors. *Frames, Fields and Contrasts: New Essays in Semantic and Lexical Organization*, eds. A. Lehrer and E. Kittay, 75–102. Hillsdale: Erlbaum.

Fillmore, C. J., and B. T. Atkins. 2000. Describing Polysemy: The Case of 'Crawl'. *Polysemy*, eds. Y. Ravin and C. Laecock, 91–110. Oxford: Oxford University Press.

Fillmore, C. J., and P. Kay. 1993. *Construction Grammar*. Manuscript. University of California at Berkeley.

Fillmore, C. J., P. Kay, and M. C. O'Connor. 1988. Regularity and Idiomaticity in Grammatical Constructions: The Case of 'let alone'. *Language* 64: 501–38.

Firth, J. R. 1957. A Synopsis of Linguistic Theory. *Studies in Linguistic Analysis*, 1–32. London: Philological Society.

Fischer, K. 1997. *German-English Verb Valency. A Contrastive Analysis*. Tübingen: Narr.

Flickinger, D. 1987. Lexical Rules in the Hierarchical Lexicon. Doctoral dissertation, Stanford University.

Fodor, J. A. 1970. Three Reasons for not Deriving 'kill' from 'cause to die'. *Linguistic Inquiry* 1: 429–38.

Foley, W., and R. V. Valin. 1984. *Functional Syntax and Universal Grammar*. Cambridge: Cambridge University Press.

Fontenelle, T. 1998. Discovering Significant Lexical Functions in Dictionary Entries. *Phraseology*, ed. A. P. Cowie, 189–208. Oxford: Oxford University Press.

Fraser, B. 1976. *The Verb-Particle Combination in English*. New York: Academic Press.

Freidin, R. 1992. *Foundations of Generative Syntax*. Cambridge: MIT Press.

Frisson, S., and M. J. Pickering. 2001. Obtaining a Figurative Interpretation of a Word: Support for Underspecification. *Metaphor and Symbol* 16: 149–71.

Fukui, N. 1986. A Theory of Category Projection and its Applications. Doctoral dissertation, MIT.

Fukui, N., and M. Speas. 1986. Specifiers and Projection. *Papers in Theoretical Linguistics, MIT Working Papers in Linguistics*, vol. 8, eds. N. Fukui, T. R. Rapoport and E. Sagey, 128–72.

Gawron, J. M. 1985. A Parsimonious Semantics for Prepositions and CAUSE. *Papers from the Parasession on Causatives and Agentivity*, 32–47. Chicago Linguistics Society.

Gawron, J. M. 1986. Situations and Prepositions. *Linguistics and Philiosophy* 9: 427–76.

Gazdar, G., E. Klein, G. K. Pullum, and I. Sag. 1985. *Generalized Phrase Structure Grammar*. Cambridge: Harvard University Press.

Geeraerts, D. 1993. Vagueness's Puzzles, Polysemy's Vagaries. *Cognitive Linguistics* 4: 223–72.

Geeraerts, D. 1994. Polysemy. *The Encyclopedia of Language and Linguistics*, eds. R. E. Asher and J. Simpson, 2337–8. Oxford: Pergamon Press.

Gentner, D. 1989. The Mechanisms of Analogical Learning. *Similarity and Analogical Reasoning*, eds. S. Vosniadu and A. Ortony, 199–241. Cambridge: Cambridge University Press.

Gibbs, R. 1984. Literal Meaning and Psychological Theory. *Cognitive Science* 8: 275–304.

Gibbs, R. 1986. Skating on thin Ice: Literal Meaning and Understanding Idioms in Conversation. *Discourse Processes* 9: 17–30.

Gibbs, R. W., and T. Matlock. 1997. Psycholinguistic Perspectives on Polysemy. *Polysemy in Cognitive Linguistics*, eds. H. Cuyckens and B. Zawada, 213–39. Amsterdam/Philadelphia: Benjamins.

Gipper, H. 1973. Der Inhalt des Wortes und die Gliederung des Wortes und die Gliederung des Wortschatzes. *Duden-Grammatik*, 415–73.

Goddard, C. 1998. *Semantic Analysis*. Oxford: Oxford University Press.

Goddard, C. 2000. Polysemy: A Problem of Definition. *Polysemy*, eds. Y. Ravin and C. Laecock, 129–51. Oxford: Oxford University Press.

Goldberg, A. E. 1995. *Constructions: a Construction Grammar Approach to Argument Structure*. Chicago: University of Chicago Press.

Goldberg, A. E. 1997a. The Relationships between Verbs and Constructions. *Lexical and Syntactical Constructions and the Construction of Meaning*, eds. M. Vespoor, K. D. Lee and E. Sweetser, 383–97. Amsterdam/Philadelphia: Benjamin's.

Goldberg, A. E. 1997b. Construction Grammar. *Concise Encyclopedia of Grammatical Categories*, eds. K. Brown and J. Miller. Amsterdam: Elsevier.

Goldberg, A. E. 2001. Patient Arguments of Causative Verbs can be omitted: The Role of Information Structure in Argument Distribution. *Language Sciences* 34: 503–24.

Green, G. 1972. Some Observations on the Syntax and Semantics of Instrumental Verbs. *CLS* 8: 83–97.

Green, G. 1989. *Pragmatics and Natural Language Understanding*. Hillsdale: Lawrence Erlbaum.

Grice, H. P. 1975. Logic and Conversation. *Syntax and Semantics*, vol. 3, *Speech Acts*, eds. P. Cole and J. Morgan, 41–58. New York: Academic Press.

Grimshaw, J. 1990. *Argument Structure*. Cambridge: MIT Press.

Grimshaw, J., and S. Vikner 1993. Obligatory Adjuncts and the Structure of Events. *Knowledge and Language*, vol. 2, *Lexical and Conceptual Structure*, eds. E. J. Reuland and W. Abraham, 143–56. Dordrecht: Kluwer Academic Publishers.

Gross, M. 1994. Constructing Lexicon Grammars. *Computational Approaches to the Lexicon*, eds. B. T. S. Atkins and A. Zampolli, 213–58. Oxford: Oxford University Press.

Gruber, J. S. 1965. Studies in Lexical Relations. Doctoral dissertation, MIT.

Gruber, J. S. 1976. *Lexical Structures in Syntax and Semantics*. Amsterdam: North-Holland.

Gueman, S. A. 1990. Secondary Predication in English and Spanish. Doctoral dissertation, University of California at Berkeley.

Guéron, J. 1990. Particles, Prepositions, and Verbs. *Grammar in Progress*, eds. J. Mascaró and M. Nespor, 153–66. Dordrecht: Foris.

Guéron, J., and T. Hoekstra 1995. The Temporal Interpretation of Predication. *Syntax and Semantics*, vol. 28, *Small Clauses*, eds. A. Cardinaletti and M. T. Guasti, 77–103. San Diego: Academic Press.

Haegeman, L. 1991. *Introduction to Government and Binding Theory*. Oxford: Basil Blackwell.

Haegeman, L. 1994. *Introduction to Government and Binding Theory*, 2nd ed. Oxford: Basil Blackwell.

Hale, K., and S. J. Keyser. 1986. Some Transitivity Alternations in English. *Lexicon Project Working Papers* #7. Cambridge: MIT Center for Cognitive Science.

Hale, K., and S. J. Keyser. 1987. A View from the Middle. *Lexicon Project Working Papers #10.* Cambridge: MIT Center for Cognitive Science.

Hale, K., and S. J. Keyser. 1991. On the Syntax of Argument Structure. *The Lexicon Project Monograph Series*. Cambridge: MIT Center for Cognitive Science.

Hale, K., and S. J. Keyser. 1992. The Syntactic Character of Thematic Structure. *Thematic Structure: Its Role in Grammar*, ed. I. M. Roca, 106–41. Berlin: Foris.

Halliday, M. A. K. 1967. Notes on Transitivity and Theme in English (Part 1). *Journal of Linguistics* 3: 37–81.

Harris, C. 1996. Recognizing Common Word Combinations: Towards a Lexicon of Variable-sized units. Manuscript. Boston University.

Harris, C. 1997. Psycholinguistic Studies of Entrenchment. Manuscript. Boston University.

Harris, C. 1998. Psycholinguistic Studies of Entrenchment. *Conceptual Structure, Discourse and Language*, ed. J.-P. Koenig, 55–70. Stanford: CSLI Publications.

Hasegawa, K. 1986. Chomsky riron no seika to tenbou (Achievements and perspectives of Chomsky's theory). *Chomsky shojiten*, ed. I. Kunihikio, 283–306. Tokyo: Taishukan.

Hasegawa, K. 1991. Secondary Predicates, VP-internal Subjects and Mutual C-command. *English Linguistics* 8: 1–15.

Haspelmath, M. 1993. More on the Typology of Inchoative/Causative Verb Alternations. *Causatives and Transitivity*, eds. B. Comrie and M. Polinksy, 87–120. Amsterdam: John Benjamins.

Hausmann, F. J. 1989. Le Dictionnaire des Collocations. *Wörterbücher /Dictionaries/Dictionnaires*, eds. F. J. Hausmann, O. Reichmann, H. E. Wiegand, and L. Zgusta, 1010–19. Berlin: Walter de Gruyter.

Hawkins, J. 1986. *A Comparative Typology of English and German. Unifying the Contrasts*. London: Croom Helm.

Hayashi, R. 1987. Another Argument that Small Clauses are S's. *Linguistic Research* 5: 29–51.

Hayashi, R. 1991. On the Constituency of Small Clauses. *Topics in Small Clauses (Proceedings of Tokyo Small Clause Festival)*, eds. H. Nakajima and S. Tonoike, 11–25. Tokyo: Kurosio Publishers.

Heid, U., and J. McNaught. 1991. *EUROTRA-7 Study: Feasibility and Project Definition Study on the Reusability of Lexical and Terminological Resources in Computerized Applications, Final Report.* Luxembourg: Commission of the European Communities.

Heim, I. 1982. The Semantics of Definite and Indefinite Noun Phrases. Doctoral dissertation, University of Massachusetts, Amherst.

Helbig, G. and W. Schenkel. 1983. *Wörterbuch zur Distribution und Valenz deutscher Verben*. Leipzig: VEB Bibliographisches Institut.

Hendrick, R. 1991. The Morphosyntax of Aspect. *Lingua* 85: 171–210.

Hendrick, R. 1995. Morphosyntax. *Government and Binding Theory and the Minimalist Program*, ed. G. Webelhuth, 297–348. Oxford: Blackwell.

Herslund, M. 1984. Particles, Prefixes, and Preposition Stranding. *Topics in Danish Syntax,* eds. F. Sørensen and L. Heltroft, 34–41. Copenhagen: Akademisk Forlag.

Higgenbotham, J. 1983. The Logic of Perceptual Reports. *Journal of Philosophy* 80: 100–27.

Higgenbotham, J. 1985. On Semantics. *Linguistic Inquiry* 16: 547–93.

Higgenbotham, J. 1987. Indefiniteness and Predication. *The Representation of (In)definiteness*, eds. E. Reuland and A. ten Meulen, 43–70. Cambridge: MIT Press.

Higgenbotham, J. 1989. Elucidation of Meaning. *Linguistics and Philosophy* 12: 465–518.

Hock, H. H. 1986. *Historical Linguistics*. Berlin: Mouton de Gruyter.

Hockett, C. F. 1964. The Proto Central Algonguin Kinship System. *Explorations in Cultural Anthropology*, ed. W. Goodenough, 329–58. New York: McGraw-Hill.

Hoeksema, J. 1991. Complex Predicates and Liberation in Dutch and English. *Linguistics and Philosophy* 14: 661–710.

Hoekstra, T. 1984. *Transitivity. Grammatical Relations in Government-Binding Theory*. Dordrecht: Foris.

Hoekstra, T. 1986. Deverbalization and Inheritance. *Linguistics* 24: 549–85.

Hoekstra, T. 1988. Small Clause Result. *Lingua* 74: 101–39.

Hoekstra, T. 1992a. Small Clause Theory. *Belgian Journal of Linguistics* 7: 125–51.

Hoekstra, T. 1992b. Subjects Inside Out. *Revue Quebecoise de Linguistique* 22: 45–75.

Hoekstra, T. 1992c. Aspect and Theta Theory. *Thematic Structure: Its Role in Grammar*, ed. I. M. Roca, 145–76. Berlin: Mouton de Gruyter.

Hoekstra, T., and R. Mulder. 1990. Unergatives as Copular Verbs: Locational and Existential Predication. *The Linguistic Review* 7: 1–79.

Hornby, A. 1954. *A Guide to Patterns and Usage in English.* Oxford: Oxford University Press.

Hornstein, N., and D. Lightfoot. 1987. Predication and PRO. *Language* 63: 23–52.

Hudson, R. 1990. *English Word Grammar*. Oxford: Basil Blackwell.

Hundsnurscher, F. 1970. *Neuere Methoden der Semantik. Eine Einführung anhand deutscher Beispiele*. Tübingen: Niemeyer.

Hunston, S., and G. Francis. 2000. *Pattern Grammar. A Corpus-driven Approach to the Lexical Grammar of English.* Amsterdam/Philadelphia: Benjamins.

Iabarretxte-Antuñano, I. 1999. Polysemy and Metaphor in Perception Verbs: A Cross-linguistic Study. Doctoral dissertation, University of Edinburgh.

Inchaurralde, C. 1997. Space, Reference and Emotional Involvement. *The Language of Emotions*, eds. S. Niemeier and R. Dirven, 135–54. Amsterdam/Philadelphia: Benjamins.

Inchaurralde, C. 2000. Lexicopedia. *The Lexicon-Encyclopedia Interface*, ed. B. Peeters, 97–114. Amsterdam: Elsevier.

Israel, M. 1996. The Way Constructions Grow. *Conceptual Structure, Discourse, and Language*, ed. A. Goldberg, 217–31. Stanford: CSLI Publications.

Iwata, S. 1998. *A Lexical Network Approach to Verbal Semantics*. Tokyo: Kaitakusha.

Iwata, S. 2002. Does MANNER Count or Not? Manner-of-Motion Verbs Revisited. *Linguistics* 40: 61–110.

Jackendoff, R. 1975. Morphological and Semantic Regularities in the Lexicon. *Language* 51: 639–71.

Jackendoff, R. 1977. *X-bar Syntax*. Cambridge: MIT Press.

Jackendoff, R. 1987. *Consciousness and the Computational Mind*. Cambridge: MIT Press.

Jackendoff, R. 1990. *Semantic Structures*. Cambridge: MIT Press.

Jackendoff, R. 1996. The Proper Treatment of Measuring Out, Telicity, and Perhaps even Quantification in English. *Natural Language and Linguistic Theory* 14: 305–45.

Jackendoff, R. 1997. *The Architecture of the Language Faculty*. Cambridge: MIT Press.

Jackson, H., and E. Amvela. 2000. *Words, Meaning, and Vocabulary*. London/New York: Cassell.

Janda, L. 1996. *Back from the Brink: A Study of how Relic Forms in Languages Serve as a Source Material for Analogical Extension.* München: Lincom Europa.

Jayaseelan, K. A. 1984. Complex Predicates and the Theory of Theta-Marking. Paper delivered at GLOW, Copenhagen.

Jespersen, O. 1924. *The Philosophy of Grammar*. London: George Allen and Urwin.

Jesperson, O. 1940. *Essentials of English Grammar*. New York: H. Holt & Company.

Jerspersen, O. 1961. *Analytic Syntax*. Copenhagen: Levin & Munksgaard.

Jespersen, O. 1965. *A Modern English Grammar on Historical Principles*. London: George Allen & Unwin Ltd.

Johnson, K. 1991. Object Positions. *Natural Language and Linguistic Theory* 9: 577–636.

Johnson-Laird, P. 1983. *Mental Models*. Cambridge: Cambridge University Press.

Johnson-Laird, P. 1988. *The Computer and the Mind*. London: Fontana.

Jones, M. A. 1988. Cognate Objects and the Case Filter. *Journal of Linguistics* 24: 89–110.

Jurafsky, D. 1992. An On-line Computational Model of Human Sentence Interpretation: A Theory of the Representation and Use of Linguistic Knowledge. Doctoral dissertation, University of California at Berkeley.

Kageyama, T. 1996. *Dooshi Imiron* (Verb Semantics). Tokyo: Kurosio.

Kathol, A. 2000. *Linear Syntax*. Oxford: Oxford University Press.

Katz, J., and J. Fodor. 1963. The Structure of a Semantic Theory. *Language* 39: 170–210.

Kaufmann, I. 1995. *Konzeptuelle Grundlagen semantischer Dekompositionsstrukturen*. Tübingen: Niemeyer.

Kaufmann, I., and D. Wunderlich. 1998. Cross-linguistic Patterns of Resultatives. Manuscript. Heinrich-Heine Universität, Düsseldorf.

Kay, P. 1996. Argument Structure: Causative ABC Constructions. Manuscript. University of California at Berkeley.

Kay, P., and C. Fillmore. 1999. Grammatical Constructions and Linguistic Generalizations: 'The What's X doing Y?' Construction. *Language* 75: 1–33.

Kay, P. 2002a. English Subjectless Tagged Sentences. *Language* 78(3): 453–81.

Kay, P. 2002b. Patterns of Coining. Invited Plenary Talk at the *Second International Conference on Construction Grammar*, University of Helsinki, Finland, September 2002.

Kayne, R. 1984. *Connectedness and Binary Branching*. Dordrecht: Foris.

Kayne, R. 1985. Principles of Particle Constructions. *Grammatical Representation*, eds. J. Gueron, H.-G. Obenauer and Jean-Yves Pollock, 101–40. Dordrecht: Foris.

Kayne, R. 1994. *The Antisymmetry of Syntax*. Cambridge: MIT Press.

Kemmer, S. 1995. Emphatic and Reflexive '–self': Expectations, Viewpoint, and Subjectivity. *Subjectivity and Subjectivization: Linguistic Perspectives*, eds. D. Stein and S. Wright, 55–82. Cambridge: Cambridge University Press.

Kemmer, S., and M. Barlow. 2000. A Usage-Based Conception of Language. *Usage-based Models of Language*, eds. S. Kemmer and M. Barlow, vii-xxviii. Stanford: CLSI Publications.

Kennedy, C. 1999. *Projecting the Adjective – The Syntax and Semantics of Gradability and Comparison: Outstanding Dissertations in Linguistics*. New York: Garland.

Kennedy, G. 1998. *An Introduction to Corpus Linguistics*. London: Longman.

Kikuchi, A., and D. Takahashi. 1991. Agreement and Small Clauses. *Topics in Small Clauses. Proceedings of Tokyo Small Clause Festival*, eds. H. Nakajima and S. Tonoike, 75–106. Tokyo: Kurosio Publishers.

Kilgarriff, A. 1992. Polysemy. Doctoral dissertation. University of Sussex.

Kilgarriff, A. 1997. I don't believe in Word Senses. *Computers in the Humanities* 31: 91–113.

Kilgarriff, A. 1999. Generative Lexicon Meets Corpus Data: The Case of Nonstandard Word Uses. Manuscript. University of Brighton.

Kim, S., and J. Maling. 1997. A Crosslinguistic Perspective on Resultative Formation. *Texas Linguistic Forum 38: The Syntax and Semantics of Predication*, eds. R. C. Blight and M. J. Moosally, 173–88.

Kitawaga, Y. 1985. Small But Clausal. *Papers from the Twenty-first Regional Meeting of the Chicago Linguistic Society*, 210–20.

Klein, D. E. 2000. *Paper has been my Ruin: On the Organization of Polysemous Senses*. Doctoral dissertation, University of Illinois at Urbana-Champaign.

Klein, D. E., and G. Murphy. 2001. The Representation of Polysemous Words. *Journal of Memory and Language* 45: 259–82.

Klein, E. 1980. A Semantics for Positive and Comparative Adjectives. *Linguistics and Philosophy* 4.1: 1–45.

Klinkenberg, J.-M. 1983. Problèmes de la Synecdoque. Du Sémantique à L'encyclopédique. *Le Français Moderne* 51: 289–99.

Kluender, R. 1985. Sätzchen: German Small Clauses as S's. *NELS* 16: 274–92.

Koch, W., and I. Rosengren. 1995. Secondary Predications: Their Grammatical and Conceptual Structure. *Sprache und Pragmatik* 35: 1–100.

Koenig, J.-P. 1999. *Lexical Relations*. Stanford: CSLI Publciations.

Koenig, J.-P., and A. Davis. 2000. Sublexical Modularity and the Structure of Lexical Semantic Representation. *Linguistics and Philosophy* 24: 71–124.

Koopman, H., and D. Sportiche. 1991. The Position of Subjects. *Lingua* 85: 211–58.

Kratzer, A. 1988. Stage-Level and Individual-Level Predicates. *Genericity in Language: Proceedings of the 1988 Tübingen Conference*, ed. M. Krifka, 247–84. Tübingen: Seminar für Natürlich-sprachliche Systeme, Universität Tübingen.

Kratzer, A. 1989. Stage-Level and Individual-Level Predicates. *Papers on Quantification*, eds. E. Bach, A. Kratzer and B. Partee, 248–84. Amherst: University of Massachusetts.

Krifka, M. 1998. The Origins of Telicity. *Events and Grammar*, ed. S. Rothstein, 197–236. Dordrecht: Kluwer.

Krohn, D. 1975. *Verbinhalt und semantische Merkmale. Studien zu paradigmatischen und syntagmatischen Relationen im Bedeutungsfeld der menschlichen Fortbewegung im heutigen Deutsch und Schwedisch.* Göteburg: Acta Universitatis.

Kunze, J. 1997. Typen der reflexiven Verbverwendung. *Zeitschrift für Sprachwissenschaft* 16: 83–180.

Labov, W. 1970. The Study of Language in its Social Context. *Studium Generale* 23: 30–87.

Labov, W. 1972. *Sociolinguistic Patterns*. Philadelphia: University of Philadelphia Press.

Lakoff, G. 1965. On the Nature of Syntactic Irregularity. Doctoral dissertation, Indiana University. Published as *Irregularity in Syntax*. New York: Rinehart & Wilson, 1970.

Lakoff, G. 1970. Global Rules. *Language* 46: 627–39.

Lakoff, G. 1976. Towards Generative Semantics. *Syntax and Semantics*, vol. 7, *Notes from the Linguistic Underground*, ed. J. D McCawley, 43–62. New York: Academic Press.

Lakoff, G. 1987. *Women, Fire, and Dangerous Things*. Chicago: University of Chicago Press.

Lakoff, G. 1993. The Contemporary Theory of Metaphor. *Metaphor and Thought*, 2nd ed., ed. A. Ortony, 202–51. Cambridge: Cambridge University Press.

Lakoff, G. 1996. Sorry, I'm Not Myself Today: The Metaphor System for Conceptualizing the Self. *Spaces, Worlds, and Grammar*, eds. G. Fauconnier and E. Sweetser, 91–123. Chicago: University of Chicago Press.

Lakoff, G., and M. Johnson. 1999. *Philosophy in the Flesh*. New York: Basic Books.

Lambrecht, K. 1990. What, me worry? Mad Magazine Sentences Revisited. *Proceedings of the 16th Annual Meeting of the Berkeley Linguistic Society. Berkeley Linguistic Society* 16: 215–28.

Lambrecht, K. 1994. *Information Structure and Sentence Form*. Cambridge: Cambridge University Press.

Lambrecht, K., and L. Michaelis. 1998. On Sentence Accent in Information Questions. *Discourse and Cognition*, ed. J.-P. Koenig, 365–86. Stanford: CLSI Publications.

Langacker, R. W. 1976. Semantic Representations and the Linguistic Relativity Hypothesis. *Foundations of Language* 14: 307–57.

Langacker, R. W. 1987. *Foundations of Cognitive Grammar*, vol. 1: *Theoretical Prerequisites*. Stanford: Stanford University Press.

Langacker, R. W. 1988. A Usage-based Model. *Topics in Cognitive Linguistics*, ed. B. Rudzka-Ostyn, 127–61. Amsterdam: Benjamins.

Langacker, R. W. 1990. The Rule Controversy: A Cognitive Grammar Perspective. *Center for Research in Language Newsletter* 4: 4–15.

Langacker, R. W. 1991. *Foundations of Cognitive Grammar*, vol. 2: *Descriptive Application*. Stanford: Stanford University Press.

Langacker, R. W. 2000. A Dynamic Usage-Based Model. *Usage-based models of language*, eds. S. Kemmer and M. Barlow, 1–63. Stanford: CSLI Publications.

Larrivée, P. 2000. Linguistic Meaning, Knowledge, and Utterance Interpretation. *The Lexicon-Encyclopedia Interface*, ed. B. Peeters, 145–67. Amsterdam: Elsevier.

Larson, R. K. 1988a. On the Double Object Construction. *Linguistic Inquiry* 19: 335–91.

Larson, R. K. 1988b. Implicit Arguments in Situation Semantics. *Linguistics and Philosophy* 11: 169–201.

Leech, G. 1991. The State of the Art in Corpus Linguistics. *English Corpus Linguistics: Studies in Honor of Jan Svartvik*, eds. K. Aijmer and B. Altenburg, 8–29. Harlow: Longman.

Leech, G. 1992. Computers and Corpus Analysis. *Computers and Written Texts*, ed. C. S. Butler, 115–40. Oxford: Blackwell.

Lees, R. B. 1957. Review of Chomsky (1957). *Language* 33: 375–408.

Lehrer, A. 1992. Polysemy, Conventionality, and the Structure of the Lexicon. *Cognitive Linguistics*: 207–46.

Leisi, E. 1954. *Der Wortinhalt. Seine Struktur im Deutschen und Englischen.* Heidelberg: Quelle & Meyer.

Leisi, E. 1955. *Das heutige Englisch: Wesenszüge und Probleme*. Heidelberg: Winter.

Leisi, E. 1961. *Der Wortinhalt. Seine Struktur im Deutschen und Englischen*, 2nd ed. Heidelberg: Quelle & Meyer.

Leisi, E. 1973. *Praxis der englischen Semantik.* Heidelberg: Winter.

Leisi, E. 1975. *Der Wortinhalt. Seine Struktur im Deutschen und Englischen*, 3rd ed. Heidelberg: Quelle & Meyer.

Leisi, E. 1978. Darstellung der Zeit in der Sprache. *Aufsätze*, ed. E. Leisi, 73–85. Heidelberg: Winter.

Leisi, E., and C. Mair. 1999. *Das heutige Englisch: Wesenszüge und Probleme*, 8th ed. Heidelberg: Winter.

LePage, R.B. 1997. The Evolution of a Sociolinguistic Theory of Language. *The Handbook of Sociolinguistics*, ed. F. Coulmas, 15–32. Oxford: Blackwell.

Levelt, W. 1989. *Speaking*. Cambridge: MIT Press.

Levin, B. 1993. *English Verb Classes and Alternations*. Chicago: University of Chicago Press.

Levin, B., and M. Rappaport. 1986. The Formation of Adjectival Passives. *Linguistic Inquiry* 17: 623–61.

Levin, B., and M. Rappaport. 1988. Non-event *-er* Nominals: A Probe into Argument Structure. *Linguistics* 26: 1067–83.

Levin, B., and M. Rappaport Hovav. 1991. Wiping the Slate Clean: A Lexical Semantic Exploration. *Cognition* 41: 123–151.

Levin, B., and M. Rappaport Hovav. 1995. *Unaccusativity: At the Syntax-lexical Semantics Interface*. Cambridge: MIT Press.

Levin, B., and M. Rappaport Hovav. 1996. Lexical Semantics. *The Handbook of Contemporary Semantic Theory*, ed. S. Lappin, 487–508. Oxford: Blackwell.

Levin, B. and J. Simpson. 1981. Quirky Case and the Structure of Icelandic Lexical Entries. *Papers from the Seventeenth Regional Meeting of the Chicago Linguistics Society*, 185–96.

Lewis, D. 1969. *Convention: A Philosophical Study*. Cambridge: Harvard University Press.

Lieber, R. 1983. Argument Linking and Compounding in English. *Linguistic Inquiry* 14: 251–86.

Lieber, R. 1990. *On the Organization of the Lexicon*. New York: Garland.

Lieber, R. 1992. *Deconstructing Morphology*. Chicago: University of Chicago Press.

Lieven, E., J. Pine, and G. Baldwin. 1997. Lexically-based Learning and early Grammatical Development. *Journal of Child Language* 24: 187–220.

Lipka, L. 1972. *Semantic Structure and Word-formation: Verb-particle Constructions in Contemporary English*. München: Wilhelm Fink.

Litvinov, V. P., and V. P. Nedjalkov. 1988. *Resultativkonstruktionen im Deutschen*. Tübingen: Gunter Narr Verlag.

Lowe, J. B., and C. F. Baker, and C. J. Fillmore. 1997. A Frame-Semantic Approach to Semantic Annotation. *Proceedings of the SIGLEX Workshop*, ed. M. Light. Held April 4-5 in Washington, D.C. in conjunction with ANLP-97.

Lüdeling, A. 1997. Strange Resultatives in German: New Evidence for a Semantic Treatment. *Proceedings of the 1997 Texas Linguistics Society Conference, The Syntax and Semantics of Predication*, eds. R. C. Blight and M. J. Moosally, 223–34. Austin: University of Texas at Austin (Linguistics Department).

Lüdeling, A. 2001. *On Particle Verbs and Similar Constructions in German*. Stanford: CSLI Publications.

Lyons, J. 1977. *Semantics*, vols. I & II. Cambridge: Cambridge University Press.

Mallén, E. 1991. A Syntactic Analysis of Secondary Predication in Spanish. *Journal of Linguistics* 27: 375–403.

Mallén, E. 1992. Secondary Predication and Lexical Identification. *Studia Linguistica*, 1–29.

Marantz, A. 1995. The Minimalist Program. *Government and Binding Theory and the Minimalist Program*, ed. G. Webelhuth, 349–81. Oxford: Blackwell.

Marantz, A. 1997. No Escape from Syntax. Don't try Morphological Analysis in the Privacy of your own Lexicon. *Proceedings of the 21st Annual Penn Linguistics Colloquium (U. Penn Working Papers in Linguistics 4:2)*, eds. A. Dimitriadis, L. Siegel, C. Surek-Clark, and A. Williams, 201–25. Philadelphia: University of Pennsylvania.

Marchand, H. 1969. *The Categories and Types of Present-Day English Word-Formation.* München: C. H. Beck Verlagsbuchhandlung.

Martinet, A. 1953. Function, Structure and Sound Change. *Word* 8: 1–32.

May, R. 1977. *The Grammar of Quantification.* Cambridge: MIT Press.

May, R. 1985. *Logical Form: Its Structure and Derivation.* Cambridge: MIT Press.

McCawley, J. 1971. Interpretive Semantics meets Frankenstein. *Foundations of Language* 7: 285–96.

McNulty, E. M. 1988. The Syntax of Adjunct Predicates. Doctoral dissertation, University of Connecticut, Storrs.

Mel'čuk, I. 1974. *Opyt Teorii Lingvisticheskikh Modelei 'Smysl ↔Tekst' [An Outline of the Meaning-Text Theory of Linguistic Models].* Moscow: Nauka.

Mel'čuk, I. 1998. Collocations and Lexical Functions. *Phraseology. Theory, Analysis, and Applications*, ed. A. P. Cowie, 23–54. Oxford: Oxford University Press.

Michaelis, L. 1998. *Aspectual Grammar and Past-Time Reference*. London, New York: Routledge.

Michiels, A. 1975. Idiomaticity in English. *Revue des Langue Vivantes* 43: 184–99.

Miller, D. G. 1993. *Complex Verb Formation.* Amsterdam: John Benjamins.

Miller, G. A. 1972. English Verbs of Motion: A Case Study in Semantics and Lexical Memory. *Coding Processes in Human Memory*, eds. A. W. Melton and E. Martin, 335–72 Washington: Winston.

Milroy, L. 1987. *Observing and Analyzing Natural Language: A Critical Account of Sociolinguistic Method.* Oxford: Blackwell.

Milroy, J., and L. Milroy. 1997. Varieties and Variation. *The Handbook of Sociolinguistics*, ed. F. Coulmas, 47–64. Oxford: Blackwell.

Milsark, G. 1976. Existential Sentences in English. Doctoral dissertation, MIT.

Minsky, M. 1975. A Framework for Representing Knowledge. *The Psychology of Computer Vision*, ed. P. H. Winston, 211–77. New York: McGraw-Hill.

Miyata, A. 2000. Object- vs. Event-Oriented Resultatives. *Tsukuba English Studies* 19: 81–98.

Moens, M., and M. Steedman. 1988. Temporal Ontology and Temporal Reference. *Computational Linguistics* 14: 15–28.

Mohanan, K. P., and T. Mohanan. 1998. Strong and Weak Projection: Lexical Reflexives and Reciprocals. *The Projection of Arguments*, eds. W. Geuder and M. Butt, 165–94. Stanford: CSLI Publications.

Mohanan, K. P., and T. Mohanan. 1999. On Representations in Grammatical Semantics. *Grammatical Semantics*, eds. T. Mohanan and L. Wee, 23–76. Stanford: CSLI Publications.

Mori, Y., S. Löbner, and K. Micha. 1992. Aspektuelle Verbklassen im Japanischen. *Zeitschrift für Sprachwissenschaft*, 216–79.

Morita, P. 1998. Some Notes on Prepositional Resultatives. *Tsukuba English Studies* 17: 319–40.

Moro, A. 1988. Per una teoria unificate delle frasi copulari. *Rivista di Grammatica Generativa* 13: 81–110.

Moro, A. 1991. The Raising of Predicates: Copula, Expletives and Existence. *MIT Working Papers on Linguistics* 15: 119–81.

Moro, A. 1995. Small Clauses with Predicative Nominals. *Syntax and Semantics*, vol. 28, *Small Clauses*, eds A. Cardinaletti and M. T. Guasti, 109–34. San Diego: Academic Press.

Moro, A. 1997. *The Raising of Predicates: Predicative Noun Phrases and the Theory of Clause Structure.* Cambridge: Cambridge University Press.

Mourelatos, A. P. D. 1978. Events, Processes, and States. *Linguistics and Philosophy* 2: 415–34.

Müller, S. 2002. *Complex Predicates. Verbal Complexes, Resultative Constructions, and Particle Verbs in German.* Stanford: CSLI Publications.

Murphy, G. L. 1997. Polysemy and the Creation of Novel Word Meanings. *Creative Thought: An Investigation of Conceptual structures and Processes*, eds. T. B. Ward, S. M. Smith, and J. Vaid, 235–65. Washington, D. C.: American Psychological Association.

Nakajima, H. 1990. Secondary Predication. *The Linguistic Review* 7: 275–309.

Nakajima, H. 1991. Reduced Clauses and Argumenthood of AgrP. *Topics in Small Clauses (Proceedings of Tokyo Small Clause Festival)*, eds. H. Nakajima and S. Tonoike, 39–58. Tokyo: Kurosio Publishers.

Nakamura, M. 1997. On Resultative Constructions. *Studies in English Linguistics. A Festschrift for Akira Ota on the Occasion of His Eightieth Birthday*, eds. M. Ukaji, T. Nakao, M. Kajita and Shuji Chiba, 492–511. Tokyo: Taishukan.

Napoli, D. J. 1988. Subjects and External Arguments. *Linguistics and Philosophy* 11: 323–54.

Napoli, D. J. 1989. *Predication Theory. A Case Study for Indexing Theory.* Cambridge: Cambridge University Press.

Napoli, D. J. 1992. Secondary Resultative Predicates in Italian. *Journal of Linguistics* 28: 53–90.

Napoli, D. J. 1999. Resultatives. *Concise Encyclopedia of Grammatical Theories*, eds. K. Brown and J. Miller, 324–29. Amsterdam: Elsevier.

Nedjalkov, V., and S. Jaxontov. 1988. The Typology of Resultative Constructions. *Typology of Resultative Constructions*, ed. V. Nedjalkov, (English Translation, B. Comrie), 3–62. Amsterdam: Benjamins.

Neeleman, A. 1995. Complex Predicates in Dutch and English. *Studies in Comparative Germanic Syntax*, eds. H. Haider, S. Olsen, and S. Vikner, 219–40.

Neeleman, A., and F. Weerman. 1993. The Balance between Syntax and Morphology: Dutch Particles and Resultatives. *Natural Language and Linguistic Theory* 11: 433–75.

Neeleman, A., and H. van de Koot. 2001. Bare Resultatives. *University College London Working Papers in Linguistics*, 1–41. London: UCL Department of Phonetics and Linguistics.

Nemoto, N. 1998. On the Polysemy of Ditransitive *save*: The Role of Frame Semantics in Construction Grammar. *English Linguistics* 15: 219–42.

Nickel, G. 1978. Complex Verbal Structures in English. *Studies in Descriptive English Grammar*, ed. D. Nehls, 63–83. Heidelberg: Julius Groos.

Nida, E. A. 1975. *Componential Analysis of Meaning: An Introduction to Semantic Structures*. The Hague: Mouton.

Nirenburg, S., and V. Raskin. 1996. *Ten Choices for Lexical Semantics* (Computing Research Laboratory Monograph MCCS-96-304). Las Cruces: New Mexico State University.

Nunberg, G. 1978. *The Pragmatics of Reference*. Bloomington: Indiana University Linguistics Club.

Nunberg, J., Sag, I., and T. Wasow. 1994. Idioms. *Language* 70: 491–538.

Onions, C. 1904. *An Advanced English Syntax*. London: Paul Kegan.

Ooi, V. B. Y. 1998. *Computer Corpus Lexicography*. Edinburgh: Edinburgh University Press.

Orgun, O. 1996. Flat vs. Branching Structures in Morphology: The Case of Suspended Affixation. *Proceedings of the 21st Annual Meeting of the Berkeley Linguistics Society*. Berkeley: Berkeley Linguistics Society.

Oya, T. 2002. Reflexives and Resultatives: Some Differences between English and German. *Linguistics* 40: 961–86.

Palmer, H. E. 1933. *Second Interim Report on English Collocations*. Tokyo: Kaitakusha.

Parsons, T. 1990. *Events in the Semantics of English*. Cambridge: MIT Press.

Pawley, A., and F. H. Syder. 1983. Two Puzzles for Linguistic Theory: Nativelike Selection and Nativelike Fluency. *Language and Communication*, eds. J. C. Richards and R. W. Schmidt, 191–225. London: Longman.

Pawley, A. 1987. Encoding events in Kalam and English: Different Logics for Reporting Experience. *Coherence and Grounding in Discourse*, ed. I. Tomlin, 329–60. Philadelphia: Benjamins.

Peeters, B. 2000. Setting the Scene: Some Recent Milestones in the Lexicon-Encyclopedia Debate. *The Lexicon-Encyclopedia Interface*, ed. B. Peeters, 1–52. Amsterdam: Elsevier.

Peirce, C. S. 1932. Speculative Grammar. *Collected Papers of Charles Sanders Peirce, Vol. II: Elements of Logic*, ed. C. Hartshorne and P. Weiss, 129–269. Cambridge: Harvard University Press.

Perlmutter, D. M. 1978. Impersonal Passives and the Unaccusative Hypothesis. *Proceedings of the Fourth Annual Meeting of the Berkeley Linguistics Society*, 157–89.

Pesetzky, D. 1995. *Zero Syntax. Experiencers and Cascades.* Cambridge: MIT Press.

Petruck, M. 1996. Frame Semantics. *Handbook of Pragmatics*, eds. J. Verschueren, J-O Östman, J. Blommaert and C. Bulcaen, 1–13. Amsterdam: Benjamins.

Pinker, S. 1989. *Learnability and Cognition.* Cambridge: MIT Press.

Pollock, J.-Y. 1989. Verb Movement, Universal Grammar and the Structure of IP. *Linguistic Inquiry* 20: 365–424.

Pollard, C., and I. Sag. 1994. *Head-Driven Phrase Structure Grammar.* Chicago: University of Chicago Press.

Prince, E. 1981. Toward a Taxonomy of Given-New Information. *Radical Pragmatics*, ed. P. Cole, 223–53. New York: Academic Press.

Pustejovsky, J. 1991. The Syntax of Event Structure. *Cognition* 41: 47–81.

Pustejovsky, J. 1995. *The Generative Lexicon.* Cambridge: MIT Press.

Pustejovsky, J. 2000. Lexical Shadowing and Argument Closure. *Polysemy*, ed. C. Leacock and Y. Ravin, 68–90. Oxford: Oxford University Press.

Quirk, R. 1972. *A Grammar of Contemporary English.* London: Longman.

Quirk, R., S. Greenbaum, G. Leech, and J. Svartvik. 1985. *A Comprehensive Grammar of the English Language.* London: Longman.

Radford, A. 1997. *Syntactic Theory and the Structure of English. A Minimalist Approach.* Cambridge: Cambridge University Press.

Ramchand, G. 1997. *Aspect and Predication: The Semantics of Argument Structure.* Oxford: Oxford University Press.

Randall, J. H. 1982. A Lexical Approach to Causatives. *Journal of Linguistic Research* 2: 77–105.

Randall, J. H. 1984. Thematic Structure and Inheritance. *Quaderni di Semantica* 5: 92–110.

Raskin, V. 1985. Linguistic and Encyclopedic Knowledge in Text Processing. *Quaderni di Semantica* 6: 92–102.

Rapoport, T. R. 1987. Copular, Nominal and Small Clauses: A Study of Israel Hebrew. Doctoral dissertation, Massachusetts Institute of Technology.

Rapoport, T. R. 1990. Secondary Predication and the Lexical Representation of Verbs. *Machine Translation* 5: 31–55.

Rapoport, T.R. 1993a. Stage and Adjunct Predicates: Licensing and Structure in Secondary Predication Constructions. *Knowledge and Language*, vol. 2, *Lexical and Conceptual Structure*, eds. E. J. Reuland and W. Abraham, 157–82. Dordrecht: Kluwer.

Rapoport, T. R. 1993b. Verbs in Depictives and Resultatives. *Semantics and the Lexicon*, ed. J. Pustejovsky, 163–84. Dordrecht: Kluwer.

Rapoport, T. R. 1995. Specificity, Objects, and Nominal Small Clauses. *Syntax and Semantics* vol. 28, *Small Clauses*, eds. A. Cardinaletti and M. T. Guasti, 153–78. San Diego: Academic Press.

Rapoport, T. R. 1999. Structure, Aspect, and the Predicate. *Language* 75: 653–77.

Raposo, E., and J. Uriagereka. 1995. Two Types of Small Clauses (Toward a Syntax of Theme/Rheme Relations). *Syntax and Semantics*, vol. 28, *Small Clauses*, eds. A. Cardinaletti and M.T. Guasti, 179–206. San Diego: Academic Press.

Rapp, I. 1997. *Partizipien und semantische Struktur*. Tübingen: Stauffenburg Verlag.

Rappaport, M., and B. Levin. 1988. What to do with Theta-Roles. *Thematic Relations, Syntax and Semantics 21*, ed. W. Wilkins, 7–36. New York: Academic Press.

Rappaport Hovav, M., and B. Levin. 1996. Two Types of Derived Accomplishments. *Proceedings of the First LFG Conference*, eds. M. Butt and T. H. King, 375–88. Grenoble, France.

Rappaport Hovav, M., and B. Levin. 1998. Building Verb Meaning. *The Projection of Arguments*, eds. M. Butt and W. Geuder, 97–134. Stanford: CSLI Publications.

Rappaport Hovav, M., and B. Levin. 1999. *Two Types of Compositionally Derived Events*. Ramat Gan, Israel, and Evanston, IL: Bar Ilan University and Northwestern University, Ms.

Rappaport Hovav, M., and B. Levin. 2001. An Event Structure Account of English Resultatives. *Language* 77: 766–97.

Rauh, Gisa. 1988. *Tiefenkasus, thematische Relationen und Thetarollen*. Tübingen: Gunter Narr.

Ravin, Y., and C. Laecock. 2000. Polysemy: An Overview. *Polysemy*, eds. Y. Ravin and C. Laecock, 1–29. Oxford: Oxford University Press.

Reinhart, T. 1976. The Syntax Domain of Anaphora. Doctoral dissertation, MIT.

Renouf, A., and J. Sinclair. 1991. Collocational Frameworks in English. *English Corpus Linguistics*, eds. K. Aijmer and B. Altenberg, 128–43. London: Longma.

Ritter, E. 1991. Functional categories in Noun Phrases. *Perspectives on Phrase Structure: Heads and Licensing. Syntax and Semantics 25*, ed. S. Rothstein, 37–62. San Diego: Academic Press.

Riehemann, S. Z. 2001. A Constructional Approach to Idioms and Word Formation. Doctoral dissertation, Stanford University.

Ritter, E., and S. T. Rosen. 1998. Delimiting Events in Syntax. *The Projection of Arguments*, eds. W. Geuder and M. Butt, 135–64. Stanford: CSLI Publications.

Roberts, I. 1988. Predicative APs. *Linguistic Inquiry* 19: 703–10.

Rochement, M. S. and P. W. Culicover. 1990. *English Focus Constructions and the Theory of Grammar*. Cambridge: Cambridge University Press.

Rosch, E. 1973. Natural Categories. *Cognitive Psychology* 4: 328–50.

Rosch, E. 1977. Human Categorization. *Studies in Crosscultural Psychology*, ed. N. Warren, 1–49. London: Academic Press.

Rosch, E. 1978. Principles of Categorization. *Cognition and Categorization*, eds. E. Rosch and B. B. Lloyd, 27–48. Hillsdale: Erlbaum.

Rosch, E. 1983. Prototype Classification and Logical Classification. *New Trends in Cognitive Representation: Challenges to Piaget's Theory*, ed. E. Scholnik, 73–86. Hillsdale: Erlbaum.

Rosen, S. T. 1990. *Argument Structure and Complex Predicates*. New York: Garland.

Rosen, S. T. 1996. Events and Verb Classification. *Linguistics* 34: 191–223.

Rosen, S. T. 1999. The Syntactic Representation of Linguistic Events. *GLOT International* 4: 3–11.

Rosenbaum, P. S. 1967. *The Grammar of English Predicate Complement Constructions*. Cambridge: MIT Press.

Ross, J. R. 1967. Constraints on Variables in Syntax. Doctoral dissertation, MIT.

Rothstein, S. 1983. The Syntactic Forms of Predication. Doctoral dissertation, Massachusetts Institute of Technology.

Rothstein, S. 1985. The Syntactic Forms of Predication. *The Linguistic Review* 5: 163–72.

Rumelhart, D. 1989. Toward a Microstructural Account of Human Reasoning. *Similarity and Anological Reasoning*, eds. S. Vosniadou and A. Ortony, 298–312. Cambridge: Cambridge University Press.

Safir, K. 1985. *Syntactic Chains*. Cambridge: Cambridge University Press.

Safir, K. 1987. What explains the Definiteness Effect? *The Representation of (in)definiteness*, eds, E. Reuland and A. Meulen, 71–97. Cambridge: MIT Press.

Salkoff, M. 1983. Bees are Swarming in the Garden. *Language* 59: 288-346.

Sapir, E. 1944. On Grading: A Study in Semantics. *Philosophy of Science* 2: 93–116.

Sato, H. 1987. Resultative Attributes and GB Principles. *English Linguistics* 4: 91–106.

Saussure, F. de. 1916. *Cours de linguistique générale*. Paris: Payot 1973.

Schank, R. C., and R. P. Abelson. 1975. *Scripts, Plans, Goals, and Understanding*. Hillsdale: Lawrence Erlbaum.

Schatte, C. 1986. Probleme der Klassifizierung von verursachten resultativen Prozessen in beschreibenden Sätzen. *Linguistica Silesiana* 9: 137–44.

Schein, B. 1995. Small Clauses and Predication. *Syntax and Semantics*, vol. 28, *Small Clauses*, eds. A. Cardinaletti and M. T. Guasti, 49–76. San Diego: Academic Press.

Schlesinger, I. M. 1995. On the Semantics of the Object. *The Verb in Contemporary English*, eds. B. Aarts and C. F. Meyer, 54–74. Cambridge: Cambridge University Press.

Selkirk, E. 1982. *The Syntax of Words*. Cambridge: MIT Press.

Shieber, S. 1986. *An Introduction to Unification-based Approaches to Grammar*. Stanford: CSLI Publications.

Simpson, J. H. 1983. Resultatives. *Papers in Lexical-Functional Grammar*, eds. B. Levin, M. Rappaport, and A. Zaenen, 143–57. Indiana University Linguistics Club.

Sinclair, J. 1991. *Corpus, Concordance, Collocation*. Oxford: Oxford University Press.

Sinclair, J. 1996. The Search for Units of Meaning. *Textus* 9: 75–106.

Slabakova, R. 1997. Bulgarian Preverbs: Aspect in Phrase Structure. *Linguistics* 35: 673–704.

Slobin, D. I. 1985. Crosslinguistic Evidence for the Language-Making Capacity. *A Crosslinguistic Study of Language Acquisition*, vol. 2, *Theoretical Issues*, ed. D. Slobin, 1157–1256. Hillsdale: Lawrence Erlbaum.

Slobin, D .I. 1996. Two Ways to Travel: Verbs of Motion in English and Spanish. *Grammatical Constructions. Their Form and Meaning*, eds. M. Shibatani and S. A. Thompson, 195–220. Oxford: Oxford University Press.

Slobin, D. I. 1997. The Origins of Grammaticizable Notions: Beyond the Individual Mind. *The Crosslinguistic Study of Language Acquisition*, vol. 5, *Expanding the Concepts*, ed. D. I. Slobin, 265–323. Mahwah: Lawrence Erlbaum Associates.

Slobin, D. I. 1998. Verbalized Events: A Dynamic Approach to Linguistic Relativity and Determinism. *LAUD Linguistic Agency*, no. 449: 1–24.

Smith, C. 1997. *The Parameter of Aspect*. Dordrecht: Kluwer.

Snell-Hornby, M. 1983. *Verb Descriptivity in German and English: A Contrastive Study in Semantic Fields*. Heidelberg: Carl Winter.

Sonnenschein, E. 1916. *A New English Grammar*. Oxford: Oxford University Press.

Speas, M. 1986. Adjunctions and Projections in Syntax. Doctoral dissertation, MIT.

Speas, M. 1990. *Phrase Structure in Natural Language*. Dordrecht: Kluwer.

Spencer, A. 1988. Lexical Rules and Lexical Representations. *Linguistics* 26: 619–40.

Sperber, D., and D. Wilson. 1986. *Relevance: Communication and Cognition*. Oxford: Blackwell.

Starke, M. 1995. On the Format of Small Clauses. *Syntax and Semantics*, vol. 28, *Small Clauses*, eds. A. Cardinaletti and M.T. Guasti, 237–70. San Diego: Academic Press.

Staudinger, B 1997. *Sätzchen: Small Clauses im Deutschen*. Tübingen: Niemeyer.

Stefanowitsch, A. 2001. Constructing Causation: A Construction Grammar Approach to Analytic Causatives. Doctoral dissertation, Rice University, Houston, Texas.

Steube, A. 1994. Syntaktische und semantische Eigenschaften sekundärer Prädikationen. *Zur Satzwertigkeit von Infinitiven und Small Clauses*, eds. A. Steube and G. Zybatow, 243–64. Tübingen: Niemeyer.

Stiebels, B. 1996. *Lexikalische Argumente und Adjunkte: Zum semantischen Beitrag von verbalen Präfixen und Partikeln*. Berlin: Akademie Verlag.

Stiebels, B., and D. Wunderlich. 1994. Morphology feeds Syntax: The Case of Particle Verbs. *Linguistics* 32: 913–68.

Stockwell, R., P. Schachter and B. Hall Partee. 1973. *The Major Syntactic Structures of English*. New York: Holt, Rinehart and Winston.

Stowell, T. 1981. Origins of Phrase Structure. Doctoral dissertation, MIT.

Stowell, T. 1983. Subject across Categories. *The Linguistic Review* 2: 285–312.

Stowell, T. 1991. Small Clause Restructuring. *Principles and Parameters of Comparative Grammar*, ed. R. Freidin, 182–218. Cambridge: MIT Press.

Stowell, T. 1995. Remarks on Clause Structure. *Syntax and Semantics*, vol. 28, *Small Clauses*, eds. A. Cardinaletti and M. T. Guasti, 271–86. San Diego: Academic Press.

Stubbs, M. 1996. *Text and Corpus Analysis: Computer-assisted Studies of Language and Culture*. Oxford: Blackwell.

Stubbs, M. 2001. *Words and Phrases: Corpus Studies of Lexical Semantics*. Oxford: Blackwell.

Suzuki, Y. 1991. Small Clauses as AgrP. *Topics in Small Clauses (Proceedings of Tokyo Small Clause Festival)*, eds. H. Nakajima and S. Tonoike, 27–37. Tokyo: Kurosio Publishers.

Sweetser, E. 1988. Grammaticalization and Semantic Bleaching. *Proceedings of the fourteenth Annual Meeting of the Berkeley Linguistics Society*, eds. S. Axmaker, A. Jassier, and H. Singmaster, 175–212.

Sweetser, E. 1990. *From Etymology to Pragmatics*. Cambridge: Cambridge University Press.

Talmy, L. 1975. Semantics and Syntax of Motion. *Syntax and Semantics 4*, ed. J. Kimball, 181–238. New York: Academic Press.

Talmy, L. 1976. Semantic Causative Types. *The Grammar of Causative Constructions*, ed. M. Shibatani, 43–116. New York: Academic Press.

Talmy, L. 1985. Lexicalization Patterns. *Language Typology and Syntactic Description*, ed. T. Shopen, 57–147. Cambridge: Cambridge University Press.

Talmy, L. 1988. Force Dynamics in Language and Cognition. *Cognitive Science* 2: 49–100.

Talmy, L. 1991. Path to Realization: Typology of Event Integration. *Buffalo Working Papers in Linguistics* 91-01: 147–87.

Talmy, L. 1996. The Windowing of Attention. *Grammatical Constructions. Their Form and Meaning*, eds. M. Shibatani and S. A. Thompson, 235–87. Oxford: Oxford University Press.

Talmy, L. 2000. *Cognitive Semantics*. Cambridge: MIT Press.

Taylor, J. 2000. Approaches to Word Meaning: The Network Model (Langacker) and the Two-word Model (Bierwisch) in Comparison. *The Lexicon-Encyclopedia Interface*, ed. B. Peeters, 115–41. Amsterdam: Elsevier.

Ten Hacken, P. 1990. Reading Distinction in Machine Translation. *Proceedings of COLING90*: 162–66.

Tenny, C. L. 1992. The Aspectual Interface Hypothesis. *Lexical Matters*, eds. I. Sag and A. Szabolsci, 1–27. Stanford: CSLI Publications.

Tenny, C. L. 1994. *Aspectual Roles and the Syntax-Semantics Interface*. Dordrecht: Kluwer Academic Publishers.

Tesnière, L. 1959. *Éléments de Syntaxe Structurale*. Paris: Éditions Klincksieck.

Tobin, Y. 1993. *Aspect and the English Verb: Process and Result in Language*. London: Longman.

Tomasello, M. 1992. *First Verbs: A Case Study in Early Grammatical Development*. Cambridge: Cambridge University Press.

Tomasello, M. 2000. A Usage-Based Approach to Child Language Acquisition. *Proceedings of the 26th Annual Meeting of the Berkeley Linguistics Society*.

Trier, J. 1931. Der deutsche Wortschatz im Sinnbezierk des Verstandes. Die Geschichte eines sprachlichen Feldes. *Wortfeldforschung. Zur Geschichte und Theorie des sprachlichen Feldes*, ed. L. Schmidt, 1–38. Darmstadt: Wissenschaftliche Buchgesellschaft.

Tsuzuki, M. 1988. Depictive Secondary Predicates versus Conditional Secondary Predicates. *English Linguistics* 5: 71-90.

Van Hout, A. 1996. Event Semantics of Verb Frame Alternations: A Case Study of Dutch and its Acquisition. Tilburg Dissertation in Language Studies, Katholieke Universiteit Brabant, Tilburg.

Van Valin, Jr., R. D. 1993. A Synopsis of Role and Reference Grammar. *Advances in Role and Reference Grammar*, ed. R. D. Van Valin, Jr., 1–164. Amsterdam: Benjamins.

Van Valin, Jr., R. D. and R. J. LaPolla. 1997. *Syntax. Structure, Meaning and Function*. Cambridge: Cambridge University Press.

Van Voorst, J. 1986. Event Structure. Doctoral dissertation, University of Ottawa.

Van Voorst, J. 1988. *Event Structure*. Amsterdam: Benjamins.

Van Voorst, J. 1991. De la Correspondance en Semantique. *Linguistica* 25: 395–419.

Van Voorst, J. 1992. The Aspectual Semantics of Psychological Verbs. *Linguistics and Philosophy* 15: 65–92.

Vendler, Z. 1967. *Linguistics in Philosophy*. Ithaca: Cornell University Press.

Verhagen, A. 2000. Interpreting Usage: Construing the History of Dutch Causal Verbs. *Usage-based Models of Language*, eds. S. Kemmer and M. Barlow, 261–86. Stanford: CSLI Publications.

Verkuyl, H. J. 1993. *A Theory of Aspectuality*. Cambridge: Cambridge University Press.

Verspoor, C. M. 1997. Contextually-Dependent Lexical Semantics. Doctoral dissertation, University of Edinburgh.

Viberg, Å. 2002. Polysemy and Disambiguation Cues across Languages: The case of Swedish få and English get. *Lexis in Contrast*, eds. B. Altenberg and S. Granger, 119–50. Amsterdam/Philadelphia: Benjamins

Vikner, S. 1994. *Verb Movement and Expletive Subjects in the Germanic Languages*. New York: Oxford University Press.

Visser, F. T. 1963. *A Historical Syntax of the English Language*, part 1, *Syntactical Units with One Verb*. Leiden: Brill.

Vosniadu, S., and A. Ortony. 1989. *Similarity and Analogical Reasoning*. Cambridge: Cambridge University Press.

Wanner, A. 1999. *Verbklassifizierungen und aspektuelle Alternationen im Englischen*. Tübingen: Niemeyer.

Washio, R. 1997. Resultatives, Compositionality and Language Variation. *Journal of East Asian Linguistics* 6: 1–49.

Wasow, T. 1977. Transformations and the Lexicon. *Formal Syntax*, eds. P. W. Culicover, T. Wasow and A. Akmajian, 327–60. New York: Academic Press.

Webelhuth, G. 1992. *Principles and Parameters of Syntactic Saturation*. New York, Oxford: Oxford University Press.

Webelhuth, G. 1995. *Government and Binding Theory and the Minimalist Program*. Oxford: Blackwell.

Wechsler, S. 1995. *The Semantic Basis of Argument Structure*. Stanford: CSLI Publications.

Wechsler, S. 1997. Resultatives and Control. *Proceedings of the 1997 Texas Linguistics Society Conference, The Syntax and Semantics of Predication*, eds. R. C. Blight and M. J. Moosally, 307–22. Austin: University of Texas at Austin (Linguistics Department).

Wechsler, S. 2001. An Analysis of English Resultatives Under the Event-Argument Homomorphism Model of Telicity. *Proceedings of the 3rd Workshop on Text Structure at the University of Texas*: 1–17.

Wechsler, S., and B. Noh. 2001. On Resultative Predicates and Clauses: Parallels between English and Korean. *Language Sciences* 23: 391–432.

Weigand, E. 1998. Contrastive Lexical Semantics. *Contrastive Lexical Semantics*, ed. E. Weigand, 25–44. Amsterdam/Philadelphia: Benjamins.

Weinreich, U. 1953. *Languages in Contact*. New York: Linguistic Circle of New York.

Weisgerber, L. 1951. *Das Gesetz der Sprache*. Heidelberg: Carl Winter.

Wierzbicka, A. 1985. *Lexicography and Conceptual Analysis*. Ann Arbor: Karoma.

Wierzbicka, A. 1986. Human Emotions: Universal or Culture-Specific? *American Anthropologist* 99: 584–94.

Wierzbicka, A. 1988. *The Semantics of Grammar*. Amsterdam: John Benjamins.

Wierzbicka, A. 1992. *Semantics, Culture, and Cognition*. Oxford: Oxford University Press.

Wierzbicka, A. 1996. *Semantics, Primes, and Universals*. Oxford: Oxford University Press.

Wilder, C. 1991. Small Clauses and Related Objects. *Groninger Arbeiten zur Germanistischen Linguistik (GAGL)* 34: 215–36.

Wilder, C. 1994. Small Clauses im Englischen und in der GB-Theorie. *Zur Satzwertigkeit von Infinitiven und Small Clauses*, eds. A. Steube and G. Zybatow, 219–41. Tübingen: Niemeyer.

Williams, E. 1975. Small Clauses in English. *Syntax and Semantics*, vol. 4, ed. J. P. Kimball, 249–73. Orlando: Academic Press.

Williams, E. 1980. Predication. *Linguistic Inquiry* 11: 203–38.

Williams, E. 1981. Argument Structure and Morphology. *The Linguistic Review* 1: 81–114.

Williams, E. 1983. Against Small Clauses. *Linguistic Inquiry* 14: 287–95.

Williams, E. 1987. Implicit Arguments, the Binding Theory, and Control. *Natural Language and Linguistic Theory* 5: 151–80.

Williams, E. 1995a. *Thematic Structure in Syntax*. Cambridge: MIT Press.

Williams, E. 1995b. Theta Theory. *Government and Binding Theory and the Minimalist Program: Principles and Parameters in Syntactic theory*, ed. G. Webelhuth, 97–124. Oxford: Blackwell.

Williams, E. 1997. Lexical and Syntactic Complex Predicates. *Complex Predicates*, eds. A. Alsina, J. Bresnan and P. Sells, 13–28. Stanford: CSLI Publications.

Winkler, S. 1997. *Focus and Secondary Predication*. Berlin: Mouton de Gruyter.

Winters, M. E. 1997. Kurylowicz, Analogical Change, and Cognitive Grammar. *Cognitive Linguistics*: 359–86.

Wittgenstein, L. 1953. *Philophical Investigations*. Oxford: Blackwell.

Wolfram, W. 1991. *Dialects and American English*. Englewood Cliffs: Prentice Hall.

Wotjak, G. 1971. *Untersuchungen zur Struktur der Bedeutung. Ein Beitrag zu Gegenstand und Methode der modernen Bedeutungsforschung unter besonderer Berücksichtigung der semantischen Konstituentenanalyse*. München: Hueber.

Wray, A. 2002. *Formulaic Language and the Lexicon*. Cambridge: Cambridge University Press.

Wunderlich, D. 1991. How do Prepositional Phrases fit into Compositional Syntax and Semantics? *Linguistics* 29: 591–621.

Wunderlich, D. 1997a. Cause and the Structure of Verbs. *Linguistic Inquiry* 28: 27–68.

Wunderlich, D. 1997b. Argument Extension by Lexical Adjunction. *Journal of Semantics* 14: 95–142.

Yamada, Y. 1987. Two Types of Resultative Constructions. *English Linguistics* 4: 73–90.

Zagona, K. 1987. *Verb Phrase Syntax*. Dordrecht: Kluwer.

Name Index

Subject Index